WITCHDOCTOR TOTEM

BOOK 3

SPIRIT WALKING, SHAMANIC JOURNEY, ASTRAL PROJECTION, AND TEACHING YOUR STUDENTS ABOUT THE PSYCHIC SELF, THE SPIRIT WORLDS, AND SHAMANIC PRACTICES

ALY CARDINALLI

WWW.OTSOSALON.COM

Austin, Texas

Cover: *Pueo Totem Journey* designed by Aly Cardinalli

Paperback ISBN 979-8-950905-00-1

e-book ISBN 979-8-950905-01-8

Be the first to know: www.otsosalon.com

CONTENTS

Trigger Warning

This book goes to difficult places that may be distressing or triggering for some readers. Topics include various forms of abuse (such as domestic violence and non-consensual acts), forced satanic rituals, the occult, addiction, substance abuse, exorcism, demonic possession, Satanism, monsters, demonology, hauntings, psychopomps, deities, spirits, ghosts, spirit walking, witchcraft, soul retrieval, past life regression, murder, human torture, conjuring entities, psychological distress and diagnoses, damaged souls, soul removal, coffins, burials, death, cultural oppression, and other intense subject matter. This book is based on real experiences and true stories. Reader discretion is strongly advised. If any of these topics are likely to cause distress, approach this book with care. Your well-being is a priority.

Disclaimer

The author and publisher make no claim that this material is complete or universally applicable. The information provided is strictly for educational purposes. By choosing to apply the ideas presented in this book, you assume full responsibility for your actions. No guarantee that using the techniques, ideas, and information presented in this book will improve your life in any way. Self-help and personal improvement depend entirely on the individual applying the ideas and techniques. Your progress and results will vary based on the time you dedicate to developing skills and your commitment to learning the concepts, techniques, and principles mentioned. The author and publisher assume no responsibility for your actions, whether the information is used for positive or negative purposes. As always, the advice of a professional should be sought. The information provided in this book is not intended to replace the guidance of health or mental health professionals. Readers are advised to use discretion before performing any rituals or spells. The author is not liable for, nor responsible in any way, for actions taken by readers as a result of the information contained in this book. Readers are encouraged to cast spells and work with spirits responsibly.

Author's Note

The information in this book was collected from experience teaching, training with leaders in the field (as I have now become), and from reading sources listed in the bibliography. The absence of individual citations is intended to maintain the flow of learning, not to claim credit for others' work. This is a stylistic choice, not a copyright claim. I encourage you to explore the referenced books, as they have greatly enriched my journey and knowledge. We should always celebrate those who laid the foundations that we build on. I hold you all in deep respect.

PRELUDE

The World Has Always Known Shamans

A Global History of Spirit Travel

Let us establish something before we go any further: you did not invent this. Neither did I. Neither did the shamanic revival of the 1980s, the New Age movement, Michael Harner's core shamanism, or any Western teacher who discovered journeying and decided to package it for modern audiences. What you are learning in this book is one of the oldest and most universal spiritual technologies in human history, found independently on every continent, in virtually every culture that has ever existed, long before any of those cultures had contact with each other.

That convergence is worth sitting with for a moment. When cultures separated by oceans and millennia arrive at the same practice through entirely different routes, something true is being pointed at. The spirit world is accessible. The human nervous system, in theta, opens a door. And people, everywhere, have always walked through it.

This chapter is a survey of that history, continent by continent, tradition by tradition. It is the lineage behind the stairs you climb.

The Word Itself: Where "Shamanism" Comes From

The term "shamanism" was first applied by Western anthropologists as outside observers of the ancient religion of indigenous Siberians and Mongols, as well as those of the neighboring Tungusic and Samoyedic-speaking peoples. The word shaman derives from the Tungus word saman, meaning, in most dialects, 'one who knows. Anthropologists suggest that shamanic practices date back to the Paleolithic era, as evidenced by ancient cave art depicting shamanistic rituals and symbols.

Here is the important caveat before we dive in: applying the word "shamanism" to every tradition we are about to discuss is imperfect, and many indigenous cultures reject the term entirely as an outside imposition that flattens the complexity and specificity of their own traditions. Every person on this list has their own name for their own practice, their own cosmology, their own protocols, and their own understanding of what is happening when a practitioner travels. The word "shamanism" is a Western umbrella that covers an enormous range of distinct traditions. We use it here for convenience, and with full acknowledgment of its limitations. What unites these traditions is the practice itself: altered states of consciousness, deliberate spirit travel, and the return with something useful for the community.

With that said, let us go around the world.

Asia: The Cradle

Siberia and Central Asia are where the anthropological study of shamanism began, and for good reason. Siberian shamanism is one of the oldest and most influential forms of shamanism, with its practices and cosmologies laying the foundational aspects of shamanic traditions worldwide. Originating from the vast, cold landscapes of Siberia, this tradition has been practiced by various ethnic groups such as the Tungusic, Yakut, Buryat, and Evenki peoples. The Siberian shaman traveled between worlds along a cosmic axis: an axis mundus, often visualized as a world tree or mountain, connecting the upper, middle, and lower realms. The yurt, a symbol of unity among the heavens, earth, and underworld, played a pivotal role in their ceremonies. Its central smoke hole was believed to be a pathway to the cosmos, guiding shamans on their spiritual quests.

The cosmology is immediately recognizable. Three worlds, a central axis connecting them, a practitioner who travels deliberately between them on behalf of their community: this is the same architecture you will use in your own journey work. The Siberian traditions did not invent this cosmology; they simply articulated it with particular clarity and left enough documentation for anthropologists to trace it.

Korea maintains one of the world's most visible and continuously living shamanic traditions. Central to the tradition are ritual specialists, the majority of them female, called mudang. The mudang serve as mediators between paying clients and the supernatural world, employing divination to determine the cause of their clients' misfortune. They also perform gut rituals, during which they offer food and drink to the gods and spirits or entertain them with storytelling, song, and dance. The calling of a mudang happens through illness: when the spirits select a person, they send a signal in the form of a devastating, incurable illness called sinbyeong. This illness cannot be treated by any medicine or therapy. It lifts only when the chosen person accepts their fate and undergoes the initiation ritual. The parallels to shamanic initiation worldwide are striking: the unwanted calling, the crisis, the death and rebirth, the emergence with power. There are over 200,000 mudang in South Korea today. This is a living tradition, actively practiced, with more practitioners per capita than most professions you could name.

China's shamanic history runs deep. Ancient historical texts described shamanistic rituals in southern China in the fourth century BC that honored mountain and river goddesses and local heroes. The ancient Wu, ecstatic mediums and ritual specialists, were active throughout early Chinese history, and shamanic practices remain alive among many of China's minority peoples: The Yi, Miao, Tujia, and Zhuang peoples all preserve strong shamanic systems. Japan's Shinto tradition contains significant shamanic elements, particularly in the figure of the miko, priestesses who historically performed possession and divination. The Ainu people of northern Japan maintain their own shamanic tradition, centered on trance and bear-spirit rituals. The itako, blind female oracles of northern Japan, work in trance states to communicate with the dead, a practice with roots going back centuries.

In Nepal and the Himalayan regions, the jhankri serves as healer, exorcist, and oracular medium, typically entering trance through drum-induced states and soul-journey work. The Indonesian island of Bali has its own rich tradition of spirit work through the figure of the balian, who navigates relationships with gods and demons through possession, dance, and ritual drama.

The Americas: North

The indigenous peoples of North America represent hundreds of distinct nations, each with their own spiritual traditions, and it would take a library instead of a chapter to do them justice. What runs through the vast majority of them is a consistent understanding that the spirit world is real, accessible, and necessary to engage with for the health of individuals and communities.

The vision quest is perhaps the most widely known practice in North American indigenous spirituality, though it takes different forms across different nations. Practiced as a rite of passage among some Indigenous cultures in North America, such as the Siksika (Blackfoot), Cree, Anishinaabe (including the Ojibwe), and Inuit, vision quests reflect the role of spirituality and contemplative thinking in Indigenous cultures and provide an important connection between the participant, the Creator, and nature.

Among the Lakota, the Hanbleceya, or "crying for a vision," was guided by elders and often lasted four days. The seeker would fast alone on a hilltop, calling out for guidance from the Great Spirit. The visions that came were carried back to the tribe and interpreted within the community. The Ojibwe practiced vision seeking as a rite of passage for young men, often involving isolation, fasting, and the hope of meeting a guardian spirit in dreams or observing signs and omens from the natural world. This guardian spirit would guide the seeker through life.

Among some Anishinaabe cultures, the "dream-fast" is considered crucial to the destiny of an individual. Dream visitors are believed to establish a relationship with the participant during the quest and serve as a guide for that person for the rest of their life. The power animal, the totem, the guardian spirit: different names for the same fundamental relationship. This is the same relationship at the heart of everything we are building in this book.

The Inuit peoples of the Arctic and subarctic maintained their own distinct shamanic traditions through the figure of the angakkuq: a practitioner who traveled to the sky and under the sea to negotiate with spirits on behalf of their community, retrieve lost souls, and address the causes of illness and misfortune. Variants of shamanism among the Inuit were once a widespread and very diverse phenomenon. The angakkuq worked with helper spirits to navigate multiple realms, a cosmological structure that echoes across every tradition on this list.

The Navajo Nation holds a sophisticated healing tradition built around the concept of hózhó: balance, beauty, and harmony between a person and the cosmos. Healing ceremonies called sings or chantways can last up to nine days, conducted by trained practitioners called hataalii, who use sand paintings, song, and ceremony to restore the patient to alignment with the natural and spiritual order. The Pueblo peoples of the American Southwest maintain kachina traditions in which spirit beings serve as intermediaries between the human and divine worlds. The Ojibwe (Anishinaabe) practice the Midewiwin, the Grand Medicine Society, which incorporates extensive knowledge of spirit travel and soul work into its healing tradition.

The Americas: South and Central

The Amazon rainforest has produced some of the most elaborate and well-documented shamanic traditions in the world. The curandero, the ayahuascero, the vegetalista: these are different titles for practitioners who work with plant medicines and spirit travel to diagnose illness, navigate spiritual crises, and maintain the health of their communities.

The Shipibo people have lived in the heart of the Amazon rain-forest for an estimated 3,000 years, and central to their way of life is the idea of an energetic world that exists beyond this physical reality. Through disciplined shamanic practices, the Shipibo believe we can travel into the energetic world to "see" and engage with the spiritual essences in nature. Shipibo shamans sing icaros, sacred healing songs, during ceremony: these songs act as bridges between the physical and spiritual worlds, their vibrations helping to "reweave" the energetic patterns of those seeking healing.

The Yanomami people of the Brazil-Venezuela border work with xapiri: a collective of spirits consulted for wisdom and guidance, accessible through trained practitioners in states of altered consciousness. The Tukano of the Colombian Amazon navigate a cosmology of multiple worlds through ritual and plant medicine, with shamans serving as the community's interface with the spiritual layers of existence. The Guaraní of Paraguay and southern Brazil practice a tradition of soul travel oriented around a concept of the divine word, the sacred center that must be sought and maintained. The Q'ero people of the Peruvian Andes, direct descendants of the Inca, work with pacos, spiritual practitioners who navigate relationships with the apus, the mountain spirits, and the layered worlds of Andean cosmology.

The Maya and Aztec civilizations of Mesoamerica maintained extensive shamanic traditions integrated with their cosmological frameworks. Maya day-keepers, the ajq'ij in K'iche', serve as calendar priests and spiritual intermediaries, tracking the 260-day sacred calendar to navigate the intersection of human life and cosmic forces. The curanderismo tradition that runs through Mexico and much of Latin America to this day has forward a lineage of folk healing that blends indigenous shamanic practice with later Spanish and African influences into something distinctly its own.

Africa: The Oldest Line

Africa is home to the San people, also called the Bushmen of the Kalahari, who represent one of the oldest surviving cultures on earth and whose shamanic tradition may be the most ancient continuously practiced form of spirit travel we have evidence for. The whole tribe takes part in dances around the fire, building in intensity until they reach a trance and communicate with the spiritual realm. San rock art, some of it 27,000 years old, depicts the rain-animals, monsters, and spirit beings encountered by dancers during out-of-body vision journeys. The San shaman enters trance through the dance, travels to other worlds, and returns with healing and information. The images on the rock walls are not decoration; they are field reports from the Other World, painted by people who had been there.

The sangoma tradition of the Zulu, Xhosa, Ndebele, and other Nguni peoples of southern Africa involves a calling through illness, an initiation, and an ongoing working relationship with ancestral spirits who provide guidance, diagnosis, and healing through the sangoma's work. The Zulu tradition of ukuthwasa describes the process of being called by ancestors, experiencing a kind of sacred sickness, and undergoing training and initiation that results in the ability to work as a healer and intermediary. The parallel to sinbyeong in Korea, to shamanic illness worldwide, is exact.

West Africa contributes the Vodou tradition (practiced in Benin, Nigeria, and brought through the diaspora to Haiti and Brazil), in which practitioners work with the Lwa, powerful spirit beings who ride their horses during possession, delivering messages and healing. The Yoruba tradition of Nigeria maintains the most elaborate surviving African cosmological framework, with its extensive pantheon of Orisha and its oracular system of Ifa. The Dagara people of Burkina Faso practice a rich tradition of ancestor communication and spirit negotiation through their own ceremonial frameworks. The Malagasy of Madagascar maintain the tradition of the ombiasy, specialists who communicate with ancestral spirits called razana. Across the continent, in tradition after tradition, the same practice: altered states, spirit contact, community healing.

Europe: Before the Erasure

Europe had its shamanic traditions too, though centuries of Christian suppression did their best to eliminate them. What survived did so at the edges, in the north, and in the fragments recorded in sagas, folklore, and the occasional ethnographic account.

The Sámi people of northern Scandinavia and the Kola Peninsula maintained one of the most robust shamanic traditions in Europe through the figure of the noaidi. The Sámi pre-Christian worldview was based on polytheism, shamanism, and animism. They held the belief that there were multiple gods and spirits inhabiting three different realms of existence: the upper, middle, and lower levels. Noaidi could travel to these different realms to heal people or contact spirits. The noaidi worked with helper spirits called gáccit, which typically manifested as animals, one for each world: a bird for the upper world, a four-legged animal for the middle world, and a fish or snake for the lower world. By the sixteenth century, Lutheran missionaries were traversing Sápmi to claim souls and establish state-system land claims. Noaidi were killed, and their drums were smashed and burned. The destruction was thorough. The survival of any of this knowledge is itself remarkable.

Norse tradition brought a form of shamanic practice called seiðr, practiced primarily by women called Völur (singular: Völva) who traveled the land offering their services. The Norse believed that the soul, called Hamr, could separate from the body and wander through the cosmos. A shaman was often aided by a Fylgja, a spirit guide often taking the form of an animal (wolf, bear, or raven), that reflected the person's character and protected them during their journey through the spirit world. The Völva worked from a high seat, attended by singers who performed the Varðlokkur, songs designed to attract spirits and hold the practitioner safe during her journey. Seidr uses seat, song, and staff to move into an altered state of consciousness to access the unseen realms. Odin himself was said to have learned seiðr from Freyja, and his ravens Huginn and Muninn, whose names mean Thought and Memory, functioned as his spirit helpers, flying across the worlds and returning with knowledge.

Celtic tradition maintained its own lineage of spirit workers under various names. The ban feasa (woman of knowledge) or ban leighis (woman of healing) could provide remedies and healing rituals, as well as cast out demons and break spells. Those who followed the creideamh si (faery faith) were known as wise wives or faery doctors, whose healing work was inspired by and devoted to the Fae. The ban chaointe or keening woman was the one entrusted with the proper commissioning of souls to the spirit world. The druids served as priest-lawyers and magicians; the bards as healers through story and song. The Celtic Otherworld, called by various names across different regions, was understood as overlapping with this world instead of being separate from it: accessible through specific liminal places and times, navigable by those trained to find their way.

Australia and Oceania: The Oldest Map

Australian Aboriginal traditions represent the longest continuous cultural history on earth, with evidence of continuous spiritual practice going back at least 50,000 years and possibly longer. The rituals that are performed enable an Aboriginal person to return to the womb of all time, which is "Dreamtime." It allows the spirit to be connected once more to all nature, to all their ancestors, and to their own personal meaning and place within the scheme of things.

The Dreaming is a concept that does not translate simply into English. It is simultaneously a creation myth, a cosmological map, a legal code, and an accessible living reality. The dreaming and traveling trails of these heroic spirit beings are the songlines, some of which could travel right across Australia, through as many as six to ten different language groupings. The songlines are literal paths across the landscape, but they are also paths through the spirit world: to know a songline is to know how to navigate, both physically and spiritually, the territory it crosses.

Aboriginal healers, called by different names across different language groups, work with the spirit dimensions of illness and country. Stanner states that Aboriginal beliefs were mystical. The Dreamtime is not a historic event. It corresponds to the whole of reality. It has a beginning, but is eternal. The Dreaming is a 'vertical line in which the past underlies and is within the present.' The spirit world and the physical world are the same world seen from different angles. Travel between them is available to those trained to make the crossing.

The Maori of Aotearoa (New Zealand) maintain a tradition of tohunga, specialists in various sacred arts including communication with atua (divine beings) and tīpuna (ancestors). The Hawaiian tradition includes the kahuna, trained specialists whose knowledge spans healing, navigation, prayer, and spirit work. Across Melanesia and Polynesia, the figure of the spiritual specialist who navigates between the human and divine worlds appears consistently, each culture having shaped the practice to their own cosmological understanding.

What This Means

Here is the thing about a practice appearing independently on every inhabited continent across tens of thousands of years: that is a data point. When something that varied in culture, language, cosmology, and method nevertheless converges on the same fundamental practice of deliberate spirit travel, of altered states used intentionally, of power animals and spirit guides, and multiple worlds accessible through the practiced human nervous system, the conclusion is not that all these people were wrong. The conclusion is that they were all right, in the way that pointing at the same mountain from different valleys is a different direction, but the same mountain.

Cross-cultural studies confirm that shamans and other shamanistic healers are found universally in human cultures: all societies have people who use altered states of consciousness to interact with the spirit world on behalf of their communities.

You are learning a practice that your ancestors practiced, whatever your ancestry.

You are learning it in one particular form, sculpted by the tradition in which I was trained and by the specific cosmological framework this book operates within. But you are joining a lineage that is as old as human consciousness itself, practiced by people on every piece of ground your feet have ever touched, under every sky you have ever seen.

The world has always known how to do this. Now you are learning too.

YOU, THE TRAVELER

Witchdoctor? I Thought You Were a Shaman?

I Thought You Were A Shaman?

I am a witchdoctor. I avoid separating the term into witch and doctor because that split creates the wrong impression. People hear doctor and assume I serve witches only. I also serve beyond the label faith healer, which Western culture tends to prefer because it feels palatable. I work in taboo spaces because... well... someone has to do it. That work belongs to my job. My title exists for accuracy; comfort comes second. My job title needs to describe what I do.

From the beginning of time, spirits have participated in our world. Yet when Indigenous people interact with spirits openly, outsiders label them fantastical or malefic, leaving no room for the everyday person to participate in the world of spirits. Meanwhile, the majority of the population believes in spirits, even when they keep their distance from religious doctrine.

When we look at tribes throughout Africa, outsiders often label them feral or savage, and we overlook their genius in connecting to spirits. These biases hide inside systemic problems around spiritual accessibility.

Blackness becomes equated with strangeness; strangeness becomes treated as exclusionary. The message becomes, for many people, spirit work is off-limits.

Witchdoctors Belong to the Shamanic Community

The role reaches far beyond the stereotype. A Voodoo priest calling on the power of ancestors functions as a witchdoctor. A griot healing through storytelling functions as a witchdoctor. A root worker advising you on plants for protection in your garden functions as a witchdoctor. Same family. A faith healer who lays hands and uses prayer to heal you with the power of energy, voice, and divine intervention is a witchdoctor. A shaman who journeys to the lower world to gather the parts of you that broke off during trauma is a witchdoctor.

Modern Western culture pushes the idea that smartphones make us more connected to ourselves, our yoga instructors, and our higher selves. We start believing we have outgrown ancient community healers. We start believing we only need them if they can fit into a schedule between a Starbucks run and a work meeting.

Where the Term Came From

Witchdoctor became the name Western cultures gave to those who mediate between humans and spirits, addressing illnesses, problems, relationships, and conflicts between two worlds. The term was slur energy then; it has it now. Yet it still points toward a real function.

Shamanic refers to those who travel between spirit worlds. People often associate shamanism with Native American cultures or Siberia. Egypt also held a shamanic culture (one of the oldest civilized societies people tend to acknowledge). The story of Isis and Osiris has journeys to and from the other world in search of life through death. Shamanism also appears within Shinto. Shinto is an Indigenous religion (its original incarnation before survival-based adaptation) of Japan, celebrating interaction with kami, nature, and animism. And of course we can name the Zulu, Lakota, Yup'ik, Candomble, Sami, Druids, Sangoma, Zande, Muism, and the Aborigines (to name a few).

Aspects of The Evolution of the Shamanic Practitioner

The history of the shaman is rooted in ancient cultures and traditions that date back thousands of years. The roles of a shaman have evolved, blending historical practices with modern interpretations. In our exploration of shamanism, let's delve into the interaction with spirits through out-of-body spirit travel, commonly referred to as journeying, spirit walking, or astral travel.

Historical Roles of a Shaman:

Shamans have held a variety of roles throughout history, each reflecting a unique aspect of their spiritual and healing capabilities. From ancient civilizations to indigenous tribes, the shaman's duties have encompassed a wide range of responsibilities:

- Ability to Disperse: Shamans possess the power to move energy, creating balance and harmony within the spiritual realm.
- Ability to be at Peace: A shaman's inner peace enables them to connect with higher realms and channel divine guidance.
- Ability to Direct: Shamans exhibit leadership qualities, guiding individuals and communities towards spiritual growth and enlightenment.
- Ability to Manifest: Through spell work and rituals, shamans can manifest intentions and bring about positive change.
- Ability to Bless: Shamans bestow blessings upon individuals, objects, and places, infusing them with divine energy.
- Ability to Empower: Shamans empower others to tap into their inner strength and innate potential.
- Ability to Create: Shamans are creators, spending their energy and artistic skills on bringing life into various vehicles.
- Being a Physician: Shamans act as healers, addressing physical, emotional, and spiritual ailments with divine intervention.

- Being a Psychotherapist: Shamans provide psychological support and guidance, aiding individuals in their journey towards wholeness.
- Being a Diagnostician: Shamans possess the ability to diagnose and understand the root causes of illness and imbalance.
- Enacting Religious Functions: Shamans serve as intermediaries between the physical world and the spirit realm, performing sacred ceremonies and rituals.
- Being a Magician: Shamans harness the power of magic to effect change and bring about healing.
- Acting as a Performing Artist: Shamans use music, dance, and storytelling to convey spiritual teachings and connect with divine energies.
- Connecting to Nature: Shamans have a deep connection to nature, drawing inspiration and wisdom from the natural world.
- Being a Sensitive: Shamans are highly attuned to subtle energies and spiritual vibrations, allowing them to navigate the unseen realms with ease.
- Acting on the Calling to Ease Pain: Shamans are called to alleviate suffering in all forms, offering comfort and healing to people, animals, and the environment.
- Acting on the Gift of Beauty: Shamans possess a vision for creating beauty in the world, infusing their surroundings with harmony and grace.
- Enjoying the Strong Relationship to Solitude: Shamans embrace solitude as a means of deepening their connection to the spiritual realms and gaining insight into their purpose.

As we embark on this journey into Shamanism and the practice of interacting with spirits through out-of-body experiences, explore all facets of becoming a shamanic practitioner. By honoring the historical and modern roles of a shaman, we can deepen our understanding of the sacred path we walk and the profound impact we have on the world around us.

What Makes Someone a Shaman

To be considered a shaman, one must possess the ability to:

- Shape-shift, or act as a storyteller
- Heal the body or spirit
- Practice ancestor or nature worship
- Serve as an intermediary between the spirit world and our world as a psychic medium, specializing in out-of-body travel
- Act as a peacemaker, or priest, with spirits
- Travel between spirit worlds and interact with spirits
- Hold rituals of peace, protection, and purification
- Use divination techniques to benefit a tribe
- Hold secret knowledge, history, and mythos
- Become a leader
- Initiate through spiritual trials

What Makes Someone a Witchdoctor

Because of this, there is a specific set of skills a witchdoctor must possess. There are a few of us because we must demonstrate proficiency across a particular set of abilities:

- Shape-shifter, or storyteller
- Psychic medium
- Exorcist
- Healer
- Manifester, or witch for hire
- Teacher, or mentor
- Mediator and counselor
- Peacemaker, or priest, with spirits
- Transitioner, meaning a spirit walker with the ability to leave the body and travel between spirit worlds or among spirits

Where does this list come from? Neolithic and Bronze Age cultures. Early folk healers often specialized in a single area. Colonization suppressed Indigenous practice; surviving healers brought more responsibilities to keep communities alive.

Witchdoctory as Practice instead of Religion

Witchdoctory is not a religion; it is a practice that encompasses skills in mysticism, psychic development, spirituality, and the occult.

Closest equivalents include the original Kahuna of Hawai'i, the Albularyo of the Philippines, and the Debtera of Ethiopia. The term witch doctor originated in England in the 1800s. The term root worker emerged in the Southern United States, a title derived from Fon faith healers kidnapped into slavery.

Globally, we can summarize the skills that various faith healers must possess:

- Mediating on behalf of spirits; removing unwanted or dangerous entities; aiding in healing afflicted spirits, whether human or otherwise; exorcist

- Healing the spirits of the forest, water, and the spirit within each community member; healer

- Divining information from weather and spirits to guide the community; psychic medium

- Comfort with transitions; walking among spirits in spirit world and around us; interacting from a shamanic platform; spirit walker

- Performing tasks by harnessing the energy of objects to shape the world around us; manifester, sorcerer

- Finding students and passing down knowledge; teacher

- Singing, dancing, or telling stories about ourselves to preserve humanity and memory, especially when books and written language remain absent; shape-shifter

- Talk story; spending time together to share and listen; allowing community members to release anguish through shared space and communication; spiritual counselor and mediator

- Passing down stories of faith, gods, spirits, and heroes to remind us of warnings, ethics, and societal structure; a priest

Yep, all of them. A person can hold the label shamanic practitioner when they do some shamanic things. A shamanic practitioner does some shamanic work. A shaman does all of it.

Who Writes the Story

Archaeology lets us unearth ancient ways that remained outside written form. Modern witchcraft cultures, such as Wicca, Golden Dawn, Theosophy, and others, often point toward the old ways through confirmation bias.

Shamanic cultures received simplification for white audiences through preconceived colonized philosophies and a lens that explains spiritual technology through comparison. You, today, can change this by not listening to sound-bite versions of things... so...

This is barbarism versus savagery. The cultures that conquer decide what holds meaning (and what doesn't). Let me say that again. The barbarian, meaning any culture that used brutality to gain power, takes technologies, even spiritual ones, interprets them through its own worldview, and passes them off as its own. In that worldview, you serve as food or follower, and that same energy still appears within communities today.

I point out that so-called savage cultures, the ones connected to plants, tribes, relationships, and industry, held a deep spiritual culture. Conquering cultures wrote the story, so conquest got celebrated.

Even your most glorified ritual, approved by church or another colonizing culture, has roots in older ways.

Those older ways trace back to the witchdoctor. Are you a brute by taking and calling it your own (especially out of context or just a sound-bite because of the convenience and laziness), or are you a savage who learns, repeats, and takes time?

Your skin color doesn't matter if you're doing it right.

A Word for Modern Practitioners

Witches and practitioners of shamanic, preternatural, and mystical ways need to shoulder responsibility for the loss of many original techniques, especially in the last twenty years. Social validation for what you know often replaces passing down what you know. Idol culture often replaces preservation. As an educator, I wag my finger. Tsk, tsk. Spread the knowledge. That intention belongs to old ways. Spread your image? That belongs to colonization. Tsk.

How Indigenous Cultures Define Healers

Indigenous peoples define healers by what they do instead of by whom they know. A healer blends call and duty, a fateful entanglement with darker spirit worlds, and an aptitude for spell weaving. Combine that with deep knowledge of psychology, storytelling, anatomy, anthropology, sociology, and metaphysics, and you have a witchdoctor.

Those who teach witchdoctory carefully select students. Western culture encourages people to decide that they will learn, then shop for a teacher. Traditional culture moves differently. Your teacher decides to teach you. They choose you, bring you under their wing, and begin the process of indoctrination. Teachers prefer students who study with respect instead of entitlement. A witchdoctor keeps mentors' names sacred and honors them through reverent demonstration of skill.

Instead of listing teachers as a colonizer method of validating skill, we describe what we can do, then prove it through action. I chose to break this tradition to keep the old ways going, but also to meet society in the Western way. I built a school. I mentor many of my students (all adults, now). Through authorship, I extend that teaching to you. By picking up this book, you have been chosen.

Psychic and Trance Definitions

Before we go further, we need to agree on our language. When terminology drifts, practice drifts with it; when words lose precision, techniques follow, and what suffers is both the practitioner and the spirits we are trying to help.

So, think of this section the way you would think of the first day of class, where I stand at the front of the room, write terms on the board, and say, " This is what I mean when I use this word, and from here on out, we all use it the same way.

Let us define the vocabulary clearly and move forward together.

Core Terms

Psychic: A psychic perceives the electromagnetic energy of the tangible world through extrasensory perception, which includes reading living people, animals, rooms, objects, and land itself, picking up emotional residue, environmental memory, and subtle energetic shifts that most people walk past without noticing. We have to be able to verify what a psychic gets psychically. Otherwise, we use the term "medium."

Medium: A medium directs that same extrasensory perception toward the intangible world and communicates with spirits, the dead, and unseen intelligences, receiving information and translating it into language the living can understand. This happens while they are conscious.

Channeler: A channeler allows a spirit to communicate through their physical body so that their voice, posture, and nervous system function as the conduit for that spirit's expression, creating a direct embodied transmission, not a conversation at a distance. It is important to note that the spirit "rides" the human. If a spirit talks "to someone," this is a medium. If a spirit takes over someone, this is channeling.

Possession: Possession occurs when a spirit inhabits part of a person and exerts control over thoughts, emotions, or movement without consent, resulting in influence that feels invasive and physically enacted. With consent(Or riding): channeling. Without: possession, even if it is temporary.

Avatar: An avatar refers to an incarnation or manifestation of a being that already exists, a word rooted in Sanskrit that describes divine descent into form, and it functions as a representation, such as a deity appearing on Earth or even a digital likeness that represents you online. Your totem or power animal is your avatar. It is an incarnation of your psychic self.

Shamanic Practitioner: A shamanic practitioner is anyone actively using shamanic rituals, tools, and techniques to engage with the spirit world and deepen their spiritual capacity, which includes you as you work through this material, but does not exhibit all of the necessary skills or life dedication that a Shaman does.

Shaman: A shaman is someone who has undergone a full initiatory transformation that permanently alters their relationship with the casual world and the spirit world and equips them to travel, mediate, and work between realms at a deep level.

Familiar: A familiar is a real animal, living or deceased, that partners with you in your craft through relationship, trust, and shared life experience.

Totem or Power Animal: A totem or power animal represents the deeper structure of your psychic and spiritual self and reveals itself through ritual or journeying as part of your development.

Spirit Animal: A spirit animal serves as an inspirational role model whose qualities you consciously cultivate in your own life.

Animal Guide: An animal guide is a spirit ally that accompanies you over time, offering protection, direction, and insight along your path. In your spiritual work, if you see *another* animal when you are journeying that is not "you" (i.e., your totem), then it may be an animal guide.

Aumakua: Aumakua are ancestral spirits who manifest in animal form and continue caring for their lineage through guidance and protection in our causal plane. That means that you will have visual omens from the same animal when you are on the right path. Mine are deer. When I see deer, I know my ancestors have sent them to tell me that I am on the right path.

Trance, Mediumship, and Astral Projection

Students often ask where psychic perception ends and shamanic travel begins, and the easiest way to explain it is to imagine a gradual shift in awareness, like turning a dial that slowly moves your attention from the physical world toward the spirit world, with each level producing a different depth of engagement, and while that happens, you lose more and more casual consciousness. So instead of treating these as separate phenomena, I teach them as stages along a continuum.

Levels of Trance

Everyday Perceptive State: At this level, you remain fully present in your body and environment while still picking up subtle impressions, which is where everyday psychic awareness functions most naturally.

Absorption State: Here, your focus narrows and deepens, your third eye engages more fully, and you begin perceiving spiritual influences while still tracking your physical surroundings, which creates the ideal condition for mediumship.

Daydream State: Your attention immerses completely in an inner stream of imagery or thought, and returning to ordinary awareness takes a moment, a state many people recognize from visualization or creative flow.

Shamanic Trance State: Awareness withdraws from the material world and settles into the otherworld; the body feels distant, and your sense of identity shifts toward the spiritual plane, creating what we traditionally call true trance.

Detached Trance State: The body rests as if sleeping while the mind remains active in the spirit world, allowing perception and interaction through the inner eye while your spirit stays tethered to the body.

Spirit Walk State or Astral Projection or Shamanic Journeying: At this depth, the body enters profound rest and awareness transfers fully to the spirit body, allowing you to travel, engage, and work directly within the otherworld instead of observing from a distance.

Learn these definitions thoroughly and use them consistently, because when your language stays clear, your thinking stays clear, and clear thinking supports safe, effective spiritual work.

What Is a Totem Animal?

Let's get one thing out of the way immediately: your totem is not your favorite animal. It is not the creature you resonate with most deeply, the one on your coffee mug, or the spirit you decided represented you after taking a quiz online. Your totem is the psychic part of yourself made visible; it is revealed to you through a specific journey, and you do not get to pick it. Whatever appears is what appears, and that animal is yours whether it flatters you or not (spoiler: sometimes it does not, and that is precisely the point).

The totem is the embodiment of your spiritual potential. Every person has within them a psychic self, a part of the spirit that operates beneath the noise of daily life, beneath the ego, beneath the stories you tell about who you are and what you deserve. That part of you simply knows. The totem is that part of you given form... your purest spiritual self, expressed as an animal.

Why An Animal?

Because animals are honest in a way human consciousness rarely manages. An animal acts from survival, care, and purpose. It does not spend time wondering whether it made the right choice or what other animals think of it. It does not spend three days wondering whether it made the right choice or what other animals think of it. When a hawk hunts, it hunts. When a wolf cares for its pack, it cares. When a bear rests, it rests fully and without guilt. There is no motive layered underneath the motive, no hidden agenda running quietly in the background. That clarity is exactly what your psychic self-possesses and what your human mind constantly struggles to achieve. The animal form of your totem is the most accurate representation of what your psychic self actually is: instinctual, purposeful, and completely without pretense.

This distinction matters enormously in practice. Your spirit guides carry their own wisdom, their own histories, and their own purposes. Your ancestors bring lineage and memory. Your totem has only you. It is a facet of your own spirit that you have yet to hear clearly. When your totem communicates with you during a journey, you are essentially in conversation with your own deepest self: the part that already knows what your thinking mind is still arguing about.

Because the totem is you, it will always act in your genuine interest. It will tell you what is true instead of what is comfortable. It is consistent in the way that the deepest parts of us are consistent, steady beneath every surface storm. Students sometimes feel disappointed when their totem seems simple, quiet, or unglamorous. They wanted an eagle and received a possum (no offense to possums, who are remarkable, by the way). The animal that appears is a mirror. Learn to look at it honestly, and you will learn something genuine about yourself.

The totem is also your navigator and your protector in the spirit worlds. Because it operates from pure instinct, not human reasoning, it perceives danger, opportunity, and direction in ways your conscious mind cannot. In journey work, your totem knows where to go, when to stop, and when to leave. When it pulls back, you pull back. This is a rule, not a suggestion. The totem has access to information your ego does not, and learning to trust that guidance is one of the foundational skills of this entire practice.

Your totem is discovered through journey, and through journey alone. It shows itself when you travel to the place where it waits, and the experience of meeting it is distinct from imagination in ways that become clear with practice. We will cover that journey in full in the chapters ahead. For now, understand what you are looking for: the honest, instinctual, agenda-free part of yourself, waiting patiently in animal form, exactly as it has always been.

Indigenous, Ancient, and Folk Italian Shamanic Spirit Walking

Astral projection, ecstasy, spirit walking, shamanic journeying, and out-of-body experiences all refer to the same condition: your spirit separates from the physical form and operates beyond the conscious experience, either among the living in the Middle World or into the spirit worlds of the other side. People argue terminology because the occult loves vocabulary drama, yet the mechanism remains consistent across cultures and eras.

I care about mechanism because mechanism gives you a repeatable skill. When you spirit walk, your body rests, and your awareness shifts, and the part of you that perceives beyond the five senses takes the lead. You can call it astral work, you can call it journeying, you can call it ecstasy, and you will still be doing the same act of purposeful departure. The only important question is whether you can do it intentionally, safely, and with results you can track.

Spirit walking appears in most indigenous cultures because it solves a universal human need: the need to commune with spirits, to retrieve information, to heal, and to negotiate the boundary between life and death.

A practitioner enters a deep meditative state, often called ecstasy, meaning a state where awareness withdraws from the physical world without collapsing into sleep. In that state, the spirit sets out to commune with the spirits of nature, the ancestors, or beings that exist on other planes. People often frame journeying as self-discovery, which it certainly can be, yet the older traditions treat it as a practical skill that supports community health and spiritual balance. That is why this practice requires respect and caution, because traveling among spirits works beautifully when you behave like a professional and becomes chaotic when you behave like a tourist. You are receiving guidance because guidance reduces risk and increases clarity.

The Call

The call to walk among spirits has been recognized in many places and many cultures, and people have always noticed patterns in who tends to receive that call. Some traditions speak of physical markers such as birthmarks, unusual moles, and culturally specific features that stand out in a family line, including hair texture, eye color, and body type. Some cultures treat twins as uniquely called, and others view a baby born with a caul as carrying a spiritual signature from the beginning. Many traditions also recognize epilepsy and certain somatic pain disorders as signs that a person lives with one foot closer to the veil, because the nervous system experiences reality in ways that the average person never has to manage. These signs do not guarantee anything, yet they show up often enough that elders have learned to pay attention.

Personality traits often reveal far more than physical markers because spirit walking requires a particular kind of inner landscape. Many called practitioners feel the need to be near trees or the ocean, and that need does not come from aesthetic preference; it comes from regulation, because nature quiets the mind and stabilizes sensitivity. Many called practitioners prefer solitude without loneliness, meaning they enjoy their own company and feel restored by quiet instead of threatened by it. High sensitivity, emotional attunement, and comfort around death also appear frequently, because the spirit walker must remain steady around themes that other people avoid. A person who panics around grief, illness, or the dead struggles to stay present in the other world. A person who respects those realities learns to travel with a clearer footing.

Reality and Imagination: Why Out of Body Work Persists Across Cultures

People love asking whether out-of-body experiences are real or imagination, and the question reveals an assumption that imagination equals unreality. Imagination is a faculty of perception, a language of the mind, and it functions as the interface through which many spiritual experiences happen. The real question involves whether the experience produces verifiable information, repeatable outcomes, and consistent sensory patterns across practitioners. A vast percentage of humans believe in spirits in some form, even among people who feel distant from organized religion, and that belief implies a widespread intuition that consciousness extends beyond flesh. When a person believes the dead can appear, they already accept that spirits can exist apart from the body. Spirit walking extends that same logic to the living, because a living spirit remains tethered to the body while still capable of operating beyond it.

If the tether exists in death, then the tether can exist in life, and that tether becomes the mechanism through which information returns to the brain for interpretation. You travel, you observe, you interact, and your nervous system translates the experience into memory and meaning when you return. That does not mean every image equals an objective fact, interpretation is required, and a mature practitioner learns to account for that and verify accordingly. Over time, you develop discernment, which means you recognize the difference between self-generated fantasy and genuine contact, and you do that through practice, documentation, and comparison with reality. The goal is competence, not belief.

The Double Life of the Witchdoctor Shaman

Witchdoctor Shamans live a double life, one in the physical world and one in the spiritual world, and the mature practitioner learns to give both worlds the respect they deserve. The physical world requires more consistent attention because bodies need food, sleep, relationships, and work.

Responsibilities do not pause for trance.

The spiritual world remains present whether people notice it or ignore it, and many people ignore it until they want something, fear something, or need help. The witchdoctor tends to remain aware of both, meaning they notice how spirits affect people and how people affect spirits. This awareness becomes a lived reality instead of an occasional curiosity. It also requires self-control, because being aware of more than the average person creates fatigue if you lack boundaries.

Spirit walking has existed since the Neolithic era and continued thriving through the Bronze Age, and as organized religions developed, many indigenous spiritualities became assimilated into larger systems. Practices survived through adaptation, secrecy, and family transmission because spiritual technology tends to outlive institutions. When institutions absorb older practices, the surface changes and the mechanism remains, and a trained eye learns to recognize that continuity. This is why the craft keeps echoing across continents and centuries. People keep discovering the same tools because the need for them has never changed.

Folk Italian Spirit Walking and the Survival of the Old Ways

If you read Charles Godfrey Leland's **Etruscan Roman Remains in Popular Tradition**, you will notice the way superstition and taboo function as spiritual law, and you will also notice parallels to Hawaiian kapu as a system of rules that inform safety and right action. Kapu means a set of rules that govern behavior, protection, and spiritual order, and the English word taboo traces back to that concept. When a culture holds a rule as untouchable, that rule functions as a spiritual boundary designed to prevent harm and preserve balance. Folk systems across the world developed their own versions of this framework because every community needed a way to encode spiritual safety into everyday life. Italy held its own frameworks through folk tradition, even when public practice had enormous risk.

During the Spanish Inquisition, many Italian folk practices were forced underground because speaking of them could lead to death. People held knowledge in stories, whispers, and private family lineages, and secrecy protected survival. The result of secrecy involves distortion over time because any tradition practiced in fear becomes fragmented, and fragmentation creates gaps. Those gaps can be repaired when a tradition reconnects with living examples of similar technology, and this is where cross-cultural exchange becomes complicated and historically real. The nineteenth century included increasing contact between Europe and Polynesia through travel, colonization, and the movement of ideas, and that period also included the violent suppression of Hawaiian religion and practice through missionary influence, legal restrictions, and cultural pressure. In that larger timeline, different cultures experienced loss, revival, and adaptation in overlapping cycles, which is why the story of survival never follows a simple straight line.

Within Italian folk practice, the strega became famously associated with leaving the body at night to work in spirit form, to perform spells, to engage in spiritual conflict, and to return home. When a witch was married, a spouse often watched the body, because the resting body remained vulnerable to interruption and harm. When a witch lived alone, the role of guardian shifted to a familiar, a household spirit, or a protective support team invoked to keep vigil. This detail matters because it reveals how seriously practitioners treated the vulnerability of trance. People protected the body because they understood the body as the anchor point that allows a safe return.

Protection: Watchtowers as the Modern Vigil

When Italians spirit walked in older folk contexts, human guardianship often served as protection, because someone physically present could prevent interference and could respond if the body reacted. They also invoked protective spirits, such as the folletti, to guard the resting body while the spirit traveled. You will do the same thing through your Watchtower Ritual of Protection, because the function remains consistent even when the form shifts. Your Watchtowers serve as sentinels, boundaries, and allies, and they create a structured perimeter around your work. You prepare the space. You establish guardianship. You travel with purpose. You return cleanly. You repeat.

When you approach spirit walking with that level of structure, you build skill that grows steadily instead of dramatically. You also build trust with the spirits who observe you, because spirits respect consistency. If you treat the work like a sacred craft instead of a thrill, the craft returns that respect through stability. That is why protection belongs at the beginning instead of as an afterthought. That is why your training includes it.

Preparing For Your First Journey

The Problem With Visualization

Visualization has three purposes in this work:

1. To jump-start your clairvoyance so you can see clearly when receiving visual information.

2. To create thought forms as an ingredient in spell work.

3. To retrain your brain's habit of negative thinking.

Visualization is not a mechanism for moving energy... at least not alone, and not with the force a witchdoctor requires. Energy is always leaving your body because we use it for everything, but focused imagination is not enough to push it where it needs to go. You need to push. Energy needs something to move it. My method is gripping my lower abdominal muscles and my ribs, the way you brace when someone is about to punch you in the stomach. Feel the energy around your temples and push out with your breath. When I ask you to push energy into something in the exercises ahead, that is exactly what I mean: brace, feel, push. Creative thinking alone will get you nowhere near it.

The same principle applies to the rest of this work. Visualization means you are making something up. A genuine psychic vision happens to you; you are the recipient, not the author. Effective spell work. is practical, not imagined. That said, the beginning of a shamanic journey does involve visualization, and here is why that is consistent: the opening visualization is a warm-up, a writing prompt, a prelude that primes the mind to receive. It triggers the canvas. After that opening, the visuals will actually get weaker and harder to see, which is exactly how you know they are real. You are experiencing something instead of generating it. If you are controlling it, you are creating it. The goal is to experience, and experience, by definition, is something that happens to you.

The Problem With Meditative Silence

Worrying about quieting your mind keeps your mind busy with worry. So we skip that entirely. You will do a mind dump at the beginning of your journey: anything distracting or weighing on you gets quickly acknowledged and set aside so you can relax into the experience of the Other World. That is all the silence you need.

Shamanic Breathing

You are probably familiar with box breathing, yogic breathing, yin and yang breathing... all of which emphasize deep, focused breath work. Shamanic breathing goes the opposite direction, and understanding why matters.

When you travel out of body, the efficiency of your breathing becomes essential. Deep, conscious breathing is something we do while awake and alert; during sleep, breathing naturally becomes shallow and subdued. Shamans, drawing from ancient Neolithic traditions, have cultivated the skill of operating on minimal oxygen intake, taking only what the body requires and using it well.

The model here is the Siberian monks. Sit comfortably and breathe slowly and shallowly: small, measured breaths that meet your body's needs without excess, exhaling gently after each inhale. As you do this, pay attention to your heart rate. A heart rate above seventy beats per minute signals agitation, which works against the state you are trying to reach. Aim for sixty beats per minute or below, breathing sparingly and efficiently. When you can journey without resorting to deep breathing, you have found the essence of shamanic breathing. That is your benchmark.

Ecstasy: The State You Are After

Ecstasy, astral travel, out-of-body experience, spirit walking, journeying... these terms all point to the same thing: the state your brain and body need to reach so your spirit can travel to the Other World. The brain produces different waves depending on what it is doing, and for the spirit to relax enough for its pieces to stretch apart and move, the brain needs to be producing theta waves specifically. Theta is that in-between state just before sleep and just after waking, heavy and drifting, and strangely aware. That is where we are headed. That is ecstasy.

Beginning Your Spirit-Walk Practice

Get comfortable, but leave just enough discomfort that you stay awake. My preference is a meditation cushion: my body softens, my posture stays upright, and I remain at that edge of alertness without effort. Cross-legged or kneeling both work well for the same reason. Christopher Penczak's book The Temple of Shamanic Witchcraft also documents other postures collected from various traditions: lying on your back, Celtic sitting (one foot slightly closer than the other, not crossed), Egyptian sitting (in a chair with feet flat on the floor and palms facing upward), lying on your side, lying face down, standing, or squatting. Choose what keeps you just slightly awake.

Here is the rule: the moment you become aware of your physical body, you are no longer traveling. An itch on your face, a dog barking, the weight of your arm on your knee... any physical awareness pulls you back. Out of body means exactly that; your attention is off your body entirely. Your body is in stasis. If you are scratching your nose and journeying simultaneously, you have a strong imagination and a lot of practice ahead of you.

Pain follows the same logic. I pass kidney stones with some regularity, and the soreness afterward is not subtle. There is no traveling through that kind of physical noise. If you live with chronic pain, working with your doctors to manage it becomes part of your spiritual practice; a body that keeps announcing itself is a body you cannot leave. We will return to this later, but the balance is important now: pain managed enough to ignore, mind clear enough to navigate.

How To Leave Your Body

You need to get your brain to theta. Here are your options:

Guided Meditation: Many students prefer this, especially at first, listening to a voice through the visualization portion until it is time to release and journey. The brain moves from alpha into theta more easily when following someone else's lead. The limitation is that when you are doing actual work in the field, you will be in beta or gamma and need to bring yourself down to theta without assistance. Build the independent skill as soon as you can.

Inebriation: Ayahuasca, mugwort, mushrooms, and other substances can bring the brain to the necessary state. Ayahuasca especially should only ever be undertaken with a trained Peruvian shaman whose job is to keep you safe while you journey; this is not a recreational experiment. In this training, inebriation as a method of travel is off the table entirely. Some of you are already mentally composing your exceptions. Save it. The reason is practical and covered in detail in the substance section below.

Sound: A drumbeat at around one hundred twenty to one hundred forty beats per minute relaxes the mind toward theta steadily and reliably. The volume keeps you awake; the repetition draws you inward. With practice, your nervous system learns the association and drops into theta faster each time you hear it. This is the method I recommend, and for most students it becomes the easiest and most consistent way to travel. Use a dedicated drumming track instead of a playlist, and use noise-canceling headphones so that your physical environment cannot yank you back mid-journey. A dog barking at the wrong moment is genuinely funny until it happens to you four sessions in a row.

A quick note on music: if the track has lyrics you understand or a melody you enjoy, your brain will engage with it and pull you back to alpha. Neutral, repetitive percussion only.

Recap: shamanic drum track, noise-canceling headphones, a space with no distractions, a comfortable posture with a trace of alertness, and your protective circle in place.

Your Environment

Your space needs to support your ability to go somewhere else entirely. External sounds are the most common disruption: neighbors, traffic, sirens, lawn mowers, anything that pulls your awareness back into the room where your body is sitting. Noise-canceling headphones handle most of this, but the headphones themselves need to be comfortable; an uncomfortable headset is just another physical distraction.

Inside the space, eliminate anything that produces light or sound: televisions, computers, LED strips, and notification lights on devices. Even through closed eyelids, flashing or shifting light registers and disrupts the state. Dim lamps or candles (set up safely) support the environment you are trying to create.

Let the people and animals in your home know what you are doing and why. Ask for the time and the quiet you need. Our ancestors journeyed with the support of their spouses, children, and animals; yours can offer the same.

Substance Use

Substances that induce altered states can bring the spirit close to the threshold of travel, and that is precisely the problem. Intoxication loosens the fibers of the soul; it creates the opening for something to come in while you are distracted and undefended. You will learn in detail later what makes a person vulnerable to spirit attachment, and inebriation is high on that list. When you are head-to-head with an entity that needs moving, you cannot afford any compromise to your clarity, your perception, or your decision-making. This is the work of an exorcist; the stakes are real.

Furthermore, training under the influence means you become dependent on that state to travel. You need to build the skill in your actual body, in your actual mind, so it is available to you under any conditions.

Clean and sober. Every time. Pain management is acceptable; mental fog is not. That balance is yours to find with your doctors, but the line itself does not move.

Relaxation Into Trance and Then Into Ecstasy

Start in your ordinary state of awareness: eyes closed, body settling, the physical world still present around you. Take a breath and let the weight of whatever is on your mind surface quickly so it can be acknowledged and released. Give it a moment, then let it go.

As you relax further, feel the quality of your awareness shift. The grip on your surroundings loosens. The room matters a little less. Your thoughts soften their edges. This is the threshold; you are approaching the space between ordinary awareness and trance.

Continue to relax. Let the drumbeat carry your attention inward. The body grows heavier and more distant. Thoughts begin to drift into imagery instead of language. The analytical mind quiets on its own, without you forcing it. This is the shamanic trance state; your awareness is withdrawing from the material world, and the spirit is beginning to stir.

Deepen further. The body is now something you are aware of in the far background; its sensations happen faintly and dissolve without pulling you back. Your breath is slow and shallow. Your heart rate is low. The Other World becomes more present than the room. This is ecstasy: that threshold between wakefulness and sleep, that pseudo-death and pseudo-sleep where the spirit steps free of the body and the journey genuinely begins.

Let the drumbeat carry you. Surrender the resistance. The spirit knows where to go.

It's Time to Journey: The Mind Dump

Start your shamanic drumming track and settle into your chosen position.

Breathe in two three, out two three, in two three, out two three.

A slow waltz tempo with your breath. Restful, gentle, natural... whatever your body does when it simply breathes. If your natural breath is shallow, let it be shallow. We are aiming for a heart rate around sixty beats per minute, and that is all we need from you right now. In two three, out two three. The Buddhist monks spent lifetimes learning to control their heart rate through breath alone; you are learning the same skill, just with less incense and more demons in your future.

Eyes closed, with your gaze directed slightly upward toward your eyebrows. No need to tilt your chin; simply let your focus drift up behind your closed lids. You will feel the difference immediately.

The Visualization Portion

This part exists to prime the canvas: to wake up the markers and crayons your mind will use to interpret and experience everything that follows. Consider it the warm-up lap.

Visualize a flame emerging from the darkness in front of you. Watch it burn and allow it to float toward you. Reach out and touch it. When you do, your energy changes its color; this flame is a reflection of you, a brightness made from your own spirit. Watch it burn brightly, then dimly. Study it. This is your energy, out in front of you where you can actually see it.

Now, let the flame float above your head. As it grows more luminous, the darkness around you begins to give way... something is visible ahead. This light is yours; you light your way.

As the flame brightens further, a staircase appears. The direction is irrelevant; up, down, sideways, Salvador Dali fever dream, it does not matter. You are taking the stairs. You have ten breaths, counting down from ten. With every inhale, take one step; with every exhale, rest on that step.

The Mind Dump: Why the Stairs Exist

Here is what the stairs are actually for, because it is more specific and more important than simply relaxing.

Your mind arrived at this journey carrying things. It always does (even in beta). The grocery run you keep forgetting, the email sitting in your drafts, the conversation from this morning that is still unresolved, the worry about your kid, the thing your boss said, the bill you meant to pay last Tuesday... all of it came with you into this space, and all of it is going to compete for your attention the moment you try to go somewhere else. This is human. This is normal. The solution is not to silence any of it, like you would in Buddhist practices (which is not shamanic). The stairs give you a specific place and a specific permission to acknowledge every single one of them, fully and without rushing, so they can be set down.

Silencing the mind is a beautiful idea that does not work in shamanic practice, and chasing it will only frustrate you. Your mind is holding onto these things because they feel unfinished, and unfinished things demand attention. The stairs give you a specific place and a specific permission to acknowledge every single one of them, fully and without rushing, so they can be set down.

So, here is what actually happens on the stairs: you take a step, you breathe, and if something surfaces in your mind, you follow it. You give it your full attention for a moment. You let it say whatever it needs to say. You look at it squarely, acknowledge it exists, and then you come back to the stairs. Back to the breath. Back to the count. You take another step. Something else surfaces; you follow it the same way. You look at it, you acknowledge it, you return. Step. Breath. Count.

This is the mind dump. You are completing each distraction instead of pushing it away, because pushed things push back. A thought you have genuinely acknowledged and set down stays down. A thought you tried to ignore will tap you on the shoulder every thirty seconds for the rest of the journey. You do not have time for that. Your client certainly does not have time for that.

Some students move through the stairs quickly because their minds are relatively clear that day. Others spend the full ten breaths (or even more) on a single persistent worry and still feel like they barely made a dent. Both experiences are valid, and both are useful pieces of information about where you are that day. The stairs accommodate all of it. Take as long as you need on each step. The drumbeat is patient; let yourself be patient too.

What you are building here is a genuine threshold: a point of transition between the ordinary world and the Other World, between the mind that manages your daily life and the spirit that travels. Every time you use this practice, that threshold becomes more defined and more reliable. Your nervous system begins to recognize the stairs as a signal: we are crossing over now, we are leaving the mundane behind, and what comes next is different. Over time, the mind dump becomes faster and more efficient because your mind learns that this is the place where things get handled, and it happens ready to cooperate.

A few things worth knowing as you practice this:

Some thoughts will come back more than once on the same staircase. That is the mind's way of telling you the thought needs more acknowledgment, a longer look, a more honest moment of sitting with it before it will agree to wait. Give it that. Two steps on the same worry is entirely fine. Three steps are fine. The goal is completion, and completion takes whatever time it takes. You don't want your distractions to shade, color, or influence your journey. Let's go in clear and clean, so filter out the water by emptying the remnants.

Some thoughts will surprise you with their urgency: you may feel relatively settled, and then something enormous surfaces that you did not realize you were carrying. This is a good sign, actually; it means the process is working and the deeper layers are releasing. Follow it. Acknowledge it fully. Come back.

Occasionally, a thought will surface that genuinely requires action before you can journey... a safety concern, something truly time-sensitive, something that your conscience will not allow you to set aside. Honor that. Put the drumbeat on pause, handle what needs handling, and start again. A journey undertaken over the top of something genuinely urgent will be compromised from the first step. Your integrity as a practitioner starts here, in the small decisions you make before you even leave your body.

By the time you reach the end, the stairs will have done their work. Your mind will be ready. There is a real difference in the quality of that quiet, and you will recognize it once you have experienced it. Forced silence is brittle and effortful; completed silence is spacious and easy. That spaciousness is what you are after. That is the doorway.

A Note on Visuals

If you are a person who struggles with visualization, try pushing your imagery further back in your head, somewhere between your ears instead of behind your eyes. Here is a test: with your eyes open and staring at a wall, can you picture your mother's face? The color blue? Do that same thing with your eyes closed. Practice those visualization muscles until you can hold the flame, even just an outline, even just a flicker. It just needs to exist.

Out-of-body work requires the ability to see in your mind. If internal visuals are genuinely beyond your reach, spirit walking will send you to the alternative methods of entity removal covered later in this book; those paths are equally valid and equally powerful. Play to your strengths.

A Note on Aphantasia

Aphantasia is the absence of voluntary visual imagery: the inability to produce a mental picture when one is not physically present in front of you. Ask someone with aphantasia to picture their mother's face, and they will know their mother's face completely, recognize her instantly in a crowd, describe her to you in accurate detail... and see nothing when they close their eyes. The screen is dark. It has always been dark. For a long time, many people with aphantasia assumed everyone experienced the world this way, because how would you know otherwise?

If this is you, first: you are in good company. The estimate is somewhere around three percent of the population, which means statistically, several of your fellow students share this experience. Second: the visualization portion of the journey, as I have described it, may simply look different for you, and different is workable.

Here is what I know from working with aphantasic students: the journey still happens. The Other World does not require your visual cortex to grant you entry. Some of my students who cannot see a single image still journey with remarkable accuracy and depth, returning with information they could have had no other way of accessing. They know where they went. They know what happened. They come back with the same certainty a sighted traveler does, just through different channels.

Some aphantasic journeyers experience the Other World as sensation: a felt sense of movement, of presence, of direction, of emotional tone. Others hear it; sounds, voices, impressions that happen with the quality of experience instead of imagination. Others simply know, the way you know your mother's face without seeing it... a direct, sourceless certainty that something is there and this is what it is. That knowing is as legitimate a form of perception as any visual, and in some ways it is more honest because there is no image to second-guess or over analyze.

The blind live fully in a world built largely for sighted people. They navigate it, know it, love it, and contribute to it in ways that have nothing to do with what they can see. A blind person who has walked through their own home a thousand times knows every corner, every threshold, every place where the floor creaks; they know it in their body and their memory and their instinct in a way that is completely its own kind of knowledge. Journeying in the dark works the same way. You go, you move through it, you come back knowing what happened, even if the lights were off the entire time.

The flame on the stairs may never appear to you as a visual. Reach for it anyway. Feel for it instead: its warmth, its pull, the slight shift in your energy when you make contact with it. The staircase may appear as a sensation of descent or ascent instead of an image. Follow it the same way. The mind dump still works; the threshold still opens; the journey still has you somewhere real.

Trust what comes through your channels, whatever those channels are. The Other World has been communicating with humans across every possible variation of human perception since long before anyone had a word for aphantasia. It knows how to reach you.

A Note on Perspective

First person, third person: let it be whatever it is. Some journeys you will experience through your own eyes; others you will watch yourself from a distance as though you are in a film. Your brain is doing its best to process a genuinely unusual experience, and perspective is one of the things that gets a little scrambled in translation. Simply continue. The perspective will sort itself out, and either way, the journey is valid.

One More Thing Before You Go

The mind dump is also quietly one of the most important habits you will build as a practitioner. You are training yourself to complete things instead of suppress them, to acknowledge instead of avoid, to clear your instrument before you play it. That habit does not stay on the stairs. It begins to move into the rest of your life: into your relationships, your healing work, your daily practice. Students who have been working with this technique for a while often tell me that the stairs changed something in how they move through the world generally... that they became faster at recognizing what they are carrying and more willing to set it down.

Which makes sense. The spirit travels more freely when the human is less encumbered (mind, soul, be quiet, it's time for the totem to shine). That is true in the Other World, and it is just as true in this one. Take care of your mind the way you take care of your tools: clean, clear, and ready for work.

The stairs are waiting. Count down from ten.

To the Mental Plane

You have completed the stairs. Your mind has done its work. Now we give you a map.

At completing the count, you arrive in a foyer: an open lobby, dim and quiet. Take a moment to orient yourself. Three directions present themselves from here, and each one leads somewhere different. You will learn them all eventually; for now, knowing they exist is enough.

To your left is a well. Dark, ancient, filled with a black cosmic liquid that looks exactly like what it is: the universe itself, vast and deep and infinite. Looking into it, you feel time the way you feel the ocean standing at its edge... the sheer scale of what is held there. This well is the passage of time; it leads to your past lives and your akashic records, everything that has ever been you across every iteration of your existence. We are heading somewhere else today, but remember where the well is.

Straight ahead is a hallway of doors. Think of the longest hotel corridor you have ever seen, then multiply it by a number that stops making sense. Every door is a memory, an event, something that has happened to you in this lifetime. Every experience you have ever had lives behind one of these doors. We are heading somewhere else today here too, but again: remember where it is.

To your right is an opening, and through it: nature. This is also known as the Mental Plane, which in it, has the Area of Consciousness. That is where we are going.

Step through.

The path ahead splits. A short trail to your left curves toward a cliff overlooking a river; this is the Area of Consciousness, where thought forms move through the air like weather, and you can connect with the energies of others or return to the current of your own. A useful place, and one we will return to. Today, we continue straight ahead, into the forest.

The longer path takes you into dense greenery: jungle, forest, the deep tangle of living things. Let the trail coil and twist as it wants to. Run if you feel like running. Let the energy of it fill you: the temperature, the sounds, the particular aliveness of trees and plants and creatures going about their business with no interest in yours. If anything remains in your mind that still needs releasing, let it go here among the roots and branches. The forest is good for that.

Halfway down the path, pause. Turn left and look into the trees. Step off the trail. Pick your way through: over branches, under low brambles, through tall weeds and undergrowth, into the density. Keep going until the trees open up. You will find a circular clearing ringed by hedges, quiet and contained. This is a spirit circle. We will do significant work here later in this book; for now, simply find it, register it, and carry it with you. Then turn around, retrace your steps back through the undergrowth, and return to the path.

Turn left and continue through the forest. Follow the trail all the way to where it curves right, where the trees thin and the rock face rises... and there, tucked around the wall of stone, is a bay. Private, secluded, connected to the open ocean beyond. The water is calm. The space is yours entirely. This is The Bay: your crossroads to the worlds, the place from which all spirit travel departs and to which all spirit travel returns. Keep this place in your body as well as your mind. You will be coming back here many times.

Before we travel anywhere from The Bay, we have one more thing to do. You need to meet your totem.

The Steps, In Order:

1. Breathe
2. Flame
3. Stairs and mind dump
4. Foyer
5. Turn right into nature
6. Take the path through the forest
7. Arrive at The Bay

Meeting Your Power Animal

Recognizing the Psychic Self and Learning to Travel Safely

Once students learn how to enter trance and successfully reach the gateway space, the very next question is almost always the same, and it usually comes with a little anxiety behind it. They ask how they are supposed to move through the spirit world safely, how they know where to go, and what keeps them from getting lost, because leaving the body for the first time can feel like stepping into a dark ocean without a shoreline. That concern is healthy and practical, and I encourage it, because caution keeps you alive and keeps your spirit intact. Out-of-body work has always involved guidance systems, and every culture that practices spirit walking builds in some form of companion or internal navigator for exactly this reason. You never travel alone, even when you think you are alone, and part of your early training involves recognizing the part of yourself that already knows how to move through those spaces. That part of you is what we call the power animal, the totem.

Let me clarify something immediately, because the language around this topic often gets tangled in fantasy, and I prefer to keep it grounded and functional. Your power animal is not an external spirit that shows up to adopt you like a stray cat, and it is not a random mascot that you pick because you like wolves or hawks or something that looks cool on a T-shirt. Your power animal represents your own psychic self, the instinctive, perceptive, deeply intuitive part of your spirit that exists beneath personality, beneath social conditioning, and beneath all the complicated human stories you carry around every day. When you encounter it in journeying, you are meeting yourself in a cleaner, more efficient form, one that communicates through instinct and sensation instead of analysis and debate. In other words, this is you without the noise. That is exactly why it functions so well as a guide.

Human thinking can be slow and complicated, especially when you are navigating unfamiliar terrain, because the analytical mind wants to label everything, question everything, and create a narrative about everything. Instinct moves faster than that. Instinct senses danger immediately, recognizes patterns, and chooses a direction without hesitation. Animals operate this way naturally, which is why the psyche often presents this deeper layer of self as an animal form instead of a human one. The animal shape communicates directly and efficiently, without ego or storytelling, and that clarity becomes incredibly useful when you are traveling through spiritual environments that shift quickly and do not follow ordinary physical rules. So when we talk about a power animal, we are really talking about your own survival intelligence given a symbolic body that you can see and interact with. That symbolic body helps the conscious mind cooperate with the psychic mind instead of arguing with it.

When you begin working with this hidden part of yourself, you will notice that it behaves less like a separate being and more like a partner that already understands the terrain. It knows when to slow down, when to leave, and when to pay attention, often before your thinking mind catches up to what is happening. Many students describe this experience as being gently guided or nudged in a certain direction, and that is exactly how it feels, like walking beside someone who knows the neighborhood better than you do. Over time, trust develops between your conscious awareness and this instinctive self, and that trust creates confidence during journeying. Instead of second-guessing every step, you begin moving with purpose. That sense of direction dramatically increases both safety and effectiveness when you are working on behalf of clients.

Because this relationship is so personal and so intimate, I always tell students to suspend expectations about what form their power animal "should" take, because preconceived ideas only get in the way. If you walk into a journey already convinced that you must have a lion because lions sound powerful, you are just projecting fantasy onto the experience, and projection blocks perception. The whole point of this exercise is to let your psyche reveal itself honestly, not to design a character you think sounds impressive. Some people meet animals that surprise them, sometimes small, sometimes quiet, sometimes completely ordinary, and that is perfectly fine. The size or drama of the animal has nothing to do with effectiveness. What matters is authenticity, because authenticity has information that imagination cannot fabricate.

When you reach the gateway during your journey protocol, instead of visualizing a flame this time, shift your attention inward and focus on sensation instead of imagery, because feeling your own energy often produces a deeper connection than watching a picture in your mind. Notice the pulse of your body, the subtle current under your skin, and the rhythm that moves through your breath and bloodstream, almost like your entire body hums quietly if you pay close attention. Let yourself sense your spirit as something tangible and present, not abstract or theoretical, but real and immediate. Then gather a small portion of that energy and allow it to move out in front of you, like a seed or a bubble that has your essence. This is still you, simply externalized so that you can observe it more clearly. Treat it gently, because you are handling your own core.

As that bubble of energy floats in front of you, allow it to glow brighter and steadier. Watch it rise above your head and illuminate the space around you, and then follow the same staircase we already practiced, breathing slowly and counting down until the ordinary world feels distant. By the time you reach the bottom, you will arrive in your mental foyer. Turn right into nature and take the fork to the left. This is your inner landscape again, which might appear as a forest, or any natural setting that feels calm and grounded. From there, give yourself time to move through the space without rushing, because the meeting happens organically. Run through the woods, feel the air on your skin, and let the environment feel alive around you. The experience should feel immersive instead of forced. This is your mental plane, so allow your mind to paint.

After spending some time running through the forest, you're going to take the path down past a huge rock wall. Follow this wall as it gets taller and taller. As it ends, the path will go around it and take you to a secluded bay. The bay is a black sand beach and is surrounded by the safety and seclusion of the wall. The bay looks out into the ocean, and it seems to go forever. This bay, the water, is the transition space between the worlds. It is your connection to the spirit worlds, to yourself, to the spirit in all things.

Take that orb of your spirit essence into your hands and launch it into the water. Watch it glow beneath the surface, changing and transforming. You are made of the veil and spirit world, and throwing your awake aura into the veil between you and the lower world, where your spirit will one day go to rest, awakens the awareness of your totem to your conscious mind (the one sitting on the shore). Remember that your totem IS YOU. Watch this part of you transform, and morph, and from the water, emerges your totem.

Your totem may flex and change. Allow your conscious analytical mind to relax and observe. Really try hard not to analyze or get overly excited. Be a passive observer, and your beta mind can analyze when you wake. The first instinct of your totem is correct.

Now, your totem might change slightly in type, but it doesn't change. For instance, I am a polar bear, but sometimes he shows himself as a brown bear or as a prehistoric bear. It doesn't really matter. Remember, don't grab on too tightly.

As it emerges, ask it to sit with you on the beach and talk to your psychic self. Find out its name and ask if there is anything you aren't listening to when it comes to your instinct.

KEEP THE NAME SECRET!

There is one rule I enforce very strongly around this work, and I say it with the same seriousness every time I teach it, because it matters. Keep the name of your power animal private. Names hold influence, and influence creates vulnerability, so this is one piece of information that stays between you and the spirit world. You can use it freely when traveling, when calling your power animal during journeying, or when working in ritual space, yet in everyday life, you keep it to yourself. Think of it the way many traditions treat sacred names, as something powerful precisely because it remains protected. Protecting that name protects your relationship with this part of yourself.

Have you seen the musical CATS? Well, there are three names for each cat. The name their family uses or gave them, the name that their tribe uses (like a wondrous nickname of self-proclaimed magic name, Stormwater Fairywolf, for instance), and then there is the name of your true essence. If anyone has this name, they have control over you. Witches would find out the secret name of a cat and then have full control over them and force them into being a familiar-slave. Do you want someone to have that power over you? No? Then keep it private. No spouse, parent, friend, or coven sister is that trustworthy. No one. If you haven't read my book, **Witchdoctor Exorcist**, let me reiterate that the worst monster of all is the human who hires you. Trust no one.

As you continue practicing, you will notice that sometimes this inner companion becomes less of a visualization and more of a felt presence, something that responds quickly and consistently whenever you travel. It will help you sense when it is time to leave a place, when something feels unsafe, or when you need to pay attention to a particular detail for your client. In many ways, it functions like an internal compass, quietly adjusting your direction without fanfare. The more you work together, the more seamless that cooperation becomes. Eventually, you will stop thinking of it as something separate at all and simply recognize it as your psychic self operating at full strength. That integration is what keeps you steady when the terrain becomes strange.

The Mirror Method

Let's say you're really struggling with your totem coming up out of the water. Remember that your totem is you. I want you to come back to the bay, and until you relax enough, keep doing this exercise instead of the water in the orb:

Reach into the sand and pull out a mirror. Hold it up to your face. Mirrors are also gateways to the spirit world, so I want you to gaze softly into the mirror and allow your human face to disappear, and in its place, allow the animal to show up. Keep doing this until he or she finally shows themself. You have finally relaxed enough to journey.

Your Totem Is Your Psychic Self

Why Instinct Guides You Better Than Thought

At some point in your training, you are going to stop thinking of your totem as a cute spirit animal that shows up to hold your hand and start recognizing it for what it actually is: far more practical, far more intelligent, and far more essential to your survival than any mascot or decorative symbol ever could be. Your totem is the psychic portion of your own consciousness given form so that your mind can interact with it. It is you. Specifically, the part of you that already knows how to navigate the spirit world without needing a lecture, a map, or a plan.

Students assume their power animal is some separate being assigned to protect them, like a cosmic babysitter. I understand why that idea is comforting, and I understand why it persists in popular spirituality. It misses the deeper truth of what is actually happening. The totem is your own psychic body. Your instinctual intelligence. The ancient animal brain that predates language and analysis. When you see it standing in front of you during a journey, you are looking at yourself: stripped of ego, stripped of social conditioning, stripped of overthinking, reduced to pure perception and survival wisdom.

This is why it appears as an animal.

Animals move through the world through instinct. They hold no committee meetings in their heads. They do not over analyze. whether the rustling in the grass is dangerous. They feel. They respond. They survive. That same instinct lives inside you, and during spirit work, it steps forward and takes the lead, because instinct functions far more efficiently in the Other World than intellect ever could.

Let me say that plainly, because this is where students get tripped up:

> **Your analytical mind is slow. Your instinct is fast. Your analytical mind debates. Your instinct knows. Your analytical mind argues. Your instinct moves.**

When you journey, you want the part that knows.

How Navigation Actually Works

When you travel to the Middle World in spirit form, you are carrying no Google Maps. You are calculating no longitude or latitude. You are building no mental blueprint of Madagascar and plotting a route to the east coast. You simply arrive. Students always ask me how this works, as if there is some hidden geometry behind it, and the answer is the answer is simpler than they expect. Your psychic self already knows how to find things. Your totem knows how to track energy the way a wolf tracks scent or a hawk tracks movement across miles of terrain.

If you are capable of finding the place physically, your totem will take you there. If you are capable of reaching the person, your totem will lead you. If the path is open and safe, you will arrive without effort. That is the job.

Students describe it differently: flying, suddenly standing in a location without remembering the travel, or being pulled by an invisible current. All of those descriptions point to the same truth. The thinking mind steps aside, and the psychic self navigates. You are being guided by the most ancient intelligence inside you: the part that predates language, culture, and fear of looking foolish.

This also explains something people tend to misunderstand about psychic ability in daily life. When you sense danger before you consciously know why, that is your totem working. When you choose a different street to drive down and later learn there was an accident on your usual route, that is your totem working. When you get a strange feeling about someone and later discover your instinct was correct, that is your totem working.

Psychic perception is instinct. Pattern recognition. The quiet animal part of you that has always kept you alive.

So when you journey, that same mechanism takes over.

When the Totem Says No

Here is the part students resist, because they assume every journey should feel like an open-world video game where every door is unlocked, and every being is available for conversation.

Sometimes you will try to reach a place and feel yourself redirected. Sometimes you will attempt to approach a spirit, and your totem will steer you away. Sometimes you will ask to meet an ancestor, and nothing happens. The beginner response is frustration: they assume they are doing something wrong, that their psychic ability is weak, that they failed the exercise.

Your totem is deciding for you. And your totem makes better decisions than your thinking mind.

A location that feels blocked has risk or interference. A spirit your totem steers you away from would serve you poorly. An ancestor your totem keeps you from may be carrying unresolved chaos, anger, or confusion that would destabilize you. The spirit world is vast, and exactly like the physical world, it contains beauty, wisdom, danger, and absolute nonsense all mixed together. You would not walk blindly into every alley in a strange city. Your totem feels the same way about certain regions of the Other World.

Some spirits are predatory. Some ancestors brought their problems into death. Some gods carry a magnitude of energy that would burn out your nervous system trying to process it. And that is fine. You are human.

The Pressure to Access Everything

There is a strange pressure in modern spirituality that tells people they should have access to everything all the time, as if enlightenment means unlimited clearance. That is ego dressed up as mysticism.

Real spiritual work includes boundaries. Real safety includes discernment. Your totem embodies that discernment automatically. It requires no explanation. It simply redirects you.

If your totem turns around and walks the other way, follow it without argument. Do not negotiate. Do not protest. Do not say, but I wanted to go over there. Your psychic self sees more than you do. It senses currents you cannot name. It reads danger long before your intellect catches up. Trusting that guidance is a skill. It is maturity. It is survival.

Instinct is older than logic. Instinct kept our species alive long before we had language sophisticated enough to write books about it. When you allow that instinct to guide your journeys, you are working with millions of years of evolution designed specifically to keep you safe. That is considerably more reliable than whatever plan you sketched out five minutes ago on your meditation cushion.

Relax

You do not have to force your way into every corner of the spirit world. You carry nothing to prove. You are collecting no experiences like trophies and meeting no entities on a checklist.

Your totem will take you where you are meant to go and will quietly steer you away from where you are meant to wait. That is protection. That is wisdom. That is the psychic part of you doing exactly what it has always done since the day you were born: keeping you alive long enough to learn, to grow, and to come home safely.

You, Your Totem, and Past Lives

Before we talk about spirit travel, trance states, or anything that resembles leaving the body, we need to slow down and define something fundamental, because if you misunderstand the structure of the soul, every technique that follows will feel vague and theatrical, instead of grounded and repeatable.

Students often come into this work carrying a cloudy, poetic idea of what a soul is, as if it were a single glowing cloud floating somewhere behind the body, doing everything all at once. That image is romantic, and it is also useless for practice. In lived spiritual systems across the world, the soul is functional. It has parts. It has responsibilities. Different aspects of you perform different tasks, and once you understand which part does what, your entire relationship to psychic work becomes clear and practical instead of mysterious and confusing.

I teach the soul the same way I teach anatomy, because clarity makes you safer. Just as the body has lungs for breathing, a heart for circulation, and a stomach for digestion, the soul has components that specialize in thinking, anchoring, and continuing across lifetimes. When you understand those distinctions, you stop lumping everything together, and you stop asking the wrong part of yourself to do the wrong job. Many frustrations in spiritual practice come from exactly that mistake, from trying to use the thinking mind for something that belongs to instinct, or trying to use memory for something that belongs to purpose. So, we begin here, at the foundation, with the simplest and most useful structure I know how to give you.

There are three parts to the soul. There is the mental part, there is the body part, and there is the totem. Each one has a different function. Each one operates on a different timeline. Each one continues differently. When you understand these three, everything else we discuss in this book will make sense without strain. While you are in this incarnation, the three are sewn together to make... you.

The Mental Self

The first part is the mental self. This is the part most people identify with when they say "me," because it is the part that thinks, remembers, learns, and changes throughout the course of this lifetime. Your mental self develops from the moment you are born and continues to accumulate experiences every single day. It collects language, education, habits, traumas, joys, preferences, fears, and beliefs. Every relationship you form, every class you take, every mistake you survive, and every success you celebrate adds another layer to this aspect of you. It is the changing and growing part of the soul, sculpted directly by what you encounter in this life.

Because it is built from experience, the mental self is temporary and specific to this incarnation. It belongs to this name, this culture, this family, this era. It is the storyteller of your life. It organizes your memories and creates the narrative that says, "This is who I am." It is brilliant at adaptation and incredibly skilled at navigating society, which is why it helps you work, study, socialize, and function as a human being in the world. At the same time, it is constantly shifting. It grows, forgets, reinvents, and reshapes itself based on new information. This part is fluid and personal, the accumulation of this lifetime and this lifetime alone. When we are injured in trauma, we need a soul retrieval to mend this part of the soul (found in my book, **Witchdoctor Kahuna Healer**).

The Body Self

The second part is the body self, and this one often surprises people because they are used to separating the body from the soul as if they were unrelated. In many indigenous and ancestral systems, the body is understood as carrying its own spiritual continuity. Your bones, your blood, your nervous system, and your genetic inheritance are not empty vessels. They carry memory. They carry lineage. They carry a connection to those who came before you. This is the part of your soul that is handed down through ancestry, the portion that ties you physically and energetically to your family line and to the earth itself.

The body self anchors you here. It is what keeps you incarnated and grounded in matter. It links you to your parents, your grandparents, and the long chain of people whose lives made yours possible. This is why burial traditions across cultures hold such weight and reverence, because the body continues to act as a point of connection even after death. When graves are disturbed, many traditions describe the spirit being called back or stirred, and symbolically, this makes sense. The body portion of the soul remains tied to the physical remains and acts like a magnet, calling the other aspects of the person back toward it. It is the tether, the gravity, the part that says, "This is home." To heal this, we have medicine and ancestral healing (also found in **Witchdoctor Kahuna Healer**).

The Totem: The Psychic Self

Then we arrive at the third part, which is the focus of this book and the part that most people misunderstand. This is the totem. This is your psychic self. This is the ongoing current of your soul that continues across lifetimes. If the mental self is the story of this life and the body self is the anchor to this lineage, the totem is the thread that keeps moving forward, regardless of what body or personality you temporarily inhabit.

The totem is not a scrapbook of memories from other lives. It does not carry detailed recollections of every person you have ever been. Those experiences belonged to the mental self of those lifetimes, and when those lives ended, those specific stories ended with them. What continues is something deeper and simpler. The totem has continuity of essence, direction, and purpose. It is the part of you that keeps traveling from one life to the next like a string passing through many beads.

Each bead is a lifetime. The string is the totem.

Because it is continuous, the totem is older than this life and will continue long after it. It is the part of you that simply keeps moving. It does not reset at birth, and it does not dissolve at death. It flows forward, carrying the underlying trajectory of your soul. You could think of it as the through line of your existence, the part that holds your deeper purpose across all incarnations. Where the mental self asks, "Who am I right now?" the totem answers, "What am I becoming across time?"

When we talk about the totem as your psychic self, this is what we mean. It is the intuitive, instinctual, ongoing part of you that operates beyond the temporary story of this lifetime. It is not constructed from what you learned in school, what job you have, or what mistakes you made last year. It is more fundamental than that. It is the part that keeps walking, life after life, carrying the core of who you are and what you are here to do.

So when you hear me say "totem," understand that I am not talking about a mascot, a symbol, or a decorative animal image. I am talking about the most continuous and enduring part of your soul. I am talking about your psychic current, the part of you that never stops moving forward. This is the aspect that we will work with when we begin spirit walking, because this is the part designed to travel. The mental self learns. The body self-anchors in the genetic code. The totem continues.

And here is the part that should make you stand a little taller in your chair, because even if your totem has walked through many lifetimes and may continue in recognizable form from one incarnation to the next, this lifetime is unprecedented. You have never before existed as this exact combination of mental accumulation, genetic inheritance, and ongoing soul string. The lessons you gather now, the grief you survive, the skills you develop, the love you offer and receive, the body you inhabit with its specific ancestral coding, and the era in which you are living create a configuration that has never occurred before and will never occur again in exactly this way. Your totem may be continuous, but the expression of it through this mind and this body is entirely original. This unique addition to the totem naturally affects it from lifetime to lifetime. This is why, from one life to another, your totem animal may shift slightly. From seahorse, to turtle, to alligator, to horse, to pegasus, to dove. It may also stay the same. I'm a polar bear in this incarnation. The protective aspect of the polar is probably because of my genetic makeup, but I'm sure I've probably been some form of bear in all my incarnations (well, maybe a fox at some point?).

You are the living intersection of what you learned in this lifetime, what was handed to you through blood and bone, and the enduring current that keeps your soul moving forward. The joys and the wounds, the talents and the flaws, the inherited tendencies and the chosen disciplines all converge into a singular expression that belongs to this moment in time.

So, while your totem has continuity, you carry uniqueness. You are not a copy of your past lives. You are the present articulation of an ancient current flowing through brand new terrain, and that makes you both timeless and entirely singular.

You are the unique conglomeration of what you learn and experience (goods and bads), what is passed down genetically to you from your ancestors, and the string that keeps them all linked, the totem.

Can't Journey?

Sick, Injured, Itchy, and Completely Human

Let me say something very plainly before we go any further, because this is one of those practical realities that people love to romanticize their way around, and it wastes an enormous amount of time. If your body hurts, you are not traveling anywhere. If you are sick, itchy, sore, inflamed, congested, or miserable, you are staying right here in your skin. That is not a spiritual failure or a lack of talent. That is biology doing exactly what biology is designed to do.

I always find it fascinating how quickly we forget this when we feel good, because when we are healthy, we walk around like floating heads pretending the body barely exists, and then the moment something slices our finger or our muscles cramp or our sinuses swell shut, our entire universe collapses into that one tiny location of pain. Vanity disappears. Social anxiety disappears. The opinions of strangers disappear. All awareness funnels directly into the body like a spotlight. Pain has a way of clarifying priorities with ruthless efficiency.

When you are sick, injured, or even mildly uncomfortable, your attention locks onto the physical form, whether you want it to or not, and that attention is the exact opposite of what we need for spirit travel. Journeying requires a gentle forgetting of the body, a loosening of identification, the same way you forget you are sitting in a theater when a movie fully absorbs you. If your knee aches or your back spasms or your skin itches from some toxic plant, you are not forgetting anything. You are hyper aware. Hyper awareness anchors you in flesh and gravity.

Astral travel depends on releasing that anchor for a little while. You soften your attention. You drift. You allow the edges of the body to blur. If instead every nerve ending screams for your focus, there is nowhere for your awareness to go. You stay parked exactly where you are, fully embodied and very awake. Which is fine, by the way, because that simply means it is a body day, not a spirit day.

So here is the boring, responsible, very adult answer that nobody wants to hear. If you feel unwell, get well first. If you are in pain, address the pain first. Rest, hydrate, stretch, see a doctor, take care of yourself like a sane person. Then travel. Journeying rewards patience and punishes stubbornness. Your body will always speak louder than any drumbeat, and learning to listen to it is part of the training.

Mana: The Fuel Behind Every Journey

Once we move past the mechanics of trance and travel, we have to talk about the thing that quietly powers all of it, because you can know every technique in the world and still go nowhere if your internal battery sits empty. Every living thing has an essential energy that sustains it, whether we are talking about plants, animals, landscapes, spirits, or humans. That foundational vitality has many names across cultures, and in Hawaiian traditions, we call it *mana*. Mana describes the life force that animates everything and gives it presence, strength, and coherence.

If you have ever played a video game where your character runs out of energy and suddenly cannot cast spells or perform actions, you already understand the metaphor. The term gets borrowed constantly in pop culture because it communicates something very intuitive. When mana runs low, nothing functions well. When mana flows strongly, everything feels easier and more responsive. Spirit travel follows the same principle.

If you ever find yourself struggling to connect, struggling to journey, or feeling like you are hitting a wall every time you try to travel, it is often not a technique problem at all. It is an energy problem. Your system may simply lack the resources required to disengage from the body and operate elsewhere. And before anyone starts preaching about trying harder or forcing it, let me say this clearly: pushing through depletion serves no one. Blaming yourself for low energy solves nothing.

Your body, mind, and spirit operate as one integrated system, which means when one part struggles, the others compensate. If your body hurts, your attention anchors. If your emotions churn, your focus scatters. If your spirit feels weak or drained, it instinctively stays close to home to recover. That instinct is protective, not lazy. Your system wants stability before exploration.

Think about physical pain again for a moment. When something hurts, you cannot simply will yourself to ignore it. Your attention keeps returning there because your body requests care. Spiritual fatigue works the same way. When mana runs low, your spirit stays grounded to repair itself. Fighting that process only creates frustration. Supporting it creates recovery.

The Mana Check: A Practical Diagnostic Tool

In Hawaiian faith, mana is the spiritual energy present in all things: the life force that moves through everything, the animating current that exists in plants and rocks and landscapes and, yes, your computer, because everything holds a kind of energy and mana is the specific quality of that energy that produces will, that generates the forward movement of a living thing toward its purpose, that gives a person the capacity to act, to create, to heal, and to practice. The 1930s called something similar ectoplasm (since reviewing what indigenous cultures have done for centuries would be savage and non-parenthetical...). Modern science calls it electromagnetic energy. Hawaiian wisdom understood it as the force behind all of those terms and beneath all of those terms simultaneously, the energy that gives will instead of simply power.

Mana is yours. It is also everyone else's. It lives in the object on your altar and the food on your table, and the relationship you tend with care, and the one you have been neglecting. It flows, it depletes, it refills, it transfers, and it responds to how you live.

When Mana Is Low

If you are struggling to connect with the spiritual realm, or finding spirit travel difficult or inconsistent, mana deserves your honest attention before anything else does. Your spirit, body, and mind are intrinsically linked, moving together as a single system, and when any one of those is unhealthy, the others register it immediately, the way a river runs differently when one of its tributaries runs dry. A spirit that is low on mana will naturally prefer to stay rooted and recover.

The Mana Check

To assess the current state of your mana, close your eyes and visualize a bowl sitting deep within your chest. Examine it: its material, its appearance, whether it has cracks, and how thick its walls are. Inside the bowl, imagine water and a tree, with the tree's roots reaching through the water and over the bowl's edge. Assess the roots: their length, their quantity, their thickness, and their strength. Examine the water: still or turbulent, clear or murky, contained or spilling? How much water is present, and what else lives in it alongside the roots? Consider the tree: its fullness, its height, its strength, its flexibility. Finally, observe the sky around the tree: the weather, the light, whether birds or, insects, or wind are present.

When you open your eyes, here is what you have just read:

The **bowl** represents your connection to community, family, and nature; the strength or fragility of those bonds shows immediately in the bowl's condition.

The **water** is your emotional state: turbulent water means turbulent emotions, overflowing water means emotions spilling into the lives of the people around you, still water means stability, and depth means emotional depth.

The **roots** represent what you feed your mind, the range and quality of what you take in, the diversity of experience and attention you bring to your own interior life.

The **tree** reflects your life's purpose and path; its health tells you something direct and honest about the state of your connection to your own direction.

The **sky** represents the external forces moving through your life: the opinions of others, the quality of your daily encounters, and the atmosphere of the world you are currently moving through.

This meditation gives you a real-time reading of the different aspects of your soul, and some of what you find will be within your own power to address; some of it will require outside help, because certain soul components ask for more than personal effort can provide, and recognizing which is which is itself a form of wisdom.

Managing Your Mana

Your mana is your energy, your spiritual essence, the current running through everything you do and everything you offer, and when you practice the craft full-time, you are managing it in every session, every interaction, every act of service, every day. One kahuna can pour their mana into another person, emptying themselves entirely, and with dedicated practice, they can refill, and it has consequences worth understanding before you attempt it.

The practices that sustain mana are the ones that sustain a person in general: faith, connection with the land, venerating the spirits, self-care, food, and healthy relationships. You need energy to cultivate energy, and the bowl fills from the same sources it always has.

If the root motivation of your practice is praise and gain, your mana will empty. Think of it this way: a person who fixes cars but spends their energy boasting about fixing cars, focusing on income instead of the actual work, bringing down other people who fix cars, and calling the whole operation a repair shop is running something entirely different from a repair shop. Mana knows the difference between the work and the performance of the work. It responds to what you are actually doing.

Misuse of your skills depletes mana as well, and in the worst case, a depleted mana creates a hole in the soul that a parasitic spirit can occupy. This is worth preventing through consistent, honest practice, which is exactly what all of this training has been building toward.

Other Causes of Mana Loss

When boasting and misuse are not the issue, other sources deserve honest examination:

- Is there something in your life that deserves celebration that you have not celebrated?
- What is holding you back from your goals, your relationships, your connections, and a thriving life?
- What does your heart actually want?
- When was the last time you were fully, genuinely yourself?
- If your totem could give you one lesson right now, what would it be?

Mana changes when you are cursed, hexed, or jinxed: it becomes thinner, shifts in color, and loses vitality. Because mana runs through everything, that interference registers in the body, the emotions, and the spirit at once.

Reciprocity matters here as well, and it matters in the most practical sense: when you receive energy and give nothing back, your mana depletes. The law is simple. Be for giving.

Mana in Objects

Some objects carry mana from the person or event that last touched or interacted with them; anything worn, handled, or used consistently during a person's lifetime becomes washed with their personal mana over time, the object holding the energetic imprint of its previous owner, the way fabric holds a scent. This is why objects that belonged to someone else require cleansing before use: you are clearing the mana residue of the previous person, which may include energetic cords still attaching that person to the object across whatever distance separates them from it now.

Mana can also be moved into objects intentionally, infused with purpose and directed toward a specific use: magical tools, ropes used for sailing, fish hooks for hunting, talismans of every kind. The same principle applied in a harmful direction produces something else entirely, and that possibility is worth knowing and worth respecting.

Your mana is yours. Tend it accordingly.

Refilling Your Mana

People always expect some exotic ritual here, some secret chant or complicated ceremony that magically fills their life force overnight, and I always disappoint them with the most ordinary answer possible. You refill your mana by taking care of yourself like a human being with needs. That means real food, real rest, real relationships, real emotional processing, and real time outside in the world. Spirit work does not replace those things. It depends on them.

Energy grows through meaningful connection, through conversations that nourish you, through creative work that engages your mind, through movement that keeps your body alive, through laughter, through quiet, through time in nature, through doing things that actually matter to you. These habits sound simple because they are simple. Simplicity does not mean trivial. Simplicity means foundational. Foundations determine everything built on top of them.

Many of us grew up in a culture that measures worth purely through productivity, which means we try to earn value through constant output while ignoring how we actually feel. That mindset quietly drains mana faster than anything else, because it disconnects you from your own humanity. You are not a machine generating results. You are a living being who requires balance, connection, and rest. When you honor that truth, your energy stabilizes.

So if you want stronger journeys, clearer visions, and more reliable travel, start here. Eat well. Sleep. Spend time with people who support you. Do work that aligns with your purpose. Step outside and touch the earth once in a while. Fill your bowl. Water your tree. Then sit down to journey. You will discover that the spirit world opens much more easily when your life force runs full.

Riding the Journey: Wu Wei and the Traveling Mind

In Taoist philosophy (Taoist is shamanic by the way), there is a concept called wu wei (� �), which translates loosely as effortless action or action-less action. The Taoists understood something that takes most of my students a frustrating amount of time to learn in practice: you hold more sand in a relaxed, open hand than in a clenched fist. Grab tighter, lose more. The same is exactly and precisely true of journeying.

About half of my students arrive at their first journeys with their analytical minds fully activated and ready to work. They want to understand what they are seeing as they are seeing it. They want to track the symbols, decode the meaning, confirm they are doing it correctly, and produce something they can report back with clarity. This feels responsible. It feels like good studentship. What it actually is... is alpha. The moment you shift from experiencing to analyzing, from receiving to producing, your brain has quietly climbed back out of theta and planted itself in ordinary waking consciousness, and the journey either dissolves entirely or becomes something you are directing instead of something that is happening to you (imagination and visualization).

Directed journeys are not journeys. They are daydreams with spiritual ambitions.

The analytical mind is a remarkable tool. It will serve you enormously in this work... after the journey. Understanding, interpretation, meaning-making: all of that belongs in the debrief, in the journal, in the conversation you have with yourself once you have returned to your body and your feet are back on the floor. During the journey itself, the analytical mind is a passenger who keeps grabbing the wheel. Your job is to let it ride without letting it drive.

This is harder than it sounds, especially for students who are intelligent, curious, and accustomed to being rewarded for producing. The instinct to understand in real time is strong. When a strange image appears in the Other World, the mind immediately wants to ask: what does that mean, is that my totem, am I doing this right, should I follow it, why does it look like that? Each of those questions is a small act of grabbing. Each one tightens the fist. Each one costs you sand.

The practice instead is this: observe, continue, trust. See what is in front of you and keep moving. Let the images come and go without immediately reaching for their meaning. Let the journey take you somewhere instead of taking the journey somewhere yourself. The difference between these two experiences is unmistakable once you have felt both; one has the quality of something unfolding, the other has the quality of something being constructed. You will know which is which. The constructed journey feels slightly too convenient, slightly too cooperative, slightly too much like what you hoped would happen. The genuine journey tends to surprise you, confuse you, and occasionally disappoint or unsettle you, because the Other World has its own agenda and does not particularly care about your expectations.

Wu wei in journeying means arriving at the theta state and then releasing the need to manage what happens next. The drumbeat has you; your totem guides you; the Other World shows you what it shows you. Your only task is to stay present and receptive, to keep the hand open, to let the sand settle into your palm without squeezing. The analysis waits. The meaning waits. The understanding waits. All of it will be there when you return, and it will be richer and more accurate for having been patient.

When students tell me their journeys feel vague or incomplete, I ask them one question: Were you watching, or were you directing? Almost every time, they already know the answer before I finish asking.

Open the hand. Receive.

Problem Solving: Why You Are Struggling to Travel

Whenever someone says that they can't journey, they assume the problem lies somewhere mystical. They assume they lack a gift. They assume their third eye is blocked. They assume their guides are silent. They assume the spirits chose everyone else first and somehow skipped them in line, like a cosmic comedy of errors.

Almost every single time, the reason is painfully ordinary.

Their bodies are exhausted. Their life is chaotic. Their emotions are unresolved. Their mana is depleted. Their nervous system is screaming.

Then they sit down, put on a drum track, close their eyes, and expect transcendence.

Spirit walking is a refined neurological and spiritual skill that requires stability, clarity, and enough internal quiet for awareness to separate from the body without panic. When your system feels unsafe, overwhelmed, underfed, or fragmented, your spirit does exactly what it is designed to do. It stays home and guards the body. It is loyal that way, even when you find it inconvenient.

Before you travel to other worlds, you handle your life in this one. That is the rule.

Repair Your Outer Life and Your Mana Repairs Itself

Students often treat spirit travel like an escape hatch. They imagine that leaving the body for a while will let them bypass the mess of daily life and float somewhere more meaningful. That fantasy sounds poetic, and it fundamentally misunderstands how the spirit actually behaves. The spirit anchors more tightly when life is unstable, because preservation always comes before exploration. Every single time.

Mana functions like your energetic savings account. Every unfinished responsibility, every unresolved conflict, every chaotic environment, and every ignored need drains that account a little at a time until you are running on fumes. When your mana runs low, your system prioritizes survival. Survival mode keeps you grounded. Grounded people stay in their bodies.

A cluttered house keeps your brain visually overstimulated. Financial disaster keeps your body anxious. Volatile relationships keep your heart braced for impact. Chronic sleeplessness keeps your nervous system from ever softening. Each of these conditions tethers you more tightly to the physical plane, and all the drum tracks in the world will not compensate for them.

Cleaning your kitchen, answering emails, finishing projects, going to therapy, drinking water, sleeping eight hours: none of these things are glamorous. All of them repair mana more effectively than any crystal or chant ever will. Stability creates trust between your body and your spirit. When the body feels safe and handled, the spirit loosens its grip and allows separation.

Before you tell me you cannot journey, look around your life and ask yourself a simple question: have you handled what is already in front of you?

Start there.

Cannabis and the Overly Flexible Spirit

This next part tends to make people defensive, and that reaction alone usually tells me everything I need to know.

Cannabis makes the spirit too flexible.

People insist that it helps them feel spiritual, open, creative, or intuitive, and altered perception is a real thing that cannabis produces. Altered perception and disciplined trance are two entirely different animals, however. Feeling floaty is a chemical state. Controlled separation is a trained skill. One you can purchase. The other, you have to earn.

When you rely on substances to enter altered states, you teach your brain that trance requires assistance. Your threshold for entering theta weakens because you have stopped building the neurological pathway through practice. instead of learning how to focus, breathe, and descend deliberately, you wait for the substance to carry you there. Your nervous system learns dependency instead of mastery.

Beyond that, cannabis softens energetic boundaries. It makes you porous. It blurs edges. In spirit work, you need clarity and precision: a clean sense of exactly where you end and the other world begins, the ability to step out of the body with intention instead of drifting out like fog through a window screen. A porous spirit wanders. It daydreams. It produces experiences that feel significant and dissolve without leaving anything useful behind.

Sobriety during practice is a requirement of mastery. Your trance comes from training. Your power animal stays sharp, alert, and ready to work. Put the substances away when you work. Respect your nervous system: let it build the real thing.

Falling Asleep Is Biology, Not Failure

The most common complaint I hear is that someone sits down to journey, immediately falls asleep, and then assumes they are spiritually blocked or doing something fundamentally wrong.

You are tired. That is the complete explanation.

Theta waves sit right on the edge of sleep. Journeying happens in that liminal state between waking and dreaming. When your body is sleep-deprived, underfed, or physically comfortable enough to fully relax, your brain chooses actual sleep every single time, because sleep keeps you alive, and your brain has excellent priorities. Your body does not care that you planned a shamanic exercise. Your body wants rest, and it will take rest the moment you give it an opening.

Look at the practical variables before anything else. Is the drumming loud enough to keep your mind lightly engaged? Are you sitting upright, or are you lying in a bed that your brain associates with unconsciousness? Did you stay up until two in the morning? Did you eat? Did you drink water? Are you simply exhausted from the relentless experience of being alive?

A meditation cushion with a straight spine keeps you alert. A steady drumbeat keeps your auditory cortex active. Nourishment stabilizes blood sugar. Hydration supports cognition. Spirit work still happens inside a body, and the body has requirements that do not pause for spiritual ambition.

If you need sleep, sleep. Rest is preparation. Come back tomorrow.

Trauma, Fragmentation, and the Need for Soul Retrieval

Sometimes the issue runs deeper than distraction or fatigue. Sometimes the reason you are struggling to travel has everything to do with protection and very little to do with discipline.

Trauma changes how the psyche organizes itself. When a person experiences intense or prolonged trauma, parts of the self withdraw as a survival strategy. Some traditions call this soul loss. Psychology calls it dissociation. The language shifts across cultures while the mechanism stays the same: a piece of you goes somewhere safe so the rest of you can endure what is happening.

When too much of your vitality is fragmented or guarded, your system resists further separation because it already feels unstable. Asking that system to leave the body willingly can feel threatening at a level far below conscious thought. The spirit clings tighter because it already knows what it feels like when pieces go missing, and it has decided that losing more pieces is not acceptable. This is loyalty, again. Inconvenient, well-intentioned loyalty.

In these cases, the path forward is healing. Therapy, somatic work, grief processing, and possibly guided soul retrieval with someone competent and grounded. Integration comes before expansion. A second story built on a cracked foundation is a demolition project waiting to happen. Repair the foundation, and traveling becomes both easier and safer.

I teach this in my book **Witchdoctor Kahuna Healer.**

Handle the Human First

There is very little that is mystical in this chapter, because the obstacles to journeying are rarely mystical. They are human. They are practical. They are solvable.

Handle your life. Feed your body. Stay sober when you practice. Rest when you are tired. Heal your wounds. Strengthen your mana. Build stability.

Then sit down. Turn on the drum. Close your eyes.
When the noise settles, the spirit moves naturally.

Watchtower Ritual of Protection

Before you go wandering into the Spirit Current like an unsupervised toddler at the edge of the ocean, we need to talk about protection, because protection is the difference between a professional and someone who ends up telling dramatic ghost stories on TikTok about how something followed them home. I do not teach fear, yet I do teach boundaries, and boundaries keep your nervous system calm and your work clean.

The purpose of the Watchtower Ritual of Protection involves creating an energetic perimeter around your workspace so that only what belongs to your intention can enter, and everything else remains politely outside. Think of it as a barricade made of relationship and authority instead of brick and mortar, an agreement between you and the spirits that this space belongs to your purpose. When done correctly, the space feels different, quieter, focused, almost pressurized, like the air has weight and attention, and that sensation tells you the room has shifted from mundane to sacred.

Shamans across many traditions cast circles for this exact reason, and although the aesthetics change from culture to culture, the mechanics remain the same. The circle marks a boundary where the practitioner can connect with spiritual forces, contain the ritual environment, and keep interference to a minimum. It separates the magical workspace from everyday noise, which allows the mind to focus fully on intention instead of distraction. Some people speak about this romantically, yet the reality stays very practical, because you cannot concentrate on exorcism, journeying, or spirit mediation while your brain keeps reacting to every stray energetic draft. The Watchtower ritual accomplishes all of this with structure, clarity, and allies stationed in each direction.

Traditionally, many mystical systems begin their circle in the East, honoring the rising sun and the beginning of life, and that works beautifully for fertility rites, blessings, and gentle devotional work.

Before you even approach the quarters, you set your intention physically and spiritually. I begin with a work candle that represents the purpose of the day, but you can use a bowl of water, a drumming ceremony, or any liniation of "it's time to work differently." I kneel before my altar, palms up, head bowed, and I offer a prayer to the gods and spirits I actually know, not whoever happens to sound impressive that week. I ask for guidance, protection, and clarity, and I extend blessings outward to my family and community because protection grows stronger when it flows both ways.

From there, you move to the quarters in order, and you build the perimeter deliberately, one direction at a time. Remember this rule and tattoo it into your brain if you must: do not call a spirit to guard a Watchtower if you plan on working with that same spirit during travel. A guardian must remain a guardian because asking someone to guard the gate while also pulling them into the room for spell work leaves the gate unattended. You also only call spirits with whom you already have a relationship, because this is not speed dating with deities. Relationship creates reliability. Random summoning creates drama.

• *East*: The East governs air, youth, beginnings, inspiration, music, art, and breath itself. This quarter invites growth and possibility, the spark of becoming that makes all change possible. You may call spirits of spring, thriving, creativity, or the angel Raphael if you prefer that structure. A yellow or orange candle works well, or feathers and light objects that move easily with the air. Light the candle and speak with warmth: ______, the easy and unplanned spirit of East, your unanticipated ways inspire me to enjoy life, for which I thank you. I light this candle and ask for your protection while I work today. Feel the space brighten.

• *South*: The South governs fire, will, blood, passion, defense, and the fierce energy that protects what matters. This quarter stands as your shield and sword, the place of strength and decisive action. You may call spirits of war, guardianship, eruption, or the angel Michael if that aligns with your practice. A red candle belongs here, nothing fancy, nothing diluted, just direct fire. Light it and speak steadily: Great spirit ______, thank you for keeping me safe, for reminding me what is worth fighting for, and for teaching me the heat of life. I ask in humble favor for your guardianship today. Let the air feel hotter, sharper, alive.

• *West*: The West governs death, endings, tides, ancestors, and the deep pull of the Spirit Current. This direction stands closest to the worlds you travel through, so you place your strongest attention here. You may call spirits of death, water, transition, or guardians of the dead, or if you prefer angelic frameworks, you may call Gabriel. A blue, black, or white candle works well, though some practitioners use a skull, a bowl of water, or a small fountain to mark the current. Light the candle and speak with reverence: I ask for the spirit of the West ______ to come and protect me while I do my work. I light this candle in reverence to you and thank you for reminding me of the sanctity of life. Feel the boundary seal.

- *North*: The North governs earth, stability, incubation, crossroads, and the quiet space between breaths where change prepares itself. This quarter holds the energy of waiting and transformation, the liminal pause before something new emerges. You may call land spirits, hunting spirits, crossroads guardians, or the angel Uriel if that language feels more familiar. A brown or green candle, or a bowl of stones or crystals, grounds the space physically. Light the candle and speak clearly: Spirit of North ______, please leave your place betwixt and between and protect me while I work today. I light this candle in homage to you and all you care for in the circle of life. Notice the weight settles.

When you close the circle, please don't rush out like someone leaving a party without saying goodbye. Return to the East and move through each quarter in the same order, extinguishing the candles and offering sincere thanks. Gratitude maintains a relationship. Relationship maintains protection. Mean it when you say thank you, because spirits recognize sincerity faster than any incantation. Then ground yourself back into the room and continue with your work.

Because I love a good historical footnote, let me point out that this concept predates modern witchcraft aesthetics by thousands of years. The Egyptian state appointed shamans who created protective fields by standing in the center of the room and projecting incantations outward so their voice struck the walls like a barrier, forming protection from the middle instead of the edges. Instead of four different guardians, they often invoked a single patron or a set of throned deities in each direction, binding sky to earth through spoken authority. You may adapt that older method if it resonates, facing each direction in turn and declaring the deity's presence with full voice, letting the echo mark the boundary. Protection does not belong to one culture or one "costume." It belongs to whoever shows up prepared, respectful, and clear about why they are stepping into the dark in the first place.

The Physiology of Trance and the Foundations of Out-of-Body Work

Before we get into spirit travel, journeying, or anything that sounds remotely exciting, let's slow down and talk about your body and your brain... because out-of-body work is a neurological and physiological state you deliberately cultivate. It is science as much as it is spirit. If you skip understanding what your nervous system is doing, you will spend a great deal of time trying very hard while absolutely nothing happens. Students who want to leap straight into "leaving the body" while their minds are still chewing on grocery lists and half-finished arguments are going to hit a wall every single time. When your brain stays busy and analytical, it stays anchored in the room: firmly attached to your senses, firmly attached to the couch, firmly attached to the very body you are trying to leave. Spirit travel needs a doorway; an occupied mind offers none. So before technique, we talk mechanics... because understanding what the brain is doing puts you in control of the process, instead of sitting there hoping something magical decides to show up.

Your brain operates through electrical rhythms, and each rhythm corresponds to a different state of consciousness. Certain states help you study; certain states help you enter trance. When you are actively learning, analyzing, taking notes, or trying to memorize something new, your brain produces mostly alpha activity: alert, focused, cognitively locked onto the world around you. Alpha is wonderful for classrooms and conversations. You are probably in it right now, reading this page.

The problem with alpha is that it keeps your attention pointed outward into the physical world. Every sound, every itch, every door that opens down the hall continues to feel important and immediate. Journeying requires the opposite direction of attention entirely: awareness turning inward, the body gradually fading into the background. Alpha makes that extremely difficult.

As the body relaxes and your thoughts soften, the brain shifts toward beta activity... calm alertness, gentle drowsiness, that particular feeling of resting on a couch staring out a window while nothing especially demands your attention. In beta, you remain awake and capable of responding to the world, yet your grip on your surroundings loosens, and your mind becomes less interested in constant commentary (what a relief). Beta is the threshold between ordinary awareness and trance: it prepares you, it softens you, but it does not yet create the altered state that allows spirit travel. Think of beta as the waiting room. You are in the right building; you are just not in the room yet.

The state we actually aim for during shamanic journeying is theta: that strange, heavy, drifting place just before sleep or immediately upon waking, where your body feels weighted, your thoughts dissolve into imagery, and you could almost fall asleep yet remain strangely aware of yourself. In theta, the analytical mind finally loosens its grip and the subconscious opens... which is precisely what allows symbols, visions, and spirit contact to emerge clearly. If you have experienced those vivid half-dreams right as you drift off, where you feel entirely somewhere else while still knowing you are in bed, you have already been in theta. That is the doorway we use intentionally. When students report that they "almost went somewhere but snapped back," they brushed against theta for a moment and then got yanked back into alpha by a thought or a sound. So close. So frustrating. So fixable.

Sound plays a surprisingly practical role in reaching theta, which is why traditional cultures rely so heavily on drumming instead of complex music or elaborate chants. A steady drumbeat around one hundred twenty to one hundred forty beats per minute gives the mind a simple, repetitive stimulus: enough to keep you from falling fully asleep, while the rhythm steadily draws your attention inward. Over time, the brain begins to associate that particular rhythm with trance automatically. Volume keeps you awake; rhythm pulls you inward; that balance creates ideal conditions for theta to emerge naturally. This is conditioning as much as it is craft; once your nervous system learns that drumbeat equals trance, you can enter the state faster each time you practice.

Music with lyrics tends to work against you... especially if you understand the language or have any emotional connection to the song. The moment your brain starts engaging with meaning, analyzing the words, remembering that one summer, or singing along internally, you are back in alpha. The doorway quietly closes. Journeying thrives on neutrality and repetition, not storytelling, not nostalgia. Simple percussion almost always serves you better than anything catchy or sentimental. Dedicated drumming tracks work better than playlists, because the goal is consistency instead of entertainment. Noise-canceling headphones also help enormously; a barking dog or a slamming door at exactly the wrong moment can snap your awareness back into the body so fast it is almost funny. Almost.

Posture affects the brain more than most people expect. The body constantly communicates with the nervous system about whether to stay alert or drift into sleep, and if you lie flat in a warm bed, your body will almost always choose sleep (as it should; you trained it well). Sitting rigidly upright, like you are waiting for a job interview, keeps the mind alert and analytical, locked in alpha. The goal is a middle ground: supported and relaxed, with enough spinal lift to maintain awareness. A meditation cushion works well because it softens the hips and legs while keeping the torso upright without effort. Some people kneel, some use a chair, some sit cross-legged; the principle is the same throughout: comfort with just a trace of alertness.

Once you settle into position, the real skill begins... and the real skill is learning to let the body fall away from your attention instead of responding to every sensation as if it is urgent. If you feel an itch and immediately scratch it, you have just told your brain that the physical body still deserves priority, and your awareness stays put. If you shift every time your leg tingles or your shirt wrinkles, you keep reinforcing the idea that the body must remain center stage. Spirit travel requires the opposite: sensations happen and dissolve without pulling you back, the way background noise in a room eventually stops registering. The body becomes something you are theoretically aware of but practically uninvested in; that detachment creates the space the spirit needs to move.

Pain adds its own layer here, and anyone living with chronic discomfort already knows how loudly the body can announce itself when something hurts. Persistent pain keeps dragging your attention back to the physical experience, which makes it genuinely harder to reach the depth of trance journeying requires. Managing your health responsibly becomes part of your spiritual practice; a distracted body creates a distracted spirit. At the same time, anything that dulls your awareness too much also interferes with the work. What you want is balance: a body calm enough to ignore and a mind clear enough to navigate.

When all of these pieces come together... steady rhythm, relaxed posture, quiet environment, inward attention... something simple happens. Something that often surprises students precisely because it lacks drama. Your awareness loosens gently from muscle and bone. The sense of the room fades. You begin to feel as though you are somewhere else, even though your body remains exactly where you left it. There is no explosion of light, no theatrical moment where you "pop out," just a quiet shift: the spirit steps forward, and the body steps back.

That quiet shift is the foundation of every journey you will ever take. Everything we build after this rests on that one skill: learning to guide your brain into the state that makes travel possible. Master this, and the rest opens up. Skip it, and you will be standing at the bay with no way into the water.

Cultural Appropriation

Remember that cultural appropriation is taking something from a culture and using it out of its historical or cultural context, or for gain by taking away from a marginalized group. Creolization is molding elements of different cultures to make a new culture. The term avatar is not being celebrated or used in its authentic form.

Cultural appropriation can be described as the act of adopting, borrowing, or imitating elements from a culture that is different from one's own out of context or without respect. This typically occurs when a dominant culture adopts aspects of a marginalized or minority culture. It encompasses the adoption of cultural practices, fashion, symbols, language, music, or any other forms of cultural expression without truly understanding or respecting the historical or cultural meaning behind them.

Cultural adoption can sometimes be an issue when it is not approached with understanding, appreciation, or permission. When done incorrectly, it may contribute to the commercialization, stereotyping, or misrepresentation of a culture. This can inadvertently reinforce harmful stereotypes, perpetuate power imbalances, and erase the cultural context and significance of certain practices or symbols. It is important to approach cultural exchange with respect and genuine curiosity.

When it comes to cultural exchange and appreciation, it's essential to approach it with kindness, sensitivity, and a genuine desire to learn. Taking the time to understand the cultural significance and history behind the elements we borrow or adopt shows respect and appreciation. Instead of appropriation, let's focus on cultural appreciation by giving credit, honoring, and respecting the cultures that inspire us.

Appreciation turns into appropriation when we engage with elements from a culture without fully understanding or respecting their historical and cultural importance. It's important to be mindful of how our actions may inadvertently lead to the commodification or exploitation of a culture. We must be cautious not to perpetuate harmful stereotypes or misrepresentations. By approaching cultural exchange with respect and genuinely seeking to understand, we can ensure that our appreciation stays true and meaningful.

It's important to clarify that adopting something from a culture you weren't born into doesn't automatically constitute cultural appropriation. What matters is how you approach it, ensuring you respect and appreciate the historical and cultural origins it comes from. It is not cultural appropriation to adopt something from a culture from which you were not born, if how you do it is done with the historical and cultural origin from which it comes from. Understanding the context and honoring the cultural significance can help ensure a respectful and meaningful exchange. That means you can add culture to your life IF AND ONLY IF it is done faithfully, with care, and in its authentic context. Let's celebrate cultural diversity in a way that fosters understanding and appreciation for one another! Mislabeling something is cultural appropriation. This is why people HATE "a turtle is my spirit animal."

To add to this, those who refuse to include and spread their culture contribute to cultural erasure. By preventing the authentic reproduction (emphasis on authentic) and spread of indigenous ways, insures that it will eventually die. If you don't plant the seed of these old ways in someone else's garden (because they don't look like you) guarantees that the plant will die. Don't gate-keep shamanic ways, as they are not closed practices. Remember that in ancient times, spirit was accessible to everyone. Let's return to those ways by making it accessible, albeit with respect and authenticity.

The Duku

One of the ignored aspects of shamanic work, especially as a witchdoctor, is storytelling, or the involvement of utilizing the performing arts. For some reason, Western culture separates and reduces performance work to entertainment; however, we all can feel how a movie can transport us to a different time or perspective, or help teach us lessons in history, taboos, or other people's experiences. We can feel how a song moves us to remember a love, or to celebrate a love we have with us now. We can feel how a dance, especially with the change of appreciation for dancers during *So You Think You Can Dance* or *Dancing With The Stars*, can make us feel things just from observing how someone controls the use of their body.

I have been a performing arts expert for over two decades, am an expert in over 18 dance forms, a trainer in seven styles of singing, and an award-winning director (from both coasts). My gifts in the transformative force of the performing arts are ignited because of my connection to my work as a witchdoctor. The purpose is always to tell the story and to figure out the best way to represent that.

In one of my classes, I taught African dance. In this class, they learned dances from throughout the continent of Africa, instead of the African dance classes, which are watered-down versions of West African dance. These dancers had lessons in culture and history from throughout Africa, and how those dances influenced or were influenced by their own cultures. In class, they also learned African-based dances, celebrating and teaching the Ring Shouts from the Afro-American enslavement era, Afro-Caribbean dances, and even dances that would be found in churches, musicals, and rock and roll.

Some days, I gave a warm-up to authentic African music, some days I played the djembe, and some days they listened to current West African pop music. The purpose of the class was to learn, discover, and represent Africa (which is massive!) through the beautiful form of dance.

During one semester, my African dance class was about to perform several numbers for a spring fair. They had a lapa of their choice over a tank top, and they were given a fabric to wear on their head. This will be worn like many people wear a towel on their head after a shower. This is called a duku.

Tabitha, a student of mine, in her forties, protested wearing a duku on her head. "I can't wear this as a white person," she said. "People will think that I am culturally appropriating. I think I should take this fabric and tie it around my ponytail instead. That way I can be a white person who is just wearing African fabric in my hair."

I was honestly shocked that this university professor did not see the issue with her statement.

"Actually," I said, "taking something from a culture and wearing it in a way that isn't how it is supposed to be worn is problematic and appropriation. An example is taking a grass skirt from Tahiti and using it as a table skirt for your lu'au-themed party. It is a garment. What if we took your wedding dress, cut it up, and wore it as wristbands? We want to respect clothing from cultures we are not a part of in the way they were meant to be worn. The problem isn't the color of your skin when wearing an African garment while demonstrating African dance. That's how we share and become a part of authentic culture and assimilation. The problem is when we piecemeal, select from a culture the parts of which we find to be a novelty or exotic, and try those things on. When dancing or telling stories from any culture, it is important to show the audience what the authentic representation actually is. Not what you feel comfortable with. If you don't feel comfortable being a part of African culture when you dance African dances, then you have no business dancing any of the pieces from this beautiful continent."

She was stunned. I have a tendency to be eloquent, intense, passionate, and specific in my words. This makes people intimidated by my presence. I also don't move frivolously. My sangfroid nature, my stillness, and my consciousness with my words, along with my stance in cultivating culture while also being a purest generally make people quite nervous with me.

She could see in my eyes that my intent was not to attack, nor did I try to bully or demean her. She considered this, and as an academic, she said, "Show me how to put it on, again?"

The Geography of the Mind and Spirit Worlds

Before you travel anywhere, you need a map.

Every journey you take in this practice begins in the same place: your own mind. Specifically, a particular layer of your mind that becomes accessible when your brain reaches theta. This is the territory we are about to chart together, and it is worth spending real time here before we move into active journeying, because a traveler who understands their landscape moves through it with confidence. A traveler who stumbles around, hoping something familiar will appear, wastes enormous energy and misses most of what is available to them.

The mind has layers. Consciousness has layers. These are the same thing said two different ways, and the map we are building here is a map of both simultaneously. Each layer is a plane of consciousness: a distinct territory with its own quality, its own access points, its own purpose. You already inhabit one of these planes right now, reading this page. The work of this practice is learning to move deliberately through the others.

Let us start where you are.

The Foyer: Hub of the Mental Plane

When you complete the stairs and accomplish your mind dump, you arrive in the foyer of your mind. Think of it as a lobby: open, dim, quiet, oriented. This is a real location within your consciousness, and with practice, it becomes as familiar and consistent as a room in your own home. Students who have been working with this geography for years describe their foyers with the same specificity they would use to describe their living rooms: the quality of the light, the temperature of the air, the particular feeling of the floor underfoot. The space develops texture and detail over time. Trust what yours shows you.

From the foyer, several directions present themselves.

To the Left: The Well

A well sits in the left side of the foyer, ancient and dark, filled with a black cosmic liquid that has the quality of deep space: vast, still, full of everything that has ever existed. Looking into it, you feel time the way you feel the ocean from a small boat. The scale is vertiginous. This is the passage to the Akashic plane, to your past lives and the full record of your soul's history. Entering requires intention; you will know when you are ready to go there. For now, know where it is.

Straight Ahead: The Hallway of Doors

Directly ahead of you stretches a hallway of doors. The longest hotel corridor you have ever seen does not come close. The doors extend beyond what the eye can follow, each one a memory or event from this lifetime: every experience you have lived, every moment stored, every version of yourself that has existed within this particular incarnation. This hallway is the library of your current life. You can enter any door and find yourself inside that memory with a completeness that ordinary recollection cannot approach. Know where it is; we have other places to be today.

To the Right: The Landing and the Mental Plane

To the right is an opening that leads to a landing and then out into the broader landscape of the mental plane. This is the direction of creation, of connection, of movement toward the spirit worlds. This is where most of your active journey work will take you, and we will map it in full shortly. For us, as shamans, this looks like a forest, jungle, or vibrant nature.

Upward: The Messianic Plane

The foyer opens upward as well. Above you is the access point to the messianic plane, to the highest version of yourself. The quality of what comes from above is different from what comes from the other directions: clearer, more distilled, carrying less of the weight of history and emotion. When you need that quality of guidance, look up.

The Center of the Room: The Channeler's Floor

For those who have trained as channelers, the center of the foyer holds one more access point. The floor itself, when approached with the right intention and training, opens. You can move through it as though it were water: downward, viscerally, through the layers of the self, into the sternum, into the spirit center that sits at the core of the body. If you have built an Adytum there, you can connect with your deity directly and channel them through the prepared vessel of yourself.

This is advanced work, and it is its own complete practice. A full book on channeling the gods, including the creation and consecration of the Adytum and everything that comes with it, is coming in **Witchdoctor Priest**. If channeling is your path, that book is where this thread continues. For now, know the floor is there and know what it leads to.

The Mental Plane Landscape

Through the right opening of the foyer, past the landing, the mental plane opens into a landscape. This is the creative plane, the plane of connection, the territory your spirit moves through on its way to the spirit worlds. It has geography, the way any place has geography: consistent, navigable, full of specific locations that serve specific purposes. This is where you create and build. This is where you grow and decay. Be out in nature because it bends and shapes the very part of you that is also made of nature (the mental plane).

A path presents itself. It forks.

The Right Fork: The Area of Consciousness

The right fork takes you to a cliff overlooking a river. This is the Area of Consciousness: the place within the mental plane where you connect to the energies of other people, to their mental planes, to the living current of consciousness that moves between all beings. When you need to read someone's energy, understand what is moving through another person, or simply remind yourself of your own energetic signature within the larger field, this is where you come. We will cover this in length in **Witchdoctor Psychic Medium.**

The quality of the Area of Consciousness is open and aerial. The cliff gives you perspective; the river below has the constant movement of thought and feeling and intention that constitutes the shared mental field of humanity. You can observe from the cliff or descend toward the river, depending on how direct a connection you need. Both positions offer real information.

The Left Fork: Into the Forest

The left fork takes you into the forest: dense, alive, coiling and twisting deeper into the green. Run through it if you feel called to run. Let the energy of living things fill you as you move: the temperature of the air, the particular quality of light through the canopy, the sounds of creatures, wind, and water. If anything remains in the mind that the staircase did not fully release, the forest tends to shake it loose. There is something about moving through dense living nature, even the mental plane's version of it, that completes what stillness sometimes cannot.

Halfway down the forest path, a place opens to your left. Step off the trail. Move through the undergrowth: over branches, under low brambles, through the density until the trees give way to a circular clearing ringed by hedges. This is the spirit circle. Quiet, contained, specifically shaped. We will do significant work here later in this book. For now, find it and carry its location with you. Then return to the path the way you came.

Continue along the path. Follow it all the way to where it curves right and the trees thin against a rock wall. Around that wall, tucked into the stone, is a bay: private, secluded, yours entirely. The water is calm. The sky above it is open. This is The Bay, and it is the primary crossroads to the spirit worlds.

The Bay: Crossroads to the Worlds

The Bay is where the mental plane meets the spirit worlds. From this single location, you can reach all three worlds, and the method of entry determines the destination.

Going into the water takes you down: into the Lower World, the vast and ancient realm beneath, where the Abyss lives and where the deeper work of exorcism and entity removal is frequently conducted.

Going into the sky takes you up: into the Upper World, where master teachers, spirit guides, and deities reside, where the highest guidance available to a practitioner can be sought and received.

Going over the cliff takes you across: into the Middle World, the spirit layer of the world we inhabit in our physical lives, where the living and the dead share territory and where much of the practical work of a witchdoctor unfolds.

The Bay is your base of operations for spirit travel. Learn it the way you learn your own kitchen: in the dark, by feel, with the confidence of someone who has been there a thousand times. You will be there a thousand times.

Methods of Travel

The geography above gives you the landscape. What follows are the methods of moving through it. Each one serves a different purpose and suits a different situation. A working practitioner eventually knows all of them and chooses instinctively based on what the journey requires.

The Bay

The most straightforward method of travel to the spirit worlds. Arrive at The Bay through the forest path, choose your direction, and go: water for the Lower World, sky for the Upper World, cliff for the Middle World. Clear, direct, reliable. This is the method most students learn first and return to most often throughout their practice.

The Spirit Circle

The spirit circle offers a different quality of entry, particularly suited to moments when you need to travel from within the mental plane instead of from The Bay. Find the clearing in the forest. Lie down in the same position your physical body is resting in during the journey. You are now your mind-body, the layer of self that inhabits the mental plane, lying in its own version of your journey position. From here, step out of that body the same way you stepped out of your physical body at the beginning of the journey. A second exit. A deeper layer. Where you arrive from here depends on your intention and your totem's guidance.

The Tree

Some people like the Druid-based way of travel. There is a giant world tree in your forest. If you climb into the tree, you can move down into the darkness and come out into the lower world. If you climb up through the trunk, you can come out of the darkness into the upper world. Or you can climb the outside of the world tree and sit on its branches. Launch yourself off to head to a location in the Middle World.

The Center of the Room: The Three Cauldrons

Let's say you don't leave the foyer of your mind, or you find a place in the jungle of the mental plane to do a different kind of journey: The three cauldrons are called upon; they arrive when you summon them. Stand in the center of the room, set your will, and call them into being: three cauldrons arranged before you, each one a portal and each one a divination tool depending on how you choose to use it.

The left cauldron connects to the Lower World. Peer into it without entering, and it offers messages about the past: images, impressions, information drawn from what has already been. Enter it, and it has you down into the Lower World entirely.

The center cauldron connects to the Middle World. Peering in gives messages about the present: the current state of a situation, the energetic reality of something happening now. Entering takes you into the Middle World.

The right cauldron connects to the Upper World. Peering in offers messages about the future: possibilities, trajectories, what is moving toward you or toward someone you are working with. Entering takes you into the Upper World.

The cauldrons give you a method of travel that requires less journey and more direct access. For a quick message, a fast check-in, a moment of orientation before deciding where to go: peer in. For full travel: enter. Both are valid tools, and both belong in your working practice.

Called up in the center of the foyer, the cauldrons offer both divination and a portal. Peer in for a message; step in for a journey. The left for the Lower World and the past, the center for the Middle World and the present, the right for the Upper World and the future. The cauldrons are particularly useful when you need speed or when the question you are carrying points clearly toward a specific world, and you want direct access without the full walk through the landscape.

The Bonfire and the Bridge

Every so often, a journey calls, and the destination simply does not announce itself. The situation is unclear, the guidance is ambiguous, and your totem is giving you that particular look that means it knows exactly where you are going and finds your confusion mildly entertaining. This is when you use the bonfire.

Find a bonfire, either in the foyer or out in the mental plane landscape. Your totem is with you. Dance around the fire together: move, let the energy build between you, let the rhythm of the dance do what dances have always done, and shift the quality of your awareness. When the two of you are ready, when the fire has done its work and the moment feels complete, blow it out.

Walk directly into it. Through the extinguished flame, into the smoke. The smoke rises around you and then clears, and when it does, a bridge stretches ahead of you: vast, solid, crossing into territory you could not have predicted from where you started. Walk the bridge. Cross it fully. When you arrive at the other side, you will be exactly where this particular journey requires you to be.

The bonfire method is the practice's way of getting your ego out of the navigation entirely. Your totem knows. The smoke knows. The bridge takes you where the work is. Experienced practitioners return to this method regularly, even after years of confident navigation, because sometimes the most important journeys are the ones you did not plan.

The Brain Behind the Map

The planes of consciousness are real territories, and the reason you can access them is both spiritual and neurological simultaneously. Your brain is the instrument through which your spirit interfaces with consciousness at every level. Understanding what it is doing while you journey is part of the spiritual work, approached from a different angle.

Your brain produces electrical activity constantly, and that activity organizes itself into rhythmic patterns called brain waves. Different wave states correspond to different qualities of consciousness, different levels of awareness, and different degrees of access to the territory we just mapped. The planes of consciousness and the brain wave states are the same system described in two different languages: one ancient and spiritual, one modern and scientific. Both descriptions are accurate. Neither one is complete without the other.

Here is what your brain is doing, from the ground up.

Delta: The Deepest Water of Dreamless Sleep

Delta waves are the slowest of all brain wave states, produced most consistently during deep, dreamless sleep. In delta, conscious awareness as you ordinarily experience it is essentially offline. The body repairs itself, the immune system does its deepest work, and the self that navigates daily life goes quiet in a way it cannot achieve any other way. Most people only encounter delta through sleep, and most people move through it without any awareness of having been there at all.

Delta is the brain's closest approximation to the Unity plane. The dissolution of individual consciousness that delta produces in sleep is a physiological echo of what the Unity plane represents spiritually: the self releasing its edges, the individual merging back into the undifferentiated ground. This is one of the reasons sleep deprivation is so profoundly destabilizing, physically and spiritually in equal measure. The body needs its nightly visit to the deep water. So does the spirit.

Advanced practitioners in certain traditions have developed the ability to maintain a thread of awareness through delta, to remain conscious in some form even in that deepest state. This is extraordinarily rare and requires years of deliberate cultivation. For the purposes of this work, delta is the horizon below the map: present, significant, and worth understanding even if you are traveling nowhere near it intentionally.

Theta: The Doorway

Theta is where we live during journeying, and by now you know it well from earlier chapters. That heavy, drifting, hypnagogic state between waking and sleep: thoughts dissolving into imagery, the body growing distant, the analytical mind finally loosening its grip on the steering wheel. Theta is the brain wave state of the mental plane. When your brain is producing theta, the foyer is accessible. The landscape is accessible. The Bay is accessible. The spirit worlds are accessible.

This is the wave state the shamanic drumbeat is designed to cultivate, the state the staircase and the mind dump are designed to stabilize, the state the breathing practice is designed to sustain. Everything in the preparation sequence of this practice points toward theta because theta is the doorway, and the doorway has to be open before anything else is possible.

Theta is also the wave state of deep meditation, of REM sleep and vivid dreaming, of the moments just before sleep when the hypnagogic imagery happens unbidden and strange. Every time you have experienced those half-dreams at the edge of sleep, the ones that feel like somewhere else entirely, you were in theta. You were standing in the doorway without knowing it was a doorway. This practice teaches you to stand there deliberately, to hold it open, and to walk through.

Alpha: The Conscious

Alpha is the wave state of relaxed wakefulness: calm, alert, present, with your attention resting gently on the world around you instead of driving through it. You move into alpha when you close your eyes and breathe slowly, when you sit quietly without a specific task demanding your focus, when you listen to music or take a walk without a destination. Alpha is pleasant. Alpha is restful. Alpha is also, for the purposes of journeying, the place where students get stuck.

Alpha sits at the threshold between ordinary consciousness and trance. The foyer waits just beyond it, and the direction is correct, but the mind finds alpha comfortable enough to stay there indefinitely, especially minds accustomed to more demanding states. Students who report that they relaxed deeply and felt peaceful but went nowhere are almost always describing a sustained alpha state. So close. The visualization portion of the journey preparation, the flame and the staircase, gives the mind just enough engagement to keep moving toward theta instead of settling into alpha and calling it a day.

Beta: The Working Mind

Beta is the wave state of active, engaged, analytical consciousness: problem-solving, decision-making, conversation, focused work, the kind of alert attention you bring to learning something new or navigating something complex. Most of your waking life is spent in beta. Reading this page right now, your brain is likely producing beta waves, with excursions into alpha when a passage gives you a moment to absorb something before continuing.

Beta is the causal plane in full operation. It is the wave state of the self that manages your life, pays your bills, argues its point, and tries very hard to understand what is happening during a journey while the journey is actively happening. That last tendency is the one to watch. The analytical beta mind lurks at the edges of theta, ready to reassert itself the moment something interesting enough to analyze appears. Every time a student starts trying to understand a journey symbol in real time, their brain is making a small climb back toward beta. Wu wei, the open hand, the riding of the journey instead of the directing of it: all of that is the practice of keeping beta in its seat while theta does the traveling.

Beta is also your greatest asset in this work, because it is what you return to after the journey. The quality of your beta processing after the fact determines how much of what you experienced you can actually use. A well-rested, well-nourished, clear beta mind integrates journey material with remarkable precision. Take care of the instrument.

Gamma: The Flash of Everything

Gamma is the fastest brain wave state, and the least understood, which is saying something because the brain remains genuinely mysterious even to those who study it most rigorously. Gamma waves appear during moments of peak concentration, during bursts of insight, and during the integration of information across different regions of the brain simultaneously. The experience of sudden understanding, the moment when something fragmented resolves into coherence, that flash of everything clicking into place at once: that is gamma.

Gamma also appears during certain states of advanced meditation. Studies of long-term meditators, particularly Tibetan Buddhist monks with decades of practice, show unusually high gamma activity during specific contemplative states, particularly those involving compassion and what the monks describe as the dissolution of the boundary between self and other. This is the neurological signature of the messianic plane: the brain firing in its highest gear, integrating across every system it has, touching briefly the experience of oneness before returning to its ordinary differentiated state.

For most practitioners at most stages of this work, gamma happens instead of being cultivated. It happens at the moment of genuine insight during a journey, at the moment when the information you received resolves into meaning, at the moment after a particularly deep session when something shifts, and you understand something in a way that goes beyond the intellectual. That flash is gamma. That flash is also, in its way, a brief visit to the upper planes: the territory where everything connects to everything else, and the self briefly stops insisting on being separate.

These five wave states are the neurological map underlying the spiritual map. Delta is at the bottom, where the deepest waters are. Theta in the middle, the working territory of this practice, the plane where the foyer waits, and the bay shines, and the spirit worlds stand ready. Alpha at the threshold, gentle and close. Beta at the surface, the ordinary self doing its ordinary work.

Gamma at the peak, the flash of integration, the brief electrical signature of oneness.

Your brain produces all of them. You move through all of them every day, most of the time without noticing or choosing. This practice teaches you to notice, to choose, and to navigate with intention. The map of the mind and the map of the brain are the same map. Now you have both.

The Planes of Consciousness

The Causal Plane

This is where you live. Waking consciousness, ordinary awareness, the experience of being a person moving through a day: appointments, conversations, hunger, the particular quality of afternoon light through a window. The causal plane is the plane of cause and effect, of linear time, of the self that manages your daily existence. When you sit down to journey, you are sitting down in the causal plane. Everything that follows is a movement away from it and, eventually, a return.

The causal plane is the plane your spirit chose when it chose this life, and it deserves the same respect you will learn to give others. The work of this practice is the ability to move fluidly between all the planes and return with something useful. You are building a skill, and the home base from which you build it is right here: ordinary, beautiful, entirely worth returning to.

The Akashic Plane

Below the causal plane, within and down, is the Akashic plane: the plane of all that has been. Every life you have ever lived, every iteration of your soul across time, every experience recorded in the vast library that some traditions call the Akashic records. The Akashic plane holds the complete history of your soul, every lifetime, every lesson, every contract, every relationship that has carried across incarnations.

Access to the Akashic plane is through the well in the foyer of the mind, which we will describe in detail shortly. This is a destination that rewards intention and patience. The information available there is dense and ancient, and it often requires significant processing time after the journey. Approach it with purpose and with generosity toward yourself for what comes back.

The Mental Plane

This is where journeying lives. When your brain reaches theta, and your spirit steps forward, you arrive in the mental plane: the plane of consciousness where thought becomes form, where creation originates, where the spirit worlds become accessible. The mental plane is the plane of the imagination in its truest and most powerful sense... the imagination as a faculty of perception instead of a faculty of invention. What you encounter here is real. You are perceiving, not producing.

The mental plane is also the plane of connection. From here, you can reach other people's energies, the spirit worlds, your own deepest self, and the layers of consciousness above. It is the great hub, the crossroads of the inner landscape, and the territory this chapter is primarily concerned with mapping.

The foyer of your mind, the landscape beyond it, the paths and the bay and the forest: all of it exists within the mental plane. This is your working territory.

The Messianic Plane

Above the mental plane is the messianic plane: the plane of your highest self, the most complete and perfected version of what you are. Every person has within them a version of themselves that has fully realized their potential, fully integrated their lessons, and fully become what they came here to be. The messianic plane is where that version exists, and connection to it offers a quality of guidance and clarity that is distinct from anything available in the planes below.

Access is upward from the foyer. We will save the deep work of this territory for later, but knowing it is above you and available to you is itself useful information. When you feel during a journey that you are reaching for something higher than your ordinary guides can offer, that direction is up.

The Unity Plane

At the top of the map, beyond the messianic plane, is the Unity plane. This is the plane of pure oneness: the undifferentiated everything that underlies all of it. Some traditions call this nirvana. Some call it the void. I've also heard it called the Buddhic plane. It is nothing and everything simultaneously, the ground state of existence before it differentiates into forms.

I will be direct with you about the Unity plane: connection to it has a real risk of conscious collapse. The individual self is a structure, and the Unity plane dissolves structures. Most practitioners will spend their entire careers working productively in the planes below it, and that is exactly as it should be. It is on this map because it exists and because you deserve a complete picture of the territory. It is the horizon at the edge of the map, the place where the known world ends. Respect that edge.

This is your map. Study it the way you would study any map before entering unfamiliar territory: with attention, with respect for what you do not yet know, and with the understanding that the territory itself will teach you things the map cannot. The foyer will develop its own character. The forest will feel different at different times. The Bay will become as familiar as your own face.

Every journey you take adds detail to this map. Every return adds confidence. That deepening is the practice, and it begins the moment you close your eyes, find your breath, and start down the stairs.

The Spirit Current and the Spirit Worlds

Understanding the Terrain of the Other World

Once you can enter trance reliably and have established a relationship with your power animal, the next practical question usually sounds very simple and very human, and it goes something like this: Where exactly am I going when I leave my body? Students often speak about the spirit world as though it were one giant, cloudy room where everything floats together in the same space, yet in practice, the Other World behaves much more like geography, with distinct environments, different kinds of inhabitants, and different rules of movement depending on where you stand. When you travel without understanding the terrain, you move like a tourist without a map, which creates unnecessary confusion and occasional risk. When you understand the layout, you move like a local, and everything becomes calmer, more efficient, and far less dramatic. So think of this chapter as orientation, the same way I would orient you to a new campus before sending you off to find your own classrooms.

I use the term *Spirit Current* to describe the overall flow of spiritual reality that surrounds and interpenetrates our physical world, because I find it helpful to imagine spirit as continuous instead of as something stacked in separate boxes. You are already standing inside this current every day, even while reading this page, because the spirit does not live somewhere else waiting for you to visit. What changes during journeying is your perception, not your location, and that shift in perception allows you to interact with layers of reality that your ordinary senses simply gloss over. Many systems describe additional realms, dimensions, timelines, or archives of memory, and those models can be useful in specific contexts, yet for the purposes of practical spirit work, I prefer to keep things focused and teach the three primary regions you will actually use. These three are commonly referred to as the Middle World, the Lower World, and the Upper World, and together they form the landscape most practitioners encounter during out-of-body travel. Once you understand these three, you can navigate most situations you will ever face in this work.

Let us begin with the *Middle World*, because it is the easiest to grasp and the one you already know intimately, even if you have never labeled it that way. The Middle World is the world we physically inhabit right now, the shared environment of streets, buildings, forests, oceans, and everyday life, yet it contains both physical and spiritual aspects woven together at the same time. Most people perceive only the physical layer because that is what the five senses evolved to prioritize, which means the spiritual activity happening here tends to go unnoticed. When you travel out of body into the Middle World, you move through the same locations with different senses, which allows you to perceive spirits, energetic imprints, and subtle presences that remain invisible to ordinary sight. This is extremely useful for practical work, such as checking on a client's home, sensing attachments in a particular space, or observing environments you cannot physically access. In many traditions, including certain Italian folk practices, witches used this kind of spirit walking for reconnaissance and protection, moving through familiar terrain with expanded perception.

The Middle World tends to feel recognizable during travel, which can be comforting for beginners, yet it still requires discipline because familiarity sometimes encourages carelessness. You might see your own house, your street, or places you visit regularly, yet the experience has a slightly altered quality, almost like looking at the same place through different lighting or through water. Spirits that inhabit this layer often include land spirits, lingering human presences, and the energetic residue left behind by strong emotional events. When working here, your role resembles that of a sensitive observer or mediator, noticing what belongs, what feels out of place, and what may need attention. Because the environment parallels the physical world, it becomes an excellent training ground for building confidence before venturing deeper into less predictable territory. Many of my students spend a good amount of time here simply practicing movement and perception.

From there, we move into the *Lower World*, which tends to feel larger, older, and more symbolic in character, and this is the region most people encounter when they first begin interacting regularly with spirits and ancestors. The Lower World has a sense of depth and density, almost like traveling into the roots of the earth or the under-layers of reality, and it often presents itself through landscapes such as caves, tunnels, forests, or vast subterranean spaces. This realm holds a strong connection to instinct, memory, and ancestry, which is why so many encounters here involve animal forms, ancestral spirits, and fragments of the self that have been forgotten or set aside. When mediums speak about contacting the veil or communicating with the dead, they are frequently interacting with this region of the Spirit Current. It functions as a gathering place for many human spirits after death, along with other entities that feel earthy, ancient, or closely tied to nature. Navigating the Lower World can feel dreamlike and surreal, yet it remains consistent enough that you learn its patterns with practice.

Because the Lower World contains such a wide range of beings, from helpful ancestors to opportunistic spirits that feed on confusion or fear, it is where your relationship with your power animal becomes especially important. This is where instinct keeps you safe, because logic alone moves too slowly when the environment shifts quickly. Some areas feel welcoming and calm, like peaceful ancestral lands or resting places, while others carry heavier, more chaotic energy that signals you to move along. Treat this realm with respect, the same way you would treat a wilderness you are hiking through for the first time, because awareness and preparation keep you steady. With guidance and practice, the Lower World becomes one of the most useful regions for healing work, soul retrieval, and ancestral communication. Many practitioners end up spending the majority of their professional journey here.

Finally, we arrive at the *Upper World*, which students often expect to feel bright and angelic, yet in my experience, it presents itself in many different ways depending on the individual, sometimes luminous and sometimes vast and dark like open space. The quality here tends to feel expansive instead of earthy, and encounters often involve teachers, guides, guardians, and beings who operate at a broader level of oversight instead of day-to-day human concerns. Where the Lower World feels rooted and instinctual, the Upper World feels spacious and abstract, like stepping into a place where ideas and archetypes take form. Many people describe meeting mentors, ancestors who have taken on protective roles, or figures who carry a strong sense of wisdom and perspective. The environment can feel immense, which is why grounding through your power animal and your own center remains important even here. Think of this realm as a place of consultation and higher guidance instead of exploration for its own sake.

When you put all three regions together, you begin to see that the Spirit Current functions less like a single destination and more like an ecosystem, with each area serving different purposes and hosting different kinds of relationships. The Middle World is about observation and practical intervention in everyday spaces. The Lower World is about healing, ancestry, and deep instinctual work. The Upper World is about guidance, teaching, and connection with larger forces that shape reality. As you continue practicing, you will naturally develop preferences and specialties depending on your temperament and the kind of work you do with clients. Understanding this layout simply gives you orientation so that when you step through the gateway, you know where you are headed and why.

All of this may sound elaborate when written out, yet in practice, it becomes intuitive very quickly, the same way you eventually learn the layout of your own neighborhood without needing a map. After enough journeys, you recognize the "feel" of each region immediately, and your body responds accordingly without much conscious thought. That familiarity is what allows you to focus on the task at hand instead of worrying about where you are. My goal in teaching you this geography is not to create rigid categories, but to give you a working framework that is about clarity and safety. Once you have that framework, the spirit world feels less mysterious and much more navigable, which is exactly how a professional practitioner prefers it.

Working the Realms

Applied Travel in the Middle, Lower, and Upper Worlds

By this point, you understand how to enter trance, how to descend through your gateway, and how to move with your power animal beside you. Which means we can finally talk about doing something useful once you arrive somewhere. Students treat journeying like sightseeing at first, wandering around, impressed by the scenery, and that is a completely understandable phase. Professional spirit work requires something more grounded and intentional, though. These realms are work spaces, and each one is about a different kind of task. Your travel needs direction.

Think of it the way you would think about entering different departments in a hospital: each floor has its own purpose and its own protocols, and you show up knowing why you are there. When you approach the spirit worlds with that mindset, everything becomes calmer and more practical, and you stop chasing every shiny thing that floats past your face. What follows is how I teach students to actually use these worlds instead of simply visit them.

The Middle World

Return to the Bay (or to your NDE location as their guide) with your power animal. By now, that place should feel familiar and steady, your launching dock instead of your final destination. The Bay is neutral ground: a calm threshold where you orient yourself, gather your focus, and decide where you are going next. Turn around and speak directly with your power animal, because this part of you already knows how to navigate terrain more efficiently than your thinking mind ever will. Have a conversation the way you would talk through directions with a trusted friend: clarify where you want to travel, and then commit to the movement together.

Once the destination is clear, jump the wall surrounding the Bay and let the shift happen naturally. Sometimes you will experience the sensation of flying. Other times, you simply arrive without any sense of distance having passed at all. Movement in the spirit world follows intention instead of mileage.

While traveling through the Middle World, you may begin noticing figures that resemble shadows moving at the edges of your perception. Here is where many people start telling ghost stories that have absolutely nothing to do with what is actually happening, so let me save you some drama. A shadow person, in most cases, simply represents another traveler whose spirit has temporarily stepped out of their body the same way yours has. Billions of people live on this planet, and many traditions practice some form of astral or dream walking. These forms appear featureless and dark, almost like silhouettes, because you perceive their presence without the physical markers of clothing, age, or identity. A lingering human spirit, by contrast, often has more recognizable traits or a particular translucence, reflecting the residue of a life once lived in a body. Understanding this difference keeps you calm and observant.

If you are spirit walking through the Middle World and someone happens to notice you, they will perceive you the same way: a vague shadow or presence instead of your full physical self, which is actually quite comforting when you think about it. Mediums sometimes pick up these movements more easily because their perception stays tuned toward spirit activity, yet even then, you remain largely anonymous and unremarkable. The idea that someone is going to recognize you specifically tends to come from imagination instead of experience, and it makes me laugh every time a student worries about it. Encountering the spirit form of a living stranger is such an unusual event that most people register it as passing energy and move on. The Middle World contains far more activity than most people realize, and your presence blends into the background just fine. That anonymity allows you to observe without interfering.

Take time during these journeys to really look around, because the Middle World reveals layers that your physical senses rarely acknowledge: displaced ghosts, elemental presences within plants and land, domicile spirits tied to homes, and the occasional darker creature that prefers to linger unnoticed. Traveling here also allows you to practice remote viewing, which simply means observing places at a distance through spirit perception instead of physical travel. You are a visitor with enhanced sight. You will witness what spirits are present and how a space feels energetically, and that information alone provides more than you might expect.

For those preparing to work as exorcists or healers, mastering the Middle World has direct practical value. You will often need to reach a client's location in spirit form before you ever meet them physically. Being able to orient yourself in their home, sense what is present, and assess the situation from a distance gives you information that shapes how you approach the session entirely. You become capable of standing beside a client in spirit even when you are miles away. In professional practice, that difference matters enormously.

Middle World Homework

Test this skill methodically instead of relying on imagination, because verification builds confidence far more effectively than fantasy. Choose real locations around the world, journey there with your power animal, and afterward research those places and compare what you perceived with photographs and descriptions. If you traveled effectively, the time of day at the location should match the time of day you experienced during your out-of-body walk. Approach it like field research. Let the journey unfold instead of directing every image, because forcing imagery produces daydreaming. When you allow the experience to develop naturally, the difference between imagination and travel becomes unmistakable.

Here are your fourteen destinations. Seven are well known, and seven are small, obscure, and genuinely unlikely to be in your mental library of pre-loaded imagery, which makes them the more rigorous test:

Well Known:

1. The Louvre, Paris, France
2. Shibuya Crossing, Tokyo, Japan
3. The Pyramids of Giza, Egypt
4. Grand Central Station, New York City, USA
5. The Sagrada Família, Barcelona, Spain
6. Machu Picchu, Peru
7. The Taj Mahal, Agra, India

Small and Unknown:

1. Gjirokastra, Albania
2. Socotra Island, Yemen
3. Tórshavn, Faroe Islands
4. Colonia del Sacramento, Uruguay
5. Matera, Basilicata, Italy
6. Takachiho Gorge, Miyazaki, Japan
7. Aksum, Ethiopia

Travel to each one. Record what you perceive before you research. The unfamiliar destinations are the most rigorous test of genuine travel.

The Lower World

Return to the Bay and treat the ocean as your doorway. Water has the psyche naturally toward depth and descent, and your spirit responds to that imagery with very little resistance. Walk straight into the water with your power animal at your side and allow yourself to submerge without hesitation. Trust that the sensation of sinking marks the transition.

As you descend, you may notice the water gradually transforming into air, and suddenly you are moving downward through open space instead of swimming. This signals that you have entered the spirit current of the Lower World. The sky often appears unfamiliar in color and texture, sometimes muted or strangely toned, and the landscape has an ancient, heavy feeling compared to the Middle World. This realm feels older and more instinctual, like the roots of existence instead of its surface. Many people sense immediately that they are somewhere deeper than ordinary reality.

Within the Lower World, you will encounter places that serve specific functions for more advanced work. One of these is the Abyss: a colorless, fog-filled expanse that feels stripped down to almost nothing, like standing on a concrete platform surrounded by emptiness. This location functions as a containment zone for troublesome entities. Spirits placed here tend to remain isolated for extended periods, which gives them time to dissipate or lose momentum without harming anyone else. Knowing how to find this place gives you an option when you encounter something that requires removal instead of negotiation. Familiarity with its location simply adds another tool to your professional practice.

Another region is sometimes called the Cavern of Lost Souls, which has a very different atmosphere and requires caution and attentiveness instead of curiosity. The environment often appears as a descending cave system with heavy energy and limited visibility, and many practitioners report that their power animal prefers to wait outside while other animal guides step forward to assist. Move quietly and softly here. Keep your energy low, soften your presence, and follow the guidance offered instead of improvising. Learning where this entrance exists is useful knowledge; lingering there serves no purpose. Respect the terrain and leave once you understand it.

The Lower World can feel vast and endless, with different areas reflecting fragments of memory, belief, and ancestral experience. You might glimpse what looks like personal heavens or regions of suffering, depending on who or what you encounter. Your power animal functions as your map through this complexity. Trust that guidance instead of trying to catalog everything you see.

Lower World Homework

Plan six separate journeys into the Lower World. In four of them, seek out and observe a cryptid: one of the great unverified creatures that exist at the boundary between the physical world and the spirit world, seen across centuries and cultures with enough consistency to suggest they are something. Observe each one from a respectful distance. Record behavior, movement, and environment. Your power animal stays close.

In your remaining two journeys, seek out ancestors. One from your known lineage and one from further back than you can name: a predecessor you carry in your blood whose face and life you have no conscious access to. Spend time with each one. Ask what they want you to know.

The Upper World

Travel to the Upper World begins again at the Bay, with movement upward. Leap over the ocean and allow yourself to rise into the sky, noticing the sensation of the air thickening around you as though it has substance. Many people describe this transition as the air turning fluid or silky, an unseen current carrying you higher without effort. Eventually, the terrain changes, and you enter a space that feels expansive and open, sometimes luminous and sometimes dark and starless, and always vast. This realm has a quieter, more contemplative quality than the Lower World. The atmosphere encourages listening.

The Upper World serves as a place of teaching and guidance, where you encounter advanced spirits, guardians, and mentors who operate at a broader level than day-to-day human concerns. Meetings here tend to feel structured and purposeful, almost like consultations instead of adventures. Many practitioners use this space to seek clarity, insight, or direction about their work. Beings who specialize in oversight and protection tend to reside here. Approach these encounters with respect and genuine curiosity, and allow information to unfold instead of demanding answers. The process feels more like dialogue than spectacle. Quiet attention has you further than force.

Upper World Homework

Plan four journeys into the Upper World.

In three of them, seek out a master: a being of advanced wisdom whose purpose is teaching instead of companionship. These are the Upper World's faculty, and they tend to meet sincerity with sincerity. Go with a genuine question instead of a general request. Your three masters may arrive in human form, in symbolic form, or as a presence more than a figure. Allow them to present themselves as they are. Record what each one offers, and return to each one more than once if the relationship opens.

In your fourth journey, seek your spirit guide: the being aligned specifically with your path, your protection, and the work you are here to do. This relationship is one you will cultivate across your entire practice. Arrive with an open mind about what form your guide takes, because preconceptions about what a spirit guide should look like will only slow the meeting down. Let them show you who they are.

As always, your power animal remains your anchor across all three worlds, in every journey, without exception. Wherever you travel, you return safely and whole.

Returning to the Body: Coming Home Cleanly and Staying Safe

At some point, every student asks the same question with a little bit of worry behind their eyes, and it usually sounds like this: What if I can't come back? The question makes complete sense because leaving your body sounds dramatic when you say it out loud. In practice, the return has always been the easiest part of the entire process. I have never had trouble returning, and I have never watched a student struggle with it either, because the body has a very strong claim on you. Staying out tends to require more effort than coming back, because we are engineered to live inside these bodies and operate through them. Spirit form feels natural in a metaphysical sense, yet biologically we belong here until death. Your system always seeks homeostasis, and for us, that home base is flesh, breath, and gravity.

When a journey concludes, most people simply become aware of their physical form again, without doing anything special, almost like waking from a nap as the room slowly comes back into focus. You feel the weight of your legs, the pressure of the floor or chair beneath you, and the sounds around you begin to register again. That transition happens organically because your consciousness remains tethered to your body the entire time, even while your perception travels elsewhere. Think of it like a rubber band stretched to its limit: the moment your attention relaxes, it snaps back. The body calls you home constantly, and the call grows louder the moment you allow it. Returning requires nothing more than allowing it to happen.

If you ever feel a little slow or foggy coming back, simple tools accelerate the process immediately. Raising your alertness shifts your brainwaves and pulls you out of trance, which means sound and emotion work in your favor here. Call your own name out loud with intention, the way someone would shout across a field to get your attention, and you will feel yourself snap back into your body very quickly. After that, refocus on the back of your eyelids, let everything go dark, and then slowly open your eyes and take in the room. Within seconds, you are fully present.

Getting Lost During Travel

Another fear that tends to show up early is the idea of getting lost somewhere in the spirit world, as though you might wander too far and forget how to return.

Your soul remains connected to your body at all times, and that connection functions like a tether, constantly maintaining orientation between the two.

Even after death, traditions all over the world describe the body calling back pieces of the spirit, which tells you how strong that relationship really is. During ordinary journeying, that bond stays intact and active throughout.

Physical stimulus pulls you back instantly, which means everyday life acts as a built-in safety system, whether you think about it or not. If someone touches your body, if a sound interrupts you, if your music cuts out, or if anything demands your physical attention, you return immediately without effort. The system works automatically. I have watched students pop back into their bodies because a dog barked or a phone vibrated, and they looked genuinely surprised at how fast it happened. Simple biology and awareness snap back into place.

The tether between spirit and body remains constant, and that tether always wins. Your body stays right here the entire time, waiting for you. Returning happens the moment your focus shifts.

On Risk, Injury, and the Realities of the Spirit Current

Here is the part I handle carefully with students, because it requires honesty and maturity in equal measure. For years, I softened this conversation because beginners tend to look for danger the moment you mention it, and looking for danger creates unnecessary problems. Most everyday spirit walking takes you through stable terrain where cooperation and observation dominate. Calm, purposeful work with clear intention and a steady power animal keeps you in the regions of the Spirit Current where routine travel and client work belong. That is the reality most of the time.

At the same time, we practice a craft that involves interacting with spirits, and they span a wide spectrum of personalities and behaviors, just as humans and animals do. Some entities behave aggressively. Some behave predatorily. Some operate on instincts that have nothing to do with human comfort or morality. A mature practitioner understands this with the same calm they bring to understanding that the ocean contains sharks: accurate, useful, and worth knowing without dramatizing.

The spirit world contains beauty, teachers, ancestors, and helpers in abundance. It also contains regions that function more like wilderness: vast, alive, and operating according to their own rules. Consider the physical world for a moment and how enormous it really is, from your house to your street to your town and then outward to oceans, deserts, and remote forests filled with creatures you will never personally encounter. You sit in your living room without concern about crocodiles because you are simply in a different territory. The same principle applies here. Harmful beings exist in their own regions, and ordinary journeying takes you nowhere near them. You would have to go out of your way and override every signal your power animal sends you to wander into that territory. Context matters enormously.

This is exactly why your power animal functions as your guide and safeguard instead of a symbolic mascot. This aspect of you has instinct, pattern recognition, and survival intelligence that operates faster than rational thought. When something feels wrong, your power animal redirects you the same way your hand pulls back from a hot stove before you consciously register the heat. Trust that guidance. It exists to keep you aligned with safe and purposeful travel, and following it keeps you steady far more effectively than any memorized list of threats ever could.

Approach this work the way you would approach hiking in genuine wilderness: with respect, preparation, and awareness. Stay focused on your intention, follow your guide, and give unfamiliar territory the same consideration you would give a trail you have never walked before. Do that, and your journeys remain steady, useful, and whole. The goal is always the same: go where you need to go, do the work, and come home. Everything we have practiced leads you back to that simple, reliable rhythm.

Animism: The Soul of All Things

The word animism comes from the Latin *anima*, meaning soul or life force. The doctrine is exactly what that etymology suggests: everything has a soul. Every living being, every plant, every rock, every river, every computer, every remote control sitting on your coffee table. All of it has a soul. In the second book of this series, **Witchdoctor Kahuna Healer**, we talk about how the soul of non-living things is just the "body," or *uhane*. If everything has a soul, every object has a life of some kind (including the crystals you tote around... which is why each crystal can do something different from the average rock), then you may have a new outlook on life. **Every soul participates in the living fabric of existence, whether you acknowledge that participation or not.**

Take a moment with that.

I came to the word animism through shamanic practice but was always taught about the soul of the plants living in Keanae, Hawai'i, and what this word gave me was a framework for something I had already felt but lacked the vocabulary to describe: the sense that the world is not a collection of objects moving around each other but a web of relationships, each thread alive and carrying information. Plants, animals, stones, water, wind, the particular quality of a place that has held human suffering or human joy for long enough that you feel it the moment you walk in: all of it is animated. All of it has something to say, if you develop the patience and the perceptual range to hear it.

This is the spiritual backbone of shamanic belief, and it is the reason spirit work is possible at all. You can communicate with the natural world because the natural world is constantly communicating. You can work with the spirit of a place because places have soul. You can negotiate with the energy of an object because objects carry energy that accumulates, shifts, and affects the people who interact with them. Animism provides the cosmological ground on which every practice in this book stands.

The interconnectedness animism describes is practical. When the soul health of your environment deteriorates, you feel it. A house where something terrible happened and was never addressed has that weight in its walls, and the people who live there absorb it gradually without knowing why they feel heavy, anxious, or depleted. A forest that has been treated with respect over generations feels different from one that has been clear-cut and left to recover: same trees, different spirit. The vitality of the living systems around you contributes to your own vitality, and your own vitality contributes back to theirs. This is the web, and you are a thread in it, pulling and being pulled.

Extending animist awareness to the objects of daily life tends to surprise people, particularly those who came to this practice from a Western secular background, where a remote control is just a remote control. And yet: consider how long human beings have understood that certain objects accumulate meaning, charge, and power. Every tradition on earth has its sacred objects, its relics, its heirlooms that carry the weight of the people who held them. The grandmother's ring that feels like her presence. The house that still holds the energy of its original family decades after they left. The tool that works better in the hands of someone who loves it. These experiences are animism confirming itself through ordinary life, available to anyone paying attention.

Shamanic practice trains that attention deliberately. Where an ordinary person might feel vaguely uncomfortable in a particular room without knowing why, a trained practitioner can identify what is present, where it came from, and what it requires. Where someone might notice that a client's home feels heavy, the practitioner can locate the specific object, relationship, or history generating that weight and address it. Animism gives you the conceptual framework; practice gives you the perceptual tools to work within it.

The ecological dimension of animism is also worth sitting with seriously, because it has weight beyond the spiritual. A worldview in which everything is alive and ensouled produces a very different relationship to the natural world than one in which nature is a collection of resources available for human use. Indigenous cultures that maintained animist frameworks over long periods also tended to maintain sustainable relationships with their ecosystems, because you treat the world differently when you understand it as a community of beings instead of a warehouse of materials. That understanding is available to contemporary practitioners, and the planet could use considerably more of it.

For the working witchdoctor, animism is the water you swim in. Every journey you take moves through a world that is alive at every level. Every entity you encounter, every landscape you traverse, every spirit you negotiate with: all of it is animated, all of it is relational, and all of it responds to the quality of attention and intention you bring. Approach the spirit world the way a skilled diplomat approaches a foreign culture: with genuine curiosity, with respect for what you do not yet understand, and with the recognition that you are a guest in a living system that was here long before you arrived and will continue long after you leave.

The soul of all things is paying attention. So should you.

Spirit Walk Alternative Journeys

Your brain still needs to reach theta for all of these. Find your posture, start your drumming track or music at one hundred twenty to one hundred fifty beats per minute, or use five hundred twenty-eight hertz tones played loudly enough to keep your mind from drifting into sleep. The mechanics of preparation stay the same regardless of which vehicle you choose.

Sometimes the visualization sequence I outlined earlier simply does not cooperate. Maybe it has temporarily stopped working for you. Maybe you are having an off day, and the stairs feel like concrete, and the bay feels like a postcard.

Maybe you are the kind of traveler who needs more than one road into the same territory. All of that is workable. What follows are alternative modalities for the journey, each one arriving at the same destination through a different door.

The Circle

This works best for Middle World travel, but can work anywhere. This is stepping out of your physical body, then stepping out of that mind-body that is getting in the way.

1. Breathe until your heart rate reaches sixty beats per minute.

2. Take the stairs through your mind dump and arrive in the foyer.

3. Turn right out of the foyer and head into nature.

4. Stop halfway down the path and turn left into the forest. Walk until you find the spirit circle: a circular clearing ringed by hedges. Step into the grass and allow it to mold itself around your body, conforming to your shape, the way your physical environment is holding your body back in the room.

5. Let your mental self close its eyes, mirroring what your physical body is doing.

6. On the count of three, pull yourself out of your mental body and into your astral body. Your power animal will be waiting.

7. Together, decide where you are going. Run toward the hedge and jump. You will land on the other side exactly where you are meant to be.

The Bonfire

This works particularly well for Upper World travel.

1. Breathe until your heart rate reaches sixty beats per minute, and take the stairs through your mind dump.

2. When you arrive in the foyer, a bonfire will be burning in the center of the room. If it is not already there, call it.

3. Dance around the fire. Your power animal will join you as you move, and the dancing itself is part of the word.

4. When you have reached ecstasy, you and your power animal blow out the bonfire together. Smoke fills the room. Walk directly into the smoke where the fire was burning. As you move through it, the smoke parts and the journey begin.

The Cauldrons

This method travels anywhere: Lower World, Middle World, Upper World. Your choice.

1. Breathe until your heart rate reaches sixty beats per minute, and take the stairs through your mind dump and arrive in the foyer.

2. Stand in the center of the room and look down at the floor. Watch it shift, becoming fluid, moving like liquid beneath your feet.

3. From the center of that fluid floor, three cauldrons rise: each one full of dark, gelatinous liquid.

4. The left cauldron has you to the Lower World, moving you through the spirit current the way the ocean does at the bay. The center cauldron takes you to the Middle World, returning you to your own environment but from the other side of the veil. The right cauldron takes you upward into the Upper World. Your power animal will be there when you land; they are always part of you and always find you.

Climbing the Breadfruit Tree

In Hawaiian tradition, the breadfruit tree holds the path to Milu, the Lower World. This method draws on that lineage while allowing your own mind to fill in the details as it sees them.

1. Breathe until your heart rate reaches sixty beats per minute.
2. Take the stairs through your mind dump and arrive in the foyer.
3. Turn right out of the foyer into nature and head toward a large tree. A breadfruit tree is the traditional form, but your mind will offer you whatever it offers you, and that is acceptable. The tree may already be growing in your foyer before you even reach the landscape; some students find it waiting for them in the center of the room.
4. Find the hole in the trunk and climb inside.
5. Climb upward through the interior of the trunk until you emerge at the top.
6. For the Lower World: sit on a branch and shake it until it breaks. Ride it down like a broomstick and let it drop you into the Lower World below.
7. For the Upper World: climb to the very top of the tree and allow your ascent to carry you up into the darkness above.
8. For the Middle World: grip the trunk, close your eyes, and jump. You will land where you need to be.

Treading the Mill

This one works differently from everything else on this list, and it requires a few additional tools:

- Your broom, or any object you can use to point at a focal point
- A plant, candle, or crystal to serve as your focal point
- Enough space to walk, run, or dance in a circle around it

Begin with your focal point placed in the center of the room. Start your music. Point your broom toward the focal point and begin moving around it counter-clockwise: walking, running, dancing, whatever your body wants to do. Keep moving for three full minutes. By the end of those three minutes, you should feel slightly dizzy, that particular quality of looseness that signals your spirit is ready to separate.

Lie down and place the broom on your chest. From here, travel.

Is It Imagination?

When students reach the point in their training where they are finally ready to meet their totem, something very predictable happens, and it happens so consistently that I can almost set my watch by it. Up until this moment, everything has felt structured and academic. There are steps to memorize, definitions to understand, brainwaves to study, postures to test, and techniques to practice. The mind feels useful there. The intellect feels helpful. The part of you that plans and organizes gets to shine. Then we arrive at the threshold of the actual journey, the moment where the spirit begins to separate from the body and the Other World starts to open, and suddenly that same brilliant mind becomes the obstacle standing squarely in the doorway.

I watch students sit down with perfect posture, headphones on, drum playing, breathe slowly and steadily, and for a few seconds, everything flows beautifully. Their shoulders soften. Their face relaxes. Their awareness begins to drift. Then the first image appears, maybe a flicker of light, maybe the suggestion of trees, maybe the sense that something is approaching, and immediately their forehead tightens like they are solving a math problem. They start asking questions. Is this right? Is this my animal? What if I am imagining this? Should it look bigger? Should it speak? Am I doing this correctly? That entire internal interrogation pulls them straight out of the trance and plants them firmly back into their body, frustrated and convinced that they failed.

Did they fail? They simply tried to drive the car while it was already driving itself.

Meeting your totem is one of the simplest experiences in this entire practice, and I mean that sincerely. It is simple because your totem already exists as part of you. It is your psychic self. It is not something you have to hunt down or summon from across the cosmos. You are not searching for a rare bird in a distant forest. You are meeting a part of your own spirit that has always been present. The difficulty comes from one thing and one thing only. Control.

Control is the habit we develop to survive daily life. Control helps you schedule your week, manage your money, plan your classes, and keep your household running. Control makes you competent, functional, and respected in the material world. Control also keeps your nervous system alert and your brain active, and that specific neurological state directly prevents spirit travel. The same mechanism that helps you succeed at work keeps you anchored to your chair when you are trying to leave your body.

This is where we return to the science for a moment, because understanding the mechanics removes the mystery and saves you a great deal of unnecessary self-criticism. Spirit walking happens in theta brainwaves. Theta is receptive, dreamy, symbolic, and fluid. Theta allows experiences to arise without commentary. Alpha brainwaves, on the other hand, govern active thinking, evaluating, analyzing, and problem-solving. Alpha is the state you use to read this book, to take notes, to plan dinner, or to decide which email to answer first. Alpha is incredibly useful for daily functioning, and it is completely incompatible with journeying.

If you are analyzing, you are in alpha. If you are planning, you are in alpha. If you are trying to "figure out" what something means while it is happening, you are in alpha. And if you are in alpha, you are not traveling.

I say that very directly because students often assume they can multitask their way into the spirit world, as if they can half-think and half-journey at the same time. You can't. Your brain doesn't work that way. You either surrender to receptivity, or you remain engaged in cognition.

This is why I gently, but firmly, tell my students to stop trying so hard. The harder you try, the less you experience. The more you grip, the less you receive. And this is where the simplest metaphor in the world explains the entire process better than any neurological lecture ever could.

Imagine you are standing on a beach with a handful of sand. If you clench your fist as tightly as possible and try to hold onto every grain, what happens? The sand slips out through your fingers. The tighter you squeeze, the faster it escapes, until you open your hand and realize you are holding almost nothing. Now turn your palm upward and relax your hand. Let the sand rest there gently, supported instead of imprisoned. Suddenly, you can hold an entire mound without effort because you stopped trying to dominate it.

Journeying works exactly like that.

When you try to grip the experience, name it, categorize it, and control its direction, it slips through you. When you soften your mind and allow the experience to rest in your awareness without interference, it gathers naturally and fully. Your totem approaches when you stop chasing it. Your path opens when you stop forcing it. Your spirit travels when your mind loosens its grip.

Students often laugh when I tell them that the most advanced technique in shamanic work is learning how to relax, yet it remains true. Children journey easily because they have not yet trained themselves to analyze every sensation. They allow the story to unfold. Adults, especially intelligent adults, try to outsmart the process. Intelligence turns into interference, curiosity into control.

So, when you sit down to meet your totem, treat the experience like floating on water. If you thrash and kick and demand to stay afloat, you exhaust yourself and sink. If you lean back and trust the water to hold you, your body rises effortlessly. Let the drum carry you. Let the images form on their own. Let the animal arrive in whatever shape it chooses.

Journey to the Pipe Foxes

The kuda-gitsune, known in Japanese mythology and folklore as the Pipe Fox, is a tiny fox spirit depicted without arms or legs: a small, sinuous creature that fits inside a bamboo pipe, something like those furry Squirmles (also marketed as Snoots, Magic Twisty Worms, Wiggle Worms, or Worm on a String) that charmed everyone at some point in their childhood. Despite its compact form, the kuda-gitsune has powerful magical abilities and a reputation for intelligence, mischief, and charm. It is one of the more delightful figures in Japanese folklore, and I decided I needed to meet one personally.

This is how that journey went, and more usefully, how you can replicate the method for any creature that captures your curiosity.

Preparation

Begin the way you always begin. Start your shamanic drumming track, settle into your chosen posture, and breathe until your heart rate reaches sixty beats per minute. Allow the stairs to carry you through your mind dump and arrive in your foyer. From there, move through the mental plane landscape, letting your mind paint the environment fully. Your power animal will join you when you are genuinely connected: when it happens, you are ready.

Choosing Your Destination

Before beginning the journey, spend time with the creature you intend to visit. Read about it. Let the imagery and mythology settle into your awareness. This primes the mental plane's canvas with the information it needs to build the appropriate environment. A journey undertaken with genuine curiosity and research behind it produces a richer and more accurate experience than one undertaken on a whim.

When your power animal joins you in the mental plane, state your intention clearly: you are traveling to find this creature in its own territory. Then follow your totem's lead on the method of travel. Your power animal may pull you toward the hedge instead of the bay, or choose a direction that surprises you entirely. Follow anyway, because ignoring your psychic self is the kind of mistake you make once. Your totem will carry you to altitude, over whatever geography belongs to the creature you are seeking, and bring you down through the appropriate entry point into the correct world.

What the Lower World Looks Like From a Non-Standard Entry Point

Entering the spirit world through a bay in a foreign country produces a specific environmental quality worth noting in your journey records. The world may invert on arrival: water appearing below you, the causal world residing beneath it, the sky carrying a color that reflects instead of matches the Middle World above. The landscape will mirror the physical location you entered through, with its own spirit-world textures replacing the ordinary ones. Grass becomes fur. Stone becomes something older. The familiar geography shifts into its spirit counterpart, consistent in structure and transformed in substance.

From the crevices and openings of that landscape, the creatures you came to find will emerge in their own time. Arrive with patience and genuine receptivity instead of expectation about what form the encounter should take. Record everything: the colors, the sounds, the quality of movement, the behavior of the beings toward you and toward your power animal. These details carry information that your beta mind will process after you return.

One practical detail worth building into every creature's journey: check the sky. When the sky in the Lower World location appears sunny, the corresponding time above in the causal world is nighttime at that geographic location. When you return to your body, check the actual time and calculate what time it would be in the region you visited. A match between the spirit world's light conditions and the real-world time at that location confirms the accuracy of your travel. Always note the sky. Always check the time afterward. Let the data speak.

Offerings and Etiquette

Creature visits in the spirit world follow the same principles of reciprocity that govern all spirit work. Arriving without an offering limits what the encounter can become. You can observe and enjoy the presence of the beings you visit, and the relationship stays at that level until a proper exchange has been established. If your intention is to develop an ongoing relationship with a spirit creature or to bring something of their energy back into your practice, research the traditional offerings associated with that being and arrive prepared. The visit on its own terms is always worthwhile. The relationship that develops through proper reciprocity over time is something considerably richer.

Applying This Method to Any Creature

Every cryptid, folklore creature, mythological animal, and spirit being from any tradition on earth is yours to visit through this method. The mechanics stay identical: research the creature thoroughly before the journey, set your intention clearly, follow your power animal to the appropriate world and entry point, and arrive with the quality of attention the encounter deserves. The Lower World tends to hold creatures that are ancient, instinctual, and deeply rooted in the earth's own memory. The Middle World holds beings that overlap with our own living reality. The Upper World holds creatures of a more luminous and rarefied nature. Your power animal knows which territory belongs to which being; trust that navigation and let the environment confirm it on arrival.

The spirit world is a territory you visit. Every creature in every mythology that has ever captured human imagination enough to be recorded and brought forward across centuries is pointing at something real. Go find out what.

Hedge Witchery

Hedge witchery sits inside the larger family of shamanic craft, and if you strip away all the modern aesthetics and marketing language, what you are looking at is a practitioner who specializes in divination, trance, and dream-based spirit travel. The hedge witch works at the threshold, standing with one foot in the physical world and one foot in the spirit current, moving back and forth with intention instead of accident. Traditionally, this work leans solitary, quiet, and personal, because traveling between worlds demands focus and self-reliance more than group ritual. You will often find hedge witches working alone or in very small circles.

The word hedge has nothing botanical about it, and I say that clearly because the internet and some non-academic writers have done some creative damage here. The hedge is the border: the boundary, the thin place between realities. Hedge witchery means learning to cross that border on purpose to send energy from items.

In this book, you will use hedge witchery in a practical way, because instead of simply journeying to explore or gather insight, you will carry your spells with you astrally and deliver them directly to the target. That shifts hedge work from passive observation into active magical intervention, which is where witchcraft and spirit walking meet each other. You are traveling with intention, with energy built between your hands, and with a task to complete. That combination of trance and spell craft is what makes this specifically witchery instead of general shamanic wandering. The hedge is the crossing. The witchery is what you do once you arrive.

Words in Spells: Why Language Matters

Before we start throwing energy around between worlds, we need to talk about something deceptively simple that students consistently underestimate: the words they use during a spell. When you open a grimoire and find prescribed phrases written out, those words were chosen with purpose, and they carry force. Anyone who has ever received a compliment that made them stand taller, or an insult that lodged itself somewhere and stayed for years, already understands this at a visceral level. Words land in the body and change you.

In spell craft, words generally appear for one of three reasons, and recognizing which reason you are dealing with makes you considerably more effective. Sometimes the words themselves function as ingredients: specific sounds or names hold energetic signatures that the spell requires, the way herbs or stones do in a recipe. Sometimes the structure and cadence matter more than the literal meaning, because rhythm creates momentum and binds energy together like a current. And sometimes the words exist primarily to evoke feeling inside you, since your emotional charge fuels the spell more than any external tool ever could. Quite often, all three factors work together simultaneously.

My responsibility as your teacher is to help you discern which situation you are dealing with, instead of having you copy scripts indefinitely. In some places, I give you exact phrases to use; in others, I tell you to write your own, because a spell that depends on personal emotional resonance needs your language. My goal is efficacy. If my wording feels flat in your mouth, test it, document the results, and adjust intelligently. Witchcraft functions like any other skill: you observe, experiment, and refine.

On Mislabeling Hedge Witchery

Let me climb onto my soapbox for a moment, because this is one of those terminology issues that makes educators twitch.

Somewhere along the way, people started relabeling green or plant-based magic as hedge witchery simply because the word hedge sounded earthy and botanical. That interpretation ignores centuries of actual usage. Hedge witchery has always referred to crossing between worlds through trance and spirit travel. It belongs to the lineage of spirit walkers, dream travelers, and those old Italian and European witches who left their bodies to work on the other side.

Definitions evolve over time, and language shifts; I accept that. Accuracy still matters when teaching foundational skills. Green magic is plant work. Hedge work is spirit travel. Blending everything into one vague aesthetic looks appealing online and produces genuine confusion in beginners who are trying to learn something real. If you practice herbs, crystals, spirit walking, and talisman craft, wonderful: say that clearly. Precision helps students. Vague labels serve aesthetics.

Hedge Witchery 101: Understanding Spell Structure

Before you carry anything astrally, you need to know what you are carrying. Every spell generally falls into one of three broad categories, and identifying which type you are casting clarifies how it should function.

Direct: The magic touches the target or environment directly, such as wearing a talisman for luck or placing protective items in a space.

Sympathetic: An object represents the person or place, and you work on that representation to create change.

Energetic Exchange: You sacrifice or transform one thing to power an unrelated result.

Inside any spell, several structural components determine effectiveness. Clear focus: holding your intention steadily instead of multitasking. Correct ingredients: materials carry specific properties and history, just as ingredients in cooking do. Follow the recipe first, then experiment later with data in hand.

You also need a casting agent: the method that actually sends the spell into motion. Many books omit this part, and without a casting action, the spell simply sits there like an unsent letter. Fire, air, water, stone, growth, time, and spirit all provide different ways to release energy, and choosing one gives the spell a clear exit point. Think of it as pressing send.

Performing a Spell Astrally: Practical Hedge Work

When you perform hedge witchery, you adjust the structure slightly because you become the casting agent. You carry the energy yourself into the Middle World instead of sending it through a candle, river, or crossroads. That means the sympathetic components tied to names or objects also fall away, since you will deliver the energy directly to the actual person or place. The final casting action also falls away, because you are the casting action. Your body and spirit replace the mechanism.

Set up your ingredients in front of you exactly as you would for an ordinary spell and build the energy between your hands until you feel it tangibly: pressure, heat, weight, some quality that tells you the charge is real. When the charge builds, begin your drumming, enter trance, and draw that energy into yourself. Carry it the way you would carry water in a vessel. Then travel.

REMOVE ALL NAMES, AND PRONOUNS.

REMOVE "so mote it be" or other word casting agents.

REMOVE the finishing step in spells that require it to be put at a crossroad, buried, thrown into a stream, or the candle to finish melting.

Move through your stairs, clear your mind, arrive in the Middle World, and go directly to your target. Deliver the energy intentionally and completely, making sure nothing lingers in your field. When the transfer feels finished, return home. Clean delivery. Clean exit.

When you return, the physical materials left behind are empty. Dispose of them practically instead of treating them as sacred relics: the energy already went where it needed to go. Crystals can be cleansed and reused. Everything else goes in the trash. Efficient. Practical. Done.

Welcome to hedge witchery.

The Past Life Journey

The well has been waiting on the left side of your foyer since the first time you took the stairs and learned about the surroundings in your mind. You have walked past it on your way to the forest, on your way to the bay, on your way to everywhere else this practice has taken you. Today, you stop at the well.

This journey goes somewhere none of the others go. That is worth explaining before you arrive at the well and wonder where your polar bear, your hawk, or your possum has gotten to, because the absence can feel disorienting if you are unprepared for it.

Your totem is the psychic self: the instinctual, agenda-free, animal expression of who you are in this life. What ties you to your past lives IS your totem. So you will be journeying through the DNA history of your totem as the portal through your past lives.

The Akashic plane holds something old: the complete record of every life your soul has inhabited across every incarnation it has taken. That lineage predates your current totem the way your DNA predates your personality. When you descend into the well, you are traveling through the genetic memory of the totem itself, and that territory belongs to you alone. Your totem cannot accompany you there because it is an expression of this particular life. What waits in the well is everything that came before this life existed. Go alone. You know the way.

Why People Seek Past Life Work

Past life regression has become one of the more mainstream entries in the alternative healing catalog, and the range of reasons people pursue it is worth understanding before you travel there yourself. People arrive at the well from many different directions.

Many seek it for unexplained fears and phobias that seem to have no basis in their current life: fears of water, heights, confined spaces, or certain animals that may trace back to traumatic deaths or experiences in previous lifetimes. Others arrive carrying recurring relationship patterns, finding themselves in the same dynamics repeatedly, regardless of how different the people involved seem. Some come with chronic pain that has no clear medical origin, or with persistent feelings of not belonging, chronic guilt without obvious cause, or a persistent sense that their life purpose remains just out of reach.

Sometimes the journey reveals happiness in a previous life instead of trauma, reminding the traveler of their own worth and capacity, showing them versions of themselves that shone in ways they have forgotten were possible. Greater self-awareness is one of the most consistently reported benefits: seeing yourself across lifetimes develops a perspective on your strengths and patterns that a single lifetime simply cannot provide.

The therapeutic community holds a range of opinions on the validity of past life regression, and I will give you that honestly instead of pretending consensus exists where it does not. Past life regression is widely rejected as a psychiatric treatment by clinical psychiatrists and psychologists, with a 2006 survey finding that a majority of doctoral-level mental health professionals rated it as discredited as a treatment for mental or behavioral disorders. The primary concern is the reliable indistinguishability of hypnotically produced memories from actual memories, and the process's susceptibility to suggestion and confabulation.

Here is my position, and you can do with it what you will: I am a witchdoctor, and I travel to the Akashic plane through the well in my own foyer with my own nervous system in theta, and what I find there is consistent, verifiable in detail, and distinct in quality from imagination in ways that any experienced traveler will recognize. The debate about whether hypnotic regression in a clinical setting produces genuine memories is a separate conversation from what happens when a trained spirit walker descends through the wormhole of their own soul's history in deliberate theta. Both conversations are worth having. They are about different experiences that happen to share a name.

What matters practically is this: people seek past-life work because something in this life points backward. A pattern that happened without explanation. A fear that predates any experience capable of producing it. A skill that came too easily. A place that felt like home before you had ever been there. A relationship that had a weight of history the two of you had never actually accumulated. These are the soul's fingerprints from other incarnations, and the well is where you go to find the hands that made them.

What Past Life Travel Reveals About This Incarnation

Every life your soul has inhabited contributed something to the version sitting in the chair reading this page. Skills developed across lifetimes come with you as aptitudes that feel innate. Wounds brought forward unresolved come as patterns that confound the people who love you and occasionally confound you as well. Relationships repeat across incarnations in different forms because the soul returns to unfinished business the way a tongue returns to a sore tooth. Understanding what happened before this life gives you the context for what is happening in it.

Specific fears that showed up without origin in this lifetime become explicable when you find the life that produced them. Chronic physical symptoms that resist treatment sometimes trace back to the manner of a previous death, the body carrying a somatic memory of something that happened to a different version of itself. Gifts that seem disproportionate to your current life's experience, languages that come too easily, skills that feel remembered instead of learned, connections to particular cultures or time periods that go beyond intellectual interest: all of these are worth bringing to the well.

The past life journey also offers something that ordinary therapy rarely reaches: the experience of your soul as a continuous entity across time instead of a self that began at birth and ends at death. That experience changes the quality of your relationship to your own life. Problems that felt permanent begin to feel like chapters. Patterns that felt like identity begin to feel like habits carried forward from a context that no longer applies. The scope of what you are expands considerably when you have felt yourself living in a different body, in a different century, in circumstances that shaped you in ways you are still navigating.

What Past Life Travel Reveals About Your Totem

Your totem is the psychic self of this incarnation: the instinctual, agenda-free expression of who you are in this particular life. What the past life journey offers, in addition to everything above, is a view of the soul history that your totem emerged from. The wormhole you descend through is the DNA of that history, and traveling it gives you access to information about why your totem takes the form it does, what it has from the lifetimes that preceded this one, and where its particular strengths and limitations originate.

A totem's strengths are the qualities your soul has developed across lifetimes with enough consistency that they have become part of the psychic self's essential nature. If your totem is a predator, look in the past lives for the lifetimes that built that quality: the survival experiences, the periods of solitary navigation, the moments when that particular kind of intelligence was what kept the soul alive and moving forward. The strength your totem has has history behind it, and understanding that history deepens your working relationship with it considerably.

A totem's limitations are the places where the soul is still learning: the qualities that have been challenged across lifetimes without yet resolving, the patterns that show up in the totem's behavior during journeys as hesitation, avoidance, or a particular kind of reactivity. Your totem is the psychic self, and the psychic self has everything the soul has accumulated, including the unfinished work. Knowing which past lives contributed to a specific limitation gives you the opportunity to address it at the root instead of working around it indefinitely.

Bring your totem to the edge of the well. It will stay behind when you drop in, but the act of standing there together before you descend, of letting your totem sense what you are about to do and why, builds a quality of trust in the relationship that journeying to the Upper World or the Middle World simply cannot replicate. You are showing your psychic self the full scope of what it is. That kind of honesty deepens everything that comes after.

The well is deep. Your history is vast. Go look at it.

The Journey

Begin the way you always begin. Start your drumming track, settle into your posture, and breathe until your heart rate reaches sixty beats per minute. Take the stairs through your mind dump, arrive in the foyer, and allow the space to become fully present around you: the quality of the light, the particular quiet of the room, the three directions you know well by now.

Turn left.

Walk to the well. Stand at its edge and look down. The liquid inside has the quality of deep space: black, vast, filled with something that feels older than your body can comfortably hold. This is the passage of time, and looking into it, you feel that passage the way you feel the ocean from a small boat in the dark. The scale is enormous. Let it be enormous. Stay with the vertigo until it becomes something more like wonder.

When you are ready, climb up onto the edge of the well and look directly down into the cosmic liquid below. Feel the pull of it. This is your history pulling at you, the accumulated weight of every life your soul has ever inhabited calling you back toward the knowledge of itself. Allow that pull to do its work.

Drop in.

The Wormhole

The descent through the well is unlike any other form of travel in this practice. There is no forest, no bay, no landscape to navigate. What you move through instead is something closer to the interior of a tunnel that is also somehow alive: the DNA of your soul's history, coiling and unspooling around you as you fall. Images, impressions, textures, and fragments of lives will move past you as you descend. Some will feel familiar in the specific way that has nothing to do with this lifetime. Some will feel foreign. Let all of it move past without grabbing. You are falling through the whole of your soul's lineage, and your destination is a specific life that calls to you from somewhere in the depths of that descent.

You will feel it when you are close to a life you can enter. Something in the movement changes: a particular current, a pull that is more specific than the general downward momentum of the wormhole. A life begins to coalesce around you instead of moving past. When that happens, stop resisting the pull and drop down into it.

First Person, Always

Here is the rule of past life journeying, and it is the most important thing in this chapter: you are looking for a first-person experience. Eyes behind someone else's eyes. Hands that are your hands in another body. The smell of a particular century, the weight of unfamiliar clothing, the specific quality of light in a place and time that predates your current existence.

If you find yourself watching the scene from a distance, observing a figure moving through a life the way you would watch a film, you have landed in the Akashic record of that life instead of in the life itself. The Akashic records are the written account: the visual documentation of what occurred, stored in that cosmic library that the well connects to. This is valuable, entirely real information, and it is the account of the life instead of the experience of it. A book about a place and the place itself are two different things.

To shift from third person to first person, close your eyes during the journey and feel your body. Where are your feet? What surface are they on? What does the air smell like? What sounds are present? Pull your awareness inward toward the physical experience of the life instead of the visual record of it, and the perspective will shift. You will feel the difference the moment it happens: the scene stops being something you are watching and becomes something you are living. That is the real journey.

What You Are Looking For

Past life journeys serve different purposes depending on what you bring to them. Some practitioners travel to the Akashic plane to understand patterns that repeat across lifetimes: relationships that appear in different forms, wounds that have never fully resolved, skills and knowledge that came with them into this incarnation already present. Others travel to retrieve specific information relevant to current healing work, their own or a client's. Others simply go because the soul is curious about itself, and that is reason enough.

Whatever draws you to the well, arrive with a genuine question instead of a demand for specific content. The life that calls to you from the wormhole is the life that holds what you currently need, and that may differ from the life you imagined visiting. Trust the pull. The soul's navigation is considerably more accurate than your planning mind's itinerary.

When a life has shown you what it holds, return through the wormhole the way you came: upward, through the coiling lineage of your soul's history, back through the well and into the foyer. Take a moment in the foyer before you ascend the stairs, because the transition from Akashic depth to ordinary consciousness can feel more significant than other returns. Give yourself the time. The body will call you home in its own reliable way.

Record everything immediately upon return, before your beta mind begins editing the memory into something more coherent and less accurate. The fragments matter. The details matter. The emotional quality of what you experienced matters as much as the narrative content. Write it all down before you analyze any of it.

The well has been waiting. Now, you know what it is for.

The Akashic Records

Reading the Record of Your Soul

Before you climb onto the edge of that well, you need to know which tool you are holding. The past life journey puts you back on the road: boots on the ground, first person, fully inside a specific body in a specific century, living it. The Akashic journey takes you to the complete archive: every map ever used, every contract ever signed, every lesson marked learned or still in progress. One gives you the feeling of the road. The other gives you an understanding of the entire journey.

Both are worth having. They answer different questions.

What the Akashic Records Are

Akasha is a Sanskrit word. It means ether: the fifth element, the substrate from which the other four emerge and to which they eventually return. In Vedic cosmology, it is the primordial substance of the universe itself, the field that holds all creation within it. It also has the quality of sound, because in Vedic understanding, sound is the first thing to emerge from pure potential, and sound requires a medium to travel through. Akasha is that medium. Every event, every thought, every emotion, every intention, every action that has ever occurred travels through it and is permanently recorded within it.

Maybe think of it this way: the Akashic Records is the cross-section of the mental plane, a recording of every wisp that moved through the winds of thought and action. The complete, continuously updating archive of everything that has ever occurred across all time, all space, all consciousness. Every soul that has ever incarnated has a record there. Every civilization that has ever risen and fallen is documented. Every agreement made between souls before incarnation, every vow spoken in grief or passion or devotion, every pattern carried forward from one lifetime into the next: all of it, accessible to any consciousness that knows how to reach it.

The records are alive. People arrive expecting a traditional library: shelves, silence, the smell of old paper, a card catalog, a librarian giving them a look over half-moon glasses.

The Akashic field is a living, breathing, continuously updating intelligence. New entries arrive constantly. The record of this exact moment, the one you are living right now, reading these words, is being written as you live it. The records hold the past, the present, and the probable trajectories of the future simultaneously. This is why Akashic readings can offer insight into what is coming as readily as what has been.

Your individual record contains everything your soul has accumulated across every incarnation: skills developed in one life that arrive in the next as inexplicable aptitude, wounds that arrive as fears with no origin story, agreements with other souls that shape your most significant relationships in ways that have absolutely nothing to do with the personalities currently involved, gifts earned through lifetimes of specific work that belong to you as permanently as your bone structure. The record also contains your soul's purpose for this particular incarnation. The blueprint. The lessons you came specifically to navigate.

The World Has Always Known This

Every major spiritual tradition in human history has pointed to this same territory, independently, across cultures that had no contact with each other. When every tradition on earth points at the same mountain from different valleys, the mountain is real (I have said that before in this book. It keeps being true.)

The oldest and most continuous traditions of accessing cosmic memory are the indigenous and shamanic ones. They belong at the beginning of this history. Western esoteric writing tends to place them in footnotes on the rare occasions it acknowledges them at all. We are fixing that right now.

The Aboriginal Australian Dreamtime is perhaps the most sophisticated framework for cosmic memory any culture has ever developed, and also one of theoldest, with roots going back at least sixty-five thousand years of continuous practice. Sixty-five thousand. Let that linger for a moment before we continue.

The Dreamtime is simultaneously the creation epoch, the living present, and the eternal field of all knowledge and story: the place where everything that has ever existed continues to exist, accessible to those trained to navigate it. The songlines are the Akashic records made geographic: energetic pathways running across the Australian landscape connecting every sacred site, every story, every ancestral event in a living network the trained practitioner can walk, sing, and read. To know a songline is to have access to the complete record of everything that has ever occurred along it. The land is the archive. Walking it with trained awareness is Akashic work, and Aboriginal Australians have been doing it longer than any other documented spiritual practice on earth.

The griot tradition of West Africa produces a different but equally remarkable form of living record-keeping. The griot is trained from childhood to hold the complete ancestral record of their people in living memory, transmitting it forward through story, song, and ceremony. They hold the energetic imprint of their community's history in their body and their voice. When a griot dies, the tradition says that a library has burned. They understand precisely what they are carrying.

Did you know that the ancient Hawaiians had this as well? They were called ʻapo. Hawaii had its own version of the living record keeper in the figure of the haku mele: a professional trained in the art of 'apo, the ability to receive the spoken word, memorize it verbatim, and recite it word for word across hours of continuous transmission. Haku mele were chosen in youth or inherited the calling, and the records they carried in their bodies covered hundreds of generations and several thousand years of lineage, history, and cosmological knowledge. They were living libraries, preserving the identity and soul memory of the Hawaiian people in the same way the griot preserved the soul memory of West Africa: in the voice, in the body, in the breath. When a haku mele was recited, the ancestors were present. The record was alive. That is Akashic work, performed standing up, from memory, in chant.

Native American traditions carry their own frameworks for cosmic memory, specific to each nation and each cosmological system. The vision quest is fundamentally an act of accessing the soul's larger record: going to the threshold, opening the self to the information the Great Mystery holds about this particular soul's purpose, and returning with clarity about the agreements and the direction of the current life. The medicine wheel maps the cyclical nature of time and experience: everything that has occurred continues to exist in the record, every cycle builds on the ones before it, and the soul navigates time as a spiral instead of a line. The Lakota concept of Mitákuye Oyás'iŋ, all my relations, expresses the Akashic truth directly: every soul is connected to every other through the shared field of cosmic memory and mutual incarnation.

The Huichol people of Mexico carry a piece of this cosmology that connects directly to the work in this book. The concept of kupuri, the life force the shaman retrieves from the spirit realm for the community, comes from a cosmic field of original energy that holds every soul's complete record and potential. The deer spirit Kauyumari serves as the first navigator of that field and the guide for shamans seeking access to its deeper territories. The Huichol shaman approaching cosmic memory does so with a guide and a specific intention, because the field is vast, and purposeful navigation matters. Sound familiar? It should. The well in the foyer of your mind is the same understanding, expressed through your own interior geography.

The Oroqen people of northeastern China maintain a shamanic tradition in which the shaman navigates ancestral memory across generations, transmitted entirely through oral tradition and personal experience. The complete record of the soul's history is accessible through trance states, with the shaman as the trained specialist who enters and reads it on behalf of the community. Ancient, specific, and entirely consistent ith what every other shamanic culture independently developed: the cosmic record exists, trance accesses it, trained practitioners navigate it with intention. Every time. Everywhere. Without exception.

Vedic philosophy gave us the word, and the concept predates the Sanskrit texts that named it. The Upanishads describe Brahman, the universal consciousness underlying all existence, as the field within which every event and every soul exists simultaneously. The individual soul's record is held within universal consciousness, the way a wave is held within the ocean: distinct in form, continuous in substance. The Vedic seers accessed this field through deep meditative states and brought back knowledge that became the foundational texts of one of the world's oldest living spiritual traditions (They were journeying. They just called it something else.).

The Judeo-Christian tradition has its own version in the Book of Life, referenced in Exodus, the Psalms, Daniel, and Revelation. God's complete knowledge of every soul across all time is a monotheistic expression of the same Akashic truth: the cosmic record exists, it is complete, and it holds the soul's full account.

Into this ancient and global lineage arrived Helena Blavatsky in the late nineteenth century, introducing the Sanskrit terminology to Western esoteric audiences and describing what she called the indestructible tablets of the astral light. C.W. Leadbeater formally named them the Akashic Records in 1899. Rudolf Steiner described the Akashic Chronicle: a super physical plane of existence containing the complete record of all past events, accessible through specific meditative states. Edgar Cayce, the sleeping prophet, delivered 14,306 readings in self-induced trance states between 1901 and 1945, describing the records as God's Book of Remembrance and the experience of accessing them as watching a cosmic film. His readings covered past lives, health, karmic patterns, and soul purpose with a consistency and specificity that remains remarkable regardless of your position on their origin.

The Suppression of Soul Memory and the Permission Myth

The Library of Alexandria burned. The Inquisition targeted practitioners who had direct access to spirit and cosmic memory, specifically and systematically. The witch trials of Europe and colonial America were, among other things, a sustained campaign against the people who held the community's direct relationship with the spirit world and the ancestral record: the hedge witches, the cunning folk, the village healers who knew how to enter trance and come back with information. The campaign was effective. Within a few generations, the knowledge of how to access that information directly had been severed from the cultures that once held it as ordinary practice.

This is the context for the permission myth.

When you sever people from their own direct access to cosmic memory over several centuries of sustained effort, and then a spiritual marketplace emerges that offers to sell that access back, the permission myth is the product. It takes the severing that was done by force and reframes it as a natural condition: of course, you need help getting there, of course, there are gatekeepers, of course, some records are locked, and some access is restricted. The fear created by centuries of persecution gets dressed up in spiritual language and sold as wisdom.

Same energy. Different costume. Worth naming every single time.

The Permission Myth: Let's Handle This

You do not need permission to access your own Akashic records. You do not need permission to access anyone else's, either.

I know that is going to make some people uncomfortable. Good. Sit with it.

The records are a field of cosmic information. They belong to the cosmos as much as they belong to any individual soul.

STOP TRYING TO ASSERT THE COLONIZING PHILOSOPHY OF "MINE" OR "MY LAND" OR "MY PROPERTY" IN A DOCTRINE OLDER THAN COLONIZING PHILOSOPHY!

The idea that a cosmic lock engages the moment you look at someone else's records is the same mythology we just dismantled, applied to a different target. The field does not work that way. Information is accessible to consciousness that can reach it. Full stop.

The records respond to readiness and intention. A beginner descending into the well with a buzzing mind and no specific question will access different layers than a practiced traveler with years of theta stability and a precise, deeply felt intention. That difference is real. It is a description of skill development, exactly the way a beginning musician hears different things in a piece of music than a concert pianist does. The music is available to both of them. Training determines the depth of access. Not permission. Not worthiness. Not a cosmic bouncer checking credentials at the door.

What guides your behavior as a practitioner is your own integrity, your purpose, and your training: the same things that guide every other aspect of this work. You read another person's records because you are working in the service of their healing, because you are doing your job, because the information serves a legitimate purpose. Your own character is the gatekeeper. The only gatekeeper that actually exists.

Soul Contracts: The Agreements That Shape This Life

Within the Akashic records lives one of the most practically useful and most frequently misunderstood categories of soul information: your contracts.

A soul contract is an agreement made before incarnation, outlining the lessons, relationships, and experiences the soul intends to navigate in a given lifetime. Some contracts are made in the between-life state, in the period of planning and rest between incarnations, with full clarity and deliberateness. Others are made in the heat of a previous life's most intense moments: vows of loyalty spoken in circumstances that ceased to exist centuries ago, commitments made in grief or rage or love that the soul carried forward without revisiting, survival strategies from one century that arrived in the next as inexplicable compulsions.

Soul contracts explain the things about your life that defy ordinary causation.

The relationship that carried a weight of history, the two of you had never actually accumulated together. The sense of obligation toward someone that has nothing to do with anything that has happened between you in this lifetime. The recurring pattern that appears in different forms across different relationships, as though the same lesson keeps walking up to different doors and knocking until you finally open one. The inexplicable draw toward a particular place, culture, period of history, or field of work that came before you had any rational basis for it.

Empowering contracts encourage your growth, your purpose, and your flourishing. The relationship that challenges you in exactly the ways you need to be challenged. The teacher who arrived at precisely the right moment with precisely the right knowledge. The creative gift you came with, earned through lifetimes of specific work, is available to you in this incarnation as part of what you came here to offer. Empowering contracts feel clean and purposeful even when they are difficult. They move you forward.

Disempowering contracts came from less deliberate circumstances: vows made in crisis, patterns chosen under duress, commitments that made sense in their original context and have been dragged forward past their usefulness into territory where they actively create suffering. The person who took a vow of poverty in a religious lifetime and now cannot hold onto money, regardless of how much happens. The person who vowed never to love again after a devastating loss and now finds intimacy inexplicably impossible. The person whose soul agreed to carry a family pattern for one generation and is still carrying it three generations later, because no one knew it could be put down. Visible in the records. Addressable once seen.

Karmic contracts are the agreements between souls with unfinished business across lifetimes: relationships in which the same dynamic replays with different personalities because the underlying lesson was never completed. The soul you keep meeting in different bodies, always in a particular dynamic, always navigating the same essential question from different angles. Karmic contracts carry an unmistakable quality: the relationship feels predetermined, the dynamic feels ancient, and the emotional charge is entirely out of proportion to the actual history between the people currently involved. The Akashic record shows you the root, the original agreement, and the lesson the two souls have been circling. That visibility changes everything about how you navigate the relationship going forward.

Contracts with the natural world are less discussed in most Akashic literature and more central to shamanic cosmology than almost anything else in this practice. Your agreements with the animal spirits, the land spirits, the elements, and the natural forces that have accompanied your soul across lifetimes are recorded in the Akashic field. Your totem's relationship with your soul predates this incarnation. The Akashic record holds the history of that relationship: the lifetimes in which you worked closely with that animal spirit's energy, the lifetimes in which the connection lay dormant, the agreements that brought your totem and your soul into the specific working relationship you are developing right now. Reading that record deepens the relationship in ways that straightforward journey work cannot replicate.

Revoking contracts is real, practical, and available to anyone willing to do the work with honesty and intention. A contract made in a previous lifetime under conditions that no longer apply, a vow that made sense in its original context and is actively creating damage in the current one: formally releasable through Akashic work. Find the contract in the record. Understand its original context completely. Acknowledge what purpose it served at the time. Then declare its completion with enough emotional reality that the release reaches the energetic level where the contract actually lives. Intellectual acknowledgment alone will not get you there. The release has to land in the body. When it does, the shifts in the current life tend to follow quickly, because the underlying pattern generating the recurring experience has been addressed at its actual root instead of its surface expression.

What the Akashic Journey Offers That Other Journeys Cannot

The past life journey puts you in the room, but the Akashic records show you the entire building: the blueprint, the architect's notes, the complete history of every person who has ever lived there, and the contracts that brought all of them to the same address.

The Akashic journey holds multiple lifetimes in view simultaneously. The lesson has appeared in different forms across five or six incarnations. The relationship repeats with different personalities, but the same essential dynamic. The gift developed across multiple lifetimes is now available to you in its most refined form. The past life journey cannot give you that view; only the records can.

For client work, the Akashic journey offers access to another person's soul history, contracts, and patterns in service of their healing. You are reading the record instead of influencing the experience, which keeps the information precise and the work clean. The practitioner who can access the Akashic field accurately has a tool of extraordinary value. That tool is available to you right now.

How to Journey to the Akashic Records

Begin the way you always begin. Drumming track, posture, breath, heart rate to sixty beats per minute. Take the stairs through your mind dump. Arrive in the foyer with your mind cleared and your awareness settled.

Stand in the foyer and orient yourself. Hallway of doors straight ahead. Right opening leading to the mental plane landscape you know well. Above you is the access point to the messianic plane. To your left: the well.

Before you approach it, set your intention. The Akashic field is vast beyond comprehension, and arriving without a specific focus is like walking into the largest library on earth and asking to see everything. You'll need to paint it as something because it is incomprehensible in what it actually is, so create a language and system to find what you're looking for. Remember that this was around *way* before there were modern libraries.

Arrive with a question

Broad works: what soul contracts are currently most active in my life?

Specific works: What is the origin of this recurring pattern?

Practical works: what gifts did I earn in previous lifetimes that are available to me in this one?

The more genuine and deeply felt the question, the more direct and useful the information that comes back.

Walk to the well. Stand at its edge. Look down into the cosmic liquid. Feel what it feels like to stand at the edge of your own complete history. The vertigo is appropriate. The scale is real. Let it land.

Climb onto the edge. Look directly down. Feel the pull. Your totem stays here: your psychic self is specific to this incarnation, and what waits in the well predates it. Say goodbye to your totem for the duration. It will be there when you return.

The Descent

The descent through the Akashic well is unlike every other form of travel in this practice. No landscape, no path, no forest or bay or bridge. What you move through is the field itself: a living, luminous, immense intelligence carrying the quality of everything simultaneously. Students describe it as moving through liquid light, falling through a tunnel lined with living memory, swimming through a substance that is simultaneously sound and image and feeling, or simply falling through something enormous that recognizes you. All of these descriptions are accurate. The field presents itself in the language each soul can most readily receive. (It is thoughtful that way.)

Fragments of your own history may move past you as you descend: faces, landscapes, flashes of experience from lifetimes you have not yet visited, the emotional residue of agreements made and patterns established across incarnations. Allow all of it to move past. You are moving through the complete record, and the complete record contains more than any single journey can examine. Your intention is your compass. The field has you toward the information your question calls for.

What You Encounter

The Akashic records present themselves differently to different practitioners. Your mind builds the interface it needs to work effectively with the available information. Many people encounter something that functions like a library: vast, organized, containing records in some form they can read or experience. Others encounter a field of pure information arriving as direct knowing instead of visual imagery: you simply find yourself knowing things you did not know before, with a certainty distinct from ordinary thought. Others encounter guides or record keepers who facilitate access and help navigate the field. These are aspects of your own consciousness serving as helpful interfaces. Use whatever your mind builds. The architecture serves the access.

Reading your contracts requires finding them in whatever form they take in your interface: a specific record, a document, a living memory, a felt sense of an agreement. When you find a contract, examine it fully before deciding what to do with it. Where did it originate? What circumstances produced it? What purpose did it serve? What is its current effect? The full picture matters before any decision about release.

Peering into the collective records, the records of civilizations, lineages, and shared human history, requires a wide focus. Many practitioners use the collective records in the service of healing work with lineage patterns, ancestral trauma, and community wounds. Advanced territory. Approach it the same way you approach all advanced work: with respect and a clear intention.

Reading Another Person's Records

Same process as reading your own, but you need to travel through their energetic signature. Arrive at the well with the specific intention of accessing this person's information. Carry that intention clearly. The field responds to the sincerity of your purpose and the stability of your theta. Report what you find with clean delivery. That is the whole protocol. Remember, this is open to all. Sorry, not sorry.

Returning

Record everything immediately upon return. Everything: the fragments, the impressions, the emotional qualities, the things that seemed too obvious or too strange or too simple to write down. The beta mind begins editing immediately, organizing material into something that makes more sense and losing the edges and details that matter most in the process. Write before you edit. Analyze after you have written. In that order, every time.

What to Do With What You Find

Information from the Akashic records falls into two categories in terms of what they can do: information that requires integration, and information that requires action.

Integration means sitting with what you learned and allowing it to change your understanding over time. Knowing that a particular fear originated in a drowning three lifetimes ago may require nothing more than the shift in perspective that comes from understanding the origin. The fear often loses a significant portion of its charge simply from being seen in context. Integration is quiet work, done over days and weeks after the journey, as the information settles into the body and the understanding deepens.

Action means addressing something that requires more than understanding: revoking a contract, releasing a vow, completing an unfinished agreement, changing a current life pattern whose Akashic root is now visible. This work is done with ceremony and intention and the full weight of your training behind it. Find the contract in the record, understand it completely, acknowledge its original purpose, and declare its completion with enough emotional reality that the release reaches the energetic level where the contract actually lives. When it does, the shifts in the current life tend to follow. The underlying pattern has been addressed at its root instead of its surface expression.

For client work: accuracy in the reading, honesty in the reporting, humility about the limits of your perception. What you read in the records is filtered through your own nervous system and your own current level of development. The more stable and clear your theta, the more accurate your access. The more honestly you hold your own development, the more useful your work becomes. Both of those things are in your control. Develop them accordingly.

The Well and the Practice

The Akashic journey is the most direct route to understanding your soul's purpose in this incarnation, the contracts shaping your most significant relationships, the patterns that have followed you across lifetimes, and the gifts you have earned and carry. It is also the most humbling journey in this entire practice. Standing inside the complete record of your soul's history across all time produces a quality of perspective on the current moment that nothing else quite generates. The concerns that feel enormous from inside one lifetime look different from the view of the complete journey. The patterns that feel permanent from inside one incarnation look different when you can see the lifetimes in which they began and the trajectories along which they are moving.

Shamanic practitioners have been walking to the well since before anyone had a word for it. The Aboriginal elder singing the songlines. The griot with their community's complete history in their voice and body. The Vedic seer sitting at the edge of universal consciousness. The Egyptian priest reading the cosmic record in the Hall of Two Truths. All of them: the same practice, the same field, the same ancient human capacity to reach past the boundary of a single lifetime and read the complete record of the soul.

The well on the left side of your foyer is your access point to that field. Built into the geography of your mind's landscape for a reason. Waiting with the patience of something that holds all of time within it.

You know where it is. You know what to bring. You know the question you have been carrying since before you knew what to do with it.

Doors: Shadow Work

The hallway of doors stretches straight ahead of you in the foyer of your mind. Every door is a memory from this lifetime: every experience you have lived, every moment stored, every version of yourself that has existed within this particular incarnation. Most journeys take you right, into the mental plane, or left, into the Akashic depths. This journey takes you straight ahead.

Welcome to shadow work.

Shadow work is the practice of going into the parts of yourself you have been avoiding. The unresolved stuff. The memories that still have teeth. The patterns you keep repeating while swearing you have no idea why. The emotions you buried so efficiently that you forgot they were there until one perfectly ordinary Tuesday, when something small happens, and suddenly you are furious in a way that has absolutely nothing to do with Tuesday.

Every serious practitioner does this work. Psychics, witches, shamans: the people working with the deepest layers of human experience cannot afford to have unexamined wreckage in their own hallways (I'm looking at you! Even leaders MUST do shadow work regularly. This is not just for "beginners." No one is fully enlightened. Do your work!). Your unresolved material bleeds. It colors your readings, creates your biases, clouds your perception, and shows up uninvited in your client sessions wearing a very convincing disguise.

Doing shadow work is how you learn the difference between what you are genuinely perceiving and what you are projecting.

Shadow work also builds something that cannot be faked: genuine empathy. When you have actually walked through your own darkness and come back with something useful, you can hold space for a client in theirs in a way that no amount of training or technique can replicate. You know the territory. You have been there. That knowing is what makes the difference between a practitioner who offers technique and one real presence.

Some people resist shadow work because they believe that engaging with pain or grief cultivates more of the same energy. That position confuses suppression with transcendence. Toxic positivity, the relentless pursuit of happiness, and the systematic denial of anything uncomfortable do not produce genuine well-being. It produces a distorted relationship with reality, a growing disconnection from authentic emotion, and a backlog of unprocessed material that keeps accumulating interest. Eventually, the account comes due, always at the worst possible moment, always louder than it needed to be.

Think of it this way: a wound with an infection does not heal by being covered up and left alone; the infection has to be addressed before genuine healing can happen underneath. Draining that wound is uncomfortable. It is unpleasant. It is also the only path to actual recovery. Shadow work operates on the same principle. The unresolved material is the infection. Looking at it directly is how you drain it. The discomfort of the process is real... and it is also temporary, because on the other side of genuine shadow work is something sustained positive thinking can never produce: actual integration. The wound closes from the inside. The pattern opens at its root. The memory loses its charge.

You become more whole. Practitioners who are more whole do better work. Every time.

So, the hallway is ahead of you. The doors are waiting. Let us talk about how to walk through them.

The Journey of the Doors

The preparation is the same as always: drumming track, posture, breath, heart rate to sixty beats per minute. Take the stairs through your mind dump and arrive in the foyer with your mind cleared and your awareness settled.

This time, walk straight ahead.

The hallway of doors begins where the foyer ends. Step over the threshold and feel what happens: the hallway extends in both directions now, forward and behind you, stretching in both directions as far as you can see. Thousands of doors, every memory you have ever lived, every moment stored from this incarnation, every experience that shaped you, whether you remember it consciously or not. All of it here, all of it accessible, all of it waiting with the particular patience of things that have been waiting a long time.

Take a breath and notice something important: this journey is a meditation journey instead of an out-of-body journey. You are working within the mind instead of traveling beyond it. Your awareness stays here, in this hallway, in this lifetime, in the material that belongs specifically to you and this incarnation. The work is interior. The work is deep.

Now: what did you come here for?

You already know. You came with something specific: a pattern that keeps repeating, a relationship that confuses you, a block that sits in the way of something you are trying to build. Money, maybe. Self-worth. A particular wound from a particular person. A version of yourself you keep bumping into that you do not fully understand yet. Whatever it is, you know it. Your body knows it. Hold it in your awareness and begin to walk.

The door will find you as much as you find it. That is how this works. You are looking for the memory at the root of the thing you came to address, and your instinct knows where it lives better than your thinking mind does. Walk until something pulls. A door that catches your attention, a handle your hand moves toward without your permission, a particular quality of energy that stops you in your tracks. That one. That is the one.

Stand in front of it for a moment. Feel what it feels like to be here: the particular weight of whatever this door holds, the quality of what is behind it. Your body already knows what is in this room. You are about to know it consciously.

When you are ready, begin the breath sequence.

Out for four. In for four.

Out for three. In for three.

Out for two. In for two.

Out for one. In for one.

Step through.

Inside the Room

You are inside the memory now. Let it be what it is. Let the scene assemble around you: the people, the environment, the emotional texture of what happened here. You are present in it the way you are present in a dream that knows it is happening. Feel what there is to feel. See what there is to see. Allow the memory its full reality instead of the edited version your mind has been carrying around.

This is the work. Being here, fully, instead of at a managed distance from it.

Some rooms will be uncomfortable. Some will be painful. Some will surprise you with what they actually contain, because memory is not always accurate, and the story you have been telling about a particular experience is sometimes quite different from the experience itself. Let whatever happens arrive. The memory has been waiting behind this door for a reason; it has something to show you. Give it the time it needs.

When you feel the room has given you what it holds, watching the entire memory, reach backwards, as if the door is there, step back through the door, and into the hallway, shutting the door.

The Flag of Integration

You are back in the hallway now, the door closed in front of you. Reach into your pocket. You will find there a small piece of paper: a tag, a flag, something that can be pressed into the surface of the door and stay there. Take it out. Press it into the door.

Now watch.

If the door changes, something in its appearance shifts, the color alters, the texture transforms, the whole thing softens or brightens or reshapes itself in some way: the memory is integrating. You are accepting this room into yourself, acknowledging what it holds, beginning the process of working it into your understanding of who you are instead of keeping it locked away where it has been quietly running things from behind the scenes. This is the shadow being brought into the light. This is the wound beginning to close from the inside.

If the door does not change, you have more work to do with this one. The memory has not finished with you yet, or you have not finished with it. Return another time. The door will still be here. It has been here this whole time, and it is going nowhere.

You can visit as many doors as feel right on a single journey. One is enough if it is the right one. Several is fine if the hallway keeps pulling you forward. Follow your instinct instead of a quota; the hallway knows what order things need to happen in. Trust the pull.

Leaving the Hallway

The hallway extends in both directions into what feels like eternity, and eternity is not a practical place to spend an entire afternoon. When you are ready to leave, here is how you do it.

Kneel down.

Focus on the floor directly in front of you. Look at it minutely: the texture, the grain, the specific quality of the surface beneath your knees. Bring your focus down so completely that the hallway and the doors begin to disappear from your peripheral vision. Keep going. Narrower. Closer. Until all you can see is the floor, just the floor, nothing but the floor in every direction of your awareness.

Then look up.

You are back in the foyer.

Take a breath. Feel the familiar quality of the space around you. The hallway of doors is straight ahead, behind the threshold you stepped back over. The well is to your left. The right opening leads to the mental plane. Everything is exactly where you left it.

Open your eyes.

After the Journey

Record everything immediately. The door you found, the memory inside it, what the room showed you that was different from the story you had been carrying, whether the door changed when you pressed the flag into it. All of it, before the beta mind begins its editorial process and smooths the edges off the things that matter most.

Give yourself time before you analyze. Integration is *not* an intellectual process. Integrating shadows tends to happen over days instead of minutes. You may find in the days following a door journey that something shifts in the area you came to address: a pattern softens, a reaction feels different, a choice that used to be automatic becomes a choice again. That is the shadow work doing what shadow work does.

Some doors will need to be visited more than once. A single journey through a memory that has been locked away for decades rarely completes the entire integration in one session, any more than a single physical therapy appointment resolves a long-standing injury. Return. Press a new flag into the door. See what changes each time. The hallway is always there, always straight ahead of you in the foyer of your mind, always full of everything you have ever lived.

The Shamanic Boat Journey

Most of what this book teaches is solitary work. You and your totem, you and the well, you and the hallway of your own memories. The work is personal because the interior landscape is personal, and there is no shortcut around that. But there is another category of shamanic work entirely, one that has been practiced across cultures and centuries: group travel. Journeying together, to the same destination, in the same vessel.

This is the shamanic boat journey.

It is one of the most remarkable experiences available to a group of accomplished practitioners, and I want to be specific about that word: accomplished. This journey requires that everyone in the boat has already developed reliable theta, has met their totem, has learned the difference between journeying and imagining, and can navigate the worlds with confidence. A boat journey with practitioners who are still learning to distinguish genuine experience from imagination produces a muddled mess where everyone half-consciously influences everyone else's experience and no one gets anything real. Do the individual work first. Then get in the boat together.

The Structure: Navigator, Crew, Herder

The group sits or lies in a single line, one behind the other. The person at the front of the line is the **navigator**. The person at the back is the **herder**.

The navigator's job is to hold the destination and lead the group there. They go first energetically, pulling the boat forward, setting the course, and maintaining it throughout the journey. The navigator needs to be your most pointed and most stable traveler: someone whose theta is deep and reliable, whose totem is a steady working partner, and who can hold a fixed intention while simultaneously navigating whatever the destination presents.

The herder's job is to watch the back of the boat. Shamanic travel done in a group produces a particular dynamic: individual practitioners, even experienced ones, will occasionally get pulled sideways by something interesting, distracted by a detail, or simply wander off down a side corridor of the experience that belongs to them alone instead of the group journey. The herder notices when this happens and brings the wanderer back. They are the rear anchor, the shepherd, the one making sure no one gets left behind or lost in territory that belongs to a different journey entirely. The herder needs patience, broad awareness, and the ability to maintain their own journey while also monitoring the group's energetic integrity.

Everyone else: follow the navigator, stay in the boat, and let the experience be what it is.

The Departure

Each practitioner begins the journey individually, the way they always begin: drumming track, posture, breath, heart rate to sixty beats per minute. Take the stairs through the mind dump, arrive in the foyer, turn right into the mental plane, take the left fork through the forest, and make your way down to the bay.

Your bay. Your black sand beach, your rock wall, your ocean going out forever.

When you arrive at the bay, you will find a boat waiting at the water's edge. It belongs to the group. Step into it. As each practitioner happens at their own bay and steps into their own boat, the boat will take off. Once the boats leave the shore and head towards the agreed-upon destination, the boats of all of the practitioners merge. This is the part that surprises people the first time they experience it, particularly if the group is not physically together in the same room. Time in the spirit world does not run at the same rate as time in the causal plane, and the rate at which each practitioner processes the experience will differ. Some will arrive at the destination quickly. Some will take longer. The boats merge regardless. The navigator holds the course, and the group assembles around that course at whatever rate their individual journeys require.

If your group is in different physical locations, this still works. Go to your bay. Get in your boat. Trust the merge. The spirit world does not require your physical proximity to assemble you in the same place. It requires your shared intention and your navigator's held course. That is enough.

What You Encounter

Here is something worth knowing before you go: the practitioners in your boat may appear to each other in different forms. Some will see their fellow travelers as the humans they are. Others will see them as their totems: the polar bear, the hawk, the possum (still remarkable), moving through the destination alongside them in animal form. Both are accurate perceptions of the same souls. Some will see them as floating shadow-people colors, like wispy cotton-candy lights. The form someone appears in tells you something about the quality of perception happening in that moment; neither is more real than the other.

Each person's journey will be genuinely different, even within the same destination. The navigator takes the group to the same place and holds that place as the shared context. What each practitioner experiences within that context, what they notice, who approaches them, what the environment shows them specifically: all of that belongs to the individual. This is the nature of the spirit world, speaking to each soul in the language that soul can most readily receive, and no two souls receive the same transmission in the same way.

This is critical to understand before the debrief: everyone's experience is valid. When the group returns and begins to compare notes, the conversation stays in the territory of sharing instead of adjudicating. No one's experience cancels out anyone else's. No one attempts to tell another practitioner what they should have experienced, what the correct interpretation of the destination is, or that their perception was wrong because it differed from someone else's. The boat journey produces a shared destination and individual experience simultaneously, and both of those things are true at the same time.

Let everyone's journey be true.

Destinations

The shamanic boat journey can go anywhere the navigator is willing to hold. I have sent groups to remarkable places over the years, and what the practitioners bring back consistently confirms the validity of the method. Here are some of the destinations I have used:

Niflheim: the primordial Norse realm of ice, mist, and cold that predates creation itself, one of the two primal forces from whose meeting all life emerged. The oldest cold. The darkness before the darkness had a name.

The River Styx: the boundary between the living world and the realm of the dead in Greek cosmology, tended by Charon, crossed by souls at the moment of transition. The navigator takes the group to the river itself, to the crossing, to the particular quality of that threshold.

Izanami's Underworld: the Japanese realm of Yomi, where the goddess Izanami retreated after her death in childbirth and from which Izanagi attempted to retrieve her. A dark, rotting, ancient underworld with its own specific atmosphere and its own specific lessons about grief, loss, and the things love cannot undo.

The Path of a Songline: traveling the energetic pathway of an Aboriginal Australian songline, following the dreaming track of an ancestral being across the Australian landscape and through the layers of cosmic memory encoded in it.

Min's Domain: the ancient Egyptian desert territory of Min, god of fertility, virility, and the eastern desert: raw generative power, ancient and elemental, presiding over the roads between worlds.

Atlantis: the submerged civilization, whatever it actually was and wherever it actually existed. Practitioners traveling here bring back a remarkable consistency of imagery and atmosphere that is worth experiencing and worth comparing across the group afterward.

Through the Pyramids of Egypt: entering the pyramid complex not as a tourist but as a spirit traveler, moving through the chambers and passages and the cosmological architecture of a structure built specifically to facilitate the transition between worlds.

These are starting points. The navigator can hold any destination that can be described with enough specificity and felt with enough genuine intention to give the group something real to travel toward. Historical locations, mythological realms, specific points on the earth's surface, specific moments in recorded history: all of it is accessible to a capable navigator with a stable group.

The Debrief

When the drumbeat signals the return, each practitioner comes back to their bay, steps out of the boat, returns through the forest path, through the foyer, up the stairs, and back into their body. Open your eyes. Take your time.

Record your experience before you share it. Write down what you encountered: the atmosphere of the destination, what you noticed, who or what approached you, what felt significant, and what surprised you. Get it on paper before the group conversation begins, because group conversations are contagious, and you want your genuine experience preserved before other people's accounts begin to influence your memory of it.

Then share. Keep the language in the territory of personal experience: what you saw, what you felt, what you perceived. Stay out of the territory of interpretation on behalf of other people's experiences. Resist the impulse to build a consensus narrative of what the destination was like, because the destination was like different things to different people, and all of those things are true simultaneously.

What you are looking for in the debrief is convergence: the specific details that multiple practitioners perceived independently without having discussed them beforehand. A particular quality of light. A specific figure who appeared to more than one traveler. An atmosphere that everyone described differently, but that points, when you look at the descriptions together, at the same underlying reality. Convergence is your verification. It tells you that the group was genuinely in the same place, each experiencing it through their own nervous system and their own perceptual range, all pointing at the same mountain from different angles.

A Final Note on Gaslighting

One more thing, and I say this directly because it matters: accomplished journeyers do not invalidate each other's experiences, i.e., gaslight.

If a practitioner reports something that differs from what you experienced, the correct response is curiosity. If a practitioner reports something that seems impossible or implausible based on your own perception of the destination, the correct response is still curiosity. The spirit world is not a consensus reality that everyone experiences identically. It is a vast, living, complex territory that presents differently to different nervous systems, different levels of development, and different individual soul histories.

The only experience worth questioning is your own: asking yourself honestly whether what you received was genuine perception or imagination, whether you followed the navigator or wandered, whether you were journeying or producing. That honest self-examination is your responsibility and yours alone.

Everyone else's experience belongs to them. Leave it there.

The Hunt

Playing Lupercus's Game in The Lower World

Before we talk about the Hunt itself, let us talk about who is overseeing it.

Lupercus is the Lord of the Hunt: The Horned One, the god of the forest and its life force, the primal intelligence that governs the survival instinct in every living thing. He is ancient, and he goes by many names across many traditions, because the force he represents predates the cultures that named him. The Romans called him Lupercus, god of fertility and the wolf, celebrated at the Lupercalia in February when the hunt was declared open, and the wild things ran. The Celts called him Cernunnos: the antlered god, lord of animals, the wild places, and the boundary between the human world and the spirit world. The Norse knew him as Herne, the Hunter, who rides the wild hunt across the winter sky. The Greeks called him Pan: the goat-footed god of the wilderness, whose presence in the forest produced the particular terror the word panic was originally coined to describe. The Romans also called him Faunus: god of the countryside, the herds, and the untamed natural world.

He is the same force in every tradition: the intelligence behind the will to survive, the patron of the hunt as sacred practice, the one who watches when predator and prey meet in the dark, and the outcome is genuinely uncertain.

He is an order emerging from wildness. He is the mind that the forest has.

If your tradition works with gods, use whichever name belongs to your path. If your tradition does not work with gods, understand him as the intelligence that manages the survival instinct: the force from which the drive to endure, adapt, and outwit originates. He is the season of winter, the space between spaces. Replace his name in any invocation with what fits your faith. Please don't replace anything else. The Hunt is cross-cultural: this force exists in every tradition because it exists in every living thing.

He oversees the Hunt. He keeps it fair. He is why the game has rules. Most spiritual practices are cooperative. You ask, the spirits answer. You travel, your totem guides you. You work with the energy available and return with something useful. The Hunt is something else entirely.

The Hunt is a game. A competition. A direct engagement with the paranormal in which you put your skill, your instinct, your prepared magic, and your wits against a spirit opponent in a course neither of you fully controls, with rules both parties have agreed to. There is a clear winner at the end. It is the most athletic thing this practice requires of you, and one of the most valuable, because nothing sharpens your magical instincts quite like being genuinely hunted.

The purposes are specific: to build alliance with paranormal forces that do not cooperate easily, to demonstrate genuine allegiance to the craft through action instead of intention, to maintain your fitness across every dimension that matters to a working practitioner (physical, psychological, spiritual, emotional, and magical), and to practice defensive and offensive magic the way it actually needs to be practiced: instinctively, under pressure, in the dark.

Two rules govern everything about this practice, and both are worth understanding before you go any further.

The first: you will only attract opponents of comparable strength to your own personal magnetism.

The spirit world does not send you more than you can handle. It sends you exactly what matches you. Which means that over time, as your skill develops, your opponents change accordingly.

The second: comparable strength does not mean identical skills. Your opponent may be stronger in certain areas than you are and weaker in others. The fight is fair; the skills are not a mirror image. You may have more offensive power and less defensive range. Your opponent may excel at disorientation and psychological pressure while your spell work outpaces theirs. The balance is in the overall match, not in a point-by-point equivalence of abilities. You will discover your opponent's specific strengths and weaknesses the same way they discover yours: in the course, under pressure, in real time.

The Hunt on the Causal Plane: Understanding the Original Game

Before we take the Hunt into the spirit world, you need to understand how it works on the causal plane, because the journey version makes considerably more sense once you have the original structure in your head.

On the causal plane, you are the one setting the terms and summoning the spirit. For example, you choose the location: a carefully bounded outdoor area with a clear starting point, a clear finishing point, and natural boundaries (roads, waterways, stone walls, tree lines) defining the edges of the course in all four directions. The course for a beginner runs no more than half a mile in any direction. Enough space to get genuinely lost, genuinely disoriented, and genuinely tested.

Here is the critical thing to understand about the causal plane version: you summoned the spirit into a course it does not necessarily know. It is unfamiliar to the terrain. You have the advantage of having chosen the location, having walked the route, and having set the terms on your ground. The spirit enters your game.

When you take the Hunt into the spirit world, everything flips. You are the one dropping in and not knowing the terrain, the boundaries, or even the end point.

What Counts as a Hit

A hit is any magical action that successfully affects your opponent, directly or indirectly.

A *direct hit* is a spell you deliberately aim at the spirit and that lands. Any spell counts: a binding, a love spell, a confusion working, a banishment, a curse, an energetic push, or a money spell. The category of spell is irrelevant. What matters is that you directed it at your opponent with intention, and it connected. If it lands, it counts.

An *indirect hit* is a spell that was not aimed at the spirit but affects them anyway through your own protection or defense. A protection spell on your neck that deflects an incoming attack counts as a hit on the spirit whose attack it turned back. A ward that causes an approaching opponent to stumble counts. A shield that reflects an assault back to its sender counts. You did not aim at the spirit directly; you protected yourself, and the protection reached them. That is an indirect hit, and it counts exactly the same as a direct one.

Three hits of either kind, in any combination, win the round.

And vice versa.

The spirit operates by the same rules. A spell aimed directly at you is a direct hit if it lands. An action that affects you indirectly through the environment or the terrain of the course counts as an indirect hit if you feel it connect. Pay attention to both categories coming in as much as you track both categories going out. The opponent is counting too.

Preparation: The Spells You Bring

Before either version of the Hunt, you prepare your offensive and defensive magic in advance. Review the Hedge Witchery chapter for the full framework of how spells work, how energy is built and held, and how magic is carried astrally. For the Hunt specifically, you are building spells before you go in and carrying them with you the way a soldier has weapons into the field. You should not build your magic under pressure in the middle of a pursuit. You should build it beforehand and deploy it when the moment requires it.

Prepare both offensive tools (spells designed to land hits on your opponent) and defensive ones (protections, deflections, shields). Know what you are carrying before you step into the course.

Setting Up the Journey Hunt

Begin in the mental plane. Connect to Lupercus: feel for his presence, hold the question of the Hunt in your awareness, and wait for the response. You are looking for a clear yes: a felt sense of assent, an energetic shift, something that happens with the quality of genuine agreement instead of your own wishful thinking. If you feel that yes, the game is on. If the response is ambiguous or absent, today is not the day. The Hunt requires two willing opponents of equal ability.

When the yes happens, carry your prepared spells with you into the journey, the way you carried them in hedge witchery. You built them before you sat down. They are with you. You know what you have.

The Departure

Begin the standard preparation: drumming track, posture, breath, heart rate to sixty beats per minute. Take the stairs through your mind dump, arrive in the foyer, turn right into the mental plane, take the left fork through the forest, and make your way down to the bay.

Stand at the bay. Your totem is with you and knows what you are about to do. Drop into the water. Descend into the Lower World. You will now be that "puff" of smoke that falls into their course.

The Course

You arrive in the Lower World, and you do not know where you are. That is the condition of the Hunt. Your totem takes the lead. Follow it with the same trust you have developed across every other journey you have taken together: immediate, complete, without second-guessing. Your totem perceives the terrain, the opponents, the hazards, and the direction of the finish line with a clarity your analytical mind cannot match under these conditions. This is the Hunt's great teaching: it forces you into a level of trust with your psychic self that nothing else in this practice quite requires. You cannot think your way through the Hunt. You have to feel your way through it.

The rules remain identical to the causal plane version. Three hits to the opponent, and the first to reach the finishing point wins. Your totem helps you navigate toward the finish and helps you land hits on the spirit opponent moving through the same course.

Remember: your opponent is your equal, not your mirror. They will be stronger than you in some areas, and you will be stronger than them in others. Pay attention to where the pressure is coming from in the early stages of the course; it tells you where their skill concentrates. Adjust accordingly.

Getting Hit

If a spirit lands a hit on you: a genuine energetic contact, a spell connecting, a direct interference that you feel land clearly... You might wake up. The journey ends. You are back in your body, eyes open. We are very fragile, so think of this as if they hit you hard enough on that side, you'll just zap back.

You lost. It is over.

If you land three hits on the spirit opponent before it lands one on you, and you reach the finishing point first, you win. The finish line is a clear sense of completion. You will know it when you reach it, the way you know the end of a race in the body.

After the Hunt

Record everything immediately. The terrain of the course, the nature of the opponent, where their skill concentrated, the hits landed and received, the moments where your totem's guidance was most critical, the spells that worked and the ones that did not. The Hunt produces some of the most practically useful information available to a working practitioner, because it tests your magic in conditions that approximate real professional work more closely than any training exercise can. Research what you encountered. Use an internet search, folklore databases, or mythology texts instead of AI tools, e.g. ChatGPT, which immediately default to Euro-centric mythos. Make a description and use "folklore," "mythology," or "cryptozoology."

Try searching in world mythos instead of the standard Anglican that is so pervasively available.

Then rest. The Hunt takes something out of you, on the causal plane and in the spirit world, both. Honor that. Eat something real, drink water, sleep. Let the body recover.

THE SPIRIT GUIDE JOURNEY

Most of the journeys in this book send you outward: through the forest, down to the bay, into the worlds. This one stays close. The spirit guide journey begins and ends in the foyer of your mind, and the distance you travel is measured in layers of consciousness instead of miles of spirit landscape.

> **Your guides have been trying to reach you this entire time. Every meditation that produced an unexpected impression, every dream that came with unusual clarity and weight, every moment of sudden knowing that came from nowhere with no rational explanation: that was the veil being thin.**

The Journey

Begin the way you always begin. Drumming track, posture, breath, heart rate to sixty beats per minute. Take the stairs through your mind dump and arrive in the foyer.

Turn back to face the stairs.

In front of the staircase, where you just came from, you will find a veil: celestial, gossamer, faintly luminous, hanging in the air with the particular quality of something that belongs to two places simultaneously. This is the connection to the upper world where your guides exist and from which they attempt to reach you in ordinary life. It has always been there.

Open the veil and step through.

Close it completely behind you. This is important: once you are through, you must close the veil completely. Nothing can enter your mind from the outside while you are in this space if and only if you completely close the veil behind you. Your mind belongs to you. The veil is the boundary that keeps it that way. But no holes, ok?

On the other side, gravity... well, doesn't exist. You are floating in darkness: spacious, quiet, completely without weight. Let yourself drift. The darkness here has a different quality than the darkness of the Lower World. You are above instead of below, and the atmosphere reflects that. Breathe into it. Allow the weightlessness to settle into the body instead of triggering the reflex to grab for something solid.

Ahead of you, a table and chairs materialize in the darkness with a light shining on it. Move toward them. Sit down.

Wait.

Meeting Your Guides

Your guides will arrive when they arrive. Do not reach for them, do not call out, do not populate the chairs with figures your imagination finds appropriate. Sit at the table the way you would sit in a waiting room where something genuinely important is about to happen: present, quiet, expectant, without demanding.

A note on what to expect, which is essentially a note on releasing expectation entirely: your guides are not necessarily angelic figures in white robes radiating gentle golden light. Some practitioners meet guides that look exactly like that, and those guides are entirely real. Others meet cryptids. Animals. Demi-gods from traditions the practitioner had no prior knowledge of. Ancient figures from cultures they have never studied. Beings that defy easy categorization and carry an unmistakable quality of genuine presence that has nothing to do with what the practitioner imagined they would find.

The guide is what it is. Your job is to recognize genuine presence instead of projection, and by now you know the difference: projected figures feel cooperative and convenient, arriving in exactly the form you hoped for with exactly the message you were already inclined to hear. Genuine presence feels distinct from you, sometimes surprising, uncomfortable, always carrying information that your imagination alone would not have generated.

Sit at the table. See who comes. Ask what you came to ask, or simply receive what is offered. Let the conversation be what it is instead of what you planned.

When the meeting feels complete, the guides will withdraw the way they came: with the quality of genuine departure instead of your decision to end the scene. Feel gravity return as you step back through the veil. Stand in the foyer. Open your eyes.

The Witch Race

Some of the oldest spirit walkers in recorded European history were not solitary mystics communing quietly with the divine. They were competitors. They lay their bodies down while their spouses watched over them in the dark, slipped out through the veil between states of consciousness, and flew: in their own form, as themselves, practitioners moving through the Middle World in human spirit form while their physical bodies lay at home completely unresponsive.

The Benandanti of Friuli in northeastern Italy, the Good Walkers, documented this practice in enough detail that it survived the Inquisition's attempts to eradicate it. They would enter trance, leave the body, and travel to their appointed locations in human spirit form while their resting forms stayed behind. One man testified about his wife during this period: he called to her ten times, and shook her, and could not wake her. Her body was there. She was somewhere else entirely, doing the work. So, he sat vigil until she came back because the local lore said she was probably fighting witches. And, eventually, she would wake from her battles.

That work, in the Benandanti tradition, was battling other witches in the Middle World sky: flying practitioners meeting flying practitioners, human form against human form, contesting for the fertility of the crops and the well-being of their communities.

There was one critical rule about the body left behind: it had to be protected and left in the correct position. If the body was turned onto its stomach while the spirit was away, the returning practitioner would have difficulty re-entering it, or could not get back in at all. The person watching over the resting body was performing a genuine protective function. They were the anchor. They were the reason the traveler could come home. This is why we do the Watchtower Ritual of Protection.

We take the Benandanti's tradition of practitioners meeting in the Middle World sky in human spirit form, and instead of battling, we race.

What the Witch Race Is

The Witch Race is a group spirit walk in the Middle World with a specific competitive structure: a shared starting point, a shared destination, and every practitioner making their own way between the two in their own human spirit form, flying, by whatever navigation and skill they possess. First one to the destination wins.

No cheating.

That rule sounds simple. In the spirit world, it requires genuine discipline because the temptation to shortcut, to skip the actual traversal of the distance, to simply arrive instead of travel, is real. The race requires that you genuinely move through the Middle World terrain between the starting point and the destination: that you feel the air beneath you, navigate the sky and the landscape below it, encounter what the Middle World presents along the route, and arrive having actually crossed the distance.

The Race

Begin the standard preparation: drumming track, posture, breath, heart rate to sixty beats per minute. Take the stairs through your mind dump, arrive in the foyer, turn right into the mental plane, take the left fork through the forest, and make your way down to the bay.

At the bay, jump the wall. This is Middle World travel: over the boundary, into the spirit current of the world you already inhabit in your physical life. Feel the shift as the Middle World assembles around you. You are in your own human spirit form here. Your totem may accompany you or may wait at the bay; this journey is yours to navigate as yourself instead of following your totem's instinct through unfamiliar terrain. You are the one flying. You are the one racing.

Navigate to the starting point.

My favorite starting location: the center of the Mediterranean Sea, in the sky above it. Arrive there in your human spirit form, feel the sea below you and the open sky in every direction, and find the other practitioners assembling at the same location. They appear as themselves: human spirit forms, the same people you know, perceived from the other side of the veil. This is the tradition the Benandanti practiced. Practitioners meeting practitioners, in human form, in the sky, ready to move.

When the group is assembled, and the starting signal happens, the race begins.

The Route

From the center of the Mediterranean in the sky, the destination is shore: any shore, the nearest landmass your navigation takes you to, arrived at by genuine traversal of the distance between the starting point and the coast.

Fly. Feel the air of the Middle World as you move across the water. The Middle World terrain will present things along the route: other spirits moving through the same space, elemental presences, and the particular quality of the sea's energy beneath you as you cross it. Pay attention to all of it without stopping.

The other practitioners are making the same crossing in their own way, through their own perception of the same territory, at their own pace, and by their own navigation. Some will move faster. Some will take routes that look different from yours but cover the same distance. The Middle World, like the physical world, offers more than one path between two points.

First one to touch shore wins.

After the Race

Check in with your body before you do anything else. Then debrief. The same rules apply as the shamanic boat journey: share what you experienced, keep the language in the territory of personal perception, and let everyone's journey be true. What you noticed along the route, what the sea looked like from the spirit side, what the flight felt like, who arrived at shore first, and what the arrival felt like: all of it goes into the record.

Look for convergence. The specific details that multiple practitioners perceived independently without prior discussion point to the genuine shared reality of the race. If three practitioners independently describe the same quality of light over the water or the same landmark along the route, that convergence is your verification. The mountain is the same mountain from every valley.

Other Starting Points

The center of the Mediterranean is one starting point among many. The race can begin and end anywhere in the Middle World that can be described with enough specificity to give the group a genuine shared location to assemble at. Some starting points I have used and recommend:

The center of the Amazon basin, racing to the mouth of the river where it meets the Atlantic. The top of the Great Pyramid at Giza, racing across the desert to the Nile. The middle of the Pacific Ocean, racing to the Hawaiian archipelago. The North Sea in the dark of a Norse winter, racing to any coast.

The destination can also be specific instead of general: not just a shore, but a particular temple, a particular bay, a particular ancient site. The more specific the destination, the more useful the post-race debrief becomes, because the practitioners can research the actual location afterward and compare what the Middle World showed them against the physical and historical reality of the place.

A Note on Cheating

I said no cheating at the beginning of this chapter, and I meant it, so let me be specific about what cheating looks like in the spirit world.

Cheating is skipping the traversal: willing yourself to the destination instead of crossing the distance. Cheating is using the spirit world's non-linear qualities to circumvent the actual race instead of flying it. Cheating is directing instead of journeying, producing instead of perceiving, arriving without having traveled.

The spirit world will allow you to cheat. It will not stop you. The other practitioners will sense something off in your debrief when your account of the route lacks the specific texture of genuine flight across genuine distance. And you will know, with the particular clarity that comes from honest self-examination, whether you flew the race or skipped it.

Fly the race. Cross the water. Touch shore.

First one there wins.

Your Shamanic Transformation

Let me tell you something about the life of a shaman that the pretty books leave out: it is largely terrible, and that is entirely the point.

I have survived several near-death experiences. On top of that, I live with chronic pain that will never fully resolve. Unfortunately, this may be the job description. The psycho-spiritual crises that connect a practitioner to the near-death reality of mortality tend to arrive through violent and frightening events or initiations, because the spirit world is not particularly interested in your comfort level when it decides you are ready to be useful.

The traditions say that a shaman experiences many deaths: repeated reminders of mortality that keep the practitioner tethered to spirit and to the cycles of life. The witch who has been wounded and healed has the knowledge of healing in their body.

The one who has died has the knowledge of the dead. The one who has moved through pain and suffering knows how to locate and remove it in others. The one who has been thrown so far out of balance that they forgot what balance felt like... that one knows what genuine health actually is, from the inside out, in a way that no amount of study can replicate.

For a witchdoctor to make this transition, the soul must invert. Picture your aura as the egg-shaped field that engulfs your physical self. In the shamanic transformation, that egg changes: tendrils reach outward from it, extending toward the world instead of simply containing the self. The practitioner becomes a conduit instead of a container. The boundary between self and world thins permanently, and deliberately, and in service of the work.

This transformation happens through one of the following:

- Enormous Fear.
- Near-Death Experience.
- Death and resuscitation.
- Extreme Trauma.
- Chronic Illness.
- Deep and sustained connection to the spirit of the natural world.

In my own history, my first transformation came through a near-death experience at Wai'anapanapa State Park. My second came through an encounter with something considerably worse, which those of you who have read **Witchdoctor Exorcist** are already familiar with. I was already a medium working with dark spirits before either of those events. Spell work alone did not make me a witchdoctor (as faith healers are first and foremost intermediaries between the spirit world and the sickness in our casual one). My spirit had to die enough that it transformed.

Now, before any of you start making plans, please do not engineer a chronic illness, manufacture unbearable fear, or attempt to die for your spiritual development. I say this sincerely, and with only moderate sarcasm. There is another way, and I am about to give it to you.

Your spirit can grow and transform into that of a shaman through diligent, repeated, committed connection to the natural world. The other pathways are, as a rule, one and done: you survive the thing, you transform, you carry on. The natural world pathway takes longer and requires more repetitions, but it is just as viable and considerably less likely to require hospitalization. Most practitioners need a minimum of twenty-five repetitions of each practice below. A commitment to daily connection for one month, one full moon cycle, should accomplish what needs accomplishing. It is worth every hour.

Rituals for Deep Connection to the Natural World

The Ritual of Land Connection

Find a location in nature where the civilized world is genuinely absent: no people, no sounds from roads or buildings, no visible evidence that humanity has been here recently and left its mark. This matters. The spirit of land that has been paved over or constantly trafficked by human activity has a different quality than the spirit of land that has been largely left alone, and you need the real thing for this work.

Sit on the ground. Directly on the earth, as close to actual contact as your circumstances allow. A blanket between you and the ground puts a buffer between you and the point of the exercise; leave it in the car.

Close your eyes and feel the ground beneath you: its actual, physical, tangible presence. From that physical contact, feel deeper. Feel the hum of the earth's energy, the immensity of what lives and moves beneath the surface, the force that makes the world continue functioning despite everything we do to it. Stay in that connection and read it. Feel its life force.

Allow your awareness to rest entirely in the deep feeling of the earth's soul. When you can hold that without your mind wandering toward grocery lists or existential spiraling, bring your attention to the points of contact between your body and the ground: hips, feet, calves, thighs. Feel how every part of you that touches her is fed by her, and how you give back in return. This is a constant cycle of receiving and offering, siphoning and gifting, and it moves in both directions simultaneously.

From that exchange, feel outward: how through her, you are connected to everything else that touches her. Every person, every plant, every rock, every living system on this planet shares this same ground. You can ride her soul and feel that connection extending in every direction, a vast and extraordinary web of feeding life energy, cleansing and being cleansed, nourishing and being nourished.

This is the Deep Connection of Strength, Stability, Death, Resurrection, and Growth Potential.

The Ritual of Sea Connection

Find a water source from nature: ocean, sea, lake, river, waterfall, stream. Sit near it or in it, with appropriate attention to your physical safety, because drowning is a setback.

Begin by connecting passively to the spirit of the water around you. Feel the constant life and movement of it. Ride the energy at whatever pace the water sets; allow it to direct the speed of your connection instead of imposing your own rhythm. Learn the energy before you try to match it.

Once you have ridden the spirit of water and have felt a sense of what it is, bring your own energy up to meet it. Race alongside the ebb and flow. What does its spell feel like? What does its texture carry? What does its spirit communicate when you are fully paying attention? Keep pace with the energy of water until you can feel, genuinely feel instead of imagine, the water in the air around you. The moisture that has yet to become rain. The spirit of water is present even when the water itself is invisible.

This is the Deep Connection of Cleansing and Movement.

The Ritual of Wind Connection

The wind destroys crops and cools a fever. It has seeds and brings storms. It bites, and it kisses, and it cares absolutely nothing about your preferences regarding either. Wind is the most fickle and the most honest of the natural forces, and connecting to it requires a particular kind of surrender.

Find a location where the sky opens wide above you, or position yourself under a tall tree that reaches upward into that openness. In either case, you want some degree of obstacle between you and the easiest possible connection: something that makes a little effort before the wind fully meets you.

Begin with your own physical body. Feel where the wind touches your skin, how it moves against you, how each moment of contact happens and departs before the next one begins. Feel your own breath and recognize it as your own version of wind: the life force you push out into the air and draw back in, the way you affect the atmosphere, even if not with the force and scope that the atmosphere affects you. In connection, the exchange is equal even when the scale is vast.

Match the wind's breath. Then allow the wind to meet you and match yours. Find the place where you and the wind are moving together instead of one simply acting upon the other.

This is the Deep Connection to Travel, Destruction, Comfort, Chaos, Fickle Adventure, and Vastness.

With consistent practice of these three rituals, your spirit will change. The soul begins to tug and pull outward, reaching toward everything in the world around you, developing the tendrils of a consciousness that has genuinely extended itself beyond the boundary of the skin. One practice of each will accomplish nothing meaningful, any more than a single Kung Fu class produces a master. Repeat, return, and trust the accumulation.

Sensory Deprivation

Another method for inverting and expanding the spirit is a full evening of wakeful sensory deprivation. At sunset, set an alarm for ten hours, with something vibrating every hour to keep you awake throughout. Noise-canceling headphones, blackout eye covering, and nothing else: no sound, no sight, for the full duration, awake. Spend that time sitting with your traumas, your history, your interior landscape without any external input to distract from it. This approach tends to trigger a fear-based altered state that, in the right practitioner at the right stage of development, produces the transformation.

This one is intense. You are deliberately removing the sensory scaffolding that most people use to keep themselves oriented and functional, and then sitting with everything you have been carrying for as long as you have been carrying it. Prepare thoughtfully, plan your aftercare, and bring genuine honesty to the question of whether you are ready for what surfaces.

The Night Outside

The most demanding transformation method in recorded human history is also, unfortunately, one of the oldest: spending the night alone in genuinely dangerous wilderness.

Across Neolithic cultures and tribal societies worldwide, children who showed signs of spiritual gifts were sent into the forest, jungle, or other untamed wilderness at the age of thirteen, alone, from sunset to sunrise. The purpose was survival through spiritual protection instead of physical combat: existing through the night in a world of dangerous creatures, under the care of the spirits instead of the protection of the human community. The ones who were genuinely called tended to survive. The experience completed the transformation that the gift had initiated.

History has recorded this practice as most common (probably because it's the most provacative). Contemporary practitioners are working within contemporary legal, ethical, and practical realities, and meaningful differences exist between a child raised within a community whose entire cosmological framework supported this rite, surrounded by a living tradition of spiritual protection, and an adult making unilateral decisions about wilderness survival based on a paragraph in a textbook.

Leading Others to Their Totem

The Witchdoctor as Guide

Your Near-Death Experience

There is something that happens when a person almost dies, something that leaves a permanent mark on the interior landscape of the mind. The place where it happened, whether physically real or spiritually significant, becomes a threshold. It becomes the place where the veil proved thinnest, where the spirit world pressed closest, where the body nearly surrendered, and the soul briefly stood at the edge of something enormous. That location does not forget you, and you do not forget it. It becomes, in the geography of your own mind, the most powerful crossing point you will ever have access to.

This is why every witchdoctor who leads others to their totem leads them somewhere different. This is where your spirit is inverted.

My near-death experience happened at the bay. The water, the black sand, the sense of the ocean going on forever: this is where I nearly left this world the first time, and it is why, in everything I teach and everything I write, I take students (including you in reading this) to the bay. That location is my place of spiritual transformation, permanently encoded into my interior landscape as the thinnest and most powerful threshold available to me. When I stand there in the mental plane, the veil is thin because it has been thin there before, in a way that changed everything. My totem emerged from that water because that water already knew what I was.

One of my students goes to a hospital elevator. That is her near-death location, transformed by the interior landscape into a gateway: the elevator descends to the Lower World, ascends to the Upper World, and her totem steps out from it when she is ready to meet. Another practitioner I know goes to a riverbank where she almost drowned, feeling when they were almost lost and then were not. Each of these locations has the same quality: the memory of the edge, the place where the spirit learned how permeable the boundary between worlds actually is.

If you have had a near-death experience, you already have your location. You may not have recognized it as such until this moment, and that recognition is worth sitting with before you continue reading. Where were you? What did it look, feel, and smell like? That place is yours, and it is more powerful than anything I could design for you. When you lead students to their totems, you will take them there, because it is the place in your interior landscape where the veil knows your name, and you are their guide.

If you have had multiple near-death experiences, you may find that one location holds more power than the others, or that different locations serve different purposes in your practice. Pay attention to which one your totem appeared from first. That is your primary threshold.

If You Have Never Had a Near-Death Experience

Some practitioners come to this work without a near-death experience in their history, and that is entirely workable. In that case, if no such experience has occurred yet, use the bay, as it goes from me onto you.

Preparing to Lead

Leading another person to their totem is a significant act of spiritual responsibility. You must have met your own totem clearly and worked with it long enough that the relationship feels stable and established.

You must also have a thorough understanding of the geography we mapped, because you will be describing it to someone who has never been there while simultaneously navigating it yourself. Your foyer may look different from your student's foyer (so don't describe yours to them, leave it open); your forest may differ from theirs in texture and detail. The geography is consistent in structure but personal in appearance, and a good guide holds the map loosely enough to accommodate variations without losing direction.

The Structure of a Guided Totem Journey

Begin the way you always begin: with the drum, with the breath, with the staircase. You want to teach them about it before they journey. If they are trying to understand while they are journeying, then they are learning and in alpha instead of accessing theta (and it's your fault). Explain everything to them ahead of time and ask for questions and any need for clarification before starting the journeys.

Guide your student through the preparation sequence exactly as you would guide yourself, using your voice to carry them down into theta while you descend alongside them. Your voice should be calm, slow, and unhurried. Rushing a student through the preparation sequence to get to the "interesting part" is one of the most common mistakes new guides make, and it costs the journey its depth. The preparation is the journey; everything that follows depends on how well the foundation was laid.

Once you have brought your student through the staircase and the mind dump, guide them to the foyer and then out into the mental plane. Take the left fork into the forest. Let them run. Give them time in the forest before moving them forward, because the forest does the work of clearing whatever the staircase left behind, and a student who has been given time in the forest happens at the threshold in a genuinely cleaner state than one who was hurried past it.

Then bring them to your threshold location. *There is no need to explain that it was your place of transformation.* Explaining this is an act of ego and wanting to be witnessed, and that is not your place at this time. Just tell them where they are going.

Guide them through the orb exercise, but have them throw it into your threshold location. Have them gather their energy, externalize it, and introduce it to the threshold in whatever form that takes in your location. The spirit essence meets the veil, the veil responds, and the totem emerges.

What to Do When Nothing Emerges

This happens to students who are trying too hard, students who are too excited, students whose beta minds are running commentary the entire time, and occasionally, students who are simply not ready yet for reasons that have nothing to do with effort or willingness. A student who is gripping too tightly, analytically directing instead of receiving, will stand at the threshold and see nothing while their imagination runs through a catalog of impressive animals they would not mind having.

The mirror method is your first tool in this situation. Guide them back to the threshold, have them reach into the sand or the ground or whatever the surface of your threshold location offers, and pull out a mirror. Have them gaze softly into it and wait for their human face to give way to the animal beneath. This bypasses the part of the mind that is trying to produce something and activates the part that simply observes.

If the mirror method also produces nothing, end the journey cleanly and try again in a subsequent session. Pushing through resistance in totem work rarely produces authentic results; it produces projections that the student will carry forward as genuine and then wonder why they feel hollow. An authentic meeting, when it finally happens, feels completely different from an imagined one, and your student will know the difference the moment they experience both. Give them the real thing, even if it takes longer to arrive.

Lastly, if they have a sense, but cannot see, then the answer lies there. They may not be clairvoyant even in the spirit world. Tell them they need to trust their "knowing."

After the Meeting

When your student returns from the journey, give them time before asking questions. Let them sit. Let them breathe. Let the experience settle into the body before the analytical mind begins its processing.

When they are ready, ask open questions instead of specific ones. What did you experience? What did you notice? Give them room to report without leading them toward a particular kind of answer. Your job at this stage is to receive what they bring back, help them recognize what is significant, and remind them of the one rule that matters most:

Keep the name secret. Every time. Without exception.

Remind them that the name they received belongs to the relationship between their conscious self and their psychic self, and that relationship is worth protecting with the same care they would give to anything genuinely sacred. Some students will be tempted to share it immediately out of excitement or intimacy, and that temptation is understandable. Let them know that the secrecy is the protection, and the protection is the gift they give themselves.

Your Threshold Is Your Transmission

The location you take your students to has your history in it. It has the particular quality of a consciousness that stood at the edge of its own ending and came back with something it did not have before. That quality transmits to the people you guide, even when they have no idea what your near-death experience involved or where it happened. They feel the thinness because the thinness is real, and it is real because you made it real with your own life.

This is why the witchdoctor's personal experience is not separate from their professional practice. Every crossing you have survived, every edge you have stood at, every moment when the veil proved thinner than you expected: all of it becomes available to the people you serve. Your history is your most powerful tool.

Leading Others in Journey

Leading someone else through a journey is a different skill from journeying yourself. When you travel alone, you navigate for yourself. When you are guiding another person, you are responsible for their entire experience from the moment they close their eyes to the moment they open them again. That responsibility requires preparation, clarity, and a specific kind of disciplined restraint.

The most important thing to understand before you guide anyone: your student happens at the journey knowing everything they need to know. They should have read this book, or received the instruction in some other form, before they ever close their eyes with you facilitating. The journey is the field trip. The teaching happens before you go. When you arrive, everyone already knows what they are looking at.

Teach Everything First

Before you guide anyone through a journey, they need to understand the following with enough clarity that none of it requires explanation mid-journey:

The preparation sequence: breath, heart rate, posture, why it matters, and what it produces. The stairs and the mind dump: what the staircase is for, how the mind dump works, what completion feels like. The foyer: the well, the hallway of doors, the right opening, the landscape beyond it. The mental plane: the two forks, the forest, the spirit circle, the bay. The bay: what it is, what the three directions of travel mean, and which direction you are going today. The totem: what it is, that it will appear when they are genuinely connected, what to do when it happens.

All of this is delivered before anyone lies down or closes their eyes. Answer every question in the teaching phase. A question that surfaces mid-journey pulls your student out of theta immediately. Questions belong in the preparation. The journey belongs to the experience.

Your Role During the Journey

Here is what you are doing while your student travels: you are the spouse watching over the empty body.

Remember the Benandanti, the Italian witches who lay their bodies down while their partners stood watch in the dark? The watcher's job was to keep the body safe, undisturbed, and in the correct position until the spirit returned. That is your job as a facilitator. Your student has left. Their body is in the chair or on the floor in front of you. You stay awake, present, and alert while they are gone.

You manage the music. You hold the space. You stay out of the journey entirely.

Your voice is the drumbeat's companion during the preparation sequence: slow, steady, unhurried, carrying your student deeper instead of pulling them back toward the surface. Speak at the pace of someone who has all the time in the world. Slow down further than feels natural. Then slow down again. Rushing communicates urgency, urgency produces beta, and neither of those serves your student.

Guide them through the preparation sequence step by step: the breath, the heart rate, the eyes directed upward behind closed lids. The flame, the staircase, the countdown. Name each step clearly and then give them time to actually experience it before moving to the next one. The most common mistake new facilitators make is moving too quickly, narrating the journey like a tour guide with a schedule instead of a practitioner holding space for a genuine altered state to develop.

When you reach the stairs, count them down slowly. Give each step its own breath. Allow the mind dump to happen. Students who feel hurried through the staircase carry unprocessed material into the journey and then struggle to go anywhere with it.

The Hand Off

There will come a point in every guided journey where your narration ends and the student's independent experience begins. This is the hand off: the moment you stop directing and start holding space.

When that moment happens, you say three words:

"Enjoy the journey."

That phrase is the signal. It means: you are where you need to be, your guide is with you, and the rest belongs to you. The narration is complete. The experience is live. After you say it, you just stop talking entirely.

You manage the music from this point: keeping the drumbeat running, monitoring the volume, ensuring nothing in the physical environment disrupts the space. You watch your student's physical state with the same attentiveness the Benandanti's spouse brought to watching their partner's resting body. You stay calm, present, and quiet.

Managing the Music

The drumbeat is your primary tool as a facilitator, and it requires active management throughout the journey. Start the track before the preparation sequence begins so the rhythm is already present when your student's breathing slows and their heart rate drops. Keep the volume loud enough to maintain awareness without being disruptive: the student needs the drum to keep them from drifting into sleep, and the volume is part of what does that.

Most shamanic drumming tracks include a callback signal near the end: a change in rhythm or a series of beats that signals the return. Know your track before you use it. Know exactly when the callback happens so you can prepare your student with a verbal cue just before it sounds. A student who hears an unexpected change in the drumbeat without context can snap out of theta abruptly instead of returning gently. Your preparation prevents that.

If you are setting the journey length manually instead of using a track with a built-in callback, watch the time and begin your return narration with enough lead time for a slow, unhurried ascent back up the stairs.

Calling Them Back

When the journey time is complete, bring your student back the same way you brought them in: with your voice, slowly, giving each step of the return its own time. Guide them back to the bay, through the forest, and back into their body.

When they are back, give them silence before you give them conversation. The transition from theta back to beta takes a moment, and a student who is immediately asked what they experienced will begin editing before they have finished arriving. Let them sit. Let them breathe. Let them feel the weight of their body and the quality of the room. Encourage them to journal.

Then ask open questions: what did you experience, what did you notice, what surprised you. Keep your own reactions out of it until they have finished reporting.

Be the spouse in the dark. Keep the watch. They will come back.

The Toxic Side of Spiritual Community: Watch Out, You!

Spiritual Bypassing

Authentic spirituality moves at the speed of digestion. Picture a plate full to the ceiling of burgers. You have to eat all of it to really understand it. So, you start with one. And after one full burger, you love the juicy deliciousness of it. You decide to grab another and another, but soon, you're full. Instead of finishing the plate, you say, "I know enough," and you let the rest sit there. You walk away, bloated and boasting about what you know.

Then there is the real master and student, who has one, rests, and leaves the plate, and comes back to consume another, and continues that steady pace.

You are not full, a master, nor complete just because you stuffed yourself quickly with burgers; in fact, you're bloated with some fake sense of accomplishment, which ends up making you too fat to apply any of it in the real world.

Real shamanic practice rarely feels rushed or romantic.

A little dabbling here and there creates a buzz of accomplishment because novelty provides a quick sense of knowingness, and that rush can feel like proof. Many people ride that contact high straight into loud certainty: speaking with the confidence of elders while carrying the emotional toolkit of a junky. The ego loves that sanctuary. Superiority feels safe when vulnerability feels risky. People get seduced by the promise of unconditional love and instant transformation, and they begin using spirituality as a shield. When spirituality becomes a costume you wear to avoid discomfort, bypassing has already begun.

What It Is

> ***Spiritual Bypassing* is the use of spiritual concepts, spiritual language, or spiritual practice as a way to avoid emotional and psychological work that demands attention.**

It looks like transcendence (but is just suppression of moving about in this world dressed up in sheepskin). Pain, shame, grief, anger, and trauma still live inside the body, whether a person chants around them or smiles through them. A person can learn beautiful ideas about compassion, divinity, forgiveness, and cosmic order while carrying unprocessed wounds that run their life from behind the curtain. This creates a false sense of progress: the person experiences spiritual stimulation while the underlying issues remain fully active.

Real growth requires spiritual practice and emotional work moving together in the same direction, like two hands pulling the same rope. And yes, I will keep saying it because it keeps people alive and sane: therapy belongs in the toolkit of every serious practitioner.

The Seduction

Bypassing begins with the desire to fast-track progress, because struggle feels slow and humility feels boring. People want a spiritual explanation for their pain that makes them special, chosen, targeted, or gifted, because that story feels considerably better than ordinary grief or ordinary responsibility. Sometimes, bypassing shows up as a belief that uniqueness equals supernatural persecution, which conveniently removes the need for self-examination. Sometimes it shows up as an obsession with enlightenment, expansion, higher being language, and personal power fantasies, because those fantasies temporarily numb insecurity.

The pattern stays the same regardless of the costume. The practitioner seeks relief from discomfort while keeping the discomfort unprocessed. That is why bypassing feels sweet at first and corrosive later.

How It Shows Up

Bypassing often feels like confidence; the confidence rests on avoidance. It often feels like compassion; the compassion functions as a way to escape accountability. It often feels like wisdom; the wisdom collapses the moment real life demands action.

Here are the forms I see repeatedly in spiritual communities:

- Avoiding emotional processing by using ritual, prayer, or metaphysical language as a substitute for grief work, anger work, and honest conversation.

- Ignoring systemic realities, racism, sexism, homophobia, poverty, violence, by retreating behind spiritual platitudes that create comfort for the speaker and abandon everyone else.

- Creating exclusionary ideas of who counts as a real practitioner, using spirituality as a social weapon instead of a path of service.

- Overemphasizing positivity until it becomes performance, leaving shadow, pain, and complexity without a place to land.

- Living inside magical thinking as a full-time worldview, replacing grounded assessment with fantasy and wish fulfillment.

- Dismissing science and medicine as though spirituality requires abandoning practical care, which increases risk for the practitioner and for the people who trust them.

- Using a spiritual reason for everything instead of the common-sense answer to a problem (like the poster falling off the wall was probably because the tape wore down instead of your ancestor hating David Bowie or wanting your attention).

Spirituality Becomes a Permission Slip

Sometimes, bypassing functions like denial dressed up as mysticism, and the example I use with students tends to land quickly. A person uses substances to cope with emotional pain, stress, or anxiety, and then justifies the use through spiritual language: the substance provides higher consciousness, deeper visions, stronger healing, and sacred initiation. The mind tells a story that sounds spiritual, while the nervous system screams for real support. The result feels like progress because altered states feel impressive. The underlying wound stays intact, and the behavior continues because the person receives spiritual validation for self-harm.

Bypassing becomes a sweet pill that goes down easily while the real work stays untouched. That is how a person can speak like a mystic while living like an untreated wound.

Confirmation Bias

Confirmation bias means favoring information that supports existing beliefs and filtering out information that challenges them. It is human, it is common, and it shows up in every field, including spirituality, because the brain loves certainty and hates dissonance. When bypassing takes hold, confirmation bias becomes the shield: the person invests emotionally in a spiritual narrative that protects them from pain. They seek teachers, books, videos, and communities that mirror their worldview. They reinterpret evidence so it fits the story they already want, and they treat discomfort as proof that outsiders simply fail to understand.

Over time, they lose objectivity and call it faith.

A serious practitioner holds a belief while still investigating reality from multiple angles. Those two things can coexist. They must.

Toxic Positivity

Toxic positivity is the social pressure to maintain a relentlessly positive outlook regardless of circumstances, which encourages emotional suppression instead of emotional honesty. Many spiritual communities encourage this through language like: everything happens for a reason, find the lesson, stay high vibe, keep smiling. Those ideas can sound supportive in the moment. The problem happens when a person uses positivity to silence pain instead of carry it.

People begin to feel shame when they experience anxiety, depression, grief, or rage, because they interpret those experiences as spiritual failure. They perform happiness and call it healing. The body holds the truth in tension, insomnia, illness, and eventual emotional collapse. A healthy practice gives the full emotional range a place to move, because joy requires honesty to stay alive.

Victim Blaming

Victim blaming enters the room when bypassing meets power, because it allows the observer to avoid the terror of randomness, injustice, and suffering. A person uses spiritual beliefs to explain away tragedy by placing responsibility on the victim: illness came from insufficient faith, poverty came from weak vibration, abuse came from poor manifestation, and oppression came from negative thinking. This gives the speaker a false sense of control because if the victim caused it, the speaker can avoid it by behaving correctly.

The idea feels comforting. It spreads quickly because fear loves simple stories. The damage is enormous because it denies reality and abandons people who need support. A witchdoctor, a healer, an exorcist: these people serve the suffering. That requires compassion and clarity, and it requires the complete absence of spiritual scapegoating.

Superiority

Bypassing frequently produces a false sense of superiority because spiritual identity can become a pedestal for the ego. People begin believing they transcend ordinary human limits. They speak as though they operate above nature. They interpret every coincidence as proof of invincibility. That posture reduces empathy, because the practitioner becomes detached from the messy reality of human emotion and starts treating pain as a failure of consciousness instead of a fact of life.

It also creates a power fantasy, where mystical experiences become currency, and the practitioner uses them to dominate conversations and communities.

There is nothing virtuous about expansion as a status symbol.

Virtue lives in integrity, service, humility, and the willingness to stay human while practicing the sacred.

The moment a person uses spirituality to rise above others, they have already lost the point.

When Spirituality Gets Uncomfortable, People Buy a Weekend Certification

Spirituality becomes real the moment it meets shadow, illness, mortality, grief, and pain, because those experiences require support that stays grounded instead of performative. When people build a relationship with discomfort, they gain authenticity: they stop running from their own interior world and learn to carry vulnerability with dignity.

Many people prefer control over humility, so when the path gets uncomfortable, they search for a shortcut that promises authority without struggle.

Weekend certifications sell that fantasy beautifully: everyone passes, everyone leaves feeling special, and nobody has to demonstrate repeatable results under pressure.

A serious practitioner learns skills through practice, feedback, and the slow earning of competence. That process takes the time it takes, and it takes longer than a weekend. Every time.

How a Healer Stays Grounded

If this work feels massive, that's because it is massive. The only sustainable approach involves humility, skepticism, and consistent self-care. A healer respects their abilities while staying grounded by holding several principles at once. These principles sound like mature adulthood instead of fantasy. They keep you honest. They keep you safe. They keep your clients safe. They keep your spirit clean:

- Acknowledge the limits of your skills with humility, and refer out when another professional serves the client better in that moment.
- Embrace failure as part of the learning process, and treat setbacks as data that improves technique instead of as personal collapse.
- Place causes where they belong: assess practical, medical, psychological, relational, and spiritual factors with equal respect.
- Practice self-care consistently so your body, emotions, and spirit remain resourced enough to serve others without resentment or burnout.
- Stay skeptical in a healthy way by looking at situations from multiple angles, including the simplest explanations that protect the client's health and safety.

Managing Outcomes, Shame, and the Reality of Healing

Every healer eventually faces the emotional aftermath of a session that produces an outcome the client did not expect. That moment tests character more than any ritual ever will. The healer may feel sadness, frustration, disappointment, or guilt, and the mind will search for reasons because the human psyche hates ambiguity. Clients may experience anger because hope feels precious and losing it feels brutal, and anger often turns toward the person holding the role of helper.

Part of professionalism involves learning to hold that reality without collapsing into self-shame and without inventing spiritual excuses. Shame behaves like a demon: it convinces a person that a single outcome defines their worth, and that belief drives avoidance, arrogance, or despair. You manage shame through honesty, supervision, community, and emotional work that stays ongoing. You also accept a difficult truth: success is owed to no one, and being liked by everyone is an impossible job requirement.

Healing deserves a definition that reflects real life instead of fantasy. Healing means returning the self to a state of wholeness, which often involves transformation instead of reversal. Some injuries create permanent change, and the person still becomes whole through adaptation, integration, and new ways of living. A tree can lose a branch and still remain a tree: alive, capable of growth, unique, itself. The loss becomes part of its story instead of the end of its life.

When you serve as a witchdoctor, you assist people and spirits through that transformation with skill, compassion, and realism. You will encounter spirits that resist removal. You will face outcomes that challenge your pride. You will continue anyway, because that is the work. You practice to serve. You practice to become dependable. You practice to remain human while walking with the sacred.

YOU ARE THE NEXT LINK

You, Sweet Shaman

You made it to the end of the book (well, almost... the rest is all the totems and is meant as a reference).

Now, I want to say a few things to you before the book closes.

If you have read this book and done the work inside it, you are a shamanic practitioner. That is the honest title. You can enter trance reliably, meet your totem, travel the worlds with protection, come home cleanly, and, in time, guide another person through the same passage. That is real. Claim it.

You are not yet a shaman.

Remember the burgers. One full burger makes you someone who has eaten a burger. Two makes you someone who enjoyed the meal. The plate in front of you holds a lifetime, and the only way to finish the plate is to keep coming back to it, rested, hungry, honest, across years. A shaman is someone who has done that. A shaman is someone who has been called, tested, broken, reassembled, and kept returning to the work long enough that spirit recognizes them by the consistency of their footsteps. That's not a weekend, nor is it a book. It's a life.

So, do not call yourself what you are not, yet. Call yourself what you are: a practitioner, a facilitator, a student of the oldest human skill.

Go Help Others

Here is the part that surprises students: you can teach now.

You can sit with someone who has never journeyed and carry them through the breath, the stairs, the mind dump, the foyer, the bay. You can watch their body while their spirit travels. You can say the three words, *enjoy the journey*, and fall silent, and manage the drum, and call them back when the time is right.

The world has plenty of people waiting to meet their totem and very few people willing to hold space for them responsibly. If you have read this book with care and practiced what is in it, you are already more prepared than most of the people currently offering this service publicly.

Typing that sentence makes me sad. The field is thin because the work is hard and the shortcuts are seductive. You refused the shortcuts. Go teach.

Teach what you know. Say plainly what you do not know. Refer out when another professional serves the person better. Keep your own mana tended. Keep doing the work on yourself, because the day you stop is the day your practice starts bleeding into your clients. Do your shadow work regularly; the hallway of doors belongs to you for your whole life, right? It's always right there. Return to the bay. Return to the bowl in your chest. Return to the land, the sea, the wind.

Go help others become shamanic practitioners, you sweet, sweet shaman.

On Pain

I want to be careful with this next part, because modern spirituality loves turning suffering into content, and I refuse to do that in this book.

You are going to encounter pain in this work. Your own and other people's. Grief that fails to lift on the schedule, new age philosophy says it should, or even our parents' religion and culture says it should. Clients will arrive carrying things that will change what you thought you knew about the human capacity for endurance. Spirits will arrive carrying their own grief, and some of it older than any of us. Your own body, which will get tired, injured, sick, old, and eventually cross to the spirit world, will ache and may even become bitter at this world we meander through. The shamanic transformations that happens through near-death, through chronic illness, through the things you survived that you did not choose.

Accept all of it. Glorify none of it. Seriously, this isn't about glory or status. This practice is about service and being that intermediary between the spirit world and your students.

The old texts and the pretty marketing want to turn pain into a rite of passage, a badge, a sign of having been chosen. That framing protects the reader from having to actually feel. It gives suffering a decorative function. It lets the practitioner stand at a flattering distance from the wound and call it wisdom. Bullshit. Pain sucks. Suffering sucks. Having your continued pain isn't something to "one-up," or to lay down as a badge. You hurt to remember to help a client get back to a baseline. You hurt to remember humanity, and empathize.

Accept pain instead. Your own, when it comes. Other people's, when they bring it. The pain of the spirits you work with, who sometimes carry injuries older than language. Accept it the way you accept weather: real, present, impersonal, carrying no judgment on your practice, measuring nothing except the simple fact that living things hurt.

A practitioner who has glorified their pain struggles to sit with another person's pain without secretly comparing, secretly ranking, secretly needing the other person to acknowledge their suffering too. A practitioner who has accepted their pain can sit with anything.

The wound stays a wound; the wound refuses to become a throne.
You will be asked, repeatedly, to witness things that most people prefer to look away from.
Your job is to stay.
To stay, and to feel it, and to keep your hands steady, and to come home whole afterward.

The Next Link

You are the next link in the chain.

This practice began long before me, and long before my teachers, and long before whoever taught them. It began before writing. It began on every continent independently, because the human nervous system can open a door, and people everywhere have always walked through. The San painted their journeys on rock walls twenty-seven thousand years ago. The Benandanti lay their bodies down while their spouses kept watch in the dark. The mudang still walk the streets of Seoul; the sangoma still receive their callings through the sacred sickness; the Sámi survived every attempt to erase them. The chain runs through all of it, unbroken in places, repaired in others, always moving forward through the people willing to carry it.

You are one of those people now.

Carry what you learned here. Add your own repetitions, your own clients, your own hard-won understanding of what works and what does not. Pass it along to the next practitioner without gatekeeping, without turning your knowledge into a product, without letting your name become more important than the practice itself. Spread the knowledge. That belongs to the old ways. Spread your image... that belongs to something else.

The Hand off

There is one last thing, and it is the part I have been waiting to say.

I have been the spouse in the dark for you.

That is what a teacher is, in this tradition. The reason I spent this many pages teaching you how to lie your body down safely, how to leave cleanly, how to navigate, how to come home: the whole book was a vigil. I watched your resting form while your spirit traveled through the material. I held the protocol steady so you had something to return to. I kept the lights low and the body in the correct position. I made sure nothing interrupted the passage. You did the traveling. I kept the watch.

Now, it is your turn.

Somewhere, someone is going to lie their body down in front of you and ask you to hold space while they travel for the first time. They will be nervous. They will be skeptical of their own perception. They will wonder whether they are making it up, whether their totem is real, whether this whole thing is a performance they are putting on for themselves in the dark. You will recognize all of it because you felt every bit of it on your first journey, too.

So ... here is how the book ends.

Enjoy the journey.

You sweet, sweet shaman.

THE TOTEMS

Albatross Totem

Core Totem Essence

Albatross has the soul memory of boundless navigation and faithful return. This totem lives across vast oceans, trusting wind, current, and inner compass over long spans of time. Across Polynesian voyaging cultures, maritime traditions, and Southern Ocean peoples, the albatross appears as a sacred navigator, a bearer of ancestral spirit, and a symbol of devotion that endures distance. Albatross medicine centers on long vision, spiritual companionship, and mastery of invisible pathways.

Strengths of the Totem

Albatross brings expansive perspective; awareness spans horizon, consequence, and deep time.

Albatross has effortless endurance; movement flows through alignment with natural forces.

Albatross embodies fidelity and devotion; bonds remain strong across separation and return.

Albatross navigates unseen pathways; wind, intuition, and subtle signals guide direction.

Albatross holds calm authority; presence reassures through steadiness and grace.

Challenges of the Totem

Albatross lives across an immense distance; grounding has connection within daily life.

Albatross commits deeply to long cycles; patience in purpose through extended journeys.

Albatross has sensitivity to environmental disruption; attunement has resilience and advocacy.

Albatross values freedom of movement; responsibility integrates best through chosen commitment.

Past Life Lessons Carried Forward

Albatross has learned to trust in invisible support; wind and current respond to alignment.

Albatross has learned devotion through return; loyalty expresses itself through coming home.

Albatross has learned navigation through memory; ancestral pathways remain accessible.

Albatross has learned companionship across distance; connection transcends proximity.

Recurring Patterns Across Lifetimes

Albatross souls often appear as navigators, guides, long-distance travelers, spiritual companions, or keepers of memory.

Albatross souls form enduring bonds; commitment unfolds across time instead of immediacy.

Albatross souls carry a calm presence; others feel steadied by their long view.

Initiations of This Lifetime

Albatross awakens during periods of relocation, pilgrimage, long-term calling, or spiritual companionship.

Albatross activates when the soul trusts its inner compass and commits to journeys that require faith and endurance.

Alligator and Crocodile Totem

Core Totem Essence

Alligators carry the soul memory of primordial guardianship. This totem rises from ancient waters where creation, survival, and law first took form. Across river civilizations, wetlands, and delta cultures, people recognize these beings as keepers of thresholds, enforcers of natural order, and witnesses to deep time. Alligator's medicine centers on patience, ancestral authority, and the power that comes from waiting, watching, and acting with precision.

Strengths of the Totem

Alligators bring profound patience; stillness sharpens awareness and conserves power.

Alligators carry ancient authority; presence alone establishes order and respect.

Alligators embody survival mastery; adaptation across land and water has longevity.

Alligators protect sacred boundaries; thresholds remain guarded with clarity and resolve.

Alligators hold emotional containment; feelings remain stored, processed, and released through deliberate action.

Challenges of the Totem

Alligators live with immense stored power; timing and discernment shape its release.

Alligators value control and territory; flexibility within changing systems requires conscious engagement.

Alligators carry deep memory; integration of ancient experience makes for ritual grounding.

Alligators move through stillness; environments that demand constant motion invite energetic adaptation.

Past Life Lessons Carried Forward

Alligators have learned guardianship of life cycles; birth, death, and renewal remain sacred responsibilities.

Alligators have learned the law of patience; power ripens through waiting.

Alligators have learned sovereignty through restraint; force gains wisdom through precision.

Alligators have learned endurance across epochs; continuity creates identity and purpose.

Recurring Patterns Across Lifetimes

Alligators' souls often appear as guardians, enforcers, elders, protectors of land, or keepers of taboo knowledge.

Alligators' souls hold authority without explanation; others sense boundaries instinctively.

Alligators' souls remain steady during chaos; crisis clarifies their role.

Initiations of This Lifetime

Alligators awaken during periods of boundary enforcement, ancestral reckoning, or power consolidation.

Alligators activate when the soul learns to trust stillness, timing, and embodied authority.

Crocodilian Variations: Current Life Expression

Alligator

Alligator reflects guardianship of home waters; the soul engages protection of family systems, emotional territory, and personal foundations. In Southeastern Indigenous cultures of North America, the alligator appears as a keeper of deep waters, a teacher of patience, and a symbol of survival through environmental change.

Nile Crocodile

Nile Crocodile reflects divine authority and cosmic law; the soul engages spiritual guardianship, life force regulation, and sacred violence held within order. In ancient Egyptian culture, crocodiles align with the god Sobek, a deity of kingship, fertility, military strength, and the living power of the Nile. This expression emphasizes the protection of civilization, the enforcement of divine law, and the balance between creation and destruction.

Saltwater Crocodile

Saltwater Crocodile reflects dominance across vast territory; the soul navigates leadership, command, and survival within expansive and unpredictable environments. In Aboriginal Australian traditions, this crocodile appears as an ancestral being tied to creation stories, water law, and respect for natural hierarchy.

Caiman

Caiman reflects adaptability within constrained systems; the soul works with resilience, vigilance, and protection inside limited or pressured environments. In Central and South American river cultures, caiman represents survival intelligence and the guarding of resources.

Ant Totem

Core Totem Essence

Ant has the soul memory of collective intelligence expressed through purposeful labor. This totem lives through cooperation, foresight, and the steady transformation of effort into lasting structure. Across Africa, the Americas, Asia, Australia, and ancient agrarian cultures, ants appear as teachers of order, provisioning, and communal survival. Ant medicine centers on shared purpose, patience across time, and the power that emerges when many act in harmony.

Strengths of the Totem

Ant brings extraordinary cooperation; individual action aligns seamlessly with the collective aim.

Ant has disciplined persistence; progress unfolds through consistency and repetition.

Ant embodies strategic foresight; preparation secures stability across seasons and cycles.

Ant has communal responsibility; care for the whole sustains each member.

Ant builds enduring systems; small actions accumulate into resilient structures.

Challenges of the Totem

Ant lives through continual duty; replenishment through rest and celebration sustains vitality.

Ant values order and routine; creativity expands expression within structure.

Ant prioritizes group needs; personal voice strengthens balance and long-term cohesion.

Ant works patiently over time; recognition develops through shared acknowledgment.

Past Life Lessons Carried Forward

Ant has learned survival through cooperation; unity multiplies strength.

Ant has learned abundance through preparation; foresight preserves life.

Ant has learned dignity in labor; effort itself holds sacred value.

Ant has learned timing through season and cycle; patience aligns reward with readiness.

Recurring Patterns Across Lifetimes

Ant souls often appear as builders, organizers, providers, caretakers, or architects of systems.

Ant souls sustain communities quietly; reliability in trust.

Ant souls think in generations; legacy creates motivation and action.

Initiations of This Lifetime

Ant awakens during periods of rebuilding, community formation, or long-term goal commitment.

Ant activates when the soul dedicates effort toward shared purpose and enduring contribution.

Formicid Variations; Current Life Expression

Worker Ant

Worker Ant reflects service and steady contribution; the soul engages in daily labor, responsibility, and reliability that support collective survival.

Queen Ant

Queen Ant reflects generative leadership and continuity; the soul engages creation, stewardship of lineage, and long vision that sustains the whole.

Soldier Ant

Soldier Ant reflects protection and boundary defense; the soul engages guardianship, readiness, and strength applied in service to community safety.

Fire Ant

Fire Ant reflects intensity and rapid mobilization; the soul engages swift response, passionate defense, and coordinated action. This expression emphasizes awareness of impact and conscious direction of force.

ANTELOPE AND GAZELLE TOTEM

Core Totem Essence

Antelope has the soul memory of alert grace, swift intuition, and survival guided by sensitivity instead of force. This totem lives through awareness sharpened into elegant motion, teaching how life thrives through responsiveness, perception, and a respectful relationship with the environment. Across African savanna cultures, Indigenous North American plains teachings, and ancient Near Eastern symbolism, antelope appears as a teacher of vigilance, sacrifice transformed into sustenance, and beauty expressed through balance with the land. Antelope medicine centers on speed guided by awareness, humility paired with confidence, and the art of staying present within open space.

Strengths of the Totem

Antelope brings heightened perception; subtle shifts register instantly.

Antelope has graceful speed; movement aligns with intuition and timing.

Antelope embodies alert calm; readiness exists without tension.

Antelope has harmony with the land; survival unfolds through respect for the terrain and cycle.

Antelope has elegant courage; confidence moves lightly and decisively.

Challenges of the Totem

Antelope lives within constant alertness; grounding has nervous system ease.

Antelope responds rapidly to stimulus; discernment refines choice and direction.

Antelope thrives in open environments; containment has rest and restoration.

Antelope values freedom of movement; rootedness strengthens continuity.

Past Life Lessons Carried Forward

Antelope has learned survival through awareness; perception preserves life.

Antelope has learned grace through speed; movement remains balanced and precise.

Antelope has learned humility through openness; visibility sharpens wisdom.

Antelope has learned to trust in instinct; intuition guides safety and success.

Recurring Patterns Across Lifetimes

Antelope souls often appear as scouts, messengers, athletes, dancers, healers of anxiety, or guides through change.

Antelope souls move ahead of danger; awareness creates outcome early.

Antelope souls bring lightness to heavy spaces; presence restores balance and clarity.

Initiations of This Lifetime

Antelope awakens during periods requiring quick adaptation, heightened awareness, or graceful exit from unsafe patterns.

Antelope activates when the soul trusts instinct, moves decisively, and maintains harmony with the environment.

Antilopine Variations: Current Life Expression

Springbok

Springbok reflects joy expressed through movement; the soul engages vitality, optimism, and emotional release through leaps and display. Southern African symbolism associates the springbok with renewal and spirited resilience.

Gazelle

Gazelle reflects elegance and sensitivity; the soul engages grace under pressure and intuitive navigation of social and environmental space. Middle Eastern and African traditions honor the gazelle as a symbol of beauty guided by awareness.

Saiga

Saiga reflects survival within harsh terrain; the soul engages endurance, adaptability, and instinct created by extreme conditions.

Impala

Impala reflects agility and versatility; the soul engages rapid decision, flexible movement, and social coordination within changing environments.

Axolotl Totem

Core Totem Essence

Axolotl has the soul memory of sacred regeneration and suspended becoming. This totem lives within water and youth, holding the power to remain whole while continuing to grow. Across Mesoamerican cosmology, especially within Mexica and earlier Nahua traditions, the axolotl appears as a divine being linked to transformation, survival, and refusal to abandon essence under pressure. Axolotl medicine centers on regeneration without loss of identity, resilience through gentleness, and the wisdom of remaining true while the world demands change.

Strengths of the Totem

Axolotl brings regenerative mastery; healing unfolds repeatedly through cellular and spiritual renewal.

Axolotl has deep adaptability; survival expresses itself through flexibility instead of force.

Axolotl embodies preservation of essence; growth occurs without sacrificing core identity.

Axolotl has gentleness as strength; softness sustains life through endurance.

Axolotl holds water-bound intuition; emotional and psychic sensing guide action and timing.

Challenges of the Totem

Axolotl lives within prolonged liminality; momentum develops through patience and trust.

Axolotl has sensitivity to the environment; protection of space has vitality.

Axolotl values continuity of self; external pressure invites conscious choice around transformation.

Axolotl moves slowly through visible change; internal growth often precedes outer expression.

Past Life Lessons Carried Forward

Axolotl has learned regeneration as sacred art; restoration repeats without diminishing essence.

Axolotl has learned survival through remaining; staying present preserves soul integrity.

Axolotl has learned transformation without abandonment; growth honors origin instead of erasing it.

Axolotl has learned water as womb and teacher; emotion sustains healing and memory.

Recurring Patterns Across Lifetimes

Axolotl souls often appear as healers, survivors, caregivers, inner world explorers, or holders of gentle resilience.

Axolotl souls move through extended healing arcs; restoration creates identity and purpose.

Axolotl souls preserve innocence and curiosity; wonder remains alive through experience.

Initiations of This Lifetime

Axolotl awakens during periods of healing, recovery, identity preservation, or refusal to harden under strain.

Axolotl activates when the soul chooses regeneration, patience, and self-preservation as sacred paths.

Neotenic and Salamander Variations: Current Life Expression

Axolotl

Axolotl reflects sacred refusal to abandon self; the soul engages healing, regeneration, and continuity of identity. In Mexica cosmology, the axolotl connects to the god Xolotl, who transformed himself into this form to remain within the world and continue his purpose. This expression emphasizes devotion to essence, survival through gentleness, and divine persistence.

Tiger Salamander

Tiger Salamander reflects emergence from hidden growth; the soul engages transition from internal development into visible action. Indigenous North American traditions observe the salamander as a being of transformation and elemental balance.

Olm

Olm reflects deep time and subterranean endurance; the soul engages patience, sensory attunement beyond sight, and survival across long darkness. Balkan cultures recognize the olm as a creature of mystery, purity, and ancient continuity.

Armadillo Totem

Core Totem Essence

Armadillo has the soul memory of protected sensitivity and grounded resilience. This totem lives through gentle presence shielded by instinctive defense, moving close to the earth while maintaining clear personal boundaries. Across Indigenous cultures of the Americas, especially in the Southwest, Mexico, Central America, and South America, the armadillo appears as a keeper of earth wisdom, a guardian of the self, and a teacher of survival through discernment. Armadillo medicine centers on self-protection that preserves softness, stability rooted in the body, and the wisdom of knowing when to open and when to shield.

Strengths of the Totem

Armadillo brings natural boundary intelligence; protection activates smoothly without aggression.

Armadillo has grounded endurance; steady pacing has survival and longevity.

Armadillo embodies emotional safety; sensitivity thrives within clear containment.

Armadillo has earth attunement; connection to soil, burrow, and body anchors calm presence.

Armadillo has self-preservation; care for personal space sustains vitality and trust.

Challenges of the Totem

Armadillo lives with heightened sensitivity; discernment guides openness and closure.

Armadillo values safety and familiarity; exploration develops through gradual trust.

Armadillo responds to threat through withdrawal; re-emergence strengthens connection and flow.

Armadillo maintains strong personal boundaries; communication has mutual understanding.

Past Life Lessons Carried Forward

Armadillo has learned protection without hardening; softness and safety coexist.

Armadillo has learned survival through grounding; body awareness preserves life.

Armadillo has learned discernment of space; knowing where to dwell sustains peace.

Armadillo has learned self-trust; instinct guides appropriate response.

Recurring Patterns Across Lifetimes

Armadillo souls often appear as protectors of personal space, healers with strong boundaries, caregivers, or quiet stabilizers.

Armadillo souls create safety for themselves and others; calm environments grow around them.

Armadillo souls value autonomy and privacy; trust unfolds through respect and patience.

Initiations of This Lifetime

Armadillo awakens during periods of boundary strengthening, emotional healing, or nervous system regulation.

Armadillo activates when the soul learns to protect sensitivity while remaining present in the world.

Badger Totem

Core Totem Essence

Badger has the soul memory of fierce persistence made with earth truth. This totem lives through determination, boundary defense, and unwavering commitment to self-sovereignty. Across Europe, North America, Asia, and Indigenous earth-based cultures, the badger appears as a guardian of territory, a keeper of underground wisdom, and a being who endures through grit and resolve. Badger medicine centers on tenacity, courage rooted in instinct, and the power of standing one's ground with integrity.

Strengths of the Totem

Badger brings relentless perseverance; effort continues until the purpose is completed.

Badger has fearless self-defense; protection activates decisively when boundaries face pressure.

Badger embodies earth strength; grounding through the body and soil stabilizes action and emotion.

Badger has independence; self-reliance has clarity and confidence.

Badger holds subterranean wisdom; hidden layers reveal truth through patience and digging.

Challenges of the Totem

Badger lives with intense determination; flexibility expands outcome without reducing resolve.

Badger has a strong territorial instinct; discernment guides response within shared spaces.

Badger commits deeply to chosen paths; recalibration has sustainability.

Badger values privacy and autonomy; communication strengthens mutual respect.

Past Life Lessons Carried Forward

Badger has learned survival through persistence; endurance preserves life and purpose.

Badger has learned courage through embodiment; standing firm creates safety.

Badger has learned protection of self and home; boundaries shape peace.

Badger has learned truth through excavation; depth reveals clarity.

Recurring Patterns Across Lifetimes

Badger souls often appear as defenders, truth seekers, protectors, healers with strong boundaries, or keepers of land.

Badger souls persist where others retreat; determination reshapes outcome.

Badger souls value autonomy and justice; integrity guides decision and action.

Initiations of This Lifetime

Badger awakens during periods of boundary challenge, perseverance testing, or reclamation of personal power.

Badger activates when the soul commits to standing firm, trusting instinct, and protecting what matters.

Mustelid Variations: Current Life Expression

European Badger

European Badger reflects community-rooted resilience; the soul engages cooperation, territory stewardship, and long-term dwelling. European folklore honors this badger as a symbol of persistence, protection, and deep connection to the land.

American Badger

American Badger reflects solitary strength and assertive independence; the soul engages self-reliance, decisive action, and boundary enforcement. Indigenous North American traditions recognize this badger as a powerful earth warrior and protector.

Honey Badger

Honey Badger reflects fearless adaptability and audacity; the soul engages bold survival, resource acquisition, and unconventional strategy. African traditions view this badger as a symbol of courage, cleverness, and unstoppable will.

Bat Totem

Core Totem Essence

The bat has the soul memory of navigation through darkness guided by inner sensing. This totem lives through attunement, rebirth cycles, and mastery of unseen pathways. Across Mesoamerica, China, Africa, Europe, and island cultures worldwide, the bat appears as a guardian of caves and thresholds, a bringer of renewal, and a keeper of night wisdom. Bat medicine centers on perception beyond sight, transformation through descent and return, and protection of liminal space where change takes form.

Strengths of the Totem

Bat brings refined inner sensing; awareness travels through vibration, sound, and subtle cues.

Bat has mastery of transition; endings open into renewal with clarity and grace.

Bat embodies adaptability; movement responds fluidly to shifting conditions and environments.

Bats have communal intelligence; coordination and shared rhythm support survival and success.

Bat protects thresholds; caves, dreams, and inner worlds remain safe passages for change.

Challenges of the Totem

Bat lives through heightened sensitivity; grounding through body and breath has ease.

Bat moves within cycles of descent and return; integration in insight into daily life.

Bat values privacy and shelter; selective visibility strengthens stability and trust.

Bat navigates complex sensory fields; rest restores balance and precision.

Past Life Lessons Carried Forward

Bat has learned renewal through release; transformation unfolds through surrender and return.

Bat has learned perception beyond sight; inner knowing guides safe passage.

Bat has learned communal rhythm; coordination amplifies strength.

Bat has learned guardianship of liminal space; thresholds remain sacred and protected.

Recurring Patterns Across Lifetimes

Bat souls often appear as healers, psychopomps, dream workers, navigators of change, or guardians of sacred sites.

Bat souls move comfortably through transition; crisis becomes a gateway to growth.

Bat souls sense unseen currents; guidance arises from inner attunement.

Initiations of This Lifetime

Bat awakens during periods of major change, identity renewal, grief integration, or spiritual initiation.

Bat activates when the soul trusts inner sensing, honors cycles, and moves confidently through the unknown.

Chiropteran Variations: Current Life Expression

Fruit Bat

Fruit Bat reflects abundance and regeneration; the soul engages nourishment, pollination, and restoration of life systems. Tropical cultures honor the fruit bat as a seed carrier and a partner in forest renewal.

Vampire Bat

Vampire Bat reflects reciprocal care and survival through sharing; the soul engages mutual support, trust, and social bonding. Mesoamerican traditions associate the bat with underworld passage, rebirth, and sacred exchange.

Little Brown Bat

Little Brown Bat reflects precision and efficiency; the soul engages focused perception, consistency, and reliable navigation within familiar territory.

Flying Fox

Flying Fox reflects expansive movement and community visibility; the soul engages leadership within large groups and stewardship of wide ranges. Island cultures recognize the flying fox as a guardian of canopy pathways and night skies.

Horseshoe Bat

Horseshoe Bat reflects refined sensing and cave guardianship; the soul engages protection of sacred interiors and mastery of echo-based navigation. East Asian traditions associate the bat with good fortune, longevity, and blessings through sound.

Bear Totem

Core Totem Essence

Bear has the soul memory of embodied wisdom. This totem moves through cycles of action and retreat with deliberate presence. Across cultures where bears live alongside humans, people recognize bears as keepers of medicine, a walker between worlds, and a guardian of life force. Bear medicine emphasizes timing, body knowing, and the authority that grows through lived experience.

Strengths of the Totem

Bear brings profound physical and spiritual endurance; this soul knows how to survive, heal, and remain present through long cycles.

Bear holds grounded authority; leadership flows from steadiness, patience, and lived knowledge instead of display.

Bear has healing intelligence; many cultures recognize bear as a teacher of herbal medicine, bone setting, and restorative rest.

Bear honors sacred timing; this totem understands when to act, when to gather, and when to withdraw for renewal.

Bear protects life fiercely; devotion to family, lineage, students, or community flows naturally through this soul.

Challenges of the Totem

Bear lives with immense internal power; this power demands conscious regulation and respect for rhythm.

Bear experiences deep emotional currents; feelings move strongly through the body and shape behavior.

Bear values sovereignty; this creates tension when environments demand constant accessibility or speed.

Bear has ancestral responsibility; the weight of care, protection, and continuity can press heavily across lifetimes.

Past Life Lessons Carried Forward

Bear has learned the sacred role of rest as medicine; withdrawal restores strength and wisdom.

Bear has learned the consequences of power; protection requires discernment and restraint.

Bear has learned devotion to lineage; care for the young, the sick, and the land shapes soul memory.

Bear has learned how healing flows through the body; wisdom lives in bone, breath, and movement.

Recurring Patterns Across Lifetimes

Bear souls often appear as healers, protectors, elders, guardians, teachers, or land stewards.

Bear souls frequently carry responsibility early in life; others lean on their stability.

Bear souls cycle between visibility and retreat; periods of solitude renew clarity and strength.

Initiations of This Lifetime

Bear awakens during times of healing, boundary formation, leadership consolidation, or ancestral repair.

Bear activates when the soul must slow, listen to the body, and reclaim authority rooted in lived truth.

Bear Variations; Current Life Expression

Polar Bear

Polar Bear reflects profound solitude and mastery within vast inner landscapes. This variation appears when the soul navigates isolation with clarity of purpose and calm authority. Polar Bear has expert movement through emotional waters; feeling runs deep, steady, and controlled beneath a composed surface. This being locates nourishment and meaning where none appears to exist, drawing sustenance from intuition, patience, and spiritual perception. Strength arises through endurance in extreme conditions, with adversity shaping resilience instead of diminishing power. Polar Bear communicates readily with spirit realms and walks as a creature of dreamers, vision holders, and deep inner travelers. Leadership emerges quietly through presence alone, offering unwavering direction, emotional steadiness, and spiritual clarity amid cold or sparse terrain.

Brown Bear

Brown Bear reflects active guardianship expressed through steady presence and practical leadership. This variation appears when the soul engages family systems, community protection, and responsibility rooted in land, routine, and daily survival. Brown Bear has grounded confidence, balancing strength with approachability and authority with care. Across European, Asian, and Northern Indigenous cultures, Brown Bear stands as a protector of hearth, forest, and kin, teaching leadership through reliability, provision, and visible stewardship. This energy emphasizes strength used in service, boundaries maintained through consistency, and protection offered through calm, enduring commitment.

Black Bear

Black Bear reflects inner work guided by self-trust, intuition, and careful navigation of personal territory. This variation appears when the soul moves through cycles of approach and retreat with awareness, honoring instinct as the primary guide. Black Bear teaches comfort with solitude balanced by selective connection, emphasizing adaptability, curiosity, and quiet intelligence. Across Indigenous cultures of North America, Black Bear appears as a teacher of introspection, plant knowledge, and personal medicine, guiding individuals to listen inward, protect inner resources, and engage the world thoughtfully instead of forcefully.

Grizzly Bear

Grizzly Bear reflects embodied strength, instinctive leadership, and grounded authority expressed through presence instead of display. This variation appears when the soul occupies space fully, protects what matters, and acts with emotional honesty guided by deep body wisdom. Grizzly Bear teaches boundary clarity, courage in confrontation, and decisive action rooted in loyalty to land, kin, and truth. Across Indigenous cultures of North America, Grizzly Bear stands as a warrior elder and medicine carrier, holding healing knowledge drawn from earth and lived experience. Leadership emerges through visible power balanced with sensitivity, shaping environments through calm dominance, protection, and unwavering resolve.

Panda Bear

Panda Bear reflects gentle power centered in peace, nourishment, and selective focus. This variation appears when the soul engages simplicity, balance, and devotion to what truly sustains life. In Chinese cultural understanding, the panda embodies harmony, diplomacy, and the strength of softness aligned with moral clarity. This expression emphasizes conservation of energy, discernment around where effort flows, and leadership expressed through calm presence instead of force.

Beaver Totem

Core Totem Essence

Beaver has the soul memory of sacred construction. This totem shapes the environment through intention, cooperation, and patient labor. Across Indigenous North American river cultures, European waterway traditions, and boreal forest peoples, the beaver appears as a master builder, a keeper of water law, and a steward of balance between land and flow. Beaver medicine centers on creation through effort, prosperity through planning, and community sustained by shared work.

Strengths of the Totem

Beaver brings constructive intelligence; vision turns into form through steady action.

Beaver has environmental mastery; land and water respond to thoughtful shaping and care.

Beaver embodies perseverance; long projects unfold through patience and consistency.

Beaver has cooperative success; shared labor strengthens bonds and outcomes.

Beaver protects home and kin; safety grows through preparation and maintenance.

Challenges of the Totem

Beaver lives with a strong drive to build; rest and pleasure support sustainable creation.

Beaver values structure and order; adaptability has harmony within change.

Beaver commits deeply to responsibility; delegation and trust strengthen longevity.

Beaver invests heavily in outcome; flexibility has resilience when plans evolve.

Past Life Lessons Carried Forward

Beaver has learned creation as devotion; work becomes prayer when guided by care.

Beaver has learned prosperity through stewardship; tending resources multiplies abundance.

Beaver has learned protection through preparation; foresight has safety and continuity.

Beaver has learned balance between effort and flow; water teaches release alongside structure.

Recurring Patterns Across Lifetimes

Beaver souls often appear as builders, organizers, planners, providers, or community architects.

Beaver souls anchor families and projects; others rely on their reliability and vision.

Beaver souls shape environments; homes, systems, and communities transform through their presence.

Initiations of This Lifetime

Beaver awakens during periods of home creation, community development, or long-term project building.

Beaver activates when the soul commits to shaping life through deliberate effort and cooperative care.

Bee Totem

Core Totem Essence

Bee has the soul memory of sacred labor, purposeful creation, and harmony born through shared effort. This totem lives through devotion to meaning, teaching how work aligned with intention generates sweetness, stability, and continuity. Across ancient Egyptian cosmology, Greek myth, Celtic lore, and Indigenous European land traditions, the bee appears as a messenger between worlds, a keeper of order, and a symbol of prosperity earned through cooperation. Bee medicine centers on contribution with purpose, balance between individuality and community, and the understanding that creation thrives through rhythm and devotion.

Strengths of the Totem

Bee brings devotion to meaningful work; effort aligns with soul purpose.

Bee has collective intelligence; cooperation multiplies strength and outcome.

Bee embodies productivity guided by rhythm; consistency sustains abundance.

Bee has prosperity through creation; sweetness emerges from aligned labor.

Bee has spiritual communication; movement between realms feels natural and guided.

Challenges of the Totem

Bee lives within a strong drive to contribute; rest preserves vitality and clarity.

Bee commits deeply to service; self-nourishment strengthens longevity.

Bee values harmony within the group; personal voice enriches the collective outcome.

Bee follows established rhythm; creative expansion broadens expression.

Past Life Lessons Carried Forward

Bee has learned abundance through service; contribution generates prosperity.

Bee has learned harmony through cooperation; unity stabilizes creation.

Bee has learned mastery through repetition; devotion refines skill.Bee has learned joy through effort; work has sweetness.

Recurring Patterns Across Lifetimes

Bee souls often appear as builders, organizers, healers, artisans, community leaders, or culture keepers.

Bee souls strengthen systems through steady contribution; others benefit from their reliability.

Bee souls value purpose-driven creation; fulfillment flows through meaningful effort.

Initiations of This Lifetime

Bee awakens during periods of vocation alignment, community responsibility, or desire to create lasting impact.

Bee activates when the soul commits to purpose, honors rhythm, and finds joy in contribution.

Bee Variations; Current Life Expression

Honey Bee

Honey Bee reflects sacred cooperation and shared abundance; the soul engages teamwork, devotion, and creation that nourishes many. Ancient Egyptian tradition honored the honey bee as a symbol of divine order, kingship, and harmony between worlds.

Carpenter Bee

Carpenter Bee reflects structural intelligence and independent craftsmanship; the soul engages in building, shaping the environment, and transforming raw material into stability. This variation emphasizes creation through focused effort and personal responsibility.

Queen Bee

Queen Bee reflects central purpose and generative authority; the soul engages leadership through presence, continuity through creation, and guidance through being instead of doing. This expression emphasizes the fertility of ideas, the anchoring of the community, and the responsibility through the embodiment of the role.

Bumble Bee

Bumble Bee reflects joyful diligence and wholehearted effort; the soul engages enthusiasm, warmth, and persistence guided by love of the work itself. This variation emphasizes emotional resilience and success driven by sincerity instead of force.

Beetle Totem

Core Totem Essence

Beetle has the soul memory of endurance, transformation through steady effort, and quiet strength rooted in earth wisdom. This totem thrives in soil, bark, leaf, and shadow, teaching how resilience, patience, and practical labor create lasting stability. Across Egyptian, African, European, Mesoamerican, and Asian traditions, beetles appear as symbols of protection, persistence, and renewal. Their hard shell and methodical movement reflect self-contained power and grounded determination. Beetle medicine centers on steadfast progress, natural armor, and the ability to shape life slowly and securely through daily action.

Strengths of the Totem

Beetle brings durability; body and spirit withstand pressure with ease.

Beetle has patient focus; small, consistent actions build lasting results.

Beetle embodies self-protection; boundaries remain strong and healthy.

Beetles have adaptability; diverse environments become home quickly.

Beetle has transformation; decay turns into fertile new growth.

Challenges of the Totem

Beetle lives through a steady routine; creative variation refreshes inspiration.

Beetle values self-containment; connection enriches shared strength.

Beetle moves deliberately; openness to speed enhances opportunity.

Beetle has strong independence; cooperation expands influence.

Past Life Lessons Carried Forward

Beetle has learned survival through resilience; persistence ensures continuity.

Beetle has learned strength through preparation; armor protects life force.

Beetle has learned renewal through earth cycles; endings nourish beginnings.

Beetle has learned mastery through repetition; daily practice creates destiny.

Recurring Patterns Across Lifetimes

Beetle souls often appear as builders, craftsmen, farmers, caretakers of land, engineers, or those who work quietly behind the scenes to stabilize systems.

Beetle souls create foundations others rely upon; their presence brings structure and reliability.

Beetle souls value practicality and sustainability; life organizes around steady progress.

Initiations of This Lifetime

Beetle awakens during periods of building security, tending land, repairing foundations, or committing to long-term projects.

Beetle activates when the soul embraces patience, strengthens boundaries, and trusts the power of consistent effort.

BETA FIGHTING FISH TOTEM

Core Totem Essence

Fighting Fish has the soul memory of territorial clarity, emotional intensity, and sovereignty expressed through presence instead of size. Known most commonly through the Siamese fighting fish within Southeast Asian waters, this totem lives through boundary awareness, self-definition, and the courage to hold space unapologetically. Fighting Fish medicine centers on knowing where one's energy belongs, defending personal territory with precision, and expressing identity boldly even within confined environments.

Strengths of the Totem

Fighting Fish brings clear territorial intelligence; personal space and energetic boundary remain unmistakable.

Fighting Fish has vivid self-expression; color, movement, and posture communicate truth and confidence.

Fighting Fish embodies emotional intensity refined into focus; feeling sharpens awareness and resolve.

Fighting Fish has sovereignty; independence strengthens identity and self-respect.

Fighting Fish maintains resilience within constraint; limited space still has full expression.

Challenges of the Totem

Fighting Fish lives with a heightened emotional charge; grounding has balance and regulation.

Fighting Fish values solitude and control of space; selective interaction strengthens harmony.

Fighting Fish responds quickly to intrusion; discernment refines reaction into mastery.

Fighting Fish has a strong self-identity; flexibility has coexistence without dilution.

Past Life Lessons Carried Forward

Fighting Fish has learned survival through boundary clarity; space protects vitality.

Fighting Fish has learned strength through self-expression; visibility asserts presence.

Fighting Fish has learned authority through containment; power concentrates within form.

Fighting Fish has learned courage through stillness; readiness replaces constant action.

Recurring Patterns Across Lifetimes

Fighting Fish souls often appear as boundary keepers, solo leaders, artists of identity, or protectors of personal domain.

Fighting Fish souls thrive in environments requiring self-definition; presence reshapes space immediately.

Fighting Fish souls teach sovereignty; self-respect establishes order.

Initiations of This Lifetime

Fighting Fish awakens during periods of boundary enforcement, identity assertion, or reclamation of personal power.

Fighting Fish activates when the soul honors its space, expresses itself fully, and defends dignity through presence instead of excess force.

Boar and Pig Totem

Core Totem Essence

Boar has the soul memory of sacred abundance made with courage. This totem moves through the earth and the root with strength, appetite, and unapologetic vitality. Across Celtic Europe, the Mediterranean, East Asia, and Indigenous agrarian cultures worldwide, people recognize the boar as a symbol of fertility, wealth, protection, and life-sustaining power. Boar medicine centers on embodiment, nourishment, fearless engagement with life, and prosperity earned through presence and effort.

Strengths of the Totem

Boar brings grounded vitality; life force flows strongly through body, appetite, and instinct.

Boar has fearless engagement; obstacles meet direct action and persistence.

Boar embodies abundance consciousness; nourishment, pleasure, and material stability align naturally.

Boars protect what they love; devotion expresses itself through fierce loyalty and defense.Boar honor earth wisdom; roots, soil, and physical reality remain sacred teachers.

Challenges of the Totem

Boars live with powerful instinctual drive; discernment creates direction and pacing.

Boar has a strong appetite for life; balance has sustainable satisfaction.

Boars engage confrontation readily; strategy refines effort and impact.

Boar value material security; trust allows flow instead of accumulation alone.

Past Life Lessons Carried Forward

Boars have learned courage through embodiment; standing ground sustains life and lineage.

Boars have learned prosperity through a relationship with the land; tending the earth yields abundance.

Boars have learned pleasure as sacred; enjoyment strengthens resilience and joy.

Boars have learned protection of kin; defense arises from devotion and care.

Recurring Patterns Across Lifetimes

Boar souls often appear as providers, warriors, farmers, builders, guardians, or keepers of resources.

Boar souls value physical presence; hands-on work and tangible results bring fulfillment.

Boar souls anchor communities; nourishment and protection flow through their efforts.

Initiations of This Lifetime

Boars awaken during periods of survival challenge, prosperity building, or boundary defense.

Boar activates when the soul claims the right to abundance, pleasure, and embodied power.

Suine Variations; Current Life Expression

Wild Boar

Wild Boar reflects fierce courage and territorial defense; the soul engages confrontation, protection of land, and assertion of presence. In Celtic cultures, wild boar symbolizes warrior strength, sacred courage, and the blessing of abundance earned through bravery.

Domestic Pig

Domestic Pig reflects nourishment, fertility, and communal wealth; the soul engages provision, comfort, and prosperity shared within the family or village. In East Asian traditions, the pig aligns with good fortune, honesty, and material blessings.

Warthog

Warthog reflects resilience and adaptability; the soul engages survival through humor, persistence, and unconventional strength. African traditions view the warthog as a symbol of tenacity and grounded endurance.

Forest Hog

Forest Hog reflects deep earth connection; the soul engages hidden abundance, root wisdom, and power drawn from dense environments. This expression emphasizes the strength that grows beneath surface visibility.

Buffalo Totem

Core Totem Essence

Buffalo has the soul memory of sacred abundance joined with collective survival. This totem lives through generosity, endurance, and reverence for life as a shared covenant. Across the Plains nations of North America and other pastoral cultures that honor great herd beings, buffalo appears as a provider, a spiritual elder, and a living embodiment of reciprocity between people, land, and spirit. Buffalo medicine centers on gratitude, communal responsibility, and prosperity that flows through respect and balance.

Strengths of the Totem

Buffalo brings profound abundance; nourishment, shelter, and resources flow through presence and stewardship.

Buffalo has immense endurance; steady movement sustains life through harsh conditions.

Buffalo embodies communal intelligence; survival strengthens through unity and shared rhythm.

Buffalo has spiritual reverence; gratitude creates the relationship with life and land.

Buffalo has grounded power; strength expresses itself through calm persistence instead of urgency.

Challenges of the Totem

Buffalo lives with great responsibility; replenishment through ceremony and rest sustains vitality.

Buffalo has collective weight; personal needs gain clarity through intentional self-care.

Buffalo values tradition deeply; adaptation has continuity across changing times.

Buffalo has deliberate pace; responsiveness strengthens alignment with present conditions.

Past Life Lessons Carried Forward

Buffalo has learned abundance through reciprocity; giving and receiving remain balanced.

Buffalo has learned survival through unity; community preserves life.

Buffalo has learned reverence as law; respect maintains harmony between worlds.

Buffalo has learned endurance as devotion; persistence honors purpose.

Recurring Patterns Across Lifetimes

Buffalo souls often appear as providers, elders, spiritual leaders, community anchors, or protectors of tradition.

Buffalo souls sustain many lives; their presence stabilizes families and cultures.

Buffalo souls value ceremony and gratitude; meaning infuses daily life and labor.

Initiations of This Lifetime

Buffalo awakens during periods of service, cultural restoration, leadership rooted in care, or reclamation of a sacred relationship with land.

Buffalo activates when the soul chooses generosity, endurance, and reverence as guiding forces.

Bovine Variations: Current Life Expression

Plains Buffalo

Plains Buffalo reflects sacred provision and spiritual covenant; the soul engages stewardship, gratitude, and responsibility to community and land. Plains Indigenous nations honor buffalo as a relative who offers life through reciprocal respect.

Water Buffalo

Water Buffalo reflects communal labor and agricultural abundance; the soul engages cooperation, strength, and prosperity created by shared effort. Asian cultures honor the water buffalo as a cornerstone of village life and ritual continuity.

Bull and Cow Totem

Core Totem Essence

Bull has the soul memory of sacred sustenance and embodied strength. This totem lives through nourishment, fertility, labor, and the quiet power that sustains civilizations. Across South Asia, the ancient Near East, Africa, the Mediterranean, and pastoral cultures worldwide, bulls appear as life givers, symbols of prosperity, cosmic order, and the disciplined force that makes survival possible. Bull medicine centers on provision, responsibility, and power expressed through steadiness instead of impulse.

Strengths of the Totem

Bull brings life-sustaining abundance; nourishment flows through body, land, and relationship.

Bull has grounded strength; endurance has long cycles of work and care.

Bull embodies fertility and creation; life multiplies through patience and stewardship.

Bull has reliability; others depend on their consistency and presence.

Bull anchor sacred labor; effort aligns with purpose, ritual, and continuity.

Challenges of the Totem

Bull lives with heavy responsibility; replenishment has vitality and longevity.

Bull has immense physical and emotional power; conscious direction refines expression.

Bull value stability; adaptation invites flexibility within tradition.

Bull holds strong instinctual drives; regulation has harmony and safety.

Past Life Lessons Carried Forward

Bulls have learned provision as a sacred duty; feeding others preserves life and lineage.

Bulls have learned power through restraint; strength serves continuity instead of domination.

Bulls have learned fertility as stewardship; abundance grows through care and rhythm.

Bulls have learned devotion to land; soil, herd, and people form one living system.

Recurring Patterns Across Lifetimes

Bull souls often appear as providers, farmers, builders, guardians, parents, or cultural anchors.

Bull souls sustain systems; families, economies, and traditions rely on their effort.

Bull souls carry visible responsibility; others look to them for stability and support.

Initiations of This Lifetime

Bulls awaken during periods of family building, resource stewardship, leadership through labor, or reclamation of embodied strength.

Bulls activate when the soul accepts responsibility for nourishment, protection, and continuity.

Bovine Variations: Current Life Expression

Cow

Cow reflects nurturing abundance and maternal continuity; the soul engages care, nourishment, patience, and sacred provision. In South Asian traditions, the cow represents life itself, moral order, generosity, and the sacred bond between humans and sustenance.

Bull

Bull reflects generative force and disciplined power; the soul engages strength, virility, protection, and purposeful action. In ancient Mesopotamian, Mediterranean, and Indus Valley cultures, the bull aligns with kingship, storm power, fertility, and cosmic vitality.

Zebu

Zebu reflects adaptation and heat mastery; the soul engages survival, resource management, and endurance within demanding environments. African and South Asian pastoral cultures honor zebu as a symbol of wealth, status, and resilience.

Butterfly Totem

Core Totem Essence

Butterfly has the soul memory of transformation through grace and timing. This totem lives through metamorphosis, beauty born from patience, and movement guided by unseen currents. Across Mesoamerica, Ancient Greece, Indigenous North American cultures, Asia, and African traditions, the butterfly appears as a symbol of the soul, rebirth, ancestral presence, and the continuity of life beyond form. Butterfly medicine centers on change embraced consciously, lightness that follows deep work, and the ability to move between states of being with elegance.

Strengths of the Totem

Butterfly brings mastery of transformation; identity evolves through clear stages guided by inner readiness.

Butterfly has soul awareness; spirit remains present through change, loss, and renewal.

Butterfly embodies grace in motion; movement reflects trust in timing instead of force.

Butterfly has beauty through authenticity; presence uplifts environments and relationships.

Butterfly navigates impermanence with wisdom; attachment softens while meaning deepens.

Challenges of the Totem

Butterfly lives through frequent change; grounding has the integration of each stage.

Butterfly moves lightly between experiences; depth strengthens continuity and fulfillment.

Butterfly responds strongly to subtle influence; discernment guides energetic engagement.

Butterfly completes cycles rapidly; rest in transformation into embodiment.

Past Life Lessons Carried Forward

Butterfly has learned renewal through surrender; release opens new form and expression.

Butterfly has learned the soul endures; essence travels beyond physical transition.

Butterfly has learned beauty follows patience; incubation precedes flight.

Butterfly has learned to trust in becoming; timing reveals itself through stillness and emergence.

Recurring Patterns Across Lifetimes

Butterfly souls often appear as artists, healers, messengers, spiritual initiates, or guides through transition.

Butterfly souls experience multiple rebirths; identity reshapes through life phases.

Butterfly souls bring hope and uplift; presence signals change aligned with growth.

Initiations of This Lifetime

Butterfly awakens during periods of identity shift, spiritual awakening, grief integration, or creative emergence.

Butterfly activates when the soul releases old form, honors the cocoon stage, and trusts flight.

Lepidopteran Variations: Current Life Expression

Monarch Butterfly

Monarch reflects ancestral migration and soul continuity; the soul engages long journeys guided by inherited memory. Mesoamerican cultures associate monarchs with returning ancestors and the sacred cycle of life and death.

Swallowtail Butterfly

Swallowtail reflects expansion and confident emergence; the soul engages visibility, creativity, and leadership following transformation. East Asian traditions associate swallowtails with prosperity and joyful change.

Blue Morpho Butterfly

Blue Morpho reflects revelation through beauty; the soul engages sudden insight, spiritual illumination, and recognition of inner brilliance. Amazonian cultures view this butterfly as a sign of spirit presence and transformation completed.

Painted Lady Butterfly

Painted Lady reflects adaptability and global movement; the soul engages resilience, travel, and renewal across varied environments. This expression emphasizes survival through flexibility and trust.

White Butterfly

White Butterfly reflects purity of transition and ancestral visitation; the soul engages spiritual messaging, gentle guidance, and reassurance during change. Many European and Indigenous traditions regard white butterflies as messengers of loved ones and spirit allies.

Camel Totem

Core Totem Essence

Camel has the soul memory of endurance guided by inner reserves, survival through preparation, and dignity sustained across vast and demanding terrain. This totem lives where heat, distance, and scarcity shape character, teaching how patience, conservation, and foresight transform hardship into mastery. Across Bedouin, Tuareg, Berber, Arabian, North African, and Central Asian cultures, the camel stands as a companion, lifeline, and wealth bearer. Entire civilizations travel and trade through their strength.

Camel medicine centers on self-sufficiency, sacred pacing, and the wisdom of carrying exactly what the journey requires.

Strengths of the Totem

Camel brings exceptional endurance; strength sustains itself across long distances and time.

Camel has powerful resource management; energy and supply remain carefully conserved.

Camel embodies patience; progress unfolds steadily without urgency.

Camel has reliability; others trust presence during difficult passage.

Camel has navigation through barren terrain; clarity arises even when guidance appears sparse.

Challenges of the Totem

Camel lives within extended responsibility; shared support enhances longevity.

Camel values self-reliance deeply; openness strengthens connection and exchange.

Camel has heavy loads; intentional release preserves balance and freedom.

Camel has a deliberate pace; flexibility has responsiveness during change.

Past Life Lessons Carried Forward

Camel has learned survival through preparation; foresight preserves life.

Camel has learned strength through conservation; wise pacing sustains vitality.

Camel has learned dignity through service; carrying others holds sacred meaning.

Camel has learned trust in the long path; endurance fulfills destiny.

Recurring Patterns Across Lifetimes

Camel souls often appear as guides, traders, providers, healers in harsh environments, or those who support others through long transitions.

Camel souls stabilize journeys; groups reach safety through their reliability.

Camel souls value sustainability and minimalism; life organizes around what truly matters.

Initiations of This Lifetime

Camel awakens during periods of extended effort, migration, rebuilding from scarcity, or learning to conserve emotional and physical energy.

Camel activates when the soul prepares wisely, travels steadily, and trusts its inner reserves.

Camelid Variations: Current Life Expression

Dromedary Camel

Dromedary reflects focused endurance and streamlined strength; the soul engages swift, efficient travel across open terrain. Middle Eastern and North African cultures honor this camel as the ship of the desert and a symbol of wealth, trade, and survival.

Bactrian Camel

Bactrian reflects resilience through extremes; the soul engages adaptability within cold and heat, scarcity and abundance. Central Asian traditions associate this camel with steadfastness and strength through varied climates.

Wild Camel

Wild Camel reflects independence and ancestral survival intelligence; the soul engages instinctive navigation, self-trust, and endurance created by untamed landscapes.

Chameleon Totem

Core Totem Essence

Chameleon has the soul memory of adaptive awareness, perception sharpened through stillness, and transformation guided by environment instead of force. This totem lives through observation before movement, teaching how survival and mastery arise through attunement, patience, and precise response. Across African, Malagasy, and Mediterranean traditions, the chameleon appears as a keeper of messages between worlds, a symbol of time, and a teacher of subtlety. In several African cosmologies, the chameleon has divine communication and the power to shift reality through timing.

Chameleon medicine centers on energetic camouflage, emotional regulation, and the wisdom of blending without losing identity.

Strengths of the Totem

Chameleon brings exceptional perception; subtle shifts register immediately.

Chameleon has adaptive intelligence; form and behavior adjust fluidly to circumstance.

Chameleon embodies patience; stillness sharpens accuracy and power.

Chameleon has strategic invisibility; presence moves unseen until action serves best.

Chameleon has independent sovereignty; identity remains steady within change.

Challenges of the Totem

Chameleon lives through constant environmental attunement; self-anchoring strengthens clarity.

Chameleon adapts easily to others; authentic expression deepens connection.

Chameleon values concealment and watchfulness; trust has openness when safety arises.

Chameleon acts with precision; integration has emotional flow after action.

Past Life Lessons Carried Forward

Chameleon has learned survival through observation; seeing precedes movement.

Chameleon has learned strength through adaptation; flexibility preserves life.

Chameleon has learned timing as sacred law; the right moment determines success.

Chameleon has learned identity within change; essence remains constant through shifting form.

Recurring Patterns Across Lifetimes

Chameleon souls often appear as diplomats, strategists, spies, healers, performers, or those who navigate many social or cultural worlds with ease.

Chameleon souls blend into systems effortlessly; environments adjust around their presence.

Chameleon souls value subtle influence; quiet shifts create lasting transformation.

Initiations of This Lifetime

Chameleon awakens during periods requiring discretion, adaptation, cultural navigation, or identity refinement.

Chameleon activates when the soul observes deeply, adjusts wisely, and moves with exact timing.

CAPYBARA AND GUINEA PIG TOTEM

Core Totem Essence

Capybara has the soul memory of social harmony rooted in calm presence. This totem lives through ease, cooperation, and emotional steadiness, moving between land and water without friction. Across Indigenous cultures of South America, the capybara appears as a being of peaceful coexistence, communal balance, and adaptive belonging. Capybara medicine centers on relational safety, nervous system regulation, and the power of gentleness that stabilizes groups.

Strengths of the Totem

Capybara brings emotional equilibrium; calm presence settles environments and people alike.

Capybara has social intelligence; group dynamics organize naturally around cooperation and shared comfort.

Capybara embodies adaptability; movement between elements has resilience and ease.

Capybara has inclusivity; diverse beings gather safely within its field.

Capybara has nervous system regulation; steadiness restores rhythm and trust.

Challenges of the Totem

Capybara lives through openness and receptivity; discernment has energetic boundaries.

Capybara values harmony deeply; direct expression of personal need makes for a conscious voice.

Capybara prioritizes group well-being; self-direction strengthens long-term balance.

Capybara moves gently through life; assertive action develops through clarity and timing.

Past Life Lessons Carried Forward

Capybara has learned peace as strength; calm presence resolves tension.

Capybara has learned survival through cooperation; shared space sustains life.

Capybara has learned adaptability through trust; change flows without resistance.

Capybara has learned safety through attunement; awareness maintains balance.

Recurring Patterns Across Lifetimes

Capybara souls often appear as mediators, caregivers, counselors, community anchors, or peacekeepers.

Capybara souls create safe environments; others relax and stabilize in their presence.

Capybara souls value shared living; community and companionship shape fulfillment.

Initiations of This Lifetime

Capybara awakens during periods of social repair, nervous system healing, or community rebuilding.

Capybara activates when the soul learns that softness has authority and calm creates survival.

Caviomorph Variations: Current Life Expression

Capybara

Capybara reflects communal harmony and emotional regulation; the soul engages peace building, inclusivity, and steady presence. Indigenous peoples of the Amazon and Orinoco regions recognize the capybara as a being of balance, coexistence, and gentle strength within shared ecosystems.

Guinea Pig

Guinea Pig reflects domestic contribution and ritual nourishment; the soul engages care, sustenance, and community ritual. Andean cultures honor the guinea pig as a sacred food animal connected to healing, ceremony, and household well-being.

Mara

Mara reflects partnership and coordinated movement; the soul engages paired devotion, mutual vigilance, and shared territory. South American grassland cultures observe mara as a symbol of cooperative endurance and relational trust.

Cardinal Totem

Core Totem Essence

Cardinal has the soul memory of vitality expressed through color, devotion made with partnership, and presence that brightens the landscape even during cold seasons. This totem lives as a spark of life within stillness, teaching how courage, faithfulness, and a clear voice sustain hope across cycles. Across Indigenous North American traditions, Appalachian and Southern folklore, and Christian and folk symbolism, the cardinal appears as a messenger of spirit, a keeper of hearth warmth, and a sign that loved ones remain near. Cardinal medicine centers on heart-centered leadership, loyalty, and the strength to stand visibly in your own truth.

Strengths of the Totem

Cardinal brings vibrant life force; energy uplifts people and places instantly.

Cardinal has unwavering loyalty; partnership and family bonds strengthen through devotion.

Cardinal embodies confident visibility; color and presence communicate truth clearly.

Cardinal has melodic communication; song restores morale and emotional clarity.

Cardinal has year-round resilience; vitality remains strong through harsh seasons.

Challenges of the Totem

Cardinal lives with a strong territorial instinct; discernment guides sharing of space.

Cardinal values partnership deeply; independence has balance within connection.

Cardinal expresses boldly; listening deepens harmony and mutual understanding.

Cardinal has constant heart energy; replenishment sustains warmth and clarity.

Past Life Lessons Carried Forward

Cardinal has learned love through loyalty; devotion preserves a relationship across time.

Cardinal has learned courage through visibility; authentic presence strengthens community.

Cardinal has learned voice as medicine; song heals and guides.

Cardinal has learned resilience through winter; life continues through faith and persistence.

Recurring Patterns Across Lifetimes

Cardinal souls often appear as partners, singers, teachers, morale keepers, or spiritual messengers within family systems.

Cardinal souls brighten environments; hope rises through their presence.

Cardinal souls value fidelity and sincerity; relationships form the center of life's purpose.

Initiations of This Lifetime

Cardinal awakens during periods of heart healing, commitment to partnership, reclaiming voice, or serving as a messenger for loved ones or spirit.

Cardinal activates when the soul stands visibly in truth, sings clearly, and leads through warmth and devotion.

Carp Totem

Core Totem Essence

Carp has the soul memory of perseverance rewarded through transformation and honor. This totem lives through steady effort, patience, and the refinement of strength over time. Across Chinese, Japanese, Korean, and broader East Asian traditions, carp appear as a symbol of determination, prosperity earned through endurance, and ascension through commitment to a chosen path. Carp medicine centers on persistence within challenge, cultivation of inner strength, and the promise that sustained effort reshapes destiny.

Strengths of the Totem

Carp brings unwavering perseverance; steady movement continues regardless of obstacles.

Carp has disciplined patience; time becomes an ally instead of a burden.

Carp embodies transformative potential; effort refines power into mastery.

Carp has prosperity through diligence; success grows from consistency and preparation.

Carp navigates turbulent current; resilience stabilizes progress and direction.

Challenges of the Totem

Carp lives through prolonged effort; replenishment through rest and reflection sustains vitality.

Carp commits deeply to ascent; flexibility has adaptation within the climb.

Carp values endurance strongly; joy expands motivation and balance.

Carp moves methodically; responsiveness enhances opportunity along the way.

Past Life Lessons Carried Forward

Carp has learned ascension through perseverance; commitment reshapes fate.

Carp has learned strength through repetition; effort refines capability.

Carp has learned prosperity through discipline; consistency multiplies reward.

Carp has learned honor through completion; arriving at the destination justifies every step of the effort.

Recurring Patterns Across Lifetimes

Carp souls often appear as climbers of systems, long-term builders, students who become masters, or leaders forged through effort.

Carp souls rise through persistence; others recognize earned authority.

Carp souls value progress through merit; dedication creates identity and purpose.

Initiations of This Lifetime

Carp awakens during periods of long challenge, vocational ascent, or commitment to mastery.

Carp activates when the soul chooses persistence, trusts gradual transformation, and continues forward despite resistance.

Cyprinid Variations: Current Life Expression

Koi

Koi reflects visible transformation and prosperity; the soul engages beauty by endurance, leadership earned through effort, and success expressed with grace. East Asian traditions honor koi as a symbol of ascension and fulfilled destiny.

River Carp

River Carp reflects resilience within changing conditions; the soul engages adaptability, patience, and strength refined by current and terrain.

Golden Carp

Golden Carp reflects abundance and recognition; the soul engages reward following perseverance and clarity of purpose. This expression emphasizes honor earned through sustained effort.

Cat Totem

Core Totem Essence

Cat has the soul memory of sovereign presence joined with subtle perception. This totem lives between worlds with ease, choosing closeness and distance through instinct and discernment. Across ancient Egypt, the Near East, Asia, Europe, and later domestic cultures worldwide, people recognize the cat as a guardian of thresholds, a keeper of mystery, and a companion who walks beside humans without surrendering autonomy. Cat medicine centers on self-possession, energetic sensitivity, and the power of quiet choice.

Strengths of the Totem

Cat brings refined awareness; subtle shifts in energy, emotion, and environment register immediately.

Cat has embodied sovereignty; autonomy expresses itself through grace, confidence, and self-trust.

Cat embodies boundary mastery; closeness and withdrawal follow inner alignment.

Cat moves through liminal space; dream, spirit, and waking reality interweave naturally.

Cat holds a protective presence; vigilance guards home, spirit, and unseen thresholds.

Challenges of the Totem

Cat lives with heightened sensitivity; energetic environments shape mood and vitality.

Cat values independence deeply; a relationship flourishes through respect and mutual choice.

Cat has a strong internal rhythm; external demands ask for conscious pacing and self-regulation.

Cat engages selective connection; trust develops through consistency and intuitive safety.

Past Life Lessons Carried Forward

Cat has learned guardianship of sacred space; home and altar hold spiritual significance.

Cat has learned power through stillness; presence alone shifts the atmosphere.

Cat has learned discernment in relationships; choice preserves dignity and balance.

Cat has learned navigation of unseen realms; spirit communication flows through intuition and dreams.

Recurring Patterns Across Lifetimes

Cat souls often appear as mystics, healers, ritual keepers, artists, or quiet observers of human systems.

Cat souls maintain personal sovereignty; they choose roles that allow autonomy and respect.

Cat souls protect thresholds; they stand watch during spiritual work, illness, or transition.

Initiations of This Lifetime

Cat awakens during periods of boundary refinement, spiritual sensitivity, or reclamation of personal space.

Cat activates when the soul honors intuition, self-possession, and quiet authority.

Feline Variations: Current Life Expression

Domestic Cat

Domestic Cat reflects companionship without submission; the soul engages in a relationship through choice, affection, and mutual respect. In ancient Egypt, the domestic cat aligned with Bastet, guardian of home, fertility, joy, and protection against spiritual and physical threat. This expression emphasizes grace, pleasure, and sacred domestic order.

Black Cat

Black Cat reflects liminal mastery and spiritual protection; the soul engages magic, threshold walking, and intuitive power. Across European folk traditions and Egyptian lineage memory, the black cat serves as a guardian of the unseen and a companion to practitioners.

White Cat

White Cat reflects clarity and spiritual sensitivity; the soul engages purification, healing presence, and emotional attunement. Many cultures associate white cats with temple spaces, blessings, and gentle guardianship.

Tabby Cat

Tabby Cat reflects ancestral continuity and adaptability; the soul has practical wisdom, survival intelligence, and ease within human environments. This expression emphasizes balance between mystery and daily life.

Catfish Totem

Core Totem Essence

Catfish has the soul memory of deep sensing, survival through perception, and nourishment drawn from shadowed places. This totem lives within murky waters and unseen channels, teaching how clarity arises through instinct instead of visibility. Across Indigenous North American river cultures, African water lore, Southeast Asian traditions, and Southern folk symbolism, catfish appears as a bottom dweller with profound awareness, a provider during scarcity, and a being who thrives where others hesitate. Catfish medicine centers on intuition sharpened by darkness, emotional endurance, and the ability to extract value, truth, and sustenance from overlooked realms.

Strengths of the Totem

Catfish brings heightened intuitive sensing; vibration, current, and subtle shift guide action.

Catfish has resilience within obscurity; survival strengthens through adaptability and patience.

Catfish embodies nourishment from depth; value emerges from places others bypass.

Catfish has emotional steadiness; calm persists despite unclear conditions.

Catfish navigates complexity with ease; murky environments become familiar terrain.

Challenges of the Totem

Catfish live within low visibility; trust in inner sensing has confidence.

Catfish values depth and concealment; selective visibility has influence and connection.

Catfish adapts continuously; intention in direction within shifting current.

Catfish holds long endurance; rest and replenishment sustain vitality.

Past Life Lessons Carried Forward

Catfish has learned survival through instinct; sensing replaces sight.

Catfish has learned nourishment through humility; abundance hides within shadow.

Catfish has learned strength through patience; waiting reveals opportunity.

Catfish has learned guidance through depth; wisdom forms below the surface.

Recurring Patterns Across Lifetimes

Catfish souls often appear as intuitives, healers, crisis navigators, providers during hardship, or keepers of unseen systems.

Catfish souls thrive during uncertainty; complexity sharpens perception.

Catfish souls stabilize environments quietly; others rely on their grounded presence.

Initiations of This Lifetime

Catfish awakens during periods of uncertainty, emotional depth work, or navigation of opaque systems.

Catfish activates when the soul trusts intuition, remains steady within obscurity, and draws nourishment from overlooked spaces.

Cecaelia Totem

Core Totem Essence

Cecaelia has the soul memory of deep sea intelligence, emotional mastery, and sovereignty expressed through fluid strength. This totem unites human awareness with octopus body wisdom, teaching how intellect, adaptability, and intuition operate together. In modern maritime folklore and mermaid mythology traditions, the cecaelia appears as a keeper of abyssal knowledge, guardian of submerged ruins, and guide through the unseen realms beneath consciousness. Symbolically, this being represents the meeting of mind and instinct, surface world and depth world. Cecaelia medicine centers on shape-shifting identity, strategic intelligence, and comfort within profound emotional and spiritual depths.

Strengths of the Totem

Cecaelia brings exceptional adaptability; the environment becomes an ally through fluid response.

Cecaelia has deep emotional intelligence; subtle currents reveal hidden truth.

Cecaelia embodies strategic thinking; many paths unfold simultaneously.

Cecaelia has independence and sovereignty; self-guidance remains strong and clear.

Cecaelia has creative problem-solving; obstacles dissolve through flexibility and innovation.

Challenges of the Totem

Cecaelia lives within intense sensitivity; grounding in clarity and direction.

Cecaelia values solitude and depth; connection strengthens shared understanding.

Cecaelia navigates multiple layers of perception; focus refines energy and intention.

Cecaelia has powerful psychic awareness; boundaries preserve vitality.

Past Life Lessons Carried Forward

Cecaelia has learned wisdom through depth; truth reveals itself beneath surface illusion.

Cecaelia has learned survival through adaptation; change becomes strength.

Cecaelia has learned sovereignty through self-trust; independence guides destiny.

Cecaelia has learned guardianship of hidden knowledge; secrets protect sacred power.

Recurring Patterns Across Lifetimes

Cecaelia souls often appear as mystics, strategists, divers, researchers, mediums, artists, or guardians of ancient knowledge.

Cecaelia souls feel drawn to water, dream states, and subconscious exploration.

Cecaelia souls value privacy and autonomy; influence flows quietly yet profoundly.

Initiations of This Lifetime

Cecaelia awakens during periods of deep emotional work, shadow integration, psychic development, or immersion into hidden systems of knowledge.

Cecaelia activates when the soul trusts its depth, moves fluidly through change, and claims sovereignty over its inner world.

Centipede Totem

Core Totem Essence

Centipede has the soul memory of instinctive action, grounded awareness, and survival through direct contact with the earth. This totem lives close to soil, stone, and root, teaching how strength develops through sensitivity to vibration and immediate response. Across African, Southeast Asian, Pacific Islander, and Indigenous forest traditions, many-legged beings appear as guardians of thresholds, warriors of the undergrowth, and protectors of hidden paths. Centipede medicine centers on decisive movement, boundary clarity, and the mastery of many coordinated parts functioning as one unified body.

Strengths of the Totem

Centipede brings rapid responsiveness; action aligns instantly with instinct.

Centipede has full body awareness; every step senses terrain and opportunity.

Centipede embodies coordinated strength; many small movements create powerful momentum.

Centipede has courage within shadowed spaces; darkness becomes familiar ground.

Centipede has territorial protection; boundaries remain clear and defended.

Challenges of the Totem

Centipede lives through heightened alertness; calm presence refines timing and precision.

Centipede values constant readiness; stillness has integration and clarity.

Centipede engages defense quickly; discernment guides proportional response.

Centipede has strong independence; cooperation expands influence when chosen intentionally.

Past Life Lessons Carried Forward

Centipede has learned survival through instinct; swift action preserves life.

Centipede has learned strength through coordination; many parts function as one body.

Centipede has learned wisdom through contact with the earth; grounding reveals truth.

Centipede has learned protection through boundaries; clarity maintains harmony.

Recurring Patterns Across Lifetimes

Centipede souls often appear as protectors, tacticians, crisis navigators, body-based healers, or those who thrive in fast-changing environments.

Centipede souls move efficiently through complexity; obstacles dissolve through momentum.

Centipede souls value sovereignty and self-reliance; independence shapes identity and direction.

Initiations of This Lifetime

Centipede awakens during periods requiring quick decision, defense of personal space, or navigation of dense or hidden systems.

Centipede activates when the soul trusts instinct, stays grounded, and moves with precise confidence.

Myriapod Variations: Current Life Expression

Millipede

Millipede reflects patient momentum and steady progress through many small, consistent steps; the soul engages endurance through repetition, grounding through contact with earth, and protection through gentle curl instead of sharp defense. This variation emphasizes calm persistence, longevity, and strength expressed through rhythm.

Giant Tropical Centipede

Giant Tropical Centipede reflects commanding presence and fearless authority; the soul engages strong boundaries, decisive action, and protective leadership within shadowed terrain.

House Centipede

House Centipede reflects silent guardianship and unseen service; the soul engages protection of home and subtle removal of imbalance through quiet vigilance.

Chipmunk Totem

Core Totem Essence

Chipmunk has the soul memory of preparation guided by joy, resourcefulness expressed through lightness, and prosperity built through small, consistent actions. This totem lives close to the ground yet moves with brightness and speed, teaching how foresight and playfulness coexist. Across Indigenous North American woodland traditions, the chipmunk appears as a gatherer, a keeper of seeds, and a messenger of cheerful resilience. Stories often portray the chipmunk as clever, quick-thinking, and spirited, a being who thrives through planning while remaining genuinely warm. Chipmunk medicine centers on readiness, optimism, and the wisdom of tending the small things that sustain life.

Strengths of the Totem

Chipmunk brings strategic preparation; resources gather steadily for future stability.

Chipmunk has bright vitality; energy uplifts and encourages others.

Chipmunk embodies quick intelligence; solutions arise through agility and observation.

Chipmunk has abundance through small actions; consistent effort multiplies results.

Chipmunk has emotional lightness; joy strengthens resilience.

Challenges of the Totem

Chipmunk lives with constant motion; grounding has calm focus.

Chipmunk values gathering and storing; trust has sharing and circulation.

Chipmunk responds rapidly to stimulation; pacing sustains energy over time.

Chipmunk has strong alertness; rest restores clarity and balance.

Past Life Lessons Carried Forward

Chipmunk has learned prosperity through preparation; foresight secures well-being.

Chipmunk has learned survival through cleverness; agility preserves life.

Chipmunk has learned joy as medicine; lightness sustains endurance.

Chipmunk has learned that small actions shape great outcomes; steady tending builds legacy.

Recurring Patterns Across Lifetimes

Chipmunk souls often appear as planners, organizers, herbalists, crafters, teachers of children, or those who quietly maintain systems behind the scenes.

Chipmunk souls brighten environments; morale rises through their presence.

Chipmunk souls value preparedness and practicality; life organizes through thoughtful detail.

Initiations of This Lifetime

Chipmunk awakens during periods of financial planning, home building, skill gathering, or creating security for self and family.

Chipmunk activates when the soul prepares wisely, has cheerfulness, and trusts that small, steady effort creates lasting abundance.

CONDOR TOTEM

Core Totem Essence

Condor has the soul memory of high altitude guardianship and ancestral oversight. This totem lives through vast perspective, purification, and sacred responsibility to life and death cycles. Across the Andes and ancient South American civilizations, especially Inca and pre-Inca cultures, the condor appears as a divine intermediary between the upper world, the living world, and the ancestral realm. Condor medicine centers on spiritual authority earned through elevation, the cleansing of what has completed its purpose, and guidance offered from a place of profound distance and compassion.

Strengths of the Totem

Condor brings expansive vision; awareness spans generations, landscapes, and spiritual realms.

Condor has sacred purification; decay transforms into renewal through respectful passage.

Condor embodies calm authority; presence stabilizes without force or urgency.

Condor has ancestral connection; guidance flows from lineage and cosmic order.

Condor guards thresholds between life and death; transition unfolds with dignity and reverence.

Challenges of the Totem

Condor lives at great emotional and spiritual altitude; grounding has embodiment and daily connection.

Condor has responsibility for collective cycles; self-care sustains long-term guardianship.

Condor values distance and overview; intimacy develops through intentional descent.

Condor moves deliberately; patience in leadership within time-bound worlds.

Past Life Lessons Carried Forward

Condor has learned stewardship of endings; completion restores balance and prepares renewal.

Condor has learned vision through elevation; distance reveals truth.

Condor has learned service through purification; honoring death sustains life.

Condor has learned authority through humility; guardianship arises from responsibility instead of dominance.

Recurring Patterns Across Lifetimes

Condor souls often appear as elders, spiritual leaders, death workers, healers of collective trauma, or cultural guardians.

Condor souls guide from above; others feel watched over and protected.

Condor souls engage themes of legacy and ancestry; long memory creates purpose.

Initiations of This Lifetime

Condor awakens during periods of ancestral healing, grief integration, cultural responsibility, or spiritual leadership.

Condor activates when the soul accepts guardianship of cycles, offers purification, and holds space for transformation.

Coyote Totem

Core Totem Essence

Coyote has the soul memory of sacred disruption and adaptive intelligence. This totem lives through humor, surprise, and the reshaping of reality through lived experience. Across Indigenous cultures of North America, especially Plains, Southwest, Great Basin, and Pacific Coast nations, Coyote appears as a culture shaper, a teacher through consequence, and a being who bends rules to reveal deeper truth. Coyote medicine centers on learning through experience, intelligence sharpened by paradox, and transformation sparked by laughter, error, and resilience.

Strengths of the Totem

Coyote brings rapid adaptability; shifting circumstances invite inventive response.

Coyote has sharp situational intelligence; awareness reads people, systems, and opportunity with clarity.

Coyote embodies humor as medicine; laughter dissolves fear and opens learning.

Coyote navigates chaos skillfully; disorder becomes a classroom instead of a threat.

Coyote has cultural evolution; stagnation gives way to movement and change.

Challenges of the Totem

Coyote lives through constant experimentation; integration in insight into wisdom.

Coyote moves quickly between roles; commitment strengthens long-term creation.

Coyote engages risk naturally; discernment refines timing and consequence.

Coyote teaches through lived outcome; reflection deepens mastery and responsibility.

Past Life Lessons Carried Forward

Coyote has learned wisdom through consequence; experience teaches what instruction cannot.

Coyote has learned survival through flexibility; rigidity dissolves under pressure.

Coyote has learned truth through inversion; mistakes reveal hidden law.

Coyote has learned teaching through story; humor has memory and meaning.

Recurring Patterns Across Lifetimes

Coyote souls often appear as tricksters, teachers, comedians, innovators, boundary walkers, or social disruptors.

Coyote souls catalyze change; systems shift after their involvement.

Coyote souls learn rapidly; repetition refines skill and awareness.

Initiations of This Lifetime

Coyote awakens during periods of upheaval, identity experimentation, or the collapse of false structure.

Coyote activates when the soul embraces learning through experience and trusts adaptability over certainty.

Crab Totem

Core Totem Essence

Crab has the soul memory of emotional protection, lateral wisdom, and survival through sensitivity and boundary intelligence. This totem lives at the meeting of land and sea, teaching how strength emerges through timing, awareness, and self-containment instead of confrontation. Across coastal Indigenous traditions, ancient Mediterranean symbolism, East Asian lore, and island cultures, crab appears as a guardian of thresholds, a keeper of cyclical time, and a being who knows when to advance, retreat, or move sideways to remain whole. Crab medicine centers on emotional discernment, self-protection without isolation, and mastery of liminal space.

Strengths of the Totem

Crab brings strong emotional boundaries; sensitivity remains protected and intact.

Crab has intuitive timing; movement aligns with tide, cycle, and moment.

Crab embodies lateral intelligence; alternate paths reveal solutions others miss.

Crab has resilience through adaptability; armor and softness coexist.

Crab has guardianship of the inner world; feelings receive respect and care.

Challenges of the Totem

Crab lives with heightened sensitivity; grounding has ease and confidence.

Crab values protective containment; openness develops through trust and pacing.

Crab responds instinctively to intrusion; discernment refines reaction into clarity.

Crab moves carefully through exposure; courage strengthens expression and connection.

Past Life Lessons Carried Forward

Crab has learned safety through boundaries; protection preserves emotional truth.

Crab has learned wisdom through timing; patience guides movement.

Crab has learned survival through adaptability; indirect paths sustain progress.

Crab has learned strength through containment; self-respect in resilience.

Recurring Patterns Across Lifetimes

Crab souls often appear as emotional protectors, counselors, guardians of family systems, or navigators of sensitive environments.

Crab souls move skillfully through change; tides guide decision instead of force.

Crab souls protect what matters quietly; others feel safer within their presence.

Initiations of This Lifetime

Crab awakens during periods of emotional boundary work, family system navigation, or protection of inner life.

Crab activates when the soul honors sensitivity as strength, trusts timing, and has emotional intelligence.

Brachyuran Variations: Current Life Expression

Hermit Crab

Hermit Crab reflects adaptive protection and identity refinement; the soul engages growth through changing forms of safety and home. This variation emphasizes evolution through conscious transition.

Blue Crab

Blue Crab reflects emotional intensity and vigilance; the soul engages responsiveness, intuition, and protection by active awareness of the environment.

King Crab

King Crab reflects authority anchored in armor and patience; the soul engages leadership through presence, endurance, and strategic pacing.

Fiddler Crab

Fiddler Crab reflects expressive signaling and social awareness; the soul engages communication, display, and rhythm within relational systems.

Crane and Heron Totem

Core Totem Essence

Crane has the soul memory of sacred balance between earth, water, and sky. This totem lives through grace, vigilance, and the steady cultivation of spiritual clarity. Across Japan, Native American nations, ancient Egypt, and Celtic lands, the crane and its close kin appear as messengers of longevity, keepers of cosmic order, and guardians of threshold spaces where worlds meet. Crane medicine centers on patience, ritual movement, and the alignment of daily life with higher law.

Strengths of the Totem

Crane brings embodied grace; posture, movement, and presence communicate dignity and calm.

Crane has watchful awareness; perception remains steady across wide fields of experience.

Crane embodies balance; emotional, spiritual, and physical realms move into harmony.

Crane has longevity and continuity; slow rhythms has endurance and wisdom.

Crane holds ceremonial intelligence; ritual action stabilizes community and spirit.

Challenges of the Totem

Crane lives through refined sensitivity; grounding has steadiness amid constant awareness.

Crane values deliberate pacing; momentum strengthens through trust in slow unfolding.

Crane has high ethical alignment; compassion has flexibility within principle.

Crane maintains vigilance; rest restores clarity and presence.

Past Life Lessons Carried Forward

Crane has learned harmony through balance; alignment preserves life and order.

Crane has learned leadership through example; grace teaches without force.

Crane has learned sacred timing; patience reveals correct action.

Crane has learned guardianship of thresholds; liminal spaces require care and respect.

Recurring Patterns Across Lifetimes

Crane souls often appear as priests, dancers, healers, diplomats, elders, or keepers of ceremony.

Crane souls move between worlds; spiritual and practical life integrate seamlessly.

Crane souls bring calm authority; environments organize around their presence.

Initiations of This Lifetime

Crane awakens during periods of spiritual refinement, ceremonial calling, or ethical leadership.

Crane activates when the soul aligns daily movement with sacred intention and higher law.

Gruiform and Wading Bird Variations; Current Life Expression

Japanese Crane

Japanese Crane reflects longevity, fidelity, and sacred order; the soul engages devotion, ritual movement, and lifelong purpose. In Japanese culture, the crane symbolizes long life, marital harmony, and the presence of kami expressed through grace and patience.

Sandhill Crane

Sandhill Crane reflects ancestral memory and migration; the soul engages endurance, cyclical return, and connection to ancient pathways. Many Native American nations honor the sandhill crane as a dancer, a healer, and a teacher of seasonal rhythm.

Whooping Crane

Whooping Crane reflects rare calling and stewardship; the soul engages protection of sacred purpose and responsibility for continuity. This expression emphasizes care for what has great meaning.

Egret

Egret reflects purity of movement and spiritual refinement; the soul engages clarity, healing, and grace within emotional waters. In Native American and Celtic symbolism, the egret aligns with balance, careful action, and spiritual cleanliness.

Heron

Heron reflects solitary vigilance and wisdom gained through stillness; the soul engages patience, discernment, and watchful presence. Celtic traditions associate the heron with prophecy, boundary walking, and the quiet strength of observation.

Ibis

Ibis reflects sacred knowledge and cosmic order; the soul engages intellect aligned with divine law. In ancient Egypt, the ibis stands as the living symbol of Thoth, keeper of writing, time, magic, and balance between chaos and order.

Cricket Totem

Core Totem Essence

Cricket has the soul memory of presence expressed through sound, timing, and attentiveness to subtle rhythm. This totem lives through vibration instead of force, teaching how small voices shape atmosphere, memory, and continuity. Across East Asian traditions, Indigenous North American teachings, Celtic hearth lore, and Mediterranean countryside belief, cricket appears as a guardian of home, a keeper of luck and prosperity, and a messenger whose song marks safety, harmony, and right order. Cricket medicine centers on listening deeply, honoring rhythm, and understanding how sound has meaning beyond words.

Strengths of the Totem

Cricket brings attunement to rhythm; timing guides action and rest with precision.

Cricket has a powerful voice within a small form; sound establishes presence and influence.

Cricket embodies vigilance through listening; awareness expands through quiet attention.

Cricket has harmony within space; song stabilizes emotional and energetic climate.

Cricket has prosperity and protection; presence signals safety, balance, and continuity.

Challenges of the Totem

Cricket lives through heightened sensory awareness; grounding has calm integration.

Cricket expresses itself consistently; discernment guides when sound serves best.

Cricket has strongly to place; adaptability has movement between environments.

Cricket responds to vibration quickly; focus refines reaction into intentional expression.

Past Life Lessons Carried Forward

Cricket has learned power through sound; vibration creates reality.

Cricket has learned safety through rhythm; harmony preserves life and home.

Cricket has learned influence through consistency; steady presence builds trust.

Cricket has learned listening as wisdom; awareness begins in stillness.

Recurring Patterns Across Lifetimes

Cricket souls often appear as musicians, speakers, listeners, healers, storytellers, or guardians of domestic space.

Cricket souls influence the atmosphere quietly; peace or alertness follows their presence.

Cricket souls value rhythm and ritual; life organizes itself through sound and timing.

Initiations of This Lifetime

Cricket awakens during periods of homemaking, voice reclamation, creative rhythm, or heightened listening.

Cricket activates when the soul learns to trust subtle expression, honor timing, and allow sound to carry intention.

Gryllid Variations: Current Life Expression

Field Cricket

Field Cricket reflects alertness and environmental awareness; the soul engages in listening, signaling, and harmony with natural cycles. Many Indigenous traditions associate the field cricket with protection and seasonal rhythm.

Katydid

Katydid reflects playful inquiry and rhythmic curiosity; the soul engages exploration, creative expression, and interaction guided by sound and timing.

Grasshopper

Grasshopper reflects momentum through intuition and forward movement; the soul engages leaps of faith, rapid adaptation, and awareness of opportunity emerging within changing conditions. This variation channels energetic responsiveness, sensitivity to environmental shifts, and the ability to advance through timing rather than force. Power moves through motion, rhythm, and decisive action, teaching mastery through trust in instinct, calculated risk, and the courage to move before certainty fully arrives.

DEER TOTEM

Core Totem Essence

Deer has the soul memory of gentle authority and alert grace. This totem lives through sensitivity that protects life, speed guided by intuition, and dignity expressed through restraint. Across Indigenous North American nations, Celtic lands, Siberia, Scandinavia, Japan, and forest cultures worldwide, deer appear as a messenger of the wild, a bridge between realms, and a keeper of heart-centered wisdom. Deer medicine centers on compassion paired with vigilance, movement aligned with instinct, and leadership that preserves harmony.

Strengths of the Totem

Deer brings refined sensitivity; awareness of subtle shift guides safety and opportunity.

Deer has graceful movement; speed and agility express elegance and efficiency.

Deer embodies heart wisdom; compassion informs choice and relationship.

Deer has intuitive navigation; paths reveal themselves through felt knowing.

Deer holds a dignified presence; calm poise stabilizes group energy and social space.

Challenges of the Totem

Deer live with heightened awareness; grounding has steadiness during constant perception.

Deer values peace and harmony; assertive action grows through clarity and timing.

Deer responds quickly to stimulus; regulation refines the response into deliberate movement.

Deer protects vulnerability; boundaries strengthen through confidence and practice.

Past Life Lessons Carried Forward

Deer has learned protection through awareness; vigilance preserves life.

Deer has learned leadership through gentleness; strength flows through compassion.

Deer has learned navigation of thresholds; forest and spirit meet through intuition.

Deer has learned dignity under pressure; grace sustains integrity.

Recurring Patterns Across Lifetimes

Deer souls often appear as healers, mediators, artists, guides, caregivers, or protectors of gentle spaces.

Deer souls move between worlds; sensitivity has spiritual and emotional translation.

Deer souls bring calm influence; environments soften and harmonize in their presence.

Initiations of This Lifetime

Deer awakens during periods of emotional refinement, boundary learning, or return to heart-centered living.

Deer activates when the soul trusts intuition, honors gentleness, and has grace through challenge.

Cervid Variations: Current Life Expression

White Tailed Deer

White Tailed Deer reflects adaptability and alert grace; the soul navigates change, family systems, and edge spaces with intuition and speed. Many Indigenous North American cultures honor this deer as a messenger, a provider, and a teacher of respectful relationships with land.

Mule Deer

Mule Deer reflects resilience and terrain mastery; the soul engages navigation across difficult landscapes and learns confidence through adaptability. This expression emphasizes endurance guided by awareness.

Elk

Elk reflects vocal authority and communal leadership; the soul engages presence, strength, and responsibility expressed through clear signaling and group cohesion. Plains and Rocky Mountain cultures recognize elk as a symbol of stamina, dignity, and protective leadership.

Red Deer

Red Deer reflects sovereignty and ancestral power; the soul engages leadership, fertility, and ritual authority. Celtic traditions associate red deer with the Otherworld, kingship, and sacred passage between realms.

Reindeer and Caribou

Reindeer and Caribou reflect migration and collective survival; the soul engages endurance, guidance, and life sustained through movement. Sámi and Arctic Indigenous cultures honor these beings as providers, spiritual companions, and teachers of seasonal rhythm.

Roe Deer

Roe Deer reflects subtlety and liminal grace; the soul engages intuition, quiet movement, and sensitivity within cultivated and wild spaces. European folklore associates roe deer with fairy paths, boundary crossing, and refined perception.

Dolphin Totem

Core Totem Essence

Dolphin has the soul memory of joyful intelligence woven through emotional mastery. This totem lives through play, communication, and cooperative brilliance expressed within fluid environments. Across Ancient Greece, Polynesia, Indigenous coastal cultures worldwide, and Mediterranean myth, the dolphin appears as a guide, a rescuer, and a sacred companion between worlds. Dolphin medicine centers on joy as wisdom, communication as a healing force, and community strengthened through empathy and shared rhythm.

Strengths of the Totem

Dolphin brings radiant joy; play restores vitality and strengthens bonds.

Dolphins carry advanced communication; sound, gesture, and emotion convey complex meaning.

Dolphin embodies cooperative intelligence; collaboration amplifies success and safety.

Dolphin has emotional fluency; feeling informs action with clarity and compassion.

Dolphin navigates liminal waters; movement between depth and surface flows with ease.

Challenges of the Totem

Dolphins live through high emotional sensitivity; grounding has balance within intensity.

Dolphin thrives on connection; solitude invites intentional restoration.

Dolphin engages curiosity constantly; focus refines creative output.

Dolphin moves rapidly through experience; integration in learning into wisdom.

Past Life Lessons Carried Forward

Dolphins have learned joy as a survival strategy; play sustains resilience.

Dolphin has learned healing through sound; vibration has care and guidance.

Dolphin has learned community as strength; collective intelligence preserves life.

Dolphin has learned navigation through trust; intuition guides safe passage.

Recurring Patterns Across Lifetimes

Dolphin souls often appear as healers, teachers, performers, mediators, or guides through emotional waters.

Dolphin souls uplift groups; morale and cohesion increase through their presence.

Dolphin souls bridge intellect and feeling; wisdom emerges through integration.

Initiations of This Lifetime

Dolphin awakens during periods of emotional healing, creative collaboration, or return to joy after hardship.

Dolphin activates when the soul trusts play, communication, and empathy as pathways to strength.

Delphinid Variations: Current Life Expression

Bottlenose Dolphin

Bottlenose Dolphin reflects adaptability and social leadership; the soul engages cooperation, teaching, and problem-solving within dynamic groups. Many coastal cultures honor this dolphin as a helper and protector of humans at sea.

Spinner Dolphin

Spinner Dolphin reflects exuberant expression and rhythmic movement; the soul engages celebration, creativity, and communal joy expressed through motion and sound. Polynesian traditions associate spinner dolphins with sunrise, ceremony, and playful vitality.

Common Dolphin

Common Dolphin reflects speed and coordinated action; the soul engages teamwork, navigation, and energetic presence across wide territories. Ancient Mediterranean cultures regarded this dolphin as a companion of sailors and a sign of protection.

River Dolphin

River Dolphin reflects adaptability within constrained environments; the soul engages sensitivity, intuition, and navigation through complex emotional or physical channels. Indigenous river cultures recognize this dolphin as a liminal being bridging freshwater and spirit realms.

Domestic Dog Totem

Core Totem Essence

The domestic dog has the soul memory of chosen devotion. This totem evolves through a relationship with humanity, shaping identity through companionship, protection, and mutual reliance. Across ancient villages, nomadic camps, agricultural societies, and modern homes, cultures recognize the dog as a guardian, guide, and faithful intermediary between worlds. Domestic Dog medicine centers on loyalty offered freely, service given with heart, and love expressed through action.

Strengths of the Totem

Domestic Dog brings unwavering loyalty; commitment flows naturally toward people, place, and purpose.

Domestic Dog has protective awareness; vigilance has safety, continuity, and emotional security.

Domestic Dog embodies service as devotion; care becomes a sacred offering instead of an obligation.

Domestic Dog has emotional attunement; sensitivity to human feeling and intention guides behavior.

Domestic Dog bridges worlds; many cultures honor the dog as a guide of souls and a keeper of thresholds.

Challenges of the Totem

The domestic dog lives through deep attachment; discernment has balance between devotion and self-direction.

Domestic Dog prioritizes others; personal needs ask for conscious honoring and expression.

Domestic Dog responds strongly to environment; stability and routine have nervous system harmony.

The domestic dog holds a protective instinct; clarity guides appropriate response and boundary setting.

Past Life Lessons Carried Forward

The domestic dog has learned love through choice; loyalty strengthens through mutual recognition.

Domestic Dog has learned guardianship of the vulnerable; protection expresses compassion.

Domestic Dog has learned service as a sacred exchange; giving and receiving sustain balance.

Domestic Dog has learned guidance between realms; its presence comforts the living and escorts the dead.

Recurring Patterns Across Lifetimes

Domestic Dog souls often appear as caregivers, protectors, aides, healers, companions, or service-oriented leaders.

Domestic Dog souls form deep bonds; trust and reliability define their relationships.

Domestic Dog souls anchor households and communities; emotional stability grows in their presence.

Initiations of This Lifetime

Domestic Dog awakens during periods of partnership, family formation, healing through relationship, or service calling.

Domestic Dog activates when the soul learns to offer loyalty while honoring personal sovereignty.

Domestic Dog Variations: Current Life Expression

Guardian Dog

Guardian Dog reflects the protection of home and kin; the soul engages boundary keeping, vigilance, and steady presence. Many ancient and modern cultures honor guardian dogs as protectors of the threshold and family lineage.

Herding Dog

Herding Dog reflects guidance and coordination; the soul has group movement, organization, and safety through attentiveness and direction.

Companion Dog

Companion Dog reflects emotional healing and presence; the soul offers comfort, grounding, and unconditional are within close relationships.

Service Dog

Service Dog reflects sacred duty and trained devotion; the soul engages assistance, advocacy, and support for those navigating vulnerability or transition.

Village Dog

Village Dog reflects communal belonging; the soul moves freely among people, offering protection, connection, and adaptability within shared space.

Donkey Totem

Core Totem Essence

Donkey has the soul memory of steadfast service joined with quiet intelligence. This totem lives through endurance, discernment, and loyalty by lived terrain instead of abstract command. Across the ancient Near East, Mediterranean basin, Africa, Central Asia, and agrarian cultures worldwide, the donkey appears as a bearer of burdens, a guardian of thresholds, and a companion of the humble and the holy. Mule extends this lineage through synthesis, resilience, and balanced strength. Donkey medicine centers on reliability, grounded wisdom, and dignity expressed through persistence.

Strengths of the Totem

Donkey brings unwavering endurance; steady effort sustains long journeys and difficult labor.

Donkey has practical intelligence; terrain, load, and timing receive careful assessment.

Donkey embodies loyalty and trustworthiness; commitment holds firm through adversity.

Donkey has humility with strength; service expresses moral clarity and inner resolve.

Donkey protects boundaries through discernment; refusal arises from wisdom instead of defiance.

Challenges of the Totem

Donkey lives with prolonged responsibility; replenishment through rest and appreciation sustains vitality.

Donkey has strong self-direction; communication aligns effort with shared intention.

Donkey commits deeply to duty; recognition has morale and longevity.

Donkey values proven paths; openness to new routes expands possibilities.

Past Life Lessons Carried Forward

Donkey has learned survival through persistence; steady presence preserves life and purpose.

Donkey has learned wisdom through terrain; experience teaches discernment better than instruction.

Donkey has learned dignity in service; humility has strength and honor.

Donkey has learned protection through refusal; stopping prevents harm and preserves integrity.

Recurring Patterns Across Lifetimes

Donkey souls often appear as helpers, laborers, guides, caretakers, or quiet stabilizers within families and communities.

Donkey souls shoulder responsibility reliably; others trust their judgment and follow their pace.

Donkey souls move history forward quietly; progress rests on their endurance.

Initiations of This Lifetime

Donkey awakens during periods of heavy responsibility, ethical testing, or long-term service.

Donkey activates when the soul chooses perseverance, discernment, and dignity over speed or recognition.

Equid Variations; Current Life Expression

Donkey

Donkey reflects grounded wisdom and patient service; the soul engages reliability, moral clarity, and discernment by lived reality. In ancient Near Eastern, African, and Mediterranean traditions, the donkey appears alongside prophets, travelers, and healers as a companion of humility, peace, and sacred duty.

Mule

Mule reflects synthesis and resilient balance; the soul engages strength joined with intelligence, endurance paired with caution. Across cultures, a mule symbolizes hybrid wisdom, adaptability, and the ability to carry complex loads through difficult terrain with steadiness and care.

Dove Totem

Core Totem Essence

Dove has the soul memory of peace embodied through presence, purity of intention, and emotional openness. This totem lives through gentleness that reshapes environments, teaching how calm steadiness creates safety and reconciliation. Across ancient Mediterranean cultures, Hebrew and early Christian symbolism, Indigenous peace traditions, and Near Eastern lore, dove appears as a messenger of harmony, a bearer of sacred breath, and a sign of covenant between worlds. Dove medicine centers on peace as an active force, love expressed through restraint, and spiritual authority through softness.

Strengths of the Totem

Dove brings peace through presence; calm energy stabilizes people and places.

Dove has purity of intention; motives remain clear and transparent.

Dove embodies emotional openness; trust flows through sincerity and warmth.

Dove has reconciliation; relationships heal through a gentle approach and listening.

Dove has spiritual communication; prayer, breath, and intention travel easily.

Challenges of the Totem

Dove lives with high sensitivity; grounding has emotional steadiness.

Dove values harmony deeply; boundary clarity strengthens self-respect.

Dove offers gentleness freely; discernment guides where energy flows.

Dove avoids confrontation by instinct; courage grows when the soul speaks instead of retreats.

Past Life Lessons Carried Forward

Dove has learned peace as strength; calm reshapes outcome.

Dove has learned love as action; gentleness has power.

Dove has learned trust through openness; sincerity builds safety.

Dove has learned spiritual authority through purity; intention directs energy.

Recurring Patterns Across Lifetimes

Dove souls often appear as mediators, healers, spiritual guides, caregivers, or peacekeepers.

Dove souls soften hardened spaces; conflict eases around them.

Dove souls carry a calming influence; others feel seen and safe.

Initiations of This Lifetime

Dove awakens during periods of reconciliation, grief healing, spiritual devotion, or peace-making.

Dove activates when the soul chooses compassion, restraint, and sincerity as guiding forces.

Columbid Variations: Current Life Expression

White Dove

White Dove reflects spiritual purity and sacred covenant; the soul engages devotion, prayerful presence, and peace offered without condition. Mediterranean and Near Eastern traditions honor the white dove as a messenger between the divine and human realms.

Turtle Dove

Turtle Dove reflects enduring love and faithful partnership; the soul engages loyalty, tenderness, and emotional constancy. Ancient Greek and Celtic traditions associate the turtle dove with devotion and sacred union.

Rock Dove

Rock Dove reflects resilience and coexistence; the soul engages peace within dense environments and shared spaces. This expression emphasizes harmony maintained through adaptability and patience.

Mourning Dove

Mourning Dove reflects grief transformed into gentle sound; the soul engages emotional healing, remembrance, and the soft expression of sorrow that soothes instead of wounds. Indigenous and folk traditions recognize the mourning dove as a companion through loss and transition.

Pigeon

Pigeon reflects intelligence in community, navigation through complexity, and belonging within the living world of people, structures, and movement. This soul engages adaptability, social awareness, memory, and the sacred skill of finding home across distance and change. Ancient Mediterranean cultures, urban folklore, messenger traditions, and wartime histories honor the pigeon as a carrier of messages, a keeper of direction, and a witness to human life in all its density. This expression emphasizes peace practiced in real conditions, devotion expressed through return, and wisdom through endurance, familiarity, and communal presence.

Dragon Totem

Core Totem Essence

Dragon has the soul memory of primordial authority. This totem arises from the meeting of earth, sky, fire, and water, embodying the creation force into conscious will. Across cultures where the dragon appears independently, people recognize the dragon as a keeper of power, wisdom, and cosmic order. Dragon medicine centers on sovereignty aligned with responsibility, mastery of elemental force, and the guardianship of sacred knowledge.

Strengths of the Totem

Dragon brings immense life force; vitality flows through breath, blood, and vision.

Dragon has elemental mastery; fire, water, wind, and earth respond to conscious command.

Dragon embodies sovereign authority; leadership expresses itself through presence, clarity, and earned power.

Dragon guards wisdom and treasure; knowledge, land, and spiritual inheritance remain protected.

Dragon moves between worlds; mythic awareness bridges human life and cosmic pattern.

Challenges of the Totem

Dragon lives with vast internal power; regulation and refinement shape sustainable expression.

Dragon has heightened perception; responsibility grows alongside awareness.

Dragon values autonomy and dominion; collaboration develops through mutual respect and shared purpose.

Dragon awakens a strong desire for truth and mastery; patience has integration over time.

Past Life Lessons Carried Forward

Dragon has learned stewardship of power; force serves balance and continuity.

Dragon has learned guardianship of sacred knowledge; wisdom remains held until the student is ready to carry it.

Dragon has learned creation through discipline; form emerges through control and vision.

Dragon has learned cosmic perspective; individual action ripples across larger systems.

Recurring Patterns Across Lifetimes

Dragon souls often appear as leaders, innovators, guardians, visionaries, magicians, or culture shapers.

Dragon souls hold positions of influence; others respond instinctively to their presence.

Dragon souls carry responsibility early; mastery unfolds through experience and restraint.

Initiations of This Lifetime

Dragon awakens during periods of power reclamation, leadership emergence, or spiritual authority consolidation.

Dragon activates when the soul learns to wield strength in service to harmony and truth.

Dragon Variations; Current Life Expression

Eastern Dragon

Eastern Dragon reflects harmony between power and benevolence; the soul engages wisdom-guided leadership, natural order, and spiritual authority expressed through care. In Chinese, Korean, Japanese, and Vietnamese traditions, the dragon governs rain, rivers, fertility, and imperial virtue. This dragon moves fluidly, teaching balance between force and compassion, and alignment with heaven and earth.

Western Dragon

Western Dragon reflects concentrated power and guardianship; the soul engages protection of territory, hoarded wisdom, and personal sovereignty. In European mythic traditions, the dragon stands as a keeper of treasure, an embodiment of raw elemental force, and a test of courage and mastery. This dragon teaches ethical command of power and the refinement of strength through discipline.

Wyvern

Wyvern reflects precision, vigilance, and focused force; the soul engages swift decision making, territorial awareness, and power directed through clarity of purpose. In medieval European heraldry and folklore, the wyvern appears as a two-legged dragon with wings, often associated with the guardianship of land and boundaries. This expression emphasizes disciplined action, awareness of space, and the ability to strike with accuracy when called.

Drake

Drake reflects grounded strength and elemental embodiment; the soul engages physical presence, endurance, and mastery of a single dominant force such as fire or earth. In Germanic and Northern European lore, drake appears as a powerful serpent or dragon rooted close to the land. This expression teaches stability, patience, and the cultivation of power through rooted existence.

Wyrm

Wyrm reflects ancient continuity and deep earth wisdom; the soul engages memory, lineage, and the slow movement of transformation beneath the surface. In Anglo-Saxon and Norse traditions, wyrm appears as a great serpent connected to burial mounds, hidden treasure, and ancestral knowledge. This expression emphasizes depth, time, and the guardianship of what lies beneath awareness.

Amphiptere

Amphiptere reflects air and lightness within dragon form; the soul engages elevated perception, swift movement, and the ability to traverse unseen pathways. In European and Near Eastern lore, amphiptere appears as a winged serpent without legs. This expression emphasizes clarity of sight, freedom of motion, and the capacity to rise above density while still carrying power.

Hydra

Hydra reflects multiplicity of power and regenerative force; the soul engages resilience, expansion, and the ability to sustain presence through challenge. In Greek mythology, the Hydra appears as a multi-headed serpent whose heads regenerate when severed. This expression teaches adaptability, persistence, and the management of power that grows through engagement.

Lindworm

Lindworm reflects a transitional form between serpent and dragon; the soul engages evolution, threshold crossing, and the shaping of identity through change. In Scandinavian and Central European folklore, the lindworm appears as a serpent-like dragon, often connected to transformation and hidden nobility. This expression emphasizes metamorphosis, inner refinement, and emergence into fuller power.

Inkanyamba

Inkanyamba expresses storm-driven dragon force; the soul engages rapid transformation, command of weather currents, and emotional power that has speed and intensity. This variation channels lightning-quick change, heightened sensitivity to energetic shifts, and the ability to direct volatile force into a purposeful outcome. Power moves through surge, release, and recalibration, teaching mastery through direct engagement with intensity.

Grootslang

Grootslang expresses primordial dragon memory; the soul engages deep instinct, accumulation of power over time, and guardianship of what holds lasting value. This variation channels ancient intelligence, physical and energetic endurance, and a steady presence rooted beneath surface awareness. Power gathers, consolidates, and protects, teaching mastery through patience, strength, and long-view perspective.

Rainbow Serpent

Rainbow Serpent expresses creation-aligned dragon force; the soul engages life-shaping movement, cyclical renewal, and the maintenance of natural order across environments. This variation channels generative power, fluid adaptability, and alignment with living systems. Power flows through continuous creation, teaching mastery through movement, rhythm, and relationship with the whole.

Wagyl

Wagyl expresses land-bound guardian dragon force; the soul engages protection of sacred space, deep attunement to environment, and relationship with place as living presence. This variation channels steady watchfulness, environmental awareness, and devotion to the spaces it inhabits. Power holds and sustains, teaching mastery through stewardship, listening, and rooted connection.

DRAGONFLY TOTEM

Core Totem Essence

Dragonfly has the soul memory of light-borne truth and perceptual clarity. This totem lives through mastery of illusion, rapid transformation, and vision that penetrates surface reality. Across Japan, Native American nations, ancient European wetlands, and Asian river cultures, dragonflies appear as messengers of insight, victory through awareness, and the revelation of what lies beneath appearances. Dragonfly medicine centers on clarity, agility of perception, and the ability to move freely between emotional depth and luminous understanding.

Strengths of the Totem

Dragonfly brings exceptional perceptual clarity; truth reveals itself quickly and cleanly.

Dragonfly has mastery of light and reflection; illusion dissolves through awareness.

Dragonfly embodies swift transformation; change integrates rapidly once insight happens.

Dragonfly has emotional maturity; feeling informs wisdom instead of confusion.

Dragonfly has multidirectional intelligence; adaptability has freedom and precision.

Challenges of the Totem

Dragonfly lives through rapid perception; grounding in insight into lived reality.

Dragonfly moves quickly through experience; integration strengthens depth and continuity.

Dragonfly engages multiple realities at once; focus refines direction and embodiment.

Dragonfly thrives in liminal space; rootedness has sustained presence.

Past Life Lessons Carried Forward

Dragonfly has learned truth through light; clarity reveals essence.

Dragonfly has learned transformation through awareness; insight reshapes identity.

Dragonfly has learned freedom through perception; understanding dissolves constraint.

Dragonfly has learned emotional depth as a foundation; water has flight.

Recurring Patterns Across Lifetimes

Dragonfly souls often appear as seers, messengers, strategists, artists, or truth bearers.

Dragonfly souls expose illusion gently; awareness shifts reality through understanding.

Dragonfly souls navigate emotional and mental realms fluidly; insight guides action.

Initiations of This Lifetime

Dragonfly awakens during periods of awakening, truth revelation, or perceptual expansion.

Dragonfly activates when the soul learns to see clearly, move lightly, and trust insight over appearance.

Duck Totem

Core Totem Essence

Duck has the soul memory of emotional balance expressed through adaptability and gentle navigation. This totem lives through ease across water, land, and sky, moving between elements with comfort and grace. Across Indigenous North American wetlands, Celtic river lore, East Asian symbolism, and Northern European traditions, the duck appears as a guide through emotional worlds, a symbol of partnership, and a teacher of staying composed while currents move beneath the surface. Duck medicine centers on emotional intelligence, versatility, and the wisdom of calm movement through layered realities.

Strengths of the Totem

Duck brings emotional fluency; feeling flows smoothly without overwhelming direction.

Duck has natural adaptability; transitions across environments unfold with ease.

Duck embodies calm surface presence; composure steadies self and others.

Duck has partnership and cooperation; bonds strengthen through mutual pacing and care.

Duck navigates multiple realms; inner emotion and outer action remain aligned.

Challenges of the Totem

Duck lives through constant emotional movement; grounding has steadiness and integration.

Duck adapts quickly to circumstances; anchoring intention strengthens continuity.

Duck values harmony deeply; assertive direction develops through clarity and confidence.

Duck responds to subtle currents; discernment guides choice of flow.

Past Life Lessons Carried Forward

Duck has learned emotional mastery through movement; flow sustains balance.

Duck has learned adaptability as a survival skill; versatility preserves life.

Duck has learned partnership through rhythm; shared pace creates safety.

Duck has learned calm as strength; composure stabilizes turbulent environments.

Recurring Patterns Across Lifetimes

Duck souls often appear as mediators, caregivers, partners, emotional guides, or travelers between worlds.

Duck souls bring ease into complex situations; presence softens tension.

Duck souls thrive within change; transition becomes familiar terrain.

Initiations of This Lifetime

Duck awakens during periods of emotional navigation, relational adjustment, or life transition.

Duck activates when the soul trusts flow, maintains composure, and moves gracefully through layered experience.

Anatid Variations; Current Life Expression

Mallard

Mallard reflects adaptability and social fluency; the soul engages cooperation, versatility, and comfort within shared environments. Many cultures view the mallard as a symbol of balance and everyday resilience.

Mandarin Duck

Mandarin Duck reflects devotion and harmony in partnership; the soul engages committed bonds and emotional fidelity. East Asian traditions honor the mandarin duck as a symbol of enduring love and balanced union.

Wood Duck

Wood Duck reflects beauty within emotional depth; the soul engages self-expression, nesting instinct, and refined perception. Indigenous North American traditions associate the wood duck with the protection of home and gentle creativity.

Teal

Teal reflects agility and light movement; the soul engages quick adaptation and responsive navigation within shifting conditions. This expression emphasizes flexibility guided by awareness.

Loon

Loon reflects profound emotional depth and ancestral calling within the Duck lineage. This variation appears when the soul engages introspection, sacred solitude, and navigation through deep feeling. Across Indigenous cultures of the northern lakes and boreal regions, the loon serves as a spirit caller, a messenger between worlds, and a guardian of ancestral memory through sound. This expression emphasizes vocal truth rising from depth, comfort with solitude balanced by devotion to mate and territory, and the ability to travel vast emotional waters with clarity and grace.

Eagle Totem

Core Totem Essence

Eagle has the soul memory of elevated vision joined with moral clarity. This totem rises above terrain to perceive pattern, destiny, and rightful action. Across the Americas, Eurasia, Africa, and Oceania, cultures recognize the eagle and its kin as emissaries of sky power, carriers of prayer, and witnesses of truth. Eagle medicine centers on perspective, courage guided by ethics, and leadership aligned with a higher order.

Strengths of the Totem

Eagle brings far-sighted vision; perception spans distance, consequence, and long arc purpose.

Eagle has spiritual authority; presence inspires trust, honor, and alignment.

Eagle embodies courage guided by clarity; decisive action follows clear seeing.

Eagle serves as messenger; prayer, intention, and word travel between realms.

Eagle maintains sovereignty of spirit; independence has integrity and responsibility.

Challenges of the Totem

Eagle lives with expansive awareness; grounding vision into daily life requires embodiment and pacing.

Eagle values autonomy and altitude; collaboration grows through shared mission and mutual respect.

Eagle holds strong ideals; discernment guides application within complex realities.

Eagle commits to truth; speech and action carry weight and consequence.

Past Life Lessons Carried Forward

Eagle has learned leadership through service; guidance flows from responsibility to the whole.

Eagle has learned the sanctity of vision; sight has the obligation to act with honor.

Eagle has learned prayer as movement; flight itself becomes devotion.

Eagle has learned balance between sky and earth; wisdom lands through embodied action.

Recurring Patterns Across Lifetimes

Eagle souls often appear as leaders, protectors, visionaries, judges, teachers, or cultural symbols.

Eagle souls stand as moral reference points; others look to them during decision-making and crisis.

Eagle souls seek wide horizons; travel, study, and perspective shape destiny.

Initiations of This Lifetime

Eagle awakens during periods of calling into leadership, truth-telling, or public responsibility.

Eagle activates when the soul aligns vision with ethical action and lived integrity.

Raptor Variations: Current Life Expression

Golden Eagle

Golden Eagle reflects sovereign leadership and mastery; the soul engages authority, guardianship, and decisive action. Many Indigenous cultures of North America and Central Asia honor the Golden Eagle as a sacred hunter, protector, and carrier of prayer.

Bald Eagle

Bald Eagle reflects communal leadership and renewal; the soul engages stewardship of people, land, and shared ideals. In many Native American traditions, the Bald Eagle stands as a sacred national and spiritual symbol tied to unity, vision, and covenant.

Harpy Eagle

Harpy Eagle reflects a formidable presence and protection; the soul engages guardianship of dense environments and powerful boundaries. Amazonian cultures recognize this eagle as a forest sovereign and protector of life.

Eel Totem

Core Totem Essence

Eel has the soul memory of fluid power, transformation, and navigation through unseen channels. This totem lives within depth, darkness, and movement without resistance, teaching how adaptability and persistence shape survival. Across Polynesian ocean lore, Japanese and East Asian river traditions, Indigenous European waters, and coastal cultures worldwide, eel appears as a guardian of currents, a being of mystery, and a keeper of liminal passage between worlds. Eel medicine centers on flexibility, emotional intelligence, and strength expressed through movement that finds the path force cannot.

Strengths of the Totem

Eel brings extraordinary adaptability; movement reshapes itself to meet any terrain.

Eel has deep emotional intelligence; feeling guides direction and timing.

Eel embodies transformation through motion; change unfolds continuously instead of abruptly.

Eel has resilience within darkness; unseen environments become pathways instead of obstacles.

Eel navigates narrow passages with mastery; complexity offers opportunity instead of confinement.

Challenges of the Totem

Eel lives within constant movement; grounding has integration and rest.

Eel values concealment and depth; selective visibility strengthens influence and connection.

Eel adapts rapidly to shifting currents; intention in direction and purpose.

Eel has long, energetic endurance; replenishment sustains vitality.

Past Life Lessons Carried Forward

Eel has learned survival through flexibility; yielding preserves strength.

Eel has learned wisdom through darkness; depth reveals truth unavailable on the surface.

Eel has learned transformation through continuity; change remains ongoing and alive.

Eel has learned navigation of thresholds; passage between worlds requires fluidity.

Recurring Patterns Across Lifetimes

Eel souls often appear as navigators, healers, boundary walkers, emotional guides, or keepers of hidden systems.

Eel souls thrive within transition; uncertainty sharpens perception instead of diminishing it.

Eel souls influence outcomes quietly; flow reshapes the environment without display.

Initiations of This Lifetime

Eel awakens during periods of transition, emotional complexity, or movement through constrained systems.

Eel activates when the soul trusts flow, embraces adaptability, and allows transformation to remain continuous.

Elephant Totem

Core Totem Essence

The Elephant has the soul memory of ancestral continuity. This totem walks the world with reverence for lineage, land, and long memory. Across Africa and South and Southeast Asia, people recognize the elephant as a bearer of wisdom, a guardian of community, and a living archive of the past carried forward through the body. Elephant medicine centers on remembrance, collective responsibility, and strength guided by care.

Strengths of the Totem

Elephant brings profound memory; experiences, teachings, and ancestral knowledge remain accessible and embodied.

Elephant has steady power; strength expresses itself through patience, presence, and deliberate movement.

Elephant has communal leadership; protection, guidance, and mentorship support the whole group.

Elephant holds emotional intelligence; feelings move through the heart with empathy and attunement.

Elephant honors sacred pathways; travel, migration, and ritual routes align with inherited wisdom.

Challenges of the Totem

Elephant lives with deep emotional depth; feelings carry weight and conscious processing through the body.

Elephant holds responsibility for many; caring for others requires replenishment and shared support.

Elephant values continuity and tradition; rapid change invites discernment and adaptive grace.

Elephant has memory vividly; integration of the past calls for ritual release and renewal.

Past Life Lessons Carried Forward

The elephant has learned stewardship of lineage; ancestors live through action, choice, and remembrance.

Elephant has learned leadership through service; authority arises from protection and devotion.

Elephant has learned grief as a sacred teacher; mourning deepens compassion and clarity.

Elephant has learned sacred patience; time reveals truth through steady presence.

Recurring Patterns Across Lifetimes

Elephant souls often appear as matriarchs, patriarchs, elders, organizers, guardians, or cultural carriers.

Elephant souls anchor families and communities; others gather around their stability.

Elephant souls maintain long commitments; projects, relationships, and vows unfold across extended cycles.

Initiations of This Lifetime

The Elephant awakens during periods of ancestral healing, leadership inheritance, or communal responsibility.

Elephant activates when the soul steps into guardianship, mentorship, or the restoration of broken lines.

Elephant Variations; Current Life Expression

African Elephant

African Elephant reflects expansive guardianship; the soul engages leadership across wide territory, complex community systems, and visible responsibility. Many African traditions honor the elephant as a symbol of chieftaincy, memory, and sovereign strength.

Asian Elephant

Asian Elephant reflects spiritual authority and sacred service; the soul engages ritual duty, devotion, and wisdom guided by compassion. In South and Southeast Asian cultures, the elephant aligns with temple service, royal power, and the remover of obstacles through steady presence.

Ferret, Weasel, Mink, and Mongoose Totem

Core Totem Essence

Ferrets carry the soul memory of agile intelligence. This totem lives through curiosity, speed, and strategic movement within tight spaces. Across Europe, Asia, Africa, and the Americas, cultures recognize mustelids and mongooses as clever survivors, pest controllers, and small beings with outsized impact. Ferret medicine centers on adaptability, quick thinking, and the ability to navigate complexity through wit and motion.

Strengths of the Totem

Ferret brings mental agility; ideas move quickly and adapt to changing conditions.

Ferret has fearless curiosity; exploration opens opportunity and insight.

Ferret embodies strategic movement; efficiency arises through speed and precision.

Ferret thrives in constrained environments; tight systems reveal creative pathways.

Ferret holds a problem-solving instinct; obstacles invite inventive solutions.

Challenges of the Totem

Ferret lives through constant motion; rest and grounding clarity.

Ferret has heightened curiosity; focus strengthens follow-through.

Ferret values independence; cooperation develops through shared purpose.

Ferret responds rapidly; discernment guides timing and direction.

Past Life Lessons Carried Forward

Ferret has learned survival through cleverness; intelligence compensates for size.

Ferret has learned adaptation through motion; movement sustains opportunity

.Ferret has learned stealth as protection; subtlety preserves safety.

Ferret has learned persistence; repeated effort yields success.

Recurring Patterns Across Lifetimes

Ferret souls often appear as problem solvers, innovators, tacticians, scouts, or boundary navigators.

Ferret souls thrive in dynamic systems; change energizes engagement.

Ferret souls influence outcomes quietly; results speak louder than visibility.

Initiations of This Lifetime

Ferret awakens during periods of rapid change, problem-solving demand, or system navigation

.Ferret activates when the soul trusts speed, curiosity, and strategic thinking.

Mustelid and Mongoose Variations; Current Life Expression

Ferret

Ferret reflects playful intelligence and exploration; the soul engages learning, experimentation, and curiosity-driven growth. European traditions associate the ferret with hunting skill, cleverness, and partnership with humans.

Weasel

Weasel reflects precision and stealth; the soul engages strategic action, quick resolution, and subtle influence. In many Eurasian folk traditions, the weasel symbolizes alertness, cunning, and survival through intelligence.

Stoat and Ermine

Stoat and Ermine reflect seasonal adaptation and dignified presence; the soul engages transformation aligned with environment and social context. Northern cultures associate ermine with purity of purpose, sovereignty, and ceremonial authority.

Mink

Mink reflects resource mastery and luxury awareness; the soul engages value creation, territory management, and refinement. Many waterway cultures recognize mink as a skilled hunter and a symbol of material intelligence.

Mongoose

Mongoose reflects courage and protective intelligence; the soul engages confrontation of threat through speed and precision. In South Asian and African traditions, the mongoose stands as a guardian figure associated with snake mastery, household protection, and bravery grounded in alert awareness.

Firefly Totem

Core Totem Essence

Firefly has the soul memory of inner light revealed through darkness, guidance offered through gentle signal, and joy expressed through illumination instead of force. This totem lives in twilight and night air, teaching how small sparks lead travelers, comfort hearts, and awaken wonder. Across Japanese summer traditions, Indigenous North American woodland lore, Appalachian folk belief, and tropical cultures, fireflies appear as a messenger of spirits, a symbol of fleeting beauty, and a reminder that light lives within every being. Firefly medicine centers on quiet radiance, intuitive guidance, and hope through even the darkest seasons.

Strengths of the Totem

Firefly brings natural inner illumination; presence glows from within without strain.

Firefly has gentle guidance; light signals direction and reassurance.

Firefly embodies joy and play; wonder renews energy and connection.

Firefly has subtle communication; small signals create a powerful effect.

Firefly has trust in cycles; darkness reveals the brilliance of light.

Challenges of the Totem

Firefly lives within sensitivity to the environment; grounding sustains a steady glow.

Firefly expresses energy in pulses; pacing has longevity and balance.

Firefly moves softly through space; confidence strengthens visibility when needed.

Firefly values beauty and moment; consistency in creation over time.

Past Life Lessons Carried Forward

Firefly has learned light arises from within; spirit guides action.

Firefly has learned influence through subtlety; small sparks shift whole landscapes.

Firefly has learned joy sustains resilience; play protects vitality.

Firefly has learned guidance through presence; shining gently leads others home.

Recurring Patterns Across Lifetimes

Firefly souls often appear as artists, healers, children's teachers, storytellers, spiritual guides, or those who uplift others quietly.

Firefly souls bring comfort in difficult times; hope rekindles through their presence.

Firefly souls value beauty and authenticity; life organizes around meaningful moments.

Initiations of This Lifetime

Firefly awakens during periods of emotional darkness, spiritual searching, creative awakening, or rediscovery of childlike wonder.

Firefly activates when the soul trusts its inner light, shares warmth gently, and guides others through simple presence.

Lampyrid Variations: Current Life Expression

Common Firefly

Common Firefly reflects a steady inner glow and communal signaling; the soul engages connection, shared rhythm, and guidance through cooperative light.

Synchronous Firefly

Synchronous Firefly reflects collective harmony; the soul engages unity, timing, and coordinated brilliance where many lights pulse as one. This variation emphasizes community resonance and shared intention.

Glowworm

Glowworm reflects grounded illumination; the soul engages stillness, earth connection, and quiet radiance that attracts through calm presence instead of motion.

Fox Totem

Core Totem Essence

Fox has the soul memory of adaptive intelligence guided by perception and timing. This totem lives through clever movement, boundary awareness, and the ability to thrive between worlds. Across East Asia, Europe, the Arctic, North America, and Indigenous cultures worldwide, the fox appears as a mediator, a trickster teacher, and a guardian of liminal space. Fox medicine centers on strategic thinking, survival through wit, and transformation achieved through awareness instead of force.

Strengths of the Totem

Fox brings sharp perception; subtle cues, shifts, and opportunities register quickly.

Fox has strategic intelligence; solutions arise through timing, flexibility, and ingenuity.

Fox embodies liminal mastery; movement between roles, identities, and environments flows with ease.

Fox has self-preservation; survival aligns with clever boundary management.

Fox expresses creative problem-solving; obstacles invite inventive response.

Challenges of the Totem

Fox lives through constant alertness; grounding has nervous system balance and rest.

Fox values independence and discretion; trust develops through earned safety and mutual respect.

Fox adapts readily to the environment; anchoring core identity strengthens continuity.

Fox navigates complex social fields; discernment refines influence and intention.

Past Life Lessons Carried Forward

Fox has learned survival through intelligence; wit protects life and purpose.

Fox has learned transformation through adaptability; change becomes an ally instead of a threat.

Fox has learned power through subtlety; quiet movement reshapes the outcome.

Fox has learned guardianship of thresholds; edges hold opportunity and protection.

Recurring Patterns Across Lifetimes

Fox souls often appear as negotiators, strategists, artists, scouts, guides, or cultural translators.

Fox souls thrive at the margins; edge spaces offer safety and creativity.

Fox souls influence outcomes indirectly; timing and placement matter more than visibility.

Initiations of This Lifetime

Fox awakens during periods of transition, identity shift, or navigation of complex systems.

Fox activates when the soul trusts perception, embraces flexibility, and chooses clever response over confrontation.

Vulpine Variations: Current Life Expression

Red Fox

Red Fox reflects adaptability and social intelligence; the soul navigates human edge spaces, change, and opportunity with wit and responsiveness. European and North American traditions associate the red fox with clever survival and boundary crossing.

Arctic Fox

Arctic Fox reflects endurance through transformation; the soul engages resilience, seasonal adaptation, and survival by environmental awareness. Arctic cultures honor this fox as a teacher of camouflage, timing, and persistence.

Fennec Fox

Fennec Fox reflects sensory refinement and heat mastery; the soul engages alert perception, nervous system regulation, and survival within extreme conditions. North African desert cultures recognize the fennec fox as a symbol of sensitivity, cleverness, and adaptability.

Gray Fox

Gray Fox reflects versatility and quiet confidence; the soul engages movement across vertical and horizontal terrain, including forest and human space. Indigenous North American traditions observe the gray fox as a teacher of flexibility and multidimensional navigation.

Kit Fox

Kit Fox reflects minimalism and efficiency; the soul engages survival through conservation of energy and precise action. Southwestern cultures recognize the kit fox as a being of restraint and intelligent resource use.

Kitsune Lineage Fox

Kitsune reflects spiritual intelligence and shape-shifting mastery; the soul engages transformation, illusion, and wisdom gained through long experience. Japanese tradition honors kitsune as spirit beings who test integrity, reward sincerity, and guard sacred places.

Frog Totem

Core Totem Essence

Frog has the soul memory of transformation through water and earth. This totem lives at the meeting place of elements, moving between states of being with natural grace. Across Mesoamerica, Africa, East Asia, Europe, and Indigenous cultures worldwide, frogs appear as bringers of rain, renewal, fertility, and alchemical change. Frog medicine centers on life cycle awareness, emotional cleansing, and the capacity to move from one form of existence into another with acceptance and timing.

Strengths of the Totem

Frogs bring transformational power; growth unfolds through stages instead of force.

Frog has water wisdom; emotional flow has healing, intuition, and renewal.

Frog embodies adaptability; shifting environments invite responsive movement and survival.

Frog has fertility and abundance; creativity, life force, and prosperity increase through alignment with natural rhythm.

Frog holds liminal mastery; transitions between worlds, roles, and identities occur with fluidity.

Challenges of the Totem

Frog lives through constant change; grounding has stability during transition.

Frog has heightened sensitivity to the environment; energetic hygiene strengthens clarity.

Frog responds to cycles deeply; patience has trust in timing.

Frog absorbs emotional atmosphere; boundaries and personal equilibrium.

Past Life Lessons Carried Forward

Frog has learned rebirth through surrender; release allows a new form to emerge.

Frog has learned healing through water; cleansing restores vitality and balance.

Frog has learned fertility as a sacred force; creation flows through attunement to cycles.

Frog has learned comfort within liminality; transition itself becomes home.

Recurring Patterns Across Lifetimes

Frog souls often appear as healers, midwives, shamans, rain callers, artists, or cycle keepers.

Frog souls move through many life phases; reinvention creates destiny.

Frog souls guide others through change; presence offers reassurance and momentum.

Initiations of This Lifetime

Frog awakens during periods of emotional release, spiritual initiation, fertility, or major life transition.

Frog activates when the soul embraces change as nourishment instead of disruption.

Anuran Variations: Current Life Expression

Tree Frog

Tree Frog reflects emotional expression and vocal truth; the soul engages communication, visibility, and resonance. Many rain-forest and island cultures associate the tree frog with rain, calling, abundance, and joyful sound.

Bullfrog

Bullfrog reflects presence and assertion; the soul engages territory, voice, and grounded authority. North American traditions recognize the bullfrog as a symbol of strength rooted in water and land alike.

Poison Dart Frog

Poison Dart Frog reflects concentrated potency and sacred defense; the soul has a strong personal force that requires conscious respect and intentional expression. Amazonian cultures view this frog as a guardian of power and a reminder of responsibility tied to potency.

Toad

Toad reflects earth-bound alchemy and hidden wisdom; the soul engages transformation through stillness, patience, and deep connection to land. European and Asian traditions associate the toad with medicine, prosperity, rain magic, and the mysteries of transmutation.

Spadefoot Toad

Spadefoot Toad reflects emergence after dormancy; the soul engages sudden activation following long preparation. Desert cultures recognize this toad as a symbol of timing, survival, and rapid renewal.

Gecko Totem

Core Totem Essence

Gecko has the soul memory of subtle mastery and adaptive presence. This totem lives through precision, sensitivity, and alignment with unseen surfaces. Across Pacific Island cultures, Southeast Asia, Africa, and parts of the Mediterranean, the gecko appears as a household guardian, a messenger of fortune, and a being who moves safely across thresholds others avoid. Gecko medicine centers on attunement, quiet effectiveness, and success achieved through alignment instead of force.

Strengths of the Totem

Gecko brings refined sensitivity; awareness registers vibration, shift, and opportunity with immediacy.

Gecko has adaptive intelligence; environments invite adjustment that preserves momentum and safety.

Gecko embodies effortless traction; progress continues even on unfamiliar or vertical terrain.

Gecko has household guardianship; presence stabilizes space, wards off imbalance, and invites prosperity.

Gecko expresses precision and timing; small actions yield meaningful results.

Challenges of the Totem

Gecko lives through heightened perception; energetic regulation has clarity and ease.

Gecko values subtle movement; visibility requires intentional choice and voice.

Gecko adapts readily to surroundings; core identity strengthens through conscious anchoring.

Gecko thrives in quiet spaces; sustained exposure to intensity calls for grounding rituals.

Past Life Lessons Carried Forward

Gecko has learned success through alignment; the right contact creates forward motion.

Gecko has learned protection through presence; guardianship works through subtle influence.

Gecko has learned navigation of thresholds; liminal spaces offer safety and opportunity.

Gecko has learned prosperity through harmony; balance attracts abundance.

Recurring Patterns Across Lifetimes

Gecko souls often appear as protectors of space, subtle healers, intuitive navigators, or quiet problem solvers.

Gecko souls influence outcomes behind the scenes; stability grows through their presence.

Gecko souls value adaptability; survival and success unfold through responsiveness.

Initiations of This Lifetime

Gecko awakens during periods of environmental change, home creation, or energetic sensitivity.

Gecko activates when the soul learns to trust subtle guidance and precise action.

Giraffe Totem

Core Totem Essence

Giraffe has the soul memory of elevated vision, gentle strength, and leadership expressed through a calm perspective. This totem lives between earth and sky, teaching how height expands awareness and compassion guides authority. Across many African cultures and savanna traditions, the giraffe appears as a quiet sentinel of the plains, a bridge between canopy and ground, and a symbol of foresight and peaceful presence. Giraffe medicine centers on long vision, graceful power, and the ability to see both the immediate step and the distant horizon at once.

Strengths of the Totem

Giraffe brings an expansive perspective; sight reaches far beyond immediate circumstance.

Giraffe has calm authority; presence reassures and stabilizes others.

Giraffe embodies gentle strength; power expresses itself through grace and steadiness.

Giraffe has intuitive awareness; subtle shifts across the landscape register clearly.

Giraffe has heart-centered leadership; compassion guides every decision.

Challenges of the Totem

Giraffe lives with wide awareness; grounding has focus on present details.

Giraffe values peaceful presence; decisive action strengthens momentum when required.

Giraffe has a measured pace; flexibility enhances responsiveness.

Giraffe holds responsibility as lookout and guide; shared support sustains energy.

Past Life Lessons Carried Forward

Giraffe has learned leadership through perspective; seeing far ahead protects many.

Giraffe has learned strength through gentleness; calm presence resolves tension.

Giraffe has learned survival through awareness; observation precedes action.

Giraffe has learned compassion as guidance; heart and vision align.

Recurring Patterns Across Lifetimes

Giraffe souls often appear as counselors, mediators, teachers, visionaries, or guardians who watch over families and communities.

Giraffe souls naturally perceive patterns and long-term outcomes; others rely on their foresight.

Giraffe souls value harmony and grace; influence flows through steady presence instead of force.

Initiations of This Lifetime

Giraffe awakens during periods requiring long-term planning, leadership through empathy, or stepping into a guiding role for others.

Giraffe activates when the soul rises above conflict, trusts its perspective, and leads through perspective instead of force, and guides with both vision and warmth.

GOAT TOTEM

Core Totem Essence

Goat has the soul memory of resilience through ascent. This totem lives through balance, persistence, and the courage to climb where footing appears scarce. Across the Mediterranean, Middle East, Central Asia, Africa, the Himalayas, and pastoral mountain cultures worldwide, the goat appears as a survivor, a boundary crosser, and a bearer of fertility and sacred appetite. Goat medicine centers on self-determination, adaptability, and progress achieved through steady effort instead of force.

Strengths of the Totem

Goat brings exceptional balance; body and instinct coordinate precisely across difficult terrain.

Goat has resilient endurance; effort continues despite challenge and exposure.

Goat embodies adaptive intelligence; resources emerge from sparse or changing environments.

Goat expresses sovereign appetite; desire, curiosity, and vitality guide engagement with life.

Goat honors elevation; perspective widens through willingness to climb beyond comfort.

Challenges of the Totem

The Goat lives through constant movement toward higher ground; rest has sustainability and reflection.

Goat values independence strongly; cooperation grows through chosen alliance instead of obligation.

Goat engages risk naturally; discernment refines assessment of terrain and timing.

Goat has a strong instinctual desire; regulation channels appetite into a purposeful direction.

Past Life Lessons Carried Forward

The Goat has learned survival through balance; footing determines success more than speed.

Goat has learned fertility through persistence; abundance grows through continued effort.

Goat has learned wisdom through ascent; a higher view reveals context and meaning.

Goat has learned self-trust; reliance on inner sense preserves life.

Recurring Patterns Across Lifetimes

Goat souls often appear as climbers, innovators, survivors, pathfinders, or keepers of marginal spaces.

Goat souls thrive in challenging environments; difficulty sharpens skill and confidence.

Goat souls resist stagnation; movement toward growth creates destiny.

Initiations of This Lifetime

Goat awakens during periods of ambition, boundary testing, survival challenge, or reclaiming personal agency.

Goat activates when the soul commits to ascent, trusts balance, and engages life with determination.

Caprine Variations: Current Life Expression

Mountain Goat

Mountain Goat reflects mastery of extreme terrain; the soul engages endurance, precision, and calm authority within high-stakes environments. Alpine and Northern cultures honor the mountain goat as a teacher of balance and perseverance.

Ibex

Ibex reflects ancient sovereignty and ritual strength; the soul engages leadership, fertility, and spiritual authority expressed through elevation. Mesopotamian and Mediterranean traditions associate the ibex with divine vitality and mountain power.

Markhor

Markhor reflects independence and rare resilience; the soul engages survival within rugged landscapes and protection of lineage. Central Asian cultures regard markhor as a symbol of strength, dignity, and ancestral endurance.

Domestic Goat

The Domestic Goat reflects adaptability and sustenance; the soul engages provision, resourcefulness, and survival alongside human communities. Pastoral cultures worldwide honor the goat as a reliable source of nourishment and resilience.

Wild Goat

Wild Goat reflects untamed autonomy; the soul engages self-directed movement, instinctual wisdom, and freedom rooted in balance instead of dominance.

Goose Totem

Core Totem Essence

Goose has the soul memory of loyalty expressed through protection, migration guided by shared purpose, and leadership that rotates for the good of the whole. This totem lives through devotion to family, territory, and collective journey, teaching how vigilance and cooperation sustain life across long distances. Across Indigenous North American teachings, Celtic river lore, Nordic migration symbolism, and East Asian seasonal traditions, the goose appears as a guardian, a guide through transition, and a keeper of relational bonds. Goose medicine centers on faithful partnership, communal leadership, and courage expressed through watchful care.

Strengths of the Totem

Goose brings fierce loyalty; bonds strengthen through commitment and presence.

Goose has protective vigilance; awareness preserves safety for the group and home.

Goose embodies shared leadership; responsibility rotates to sustain endurance.

Goose has coordinated movement; collective rhythm has long journeys.

Goose has vocal signaling; communication maintains order and cohesion.

Challenges of the Totem

Goose lives with a strong territorial instinct; discernment refines response within shared space.

Goose commits deeply to group well-being; personal replenishment sustains longevity.

Goose responds quickly to a threat; calm integration has emotional balance.

Goose values tradition and routine; flexibility has adaptation during change.

Past Life Lessons Carried Forward

Goose has learned survival through cooperation; unity preserves life.

Goose has learned leadership through service; taking turns sustains strength.

Goose has learned protection through vigilance; awareness prevents harm.

Goose has learned devotion through return; home and kin guide direction.

Recurring Patterns Across Lifetimes

Goose souls often appear as family protectors, coordinators, community guardians, or guides through transition.

Goose souls stabilize groups during movement; others feel safer within formation.

Goose souls value partnership and continuity; loyalty creates identity and purpose.

Initiations of This Lifetime

Goose awakens during periods of relocation, family protection, shared leadership, or long-term commitment to a collective goal.

Goose activates when the soul embraces cooperation, signals clearly, and leads through faithful presence.

Gorilla Totem

Core Totem Essence

Gorilla has the soul memory of grounded authority rooted in protection and calm presence. This totem lives through strength held with restraint, leadership expressed through care, and power made with emotional intelligence. Across Central African forests and the cultures that live in relationship with them, the gorilla appears as a forest guardian, a family leader, and a symbol of strength that stabilizes instead of overwhelms. Gorilla medicine centers on peaceful power, devotion to kin, and leadership that arises through steadiness and responsibility.

Strengths of the Totem

Gorilla brings immense physical and emotional strength; power expresses itself through stability and containment.

Gorilla has protective leadership; guardianship flows toward family, community, and vulnerable members.

Gorilla embodies calm authority; presence alone establishes order and safety.

Gorilla has deep emotional attunement; empathy guides decision and response.

Gorilla has grounded wisdom; connection to land and body creates clarity and endurance.

Challenges of the Totem

The Gorilla lives with great responsibility; leadership makes for continual emotional regulation and self-care.

Gorilla has a strong protective instinct; discernment guides response and timing.

Gorilla values harmony within the group; confrontation requires conscious channeling of force.

Gorilla holds deep feelings; expression has relational balance and inner ease.

Past Life Lessons Carried Forward

Gorilla has learned leadership through protection; strength serves safety and continuity.

Gorilla has learned restraint as wisdom; calm presence prevents harm.

Gorilla has learned devotion to kin; family bonds anchor purpose across lifetimes.

Gorilla has learned authority through embodiment; grounded presence creates trust.

Recurring Patterns Across Lifetimes

Gorilla souls often appear as protectors, leaders, caregivers, elders, or stabilizing figures within families and communities.

Gorilla souls hold space for others; emotional safety grows in their presence.

Gorilla souls assume responsibility naturally; others rely on their steadiness and strength.

Initiations of This Lifetime

Gorilla awakens during periods of leadership responsibility, family protection, or community guardianship.

Gorilla activates when the soul learns to hold power with gentleness, patience, and emotional clarity.

Griffin Totem

Core Totem Essence

Griffin has the soul memory of sacred guardianship, sovereign authority, and mastery of both sky and earth. This totem unites lion and eagle, teaching how strength and vision integrate into balanced leadership. Across ancient Persia, Egypt, Greece, Scythia, and medieval Europe, the griffin appears as protector of treasure, defender of sacred sites, and sentinel of divine law. Griffin medicine centers on vigilant guardianship, moral clarity, and the courage to defend what holds true value: land, spirit, lineage, and wisdom.

Strengths of the Totem

Griffin brings a commanding presence; authority establishes safety and order immediately.

Griffin has dual awareness; ground strength and sky vision operate together.

Griffin embodies fearless guardianship; protection arises naturally and decisively.

Griffin has discernment; true treasure reveals itself through inner knowing.

Griffin has sovereign leadership; responsibility guides power with integrity.

Challenges of the Totem

Griffin lives with intense vigilance; rest renews clarity and steadiness.

Griffin values the protection of sacred territory; openness has trust and alliance.

Griffin holds a strong moral code; flexibility encourages compassion without judgment.

Griffin has great strength; a gentle presence deepens the connection with others.

Past Life Lessons Carried Forward

Griffin has learned protection as a sacred duty; guardianship preserves what matters most.

Griffin has learned strength through balance; earth and sky wisdom operate together.

Griffin has learned authority through integrity; truth stabilizes leadership.

Griffin has learned discernment through watchfulness; value shines clearly to the trained eye.

Recurring Patterns Across Lifetimes

Griffin souls often appear as protectors of knowledge, guardians of temples or land, ethical leaders, warriors with spiritual codes, or keepers of lineage treasure.

Griffin souls sense when something sacred requires defense; presence alone deters harm.

Griffin souls value honor and responsibility; leadership flows naturally toward them.

Initiations of This Lifetime

Griffin awakens during periods requiring the protection of family, culture, knowledge, or sacred purpose.

Griffin activates when the soul claims its authority, stands watch with clarity, and defends truth with courage and restraint.

Groundhog and Prairie Dog Totem

Core Totem Essence

Groundhog has the soul memory of cyclical wisdom, deep rest, and emergence guided by timing instead of urgency. This totem lives between burrow and open field, teaching how retreat restores strength and how reappearance signals renewal. Across Indigenous North American woodland traditions and seasonal agricultural lore, the groundhog appears as a keeper of weather knowledge, a reader of earth rhythms, and a gentle guardian of the threshold between winter and spring. Groundhog medicine centers on hibernation as sacred restoration, preparation through stillness, and trust in natural cycles of withdrawal and return.

Strengths of the Totem

Groundhog brings intuitive timing; emergence aligns with season and opportunity.

Groundhog has a strong earth connection; grounding stabilizes body and spirit.

Groundhog embodies restorative rest; retreat replenishes vitality fully.

Groundhog has preparation through quiet work; security builds beneath the surface.

Groundhog has gentleness and steadiness; calm presence reassures others.

Challenges of the Totem

Groundhog lives within long periods of solitude; engagement strengthens connection and shared experience.

Groundhog values the safety of the burrow; exploration expands growth and perspective.

Groundhog has deliberate pace; responsiveness enhances adaptability.

Groundhog has a strong cyclical rhythm; balance has steady productivity throughout the year.

Past Life Lessons Carried Forward

Groundhog has learned strength through retreat; rest restores power.

Groundhog has learned wisdom through cycles; every season serves a purpose.

Groundhog has learned preparation through patience; steady tending ensures survival.

Groundhog has learned renewal through emergence; each return brings fresh possibility.

Recurring Patterns Across Lifetimes

Groundhog souls often appear as herbalists, healers, planners, land tenders, or those who work quietly behind the scenes to create stability.

Groundhog souls value home and sanctuary; safe spaces anchor their purpose.

Groundhog souls understand timing deeply; they sense when to act and when to wait.

Initiations of This Lifetime

The Groundhog awakens during periods of recovery, seasonal transition, or the need to rebuild foundations.

Groundhog activates when the soul honors rest, prepares carefully, and trusts the rhythm of retreat and return.

Marmot and Burrower Variations; Current Life Expression

Woodchuck

Woodchuck reflects practical preparation and earth stewardship; the soul engages in building, storing, and tending land with care. North American folklore honors the woodchuck as a seasonal guide and weather reader.

Marmot

Marmot reflects social cooperation and alpine resilience; the soul engages community vigilance, shared burrows, and survival by high elevation environments.

Prairie Dog

Prairie Dog reflects collective awareness and communication; the soul engages signaling, teamwork, and protection of extended family systems through coordinated effort.

Pika

Pika reflects industrious gathering and bright persistence; the soul engages preparation through small, steady actions and cheerful resilience within rugged terrain.

Hawk and Falcon Totem

Core Totem Essence

The Hawk has the soul memory of divine sight and heroic guidance. This totem lives through elevated vision, moral clarity, and the courage to act as a bridge between the human world and a higher order. In ancient Egypt, hawks and falcons stand as sacred guides and heroic protectors, embodying the living eye of divine intelligence that watches, defends, and leads. Across

Egypt, the Near East, Central Asia, Celtic lands, and Indigenous North American cultures, the Hawk appears as messengers of the Sun, guardians of kingship, and champions of truth who guide souls toward rightful action. Hawk medicine centers on vision aligned with justice, leadership rooted in responsibility, and heroic service to cosmic balance.

Strengths of the Totem

Hawk brings sacred sight; perception pierces illusion and reveals divine order.

Hawk has heroic courage; action rises in service of protection and truth.

Hawk embodies moral authority; leadership flows from alignment with higher law.

Hawk has guidance and direction; others follow their clarity and steadiness.

Hawk protects balance; vigilance maintains harmony between worlds.

Challenges of the Totem

Hawk lives through elevated responsibility; grounding sustains endurance and humility.

Hawk has strong drive toward action; patience refines timing and consequence.

Hawk values independence; collaboration strengthens reach and guardianship.

Hawk holds intense vision; compassion has connection with those guided.

Past Life Lessons Carried Forward

Hawk has learned leadership through service; authority exists to protect and guide.

Hawk has learned heroism through vigilance; watching preserves life and order.

Hawk has learned vision as a sacred trust; sight has responsibility.

Hawk has learned alignment with divine law; justice creates destiny.

Recurring Patterns Across Lifetimes

Hawk souls often appear as leaders, guardians, guides, warriors of principle, or spiritual sentinels.

Hawk souls intervene during moments of disorder; presence restores direction and truth.

Hawk souls carry heroic lineage; duty to protect and guide repeats across incarnations.

Initiations of This Lifetime

Hawk awakens during periods of leadership calling, ethical testing, or need for clear guidance.

Hawk activates when the soul accepts responsibility to see clearly, act justly, and protect balance.

Raptor Variations: Current Life Expression

Falcon

Falcon reflects divine kingship and heroic protection; the soul engages leadership, precision, and guardianship aligned with cosmic order. In ancient Egypt, the falcon embodies Horus, the divine hero who restores balance, protects the throne, and guides the land through righteous vision. Falcon energy appears when the soul steps into visible leadership with sacred responsibility.

Hawk

Hawk reflects guidance and vigilant heroism; the soul engages watchful protection, moral clarity, and steady oversight. In Egyptian understanding, hawks serve as guides of the living and the dead, carrying prayers, watching over travelers, and embodying the heroic aspect of divine sight that guards humanity.

Kestrel

Kestrel reflects precision and disciplined watchfulness; the soul engages stillness, focus, and heroic restraint. This expression emphasizes seeing fully before acting.

Hornet and Wasp Totem

Core Totem Essence

Hornet has the soul memory of fierce protection, precision response, and communal defense guided by instinct and law. This totem lives through immediate action aligned with purpose, teaching how boundaries preserve life, order, and continuity. Across Indigenous North American teachings, Japanese symbolism, African village lore, Mediterranean countryside tradition, and ancient warrior cultures, Hornet appear as guardians of threshold, enforcers of consequence, and keepers of collective safety. Hornet medicine centers on clarity of boundary, courage expressed through action, and loyalty to group and purpose.

Strengths of the Totem

Hornet brings instant boundary awareness; intrusion registers without delay.

Hornet has precision in action; response aligns exactly with need and moment.

Hornet embodies communal defense; protection strengthens through coordinated effort.

Hornet has courage through presence; fear dissolves into decisive movement.

Hornet has order through consequence; clarity restores balance.

Challenges of the Totem

Hornet lives with heightened reactivity; discernment refines timing and scale of response.

Hornet guard territory fiercely; flexibility has coexistence within shared space.

Hornet commits deeply to group safety; personal rest sustains effectiveness.

Hornet moves rapidly into action; reflection deepens strategic mastery.

Past Life Lessons Carried Forward

Hornet has learned protection through action; delay invites harm.

Hornet has learned loyalty through defense; group survival creates identity.

Hornet has learned power through precision; focused force restores order.

Hornet has learned courage through clarity; certainty guides movement.

Recurring Patterns Across Lifetimes

Hornet souls often appear as defenders, boundary enforcers, guardians of law, activists, or protectors of vulnerable groups.

Hornet souls respond when lines are crossed; presence re-establishes safety.

Hornet souls value justice through action; balance returns through consequence.

Initiations of This Lifetime

Hornet awakens during periods requiring strong boundary enforcement, defense of the community, or a decisive response to a threat.

Hornet activates when the soul stands firm, protects what matters, and acts with precision instead of hesitation.

Vespid Variations: Current Life Expression

Wasp

Wasp reflects social intelligence and layered cooperation; the soul engages shared construction, vigilance, and adaptive defense. Many cultures associate the paper wasp with strategic teamwork and community guardianship.

Yellow-jacket

Yellow jacket reflects assertive boundary enforcement; the soul engages rapid response, protection of resources, and clarity of territorial law.

Bald Faced Hornet

Bald Faced Hornet reflects commanding guardianship; the soul engages authority, decisive defense, and leadership within communal structures.

European Hornet

European Hornet reflects endurance and ancestral defense; the soul engages protection created from lineage, territory, and long memory.

Mud Dauber Wasp

Mud Dauber reflects solitary precision and craftsmanship; the soul engages focused effort, individual responsibility, and protection through preparation instead of confrontation.

Horse Totem

Core Totem Essence

Horse has the soul memory of freedom joined with service. This totem moves through wide landscapes with strength, rhythm, and devotion to a shared journey. Across the Eurasian steppe, the Americas, the Middle East, and Celtic lands, people recognize the horse as a life companion, a bridge between worlds, and a carrier of spirit across distance. Horse medicine centers on movement as prayer, partnership as power, and the alignment of will, body, and breath.

Strengths of the Totem

Horse brings vital momentum; energy flows through motion, travel, and purposeful direction.

Horse has loyalty and devotion; bonds form through trust, consistency, and shared labor.

Horse embodies endurance; long journeys unfold through steady pacing and resilience.

Horse expresses emotional intelligence; sensitivity to the environment and companions guide action.

Horse serves as a spiritual carrier; many cultures honor the horse as a psychopomp and a messenger between realms.

Challenges of the Totem

Horse lives through high sensitivity; attunement to others makes for self-awareness and energetic care.

Horse commits deeply; service and responsibility require balance with personal freedom.

Horse moves powerfully through emotion; regulation through breath, movement, and grounding has harmony.

Horse thrives in partnership; clarity around direction strengthens shared purpose.

Past Life Lessons Carried Forward

Horse has learned freedom through relationship; trust expands instead of restricts movement.

Horse has learned strength through rhythm; pacing sustains long vision and vitality.

Horse has learned service as a sacred duty; carrying others honors shared destiny.

Horse has learned navigation between worlds; travel holds spiritual meaning beyond distance.

Recurring Patterns Across Lifetimes

Horse souls often appear as guides, travelers, teachers, messengers, healers, or companions in service roles.

Horse souls form deep bonds; loyalty and mutual reliance shape life paths.

Horse souls seek wide horizons; exploration and expansion bring fulfillment.

Initiations of This Lifetime

Horse awakens during periods of transition, relocation, calling into service, or reclamation of personal freedom.

Horse activates when the soul aligns movement with purpose and partnership with trust.

Horse Variations: Current Life Expression

Wild Horse

Wild Horse reflects freedom and self-direction; the soul engages autonomy, instinct, and unclaimed territory. Many Plains Indigenous cultures honor the wild horse as a symbol of power reclaimed and spirit returned to the people.

Draft Horse

Draft Horse reflects strength in service; the soul has responsibility, labor, and steadfast contribution. European agrarian traditions honor this horse as a pillar of community survival and endurance.

War Horse

War Horse reflects courage and disciplined action; the soul engages protection, strategy, and readiness. Across ancient Eurasian and Middle Eastern cultures, the war horse stands as a sacred partner in defense and honor.

Steppe Horse

Steppe Horse reflects partnership with vastness; the soul navigates long journeys, nomadic cycles, and ancestral movement. Central Asian cultures recognize the horse as kin and a spiritual ally.

Hummingbird Totem

Core Totem Essence

Hummingbird has the soul memory of joy sustained through precision and presence. This totem lives through lightness paired with immense effort, reminding the soul that sweetness and endurance coexist. Across Mesoamerica, the Andes, the Caribbean, and Indigenous cultures of the Americas, the hummingbird appears as a sacred messenger, a bearer of love, and a warrior of the heart whose power comes from devotion to life's nectar. Hummingbird medicine centers on vitality drawn from beauty, resilience powered by joy, and focus refined to the present moment.

Strengths of the Totem

Hummingbird brings radiant joy; delight fuels stamina and purpose.

Hummingbird has extraordinary focus; attention remains fully anchored in the present.

Hummingbird embodies energetic mastery; rapid movement aligns with precision and control.

Hummingbird has heart-centered courage; love motivates action and perseverance.

Hummingbird navigates subtle realms; spirit messages travel through color, sound, and motion.

Challenges of the Totem

Hummingbird lives through intense energetic expenditure; nourishment and rest sustain balance.

Hummingbird moves quickly between experiences; integration deepens meaning and continuity.

Hummingbird follows sweetness instinctively; discernment guides sustainable sources of joy.

Hummingbird maintains constant alertness; grounding has calm within motion.

Past Life Lessons Carried Forward

Hummingbird has learned survival through joy; sweetness preserves life force.

Hummingbird has learned devotion through effort; persistence honors what the heart loves.

Hummingbird has learned presence as power; the moment holds everything required.

Hummingbird has learned beauty as medicine; color and light restore spirit.

Recurring Patterns Across Lifetimes

Hummingbird souls often appear as messengers, healers, artists, lovers of life, or warriors of the heart.

Hummingbird souls uplift others; morale and hope rise through their presence.

Hummingbird souls travel widely; movement connects places, people, and purpose.

Initiations of This Lifetime

Hummingbird awakens during periods of heart healing, grief softening, or rediscovery of joy.

Hummingbird activates when the soul chooses sweetness, presence, and devotion despite intensity.

Hyena Totem

Core Totem Essence

Hyena has the soul memory of intelligence sharpened through survival, laughter that dissolves fear, and strength expressed through cooperation instead of solitary dominance. This totem lives within the savanna's edge spaces, teaching how adaptability, strategy, and communal bonds sustain life where conditions shift quickly. Across many African traditions, the hyena appears as a trickster, guardian, night traveler, and keeper of hidden knowledge. Some stories portray the hyena as foolish to teach humility; others portray it as a wise survivor who thrives through wit and teamwork. Hyena medicine centers on social intelligence, fearless engagement with shadow, and resilience through collective strength.

Strengths of the Totem

Hyena brings sharp strategic thinking; solutions arise through observation and timing.

Hyena has strong communal loyalty; cooperation multiplies power and safety.

Hyena embodies a fearless relationship with shadow; darkness reveals opportunity and truth.

Hyena has adaptability; scarcity transforms into resourcefulness.

Hyena has emotional resilience; laughter and levity restore courage and morale.

Challenges of the Totem

Hyena lives within intense social structures; personal boundaries strengthen clarity.

Hyena values constant alertness; rest sustains vitality and balance.

Hyena engages conflict directly; discernment guides when to act and when to watch.

Hyena has a strong survival instinct; trust deepens connection and openness.

Past Life Lessons Carried Forward

Hyena has learned survival through intelligence; wit preserves life.

Hyena has learned strength through community; pack bonds create stability.

Hyena has learned courage through shadow; facing darkness builds power.

Hyena has learned renewal through humor; laughter dissolves fear and tension.

Recurring Patterns Across Lifetimes

Hyena souls often appear as protectors of a group, mediators in tense environments, social strategists, healers through humor, or those who thrive within complex systems.

Hyena souls read dynamics quickly; they sense power shifts and adapt with ease.

Hyena souls value loyalty and realism; life organizes around what truly works.

Initiations of This Lifetime

Hyena awakens during periods requiring resilience, group coordination, or navigation of shadow aspects within self or community.

Hyena activates when the soul trusts its intelligence, embraces teamwork, and meets difficulty with courage and humor.

Iguana Totem

Core Totem Essence

Iguana has the soul memory of solar embodiment and ancestral stillness. This totem lives through warmth, patience, and attunement to environmental rhythm. Across Mesoamerica, the Caribbean, South America, and island cultures, the iguana appears as a sun-aligned being, a guardian of fertility, and a witness to continuity through slow time. Iguana medicine centers on regulation through warmth, presence through stillness, and wisdom gained by observing life instead of forcing it.

Strengths of the Totem

Iguana brings solar attunement; vitality rises through warmth, light, and rest.

Iguana has patient awareness; observation reveals timing and opportunity.

Iguana embodies environmental harmony; body and surroundings move into balance together.

Iguana has grounded presence; stillness in clarity and strength.

Iguana holds ancestral continuity; endurance flows through calm persistence.

Challenges of the Totem

Iguana lives through deliberate pacing; momentum develops through patience instead of urgency.

Iguana values comfort and stability; adaptability grows through gentle expansion beyond familiar zones.

Iguana has strong sensitivity to temperature and environment; self-care has resilience.

Iguana maintains a quiet presence; expression strengthens influence when chosen consciously.

Past Life Lessons Carried Forward

Iguana has learned survival through regulation; warmth, rest, and timing preserve life.

Iguana has learned power through stillness; waiting reveals advantage.

Iguana has learned fertility through alignment; abundance grows through harmony with land and season.

Iguana has learned observation as wisdom; seeing precedes action.

Recurring Patterns Across Lifetimes

Iguana souls often appear as watchers, elders in training, land stewards, gardeners, or quiet stabilizers.

Iguana souls influence pace and atmosphere; calm presence reshapes the environment.

Iguana souls value sustainability; long-view decisions guide their path.

Initiations of This Lifetime

Iguana awakens during periods of nervous system regulation, health restoration, or return to embodied rhythm.

Iguana activates when the soul learns to trust stillness, warmth, and environmental attunement.

Lizard Variations: Current Life Expression

Green Iguana

Green Iguana reflects fertility, growth, and arboreal awareness; the soul engages nourishment, renewal, and alignment with lush environments. Mesoamerican cultures associate the green iguana with life force, food security, and seasonal abundance.

Marine Iguana

Marine Iguana reflects adaptability across elements; the soul navigates emotional depth and physical endurance while maintaining inner equilibrium. Indigenous Galapagos understanding views this iguana as a testament to survival through innovation and patience.

Desert Iguana

Desert Iguana reflects heat mastery and endurance; the soul engages resilience, clarity, and vitality under intense conditions. Southwestern cultures recognize this being as a teacher of sun wisdom and efficient energy use.

Jaguar and Panther Totem

Core Totem Essence

Jaguar has the soul memory of sovereign power held in silence. This totem moves through shadow with precision, patience, and embodied authority. Across Central and South America, Africa, and parts of Asia, cultures recognize the Jaguar as guardians of thresholds, rulers of night, and keepers of sacred force tied to land and blood. This medicine centers on mastery of instinct, disciplined strength, and the courage to walk unseen paths with purpose.

Strengths of the Totem

Jaguar brings focused power; energy gathers, waits, and steadies with impeccable timing.

Jaguar has shadow mastery; the soul navigates darkness with clarity, confidence, and control.

Jaguar embodies sovereignty; authority arises from inner alignment instead of external approval.

Jaguar has precision; action expresses efficiency, decisiveness, and impact.

Jaguar protects sacred territory; boundaries hold firm through presence and readiness.

Challenges of the Totem

Jaguar lives with intense inner force; containment and direction shape sustainable expression.

Jaguar values privacy; visibility and exposure invite conscious choice and energetic discernment.

Jaguar has deep instinctual drives; integration with emotional awareness has balance.

Jaguar walks alone by nature; connection develops through trust and earned proximity.

Past Life Lessons Carried Forward

Jaguar has learned command of fear; stillness transforms threat into clarity.

Jaguar has learned the ethics of power; restraint refines strength into wisdom.

Jaguar has learned guardianship of sacred space; land, body, and lineage receive protection.

Jaguar has learned initiation through descent; entering the shadow yields transformation and authority.

Recurring Patterns Across Lifetimes

Jaguar souls often appear as protectors, warriors, ritual leaders, shamans, or boundary keepers.

Jaguar souls attract initiatory paths; trials forge mastery and confidence.

Jaguar souls value autonomy; relationships form through respect, loyalty, and depth.

Initiations of This Lifetime

Jaguar awakens during periods of power reclamation, shadow integration, or territorial defense.

Jaguar activates when the soul claims authority, refines instinct, and acts with precision.

Felid Variations: Current Life Expression

Jaguar

Jaguar reflects spiritual kingship and shamanic passage; the soul engages death-rebirth cycles, dream travel, and command of liminal realms. In Mesoamerican cultures, the Jaguar serves as a ruler of the night, a protector of temples, and a guide through underworld initiation.

Panther

Panther reflects stealth and strategic movement; the soul navigates influence, protection, and power within unseen currents. In African and diasporic traditions, Panther aligns with guardianship, courage, and disciplined strength with grace.

Jay and Bluebird Totem

Core Totem Essence

Jays carry the soul memory of voice, signaling, and truth expressed through sound and color. This totem lives through communication that protects, alerts, and inspires, balancing intelligence with social awareness. Across Indigenous North American traditions, Celtic bird lore, and Northern forest cultures, jays appear as messengers, imitators, and defenders of territory, while bluebirds appear as bringers of joy, renewal, and hopeful continuity. This medicine centers on truthful expression, social intelligence, and the courage to be seen and heard.

Strengths of the Totem

Jays bring powerful communication; voice creates safety, clarity, and connection.

Jays carry keen social awareness; group dynamics and signals register quickly.

Jays embody confidence in visibility; presence claims space without apology.

Jays have protection through sound; warning and truth preserve harmony.

Jays have optimism grounded in awareness; joy rises from clarity instead of denial.

Challenges of the Totem

Jays live with strong expressive energy; discernment guides timing and tone.

Jays respond quickly to social stimulus; grounding has calm authority.

Jays hold leadership within group space; humility has balanced influence.

Jays thrive in interaction; solitude restores vocal and emotional clarity.

Past Life Lessons Carried Forward

Jays have learned protection through voice; sound creates safety.

Jays have learned truth through expression; silence and speech both carry power.

Jays have learned joy as resilience; hope sustains community.

Jays have learned leadership through signaling; awareness guides others.

Recurring Patterns Across Lifetimes

Jays souls often appear as speakers, teachers, advocates, singers, storytellers, or social guardians.

Jays souls influence group direction; communication reshapes outcome.

Jays souls hold responsibility for tone and truth; voice has consequence.

Initiations of This Lifetime

Jays awaken during periods of self-expression, advocacy, social leadership, or reclamation of voice.

Jays activate when the soul speaks clearly, signals truth, and trusts its presence within the community.

Corvid and Thrush Variations: Current Life Expression

Blue Jay

Blue Jay reflects assertive communication and territorial guardianship; the soul engages protection, mimicry, and social intelligence. Indigenous North American traditions honor the blue jay as a truth teller and alert keeper who warns the community and challenges dishonesty through sound and presence.

Steller's Jay

Steller's Jay reflects dramatic expression and forest authority; the soul engages bold voice, visibility, and leadership within layered environments. This expression emphasizes confidence by wilderness awareness.

Scrub Jay

Scrub Jay reflects strategic memory and planning; the soul engages foresight, resource caching, and long-term thinking. This variation emphasizes intelligence expressed through preparation and adaptability.

Florida Scrub Jay

The Florida Scrub Jay reflects cooperative guardianship; the soul engages shared responsibility, family systems, and social loyalty. This expression emphasizes protection through group coordination.

Bluebird

Bluebird reflects joy, renewal, and emotional openness; the soul engages hope, gentle expression, and the return of light after hardship. Celtic and European traditions associate the bluebird with happiness, song, and the promise of continuity.

Mountain Bluebird

Mountain Bluebird reflects expansive optimism and freedom; the soul engages clarity, openness, and trust within wide emotional and physical landscapes.

Eastern Bluebird

Eastern Bluebird reflects home-based joy and gentle leadership; the soul engages community harmony, nurturing presence, and emotional reassurance.

Jellyfish Totem

Core Totem Essence

The Jellyfish has the soul memory of ancient consciousness, emotional transparency, and power expressed through surrender to flow. This totem lives without resistance, teaching how survival, influence, and navigation arise through attunement instead of force. Across Pacific Islander ocean knowledge, Japanese sea lore, Indigenous coastal teachings, and modern mythic symbolism, jellyfish appear as a being of primordial time, a carrier of soft power, and a reminder that presence shapes outcome even without structure. Jellyfish medicine centers on sensitivity guided by awareness, emotional truth revealed through transparency, and trust in the current instead of control.

Strengths of the Totem

Jellyfish brings deep emotional attunement; feeling guides movement and decision.

Jellyfish carry ancient awareness; memory flows beyond linear time.

Jellyfish embodies soft power; influence emerges through presence instead of effort.

Jellyfish has adaptability; currents become allies through surrender.

Jellyfish has transparency; truth expresses itself without armor.

Challenges of the Totem

Jellyfish live within heightened sensitivity; grounding has safety and clarity.

Jellyfish move through collective currents; intention in direction within flow.

Jellyfish lack a rigid structure; boundary awareness strengthens navigation.

Jellyfish absorbs surrounding emotion; discernment preserves energetic integrity.

Past Life Lessons Carried Forward

Jellyfish have learned survival through yielding; flow preserves life.

Jellyfish have learned power through softness; transparency has authority.

Jellyfish have learned awareness through sensation; feeling reveals truth.

Jellyfish have learned continuity through time; ancient memory guides present movement.

Recurring Patterns Across Lifetimes

Jellyfish souls often appear as empaths, mystics, emotional navigators, artists, or keepers of ancestral memory.

Jellyfish souls influence the atmosphere subtly; emotion shifts through proximity.

Jellyfish souls value presence over control; life unfolds through trust.

Initiations of This Lifetime

Jellyfish awakens during periods of emotional surrender, identity softening, or return to instinctual wisdom.

Jellyfish activate when the soul refuses rigidity, honors sensitivity, and moves with current instead of against it.

Kangaroo Totem

Core Totem Essence

Kangaroo has the soul memory of forward momentum guided by land law. This totem lives through balance, directional movement, and embodied trust in the next step. Across Aboriginal Australian cultures, the kangaroo appears as a food giver, a teacher of travel across Country, and a being aligned with Dreaming tracks that map responsibility, kinship, and survival. Kangaroo medicine centers on progress through commitment, strength rooted in balance, and movement that honors ancestral pathways.

Strengths of the Totem

Kangaroo brings powerful forward motion; energy commits fully to direction and purpose.

Kangaroo has exceptional balance; body awareness stabilizes speed and strength.

Kangaroo embodies endurance through rhythm; steady movement sustains long journeys.

Kangaroo has land attunement; navigation follows ancestral tracks and environmental signals.

Kangaroo protects lineage; care for young and kin creates instinct and action.

Challenges of the Totem

The Kangaroo lives through forward-focused momentum; flexibility has adjustment when terrain shifts.

Kangaroo commits strongly once direction sets; discernment refines choice before movement begins.

Kangaroo has physical intensity; recovery and rest sustain longevity.

Kangaroo values open space; confinement invites conscious boundary setting and grounding.

Past Life Lessons Carried Forward

Kangaroo has learned trust in movement; progress unfolds through action instead of hesitation.

Kangaroo has learned balance as survival skill; alignment preserves strength.

Kangaroo has learned responsibility to Country; land and soul move together.

Kangaroo has learned protection of the young; continuity creates purpose across lifetimes.

Recurring Patterns Across Lifetimes

Kangaroo souls often appear as path finders, providers, travelers, protectors of family, or carriers of tradition.

Kangaroo souls move life forward; stagnation dissolves through decisive action.

Kangaroo souls honor ancestral obligation; duty and movement intertwine.

Initiations of This Lifetime

Kangaroo awakens during periods of relocation, decisive change, or commitment to a clear life path.

Kangaroo activates when the soul chooses direction, trusts balance, and moves with purpose.

Macropod Variations: Current Life Expression

Red Kangaroo

Red Kangaroo reflects endurance across vast terrain; the soul engages resilience, leadership, and strength by open land. Aboriginal Australian traditions honor red kangaroo as a primary food source and a being tied to survival law and respect for Country.

Eastern Grey Kangaroo

Eastern Grey Kangaroo reflects social navigation and adaptability; the soul engages group awareness, cooperation, and balance within shared space.

Wallaby

Wallaby reflects agility and quick adjustment; the soul engages responsiveness, smaller scale movement, and flexible strategy. This expression emphasizes adaptation within varied terrain.

KAPPA TOTEM

Core Totem Essence

Kappa has the soul memory of water intelligence, mischievous boundary testing, and power through etiquette and respect. This totem lives in rivers, ponds, and liminal waters, teaching how awareness of unseen currents protects life and how courtesy stabilizes the relationship between worlds. In Japanese folklore, a kappa appears as a river spirit who challenges arrogance, rewards humility, and upholds agreements once respect is shown. Kappa medicine centers on playful testing, sacred reciprocity, and mastery of emotional waters through discipline and awareness.

Strengths of the Totem

Kappa brings sharp awareness of emotional current; shifts in atmosphere register instantly.

Kappa has strategic intelligence; cleverness solves complex situations.

Kappa embodies respect for ritual and agreement; honor sustains power.

Kappa has physical and energetic strength; water becomes an ally and a teacher.

Kappa has boundary enforcement; sacred spaces remain protected.

Challenges of the Totem

Kappa lives within playful provocation; discernment guides humor toward harmony.

Kappa values cleverness strongly; compassion deepens connection

.Kappa tests boundaries readily; balanced interaction strengthens trust.

Kappa has a strong attachment to territory; flexibility expands relationships.

Past Life Lessons Carried Forward

Kappa has learned power through respect; courtesy creates destiny.

Kappa has learned survival through awareness; water reveals hidden truth.

Kappa has learned intelligence through mischief; challenge refines wisdom.

Kappa has learned strength through discipline; ritual stabilizes instinct.

Recurring Patterns Across Lifetimes

Kappa souls often appear as tricksters with ethical codes, guardians of water, martial artists, strategists, or teachers who provoke growth through challenge.

Kappa souls test integrity; those who respond with humility gain alliance.

Kappa souls value reciprocity; agreements hold sacred weight.

Initiations of This Lifetime

Kappa awakens during periods requiring emotional mastery, respect for boundaries, or disciplined engagement with power.

Kappa activates when the soul honors ritual, maintains integrity, and navigates emotional waters with both strength and humor.

Kelpie Totem

Core Totem Essence

Kelpie has the soul memory of liminal water, emotional depth, and transformation through encounter with the unseen. This totem lives where river meets mist, and land meets current, teaching how intuition guides safe passage through mystery. In Scottish and Celtic folklore, a kelpie appears as a shape-shifting water spirit who tests awareness, rewards respect, and guards the threshold between worlds. Kelpie medicine centers on discernment, emotional sovereignty, and mastery of currents that pull at the soul. This being teaches that clear intention protects and that intuition guides every crossing.

Strengths of the Totem

Kelpie brings powerful intuition; hidden currents reveal themselves through feeling and instinct.

Kelpie has strong boundary awareness; discernment protects energy and direction.

Kelpie embodies adaptability; form shifts fluidly to meet circumstance.

Kelpie has courage within shadowed spaces; mystery becomes teacher instead of threat.

Kelpie has safe passage; guidance emerges during transition and crossing.

Challenges of the Totem

Kelpie lives within deep emotional waters; grounding has clarity and steadiness.

Kelpie values independence strongly; trust strengthens meaningful partnerships.

Kelpie engages intense transformation; pacing has integration.

Kelpie moves between worlds frequently; anchoring preserves continuity and identity.

Past Life Lessons Carried Forward

Kelpie has learned wisdom through testing; awareness sharpens through challenge.

Kelpie has learned protection through intuition; instinct preserves life.

Kelpie has learned transformation through surrender; change refines strength.

Kelpie has learned guardianship of thresholds; safe crossing has sacred responsibility.

Recurring Patterns Across Lifetimes

Kelpie souls often appear as guides through grief or transition, therapists, shamans, travelers between cultures, or protectors of emotional boundaries.

Kelpie souls sense hidden motives and unseen influences quickly; perception runs deep.

Kelpie souls value sovereignty; self-trust creates every step forward.

Initiations of This Lifetime

Kelpie awakens during periods of emotional healing, relocation, rites of passage, or stepping into unknown terrain.

Kelpie activates when the soul trusts intuition, honors boundaries, and moves through change with courage and clarity.

Koala Totem

Core Totem Essence

Koala has the soul memory of gentleness sustained through discernment, rest, and deep attunement to environments. This totem lives through selective engagement, teaching how conservation of energy preserves clarity, health, and longevity. Across Aboriginal Australian cultures, the koala appears as a guardian of ancestral land, a teacher of listening to the body, and a being whose survival depends on intimate relationships with place and plant. Koala medicine centers on self-regulation, emotional calm, and wisdom expressed through stillness instead of action.

Strengths of the Totem

Koala brings profound self-regulation; energy flows toward what truly sustains life.

Koala has deep environmental attunement; place, plant, and body communicate clearly.

Koala embodies emotional calm; presence soothes tension and restores balance.

Koala has discernment; selective focus preserves vitality and clarity.

Koala has ancestral continuity; land memory and lineage shape identity and purpose.

Challenges of the Totem

Koala lives through narrow ecological preference; adaptability expands resilience during change.

Koala values rest and containment; gentle engagement has connection and expression.

Koala moves slowly through transition; trust in timing sustains confidence and flow.

Koala has sensitivity to disruption; grounding strengthens stability and security.

Past Life Lessons Carried Forward

Koala has learned survival through discernment; choice preserves life force.

Koala has learned wisdom through stillness; listening reveals correct action.

Koala has learned harmony through place; belonging sustains identity.

Koala has learned care through conservation; rest holds sacred value.

Recurring Patterns Across Lifetimes

Koala souls often appear as caretakers of self and land, healers through presence, or guardians of quiet spaces.

Koala souls influence others through calm; nervous systems settle in their company.

Koala souls value sustainability; life organizes around what can be maintained gently.

Initiations of This Lifetime

Koala awakens during periods of burnout recovery, boundary setting, nervous system healing, or return to ancestral values.

Koala activates when the soul honors rest, chooses carefully, and aligns life with what truly nourishes.

Komodo Dragon Totem

Core Totem Essence

Komodo Dragon has the soul memory of primordial authority and ancestral endurance. This totem lives through embodied command, territorial wisdom, and the quiet certainty of ancient survival. Indigenous cultures of the Indonesian islands, especially Komodo, Rinca, Flores, and surrounding regions, regard the Komodo Dragon as a guardian ancestor and a being of shared lineage with humans. Komodo Dragon medicine centers on sovereignty rooted in age, power held without excess, and the responsibility that comes with occupying space as an elder force within the living world.

Strengths of the Totem

Komodo Dragon brings an undeniable presence; authority emanates naturally through embodiment.

Komodo Dragon has ancestral endurance; survival spans generations through instinct and restraint.

Komodo Dragon embodies territorial mastery; space organizes itself around clear ownership and respect.

Komodo Dragon has strategic patience; stillness precedes decisive and effective action.

Komodo Dragon holds primal wisdom; ancient knowing guides modern circumstance.

Challenges of the Totem

Komodo Dragon lives with immense power; conscious regulation refines impact and responsibility.

Komodo Dragon values autonomy and territory; relationships develop through mutual respect and clear boundaries.

Komodo Dragon has a slow metabolic rhythm; pacing has alignment with faster environments.

Komodo Dragon commands attention through presence; humility has harmonious leadership.

Past Life Lessons Carried Forward

Komodo Dragon has learned survival through patience; waiting preserves strength.

Komodo Dragon has learned authority through embodiment; power resides within the body instead of being displayed.

Komodo Dragon has learned guardianship of land; territory has ancestral memory and duty.

Komodo Dragon has learned restraint as wisdom; conservation of energy ensures longevity.

Recurring Patterns Across Lifetimes

Komodo Dragon souls often appear as elders, protectors of land, boundary enforcers, or figures of quiet dominance.

Komodo Dragon souls carry ancestral responsibility; lineage and place shape identity and purpose.

Komodo Dragon souls influence through presence; action occurs rarely and decisively.

Initiations of This Lifetime

Komodo Dragon awakens during periods of power reclamation, boundary defense, or assumption of elder authority.

Komodo Dragon activates when the soul accepts responsibility for space, strength, and the stewardship of ancient force.

Ladybug Totem

Core Totem Essence

Ladybug has the soul memory of gentle protection, quiet blessing, and prosperity arriving through a small sacred presence. This totem lives among leaves and gardens, teaching how delicate form can hold powerful influence. Across European folk tradition, Slavic lore, Mediterranean countryside belief, and agricultural symbolism worldwide, the ladybug appears as a sign of good fortune, divine favor, and protection of crops. Many traditions associate the ladybug with blessings from the Mother, the Virgin, or benevolent sky forces who safeguard harvest and home. Ladybug medicine centers on innocence strengthened by trust, protection expressed through subtle power, and abundance that happens through grace.

Strengths of the Totem

Ladybug brings quiet protection; unseen forces guard and stabilize life.

Ladybug has natural good fortune; synchronicity aligns gently and consistently.

Ladybug embodies gentle strength; small presence influences large systems.

Ladybug has optimism; hope renews faith and direction.

Ladybug has harmony within environments; balance restores naturally through subtle action.

Challenges of the Totem

Ladybug lives through softness; a confident presence strengthens visibility and impact.

Ladybug values peaceful surroundings; boundary clarity preserves safety and stability.

Ladybug moves lightly through life; commitment deepens lasting creation.

Ladybug has delicate sensitivity; grounding in energy and resilience.

Past Life Lessons Carried Forward

Ladybug has learned blessing through simplicity; grace sustains prosperity.

Ladybug has learned protection through alignment; harmony shields naturally.

Ladybug has learned influence through small acts; subtle gestures shift destiny.

Ladybug has learned to trust in benevolent forces; faith has abundance.

Recurring Patterns Across Lifetimes

Ladybug souls often appear as gardeners, healers, caregivers, artists, or quiet benefactors whose presence brings peace and good fortune.

Ladybug souls uplift the atmosphere gently; environments feel lighter and safer around them.

Ladybug souls value beauty, kindness, and steady tending; prosperity grows through patient care.

Initiations of This Lifetime

Ladybug awakens during periods of rebuilding faith, cultivating abundance, or restoring harmony within homes or communities.

Ladybug activates when the soul trusts in grace, honors small blessings, and brings quiet protection to those it loves.

Lion Totem

Core Totem Essence

Lion has the soul memory of sovereign leadership expressed through courage, presence, and responsibility to the collective. This totem lives through heart-centered authority, teaching how power stabilizes when guided by protection, honor, and dignity. Across African cultures, ancient Near Eastern kingdoms, Indian tradition, and Mediterranean myth, the lion appears as a guardian of law, a symbol of rightful rule, and a keeper of sacred order. Lion medicine centers on leadership that serves life, strength guided by compassion, and visibility grounded in purpose.

Strengths of the Totem

Lion brings a commanding presence; authority arises naturally through embodiment and confidence.

Lion has courageous heart energy; fear yields to clarity and decisive action.

Lion embodies protective leadership; safety and order grow through guardianship.

Lion has collective cohesion; group strength organizes around a steady direction.

Lion holds dignity and honor; integrity creates action and reputation.

Challenges of the Totem

Lion lives with great responsibility; replenishment through rest and trust sustains vitality.

Lion occupies visible leadership; humility deepens connection and loyalty.

Lion protects territory and pride; discernment refines response within shared space.

Lion has intense drive; patience has timing and long view.

Past Life Lessons Carried Forward

Lion has learned leadership through service; authority exists to protect and uphold life.

Lion has learned courage through heart alignment; love fuels strength.

Lion has learned order through presence; calm command stabilizes chaos.

Lion has learned visibility as duty; being seen has responsibility.

Recurring Patterns Across Lifetimes

Lion souls often appear as leaders, protectors, heads of family, cultural figures, or guardians of law.

Lion souls shape group morale; confidence and safety rise through their presence.

Lion souls hold responsibility for many; collective well-being guides decisions.

Initiations of This Lifetime

Lion awakens during calls to leadership, protection of others, or reclamation of personal sovereignty.

Lion activates when the soul leads with courage, steadiness, and heart-centered authority.

Lizard Totem

Core Totem Essence

Lizard has the soul memory of instinctual awareness and regenerative presence. This totem lives close to the earth and sun, guiding survival through sensitivity, timing, and rapid renewal. Across Indigenous cultures of the Americas, Australia, Africa, the Middle East, and South Asia, the lizard appears as a guardian of thresholds, a keeper of dreamtime knowledge, and a teacher of regeneration through awareness. Lizard medicine centers on perception sharpened by stillness, survival guided by instinct, and renewal achieved through shedding and return.

Strengths of the Totem

Lizard brings heightened sensory awareness; subtle vibration, movement, and change register clearly.

Lizard has regenerative power; renewal unfolds through natural cycles of release and regrowth.

Lizard embodies instinctual intelligence; body knowing guides timing and response.

Lizard has adaptability; survival thrives through responsiveness to environments.

Lizard holds dream and vision wisdom; insight arises through altered states and symbolic perception.

Challenges of the Totem

Lizard lives through heightened sensitivity; grounding has nervous system balance.

Lizard moves between stillness and sudden action; integration in momentum and clarity.

Lizard values safety and concealment; visibility develops through trust and readiness.

Lizard responds quickly to stimulus; discernment refines reaction into choice.

Past Life Lessons Carried Forward

Lizard has learned survival through awareness; perception preserves life.

Lizard has learned renewal through shedding; release restores vitality and strength.

Lizard has learned power through stillness; waiting reveals opportunity.

Lizard has learned navigation of thresholds; dream and waking worlds inform each other.

Recurring Patterns Across Lifetimes

Lizard souls often appear as scouts, healers, dream interpreters, intuitive navigators, or guardians of liminal space.

Lizard souls thrive in changeable environments; adaptability defines resilience.

Lizard souls protect vital energy; awareness guides conservation and use of life force.

Initiations of This Lifetime

Lizard awakens during periods of heightened intuition, survival challenge, or sensory awakening.

Lizard activates when the soul learns to trust instinct, read subtle cues, and regenerate through conscious release.

Lizard Variations: Current Life Expression

Desert Lizard

Desert Lizard reflects heat mastery and endurance; the soul engages resilience, energy efficiency, and survival within demanding conditions. Indigenous desert cultures honor the lizard as a teacher of sun wisdom and instinctual timing.

Horned Lizard

Horned Lizard reflects protective awareness and boundary clarity; the soul engages defense through presence, camouflage, and strategic stillness. Southwestern traditions recognize this lizard as a guardian spirit tied to land and self-protection.

Monitor Lizard

Monitor Lizard reflects vigilance and territorial intelligence; the soul engages observation, authority, and strategic movement. African and South Asian cultures associate the monitor lizard with watchfulness and ancient power.

Skink

Skink reflects regenerative ease and rapid renewal; the soul engages adaptability, tail shedding symbolism, and swift recovery following disruption. Many cultures view skink as a sign of resilience and restoration.

Anole

Anole reflects perceptual adaptation; the soul engages responsiveness to social and environmental shifts through color and behavior. This expression emphasizes awareness made by context.

Llama and Alpaca Totem

Core Totem Essence

The Llama has the soul memory of gentle service, cooperative strength, and prosperity sustained through steady contribution. This totem lives in high places and thin air, teaching how endurance, humility, and mutual reliance allow life to flourish even in demanding terrain. Across Andean cultures, especially Quechua and Aymara traditions, Llama stands as sacred companions to humanity, providers of fiber, food, transport, and ceremonial offering. They represent reciprocity between people and land, where care flows in both directions. Llama medicine centers on shared burden, peaceful resilience, and abundance created through relationship.

Strengths of the Totem

Llama brings calm endurance; steady pacing sustains long journeys.

Llama has cooperative intelligence; teamwork multiplies strength.

Llama embodies gentle presence; peace diffuses tension and restores harmony.

Llama has provision; resources flow through sustainable care and reciprocity.

Llama has high altitude vision; clarity strengthens perspective and foresight.

Challenges of the Totem

Llama lives through service to others; self-nourishment sustains vitality.

Llama values group harmony; personal voice strengthens balance.

Llama has deliberate pace; responsiveness enhances opportunity.

Llama has shared responsibility; boundary clarity preserves energy.

Past Life Lessons Carried Forward

Llama have learned prosperity through reciprocity; giving and receiving remain equal.

Llama have learned strength through humility; quiet service has power.

Llama have learned survival through cooperation; shared burden lightens the path.

Llama have learned devotion to land; place anchors identity and purpose.

Recurring Patterns Across Lifetimes

Llama souls often appear as caretakers, providers, community supporters, textile workers, healers, or those who carry responsibility for many.

Llama souls stabilize groups through calm presence; others trust their reliability.

Llama souls value sustainability and mutual aid; life organizes through partnership instead of competition.

Initiations of This Lifetime

Llama awakens during periods of service, community building, shared labor, or reconnection to ancestral land and craft.

Llama activates when the soul embraces cooperation, has responsibility with grace, and creates abundance through steady contribution.

Camelid Variations: Current Life Expression

Llama

Llama reflects strength in service and burden carrying; the soul engages leadership through reliability, guardianship of community resources, and calm authority during long journeys. Andean traditions regard llama as a sacred transport and ceremonial companion, a bridge between human and mountain spirit.

Alpaca

Alpaca reflects nurturing provision and softness; the soul engages warmth, protection, and abundance expressed through fiber, craft, and care. This variation emphasizes gentleness, sensitivity, and prosperity generated through sustainable tending.

Lobster Totem

Core Totem Essence

Lobster has the soul memory of protection through structure, growth through shedding, and survival created from depth and pressure. This totem teaches how to build a strong exterior while continuing to evolve internally. Lobsters live along the ocean floor, navigating darkness, rock, and shifting terrain with patience and awareness. Its life cycle centers on molting, a process where it outgrows its shell, sheds it, and remains vulnerable until a new one hardens. Lobster medicine centers on boundaries, renewal, and the understanding that growth requires periods of exposure.

Strengths of the Totem

Lobster brings strong natural protection; boundaries remain firm and clear.

Lobster has resilience; harsh environments do not disrupt long-term survival.

Lobster embodies adaptability; it navigates changing conditions with steady awareness.

Lobster has regeneration through cycles; growth happens again and again.

Lobster has patience; timing governs survival and success.

Challenges of the Totem

Lobster lives within protective armor; openness strengthens connection.

Lobster values defense; trust allows for expansion beyond survival mode.

Lobster experiences vulnerable transitions during growth; courage has these phases.

Lobster moves cautiously; decisive action enhances opportunity when needed.

Past Life Lessons Carried Forward

Lobster has learned protection through structure.

Lobster has learned growth through shedding.

Lobster has learned survival through patience.

Lobster has learned awareness through navigating dark environments.

Recurring Patterns Across Lifetimes

Lobster souls often appear as protectors, strategists, survivors, or individuals who rebuild themselves repeatedly through life phases.

Lobster souls develop strong external boundaries while maintaining internal depth.

Lobster souls move through life in cycles of withdrawal, transformation, and reemergence.

Initiations of This Lifetime

Lobster awakens during periods of major personal growth, identity shifts, or situations that require shedding old structures.

Lobster activates when the soul allows itself to outgrow protection, move through vulnerability, and form a new sense of strength.

Lynx Totem

Core Totem Essence

Lynx carry the soul memory of perceptive sovereignty. This totem lives through heightened sight, discretion, and confident independence. Across Northern Europe, Siberia, North America, and Indigenous cultures of forest and edge land, Lynx appear as keepers of hidden knowledge, guardians of thresholds, and teachers of self-trust. Lynx medicine centers on discernment, quiet authority, and the ability to move unseen while remaining fully aware.

Strengths of the Totem

Lynx bring exceptional perception; subtle movement, truth, and opportunity reveal themselves clearly.

Lynx carry confident independence; self-trust guides action without hesitation.

Lynx embody boundary mastery; territory, time, and energy remain protected through awareness.

Lynx move with precision; action expresses efficiency and accuracy.

Lynx hold guardianship of secrets; wisdom remains safe until the moment of use.

Challenges of the Totem

Lynx live with a strong preference for autonomy; connection grows through mutual respect and choice.

Lynx value discretion; expression strengthens impact when offered intentionally.

Lynx carry heightened alertness; rest and grounding nervous system balance.

Lynx move comfortably alone; collaboration develops through aligned purpose.

Past Life Lessons Carried Forward

Lynx have learned the power of sight beyond surface; truth reveals itself through patience.

Lynx have learned sovereignty through self-trust; authority arises internally.

Lynx have learned protection through awareness; foresight prevents harm.

Lynx have learned timing as wisdom; waiting sharpens success.

Recurring Patterns Across Lifetimes

Lynx souls often appear as scouts, guardians, trackers, intuitives, or keepers of specialized knowledge.

Lynx souls value independence; they thrive in roles that reward discretion and skill.

Lynx souls intervene selectively; presence reshapes outcome at critical moments.

Initiations of This Lifetime

Lynx awaken during periods of boundary refinement, intuitive development, or personal authority consolidation.

Lynx activate when the soul trusts perception, protects sovereignty, and has quiet confidence.

Felid Variations: Current Life Expression

Lynx

Lynx reflects deep perceptual mastery and secret knowledge; the soul engages intuition, inner sight, and guardianship of wisdom. In Northern European and Siberian traditions, the lynx associates with the ability to see through illusion, protect hidden truths, and move safely between worlds.

Bobcat

Bobcat reflects adaptability at the edge; the soul navigates independence, clever survival, and confident presence within shared human and wild territory. Indigenous North American cultures recognize the bobcat as a teacher of self-reliance, curiosity, and quiet strength expressed through flexibility.

Manatee Totem

Core Totem Essence

Manatee has the soul memory of peaceful strength expressed through gentleness, emotional warmth, and steady presence. This totem lives through slow movement and deep sensitivity, teaching how safety and harmony arise through calm engagement instead of force. Across Indigenous Caribbean traditions, West African water lore, Amazonian river cultures, and coastal teachings of the Americas, manatee appears as a water elder, a guardian of gentle passage, and a being whose presence soothes emotional and communal currents. Manatee medicine centers on compassion embodied, emotional regulation through softness, and leadership expressed through reassurance and care.

Strengths of the Totem

Manatee brings profound emotional calm; presence lowers tension and restores equilibrium.

Manatee has gentle resilience; endurance unfolds through patience and steady movement.

Manatee embodies nurturing intelligence; care flows naturally toward others and environments.

Manatee has harmony within groups; peace spreads through quiet interaction.

Manatee navigates emotional waters with grace; depth remains safe and supportive.

Challenges of the Totem

Manatee lives within tender sensitivity; boundary clarity has safety and well-being.

Manatee moves slowly through change; trust in rhythm sustains confidence.

Manatee offers gentleness freely; discernment guides where energy flows.

Manatee values connection deeply; solitude restores balance and clarity.

Past Life Lessons Carried Forward

Manatee has learned strength through gentleness; softness preserves life.

Manatee has learned leadership through reassurance; calm steadies collective emotion.

Manatee has learned harmony through care; nurturing sustains continuity.

Manatee has learned navigation through trust; flow replaces resistance.

Recurring Patterns Across Lifetimes

Manatee souls often appear as healers, caregivers, emotional anchors, or peace holders within families and communities.

Manatee souls soothe conflict; emotional waters settle around them.

Manatee souls value safety and belonging; presence creates sanctuary.

Initiations of This Lifetime

Manatee awakens during periods of emotional healing, care-giving responsibility, or restoration after stress.

Manatee activates when the soul chooses gentleness, patience, and compassion as sources of strength.

Manta Ray Totem

Core Totem Essence

Manta Ray has the soul memory of graceful strength, expansive presence, and wisdom that flows through vast emotional waters. This totem moves like a living wing beneath the sea, teaching how gentleness and magnitude coexist in harmony. Across Polynesian, Hawaiian, Melanesian, and coastal Indigenous traditions, manta ray appears as an ancestral guardian, a spirit guide, and a symbol of protection and safe passage. Many Pacific cultures honor manta as a family protector and navigator of deep ocean pathways. Manta Ray medicine centers on calm authority, emotional intelligence, and leadership expressed through steady presence instead of force.

Strengths of the Totem

Manta Ray brings serene power; strength radiates through calm movement.

Manta Ray has expansive awareness; perception spans wide emotional and energetic fields.

Manta Ray embodies grace; motion flows effortlessly through complex currents.

Manta Ray has protective guardianship; loved ones feel sheltered and supported.

Manta Ray has deep intuition; inner guidance directs safe passage through life's waters.

Challenges of the Totem

Manta Ray lives within vast emotional depth; grounding has clarity and direction.

Manta Ray values peaceful presence; decisive action strengthens momentum when needed.

Manta Ray moves gently through conflict; clear boundaries preserve energy.

Manta Ray has strong sensitivity to environment; intentional solitude restores balance.

Past Life Lessons Carried Forward

Manta Ray has learned leadership through calm; steady presence guides many.

Manta Ray has learned survival through flow; resistance transforms into cooperation with current.

Manta Ray has learned wisdom through depth; emotional truth reveals guidance.

Manta Ray has learned protection through guardianship; family and lineage receive sacred care.

Recurring Patterns Across Lifetimes

Manta Ray souls often appear as protectors, navigators, healers, lifeguards, counselors, or those who guide others through emotional or spiritual waters.

Manta Ray souls carry quiet authority; others follow naturally without pressure.

Manta Ray souls value harmony and spaciousness; life organizes around peace and connection.

Initiations of This Lifetime

Manta Ray awakens during periods of emotional healing, ancestral connection, or stepping into leadership through gentleness and wisdom.

Manta Ray activates when the soul trusts its depth, has grace, and guides others through calm presence.

Mobulid Variations: Current Life Expression

Manta Ray

Oceanic Manta Ray reflects vast range and open water mastery; the soul engages global vision, long journeys, and expansive leadership across wide horizons. Reef Manta Ray reflects community guardianship; the soul engages protection of home waters, close relationships, and stewardship of local ecosystem.

Stingray

Stingray reflects grounded sensitivity and boundary protection; the soul engages quiet presence along the ocean floor, precise defense, and a strong connection to the earth element within water.

Marmoset Totem

Core Totem Essence

Marmoset has the soul memory of communal intimacy, bright curiosity, and survival through cooperation within small close knit groups. This totem lives among branches and canopy, teaching how connection, communication, and shared care-giving sustain life. Across Amazonian and Central and South American forest cultures, small monkeys such as marmosets appear as clever watchers, playful teachers, and guardians of family bonds. Their societies revolve around cooperation, shared parenting, and constant vocal contact.

Marmoset medicine centers on relational intelligence, joyful exploration, and the strength that grows through collective care.

Strengths of the Totem

Marmoset brings strong social attunement; communication flows clearly and frequently.

Marmoset has playful curiosity; learning unfolds through exploration and experimentation.

Marmoset embodies cooperative care-giving; responsibility is distributed evenly across the group.

Marmoset has agility and adaptability; quick movement navigates complex environments with ease.

Marmoset has emotional warmth; affection strengthens trust and belonging.

Challenges of the Totem

Marmoset lives within a close community; personal space and solitude restore clarity.

Marmoset values constant interaction; focused stillness deepens inner awareness.

Marmoset engages many interests at once; prioritization strengthens follow-through.

Marmoset has high sensitivity to group energy; grounding preserves balance.

Past Life Lessons Carried Forward

Marmoset has learned survival through cooperation; shared care sustains life.

Marmoset has learned wisdom through play; curiosity reveals opportunity.

Marmoset has learned protection through connection; bonds create safety.

Marmoset has learned joy as medicine; lightheartedness strengthens resilience.

Recurring Patterns Across Lifetimes

Marmoset souls often appear as teachers of children, caregivers, mediators, performers, communicators, or those who build tight, supportive communities.

Marmoset souls thrive in collaborative spaces; teamwork feels natural and energizing.

Marmoset souls value intimacy and trust; life organizes around chosen family and shared experience.

Initiations of This Lifetime

Marmoset awakens during periods of building community, learning new skills rapidly, or strengthening family bonds.

Marmoset activates when the soul embraces play, communicates openly, and creates safety through connection and shared responsibility.

Callitrichid Variations: Current Life Expression

Marmoset

Marmoset reflects social harmony and vocal leadership; the soul engages constant communication and emotional closeness within group.

Tamarin

Tamarin reflects cooperative guardianship and spirited energy; the soul engages teamwork, bold curiosity, and shared protection of young and territory.

MEERKAT TOTEM

Core Totem Essence

Meerkat has the soul memory of communal vigilance, shared responsibility, and survival through cooperation and constant awareness. This totem lives in open grasslands and desert edges where visibility and teamwork preserve life. Across southern African traditions and North American Plains cultures, these small burrowing guardians symbolize collective safety, communication, and social intelligence. Both species thrive through coordinated watchfulness and intricate underground homes. Meerkat medicine centers on mutual care, clear signaling, and the understanding that community forms the strongest defense.

Strengths of the Totem

Meerkat brings collective awareness; many eyes protect the whole.

Meerkat has strong communication; signals travel quickly and clearly.

Meerkat embodies cooperative labor; shared effort builds lasting security.

Meerkat has loyalty; bonds strengthen through trust and presence.

Meerkat has joyful resilience; play renews morale even in demanding conditions.

Challenges of the Totem

Meerkat live in constant alertness; rest restores balance and vitality.

Meerkat value group cohesion; personal sovereignty strengthens identity.

Meerkat respond quickly to disturbance; discernment refines reaction into strategy.

Meerkat has strong attachment to home bases; exploration expands perspectives.

Past Life Lessons Carried Forward

Meerkat have learned survival through unity; cooperation sustains life.

Meerkat have learned protection through vigilance; awareness preserves safety.

Meerkat have learned prosperity through shared labor; community builds abundance.

Meerkat have learned joy through connection; play strengthens spirit.

Recurring Patterns Across Lifetimes

Meerkat souls often appear as organizers, teachers, communicators, neighborhood protectors, or those who create strong family or chosen family networks.

Meerkat souls sense shifts in environments quickly; they guide others toward safety and preparedness.

Meerkat souls value belonging and cooperation; life organizes around mutual support.

Initiations of This Lifetime

Meerkat awakens during periods of community building, neighborhood leadership, cooperative projects, or strengthening family systems.

Meerkat activates when the soul embraces teamwork, communicates clearly, and protects collective well-being.

Burrower Variations: Current Life Expression

Meerkat

Meerkat reflects sentinel leadership and rotating guardianship; the soul engages watchfulness, shared responsibility, and courageous defense of kin. Southern African symbolism associates meerkats with loyalty and clever teamwork.

Prairie Dog

Prairie Dog reflects complex community structure and vocal communication; the soul engages collaborative living, intricate social bonds, and coordinated protection of home. Plains traditions recognize prairie dog towns as symbols of interdependence and shared survival.

Merfolk Totem

Core Totem Essence

Merfolk has the soul memory of deep emotion, ancestral waters, and consciousness that flows between worlds. This totem bridges sea and shore, spirit and body, dream and waking life. Across Celtic coastal lore, West African and Caribbean traditions of Mami Wata and Yemaya, Mediterranean siren myths, Pacific Islander sea guardians, and northern selkie and merrow stories, mer beings appear as guides, healers, protectors of the ocean, and keepers of memory older than land. Merfolk medicine centers on emotional mastery, intuitive navigation, and the ability to move gracefully between realms while remaining anchored in soul truth.

Strengths of the Totem

Merfolk bring deep emotional intelligence; feeling guides wisdom and choice.

Merfolk carry strong intuitive perception; unseen currents reveal themselves clearly.

Merfolk embody fluid adaptability; form and role shift smoothly with circumstance.

Merfolk have healing presence; water energy restores body and spirit.

Merfolk have ancestral connection; memory flows through lineage and dream.

Challenges of the Totem

Merfolk live within powerful emotional tides; grounding has clarity and direction.

Merfolk value solitude within deep waters; community connection strengthens balance.

Merfolk move between realms frequently; anchors in daily life sustain stability.

Merfolk carry strong sensitivity to collective feeling; energetic boundaries preserve vitality.

Past Life Lessons Carried Forward

Merfolk have learned survival through flow; cooperation with the current sustains life.

Merfolk have learned wisdom through depth; truth rises from emotional honesty.

Merfolk have learned guidance through song and signal; voice directs safe passage.

Merfolk have learned guardianship of sacred waters; protection of life sources holds sacred duty.

Recurring Patterns Across Lifetimes

Merfolk souls often appear as healers, mediums, dreamers, artists, travelers between cultures, or those who guide others through grief, birth, and transformation.

Merfolk souls feel drawn to water environments; oceans, lakes, and rivers restore their strength.

Merfolk souls value empathy and connection; relationships form through emotional truth instead of surface exchange.

Initiations of This Lifetime

Merfolk awaken during periods of emotional healing, spiritual awakening, ancestral reconnection, or major life transitions.

Merfolk activate when the soul trusts intuition, honors feeling as guidance, and moves through life with grace and compassion.

Mole Totem

Core Totem Essence

Mole has the soul memory of subterranean wisdom and intuitive navigation through unseen realms. This totem lives beneath surface reality, guiding survival through touch, vibration, and inner knowing instead of sight. Across European folk traditions, Indigenous North American earth lore, East Asian symbolism, and agrarian cultures worldwide, mole appears as a keeper of underground pathways, a guardian of hidden labor, and a teacher of persistence that shapes land from within. Mole medicine centers on depth over display, intuition over visibility, and progress achieved through patient excavation of truth.

Strengths of the Totem

Mole brings profound intuitive sensing; touch, vibration, and subtle signals guide movement and choice.

Mole has tireless persistence; steady effort reshapes environments over time.

Mole embodies comfort with darkness; inner worlds offer safety, clarity, and direction.

Mole has focused purpose; attention remains anchored to tasks without distraction.

Mole creates foundations; work done beneath the surface creates visible stability above.

Challenges of the Totem

Mole lives deeply inward; intentional emergence has connection and recognition.

Mole commits intensely to inner focus; flexibility has responsiveness to outer change.

Mole values privacy and containment; communication strengthens shared understanding.

Mole works continuously beneath the surface; rest renews strength and clarity.

Past Life Lessons Carried Forward

Mole has learned survival through intuition; sensing guides safe passage.

Mole has learned creation through persistence; foundations form through repeated effort.

Mole has learned trust in the unseen; progress unfolds beyond visibility.

Mole has learned stewardship of earth; soil, root, and tunnel sustain life above.

Recurring Patterns Across Lifetimes

Mole souls often appear as researchers, healers, builders of systems, protectors of roots, or keepers of hidden knowledge.

Mole souls influence outcomes quietly; stability grows from their unseen labor.

Mole souls value depth and privacy; meaning develops through inner work.

Initiations of This Lifetime

Mole awakens during periods of inner excavation, trauma processing, research, or foundation building.

Mole activates when the soul commits to patient work, trusts intuition, and honors progress that occurs out of sight.

Monkey Totem

Core Totem Essence

Monkey has the soul memory of adaptive intelligence expressed through play, curiosity, and social awareness. This totem lives through learning by interaction, exploration, and creative problem-solving. Across South and Southeast Asia, Africa, Central and South America, and island cultures, monkeys appear as clever mediators between forest, village, and spirit realms. Monkey medicine centers on curiosity as a survival skill, intelligence expressed through movement and humor, and wisdom gained through engagement instead of withdrawal.

Strengths of the Totem

Monkey brings rapid learning; observation and imitation translate quickly into skill.

Monkey has inventive intelligence; tools, tricks, and strategies emerge through experimentation.

Monkey embodies social fluency; relationships form through play, communication, and awareness of hierarchy.

Monkey expresses joy as vitality; laughter and movement sustain resilience.

Monkey navigates complex environments; adaptability has success within layered systems.

Challenges of the Totem

Monkey lives through constant stimulation; focus and integration strengthen follow-through.

Monkey moves quickly between interests; completion develops through conscious pacing.

Monkey mirrors social dynamics strongly; discernment guides identity stability.

Monkey thrives on interaction; solitude invites intentional grounding and reflection.

Past Life Lessons Carried Forward

Monkey has learned survival through intelligence; cleverness preserves life.

Monkey has learned community navigation; awareness of roles and alliances creates safety.

Monkey has learned learning through play; curiosity opens pathways to mastery.

Monkey has learned balance between humor and responsibility; joy has wisdom.

Recurring Patterns Across Lifetimes

Monkey souls often appear as teachers, performers, innovators, negotiators, storytellers, or social connectors.

Monkey souls energize groups; creativity and morale rise in their presence.

Monkey souls thrive within dynamic environments; change stimulates growth and engagement.

Initiations of This Lifetime

Monkey awakens during periods of learning, social navigation, cultural adaptation, or creative expansion.

Monkey activates when the soul uses curiosity, humor, and intelligence to meet complexity with agility.

Cercopithecoid and Platyrrhine Variations: Current Life Expression

Rhesus Monkey

Rhesus Monkey reflects adaptability within human systems; the soul engages resilience, learning, and survival alongside dense populations. South Asian cultures recognize this monkey through association with daily life, temple spaces, and enduring intelligence.

Langur

Langur reflects spiritual observation and restraint; the soul engages watchfulness, devotion, and elevated perspective. In Indian tradition, langur aligns with Hanuman energy, emphasizing service, loyalty, and disciplined strength expressed through humility.

Howler Monkey

Howler Monkey reflects vocal authority and territorial communication; the soul engages presence, boundary declaration, and identity through sound. Mesoamerican cultures recognize this monkey as a solar and wind-aligned being tied to timekeeping and ritual voice.

Spider Monkey

Spider Monkey reflects agility and relational networking; the soul engages connection, flexibility, and movement through social and physical space. Amazonian cultures observe this monkey as a master of canopy travel and cooperative awareness.

Capuchin Monkey

Capuchin Monkey reflects tool use and strategic intelligence; the soul engages problem solving, innovation, and practical creativity. Central and South American traditions recognize the capuchin as a symbol of cleverness and adaptive learning.

Golden Snub-Nosed Monkey

Golden Snub-Nosed Monkey reflects harmony within harsh environments; the soul engages resilience, cooperation, and beauty sustained through difficulty. East Asian cultures observe this monkey as a symbol of endurance, social cohesion, and seasonal intelligence.

Lemur

Lemur reflects ancestral awareness and liminal perception; the soul engages heightened sensitivity, rhythmic awareness, and connection between visible and unseen realms. This variation channels intuitive intelligence, nocturnal perception, and a strong attunement to cycles of light, sound, and environment. Power moves through quiet observation, subtle communication, and deep listening, teaching mastery through presence within threshold spaces and relationship with ancestral memory.

Moose Totem

Core Totem Essence

Moose has the soul memory of solitary authority created from emotional depth and quiet command. This totem lives through still strength, deliberate movement, and presence that reshapes space without force. Across Northern Indigenous cultures of North America, Siberia, and boreal forest peoples, moose appears as a forest elder, a water walker, and a being whose size and sensitivity coexist in powerful balance. Moose medicine centers on self-possessed leadership, emotional maturity, and the capacity to stand alone without isolation.

Strengths of the Totem

Moose brings profound embodied authority; presence alone establishes respect and boundary.

Moose has emotional depth; feeling informs wisdom instead of reaction.

Moose embodies calm dominance; strength expresses itself through restraint and steadiness.

Moose has independence; self-direction guides movement and choice.

Moose navigates water and forest with equal skill; emotional and physical realms integrate smoothly.

Challenges of the Totem

Moose lives with immense internal power; conscious pacing has harmony and safety.

Moose values solitude deeply; connection grows through intentional invitation instead of proximity.

Moose moves deliberately; environments driven by urgency require grounded adjustment.

Moose has sensitivity beneath strength; emotional regulation has clarity and ease.

Past Life Lessons Carried Forward

Moose has learned leadership through presence; authority arises without assertion.

Moose has learned balance between power and sensitivity; feeling strengthens command.

Moose has learned survival through self-trust; independence preserves integrity.

Moose has learned stewardship of territory; land and water respond to respectful presence.

Recurring Patterns Across Lifetimes

Moose souls often appear as solitary leaders, protectors, elders, or figures of quiet command.

Moose souls influence through stillness; others adjust their behavior in their presence.

Moose souls carry responsibility for space; boundaries and order follow naturally.

Initiations of This Lifetime

Moose awakens during periods of leadership without support, emotional maturation, or reclamation of personal authority.

Moose activates when the soul stands fully in its own space, honors sensitivity, and leads through embodied calm.

Moth Totem

Core Totem Essence

Moth has the soul memory of quiet transformation, devotion to inner light, and wisdom gained through night travel. This totem moves through shadow and moon glow, teaching how guidance arises through intuition instead of daylight clarity. Across Indigenous American traditions, Celtic and European countryside lore, Mexican symbolism, and Himalayan and Asian night spirit stories, the moth appears as a messenger of ancestors, a keeper of dreams, and a companion of thresholds between life and spirit. Moth medicine centers on gentle navigation through darkness, faith in unseen guidance, and transformation through surrender and trust.

Strengths of the Totem

Moth brings strong intuition; inner light directs movement and decision.

Moth has deep sensitivity; subtle signals reveal hidden truth.

Moth embodies quiet perseverance; steady flight sustains long journeys through the night.

Moth has transformation; cycles of change unfold naturally and gracefully.

Moth has dream and ancestral connection; messages flow through symbol and feeling.

Challenges of the Totem

Moth lives within heightened sensitivity to light and energy; grounding stabilizes focus.

Moth values inward guidance strongly; clear boundaries protect vitality.

Moth moves toward illumination with devotion; discernment refines which lights serve growth.

Moth has a gentle presence; confident visibility strengthens expression when needed.

Past Life Lessons Carried Forward

Moth has learned trust through darkness; intuition guides safely.

Moth has learned rebirth through metamorphosis; change renews spirit.

Moth has learned wisdom through dreams; inner vision reveals truth.

Moth has learned devotion to light; purpose attracts the path forward.

Recurring Patterns Across Lifetimes

Moth souls often appear as mystics, artists, dream workers, mediums, herbalists, or those who guide others through grief, transition, and shadow work.

Moth souls feel at home in twilight and reflective spaces; quiet environments restore energy.

Moth souls value subtlety and emotional honesty; influence flows through softness instead of force.

Initiations of This Lifetime

Moth awakens during periods of inner transformation, spiritual awakening, grief processing, or reconnection to dream and intuition.

Moth activates when the soul trusts its inner glow, follows instinctual guidance, and embraces change with grace.

Mouse Totem

Core Totem Essence

Mouse has the soul memory of attentiveness expressed through humility and care. This totem lives through close observation, precise action, and the quiet shaping of survival through small choices that accumulate into lasting impact. Across Indigenous North American teachings, Celtic folklore, Asian agrarian symbolism, and European earth lore, the mouse appears as a keeper of detail, a guardian of stored knowledge, and a teacher of how gentleness and awareness sustain life. Mouse medicine centers on mindfulness, stewardship of resources, and strength found in subtle presence.

Strengths of the Totem

Mouse brings exceptional attention to detail; small signals guide effective action.

Mouse has careful stewardship; resources receive thoughtful use and preservation.

Mouse embodies humility paired with intelligence; awareness compensates for size and visibility.

Mouse has adaptability; quick adjustment has survival and continuity.

Mouse protects stored wisdom; memory and preparation secure future stability.

Challenges of the Totem

Mouse lives with heightened alertness; grounding has calm within constant awareness.

Mouse values safety and concealment; confidence grows through gradual visibility.

Mouse responds swiftly to environments; discernment refines reaction into choice.

Mouse commits deeply to preparation; trust has the enjoyment of present moments.

Past Life Lessons Carried Forward

Mouse has learned survival through awareness; detail preserves life.

Mouse has learned abundance through preparation; foresight ensures continuity.

Mouse has learned humility as strength; quiet presence creates outcome.

Mouse has learned care as devotion; tending small things creates lasting security.

Recurring Patterns Across Lifetimes

Mouse souls often appear as planners, caretakers, archivists, healers of subtle imbalance, or guardians of domestic space.

Mouse souls influence outcomes quietly; systems remain stable through their diligence.

Mouse souls value safety and continuity; harmony grows through careful tending.

Initiations of This Lifetime

Mouse awakens during periods of detail-oriented work, resource management, healing through routine, or rebuilding after disruption.

Mouse activates when the soul honors small actions, trusts attentiveness, and allows gentle persistence to guide progress.

Nāga Totem

Core Totem Essence

Nāga has the soul memory of primordial waters, sacred guardianship, and wisdom coiled within Earth and River. This totem lives at the meeting of serpent and dragon, teaching how life force flows through both depth and elevation. Across Hindu, Buddhist, Jain, Thai, Khmer, Balinese, Tibetan, and broader Southeast Asian traditions, nāga appears as a protector of springs, rivers, rain, treasure, and spiritual knowledge. Nāga shelters temples, crowns gateways, and coils beneath the roots of the world tree. Nāga medicine centers on sovereignty of energy, guardianship of sacred space, and mastery of emotional and spiritual currents.

Strengths of the Totem

Nāga brings a powerful life force; vitality moves like water and lightning through the body.

Nāga has deep ancestral wisdom; memory extends across generations and realms.

Nāga embodies guardianship; sacred knowledge and places remain protected.

Nāga has intuitive mastery of water and emotion; currents reveal hidden truth.

Nāga has spiritual authority; presence commands respect through calm strength.

Challenges of the Totem

Nāga lives within intense energy; grounding has clarity and steadiness.

Nāga values sovereignty strongly; compassionate connection deepens harmony.

Nāga engages powerful protective instinct; discernment refines response.

Nāga moves between realms frequently; because of this, balance is important.

Past Life Lessons Carried Forward

Nāga has learned protection through vigilance; sacred spaces remain intact.

Nāga has learned wisdom through depth; hidden knowledge creates destiny.

Nāga has learned renewal through shedding; transformation strengthens essence.

Nāga has learned harmony with water and rain; flow sustains all life.

Recurring Patterns Across Lifetimes

Nāga souls often appear as temple guardians, healers, priests, rain callers, energy workers, martial artists, or keepers of lineage memory.

Nāga souls feel drawn to rivers, lakes, springs, and monsoon seasons; water restores their strength.

Nāga souls value sovereignty and sacred duty; they naturally protect what holds spiritual importance.

Initiations of This Lifetime

Nāga awakens during periods of emotional purification, ancestral healing, or guardianship of knowledge and land.

Nāga activates when the soul claims its power, protects sacred truth, and flows gracefully between worlds.

Newt Totem

Core Totem Essence

Newt has the soul memory of renewal, quiet transformation, and healing through water and earth together. This totem lives between pond and forest floors, teaching how life regenerates through softness, patience, and steady adaptation. Across Celtic countryside lore, European folk magic, and woodland traditions, the newt appears as a creature of wells, springs, and moss-covered stones, often associated with restoration, alchemy, and subtle enchantment. Newt medicine centers on regeneration, emotional cleansing, and the ability to rebuild self and spirit after change.

Strengths of the Totem

Newt brings powerful regenerative energy; recovery unfolds quickly and completely.

Newt has gentle adaptability; body and spirit adjust easily to shifting environments.

Newt embodies quiet resilience; survival thrives through calm persistence.

Newt has connection to water and land; balance stabilizes emotion and action.

Newt has subtle healing presence; restoration occurs through touch and proximity.

Challenges of the Totem

Newt lives within sensitivity to environments; grounding has stability and confidence.

Newt values solitude and hidden spaces; connection deepens shared experience.

Newt moves softly through life; assertive action strengthens momentum when required.

Newt has cyclical transformation; integration has clarity between phases.

Past Life Lessons Carried Forward

Newt has learned renewal through regeneration; loss transforms into growth.

Newt has learned wisdom through patience; slow change creates lasting strength.

Newt has learned healing through water; cleansing restores vitality.

Newt has learned survival through subtlety; gentle presence sustains life.

Recurring Patterns Across Lifetimes

Newt souls often appear as healers, herbalists, energy workers, caretakers, or those who guide others through recovery and emotional repair.

Newt souls feel drawn to springs, rain, forests, and quiet places where life renews itself.

Newt souls value peace and restoration; environments grow healthier around them.

Initiations of This Lifetime

Newt awakens during periods of physical healing, emotional recovery, life rebuilding, or returning to a more natural and gentle rhythm.

Newt activates when the soul trusts its ability to regenerate, releases old skin, and embraces steady renewal.

Octopus and Squid Totem

Core Totem Essence

Octopus has the soul memory of distributed intelligence. This totem lives through many minds within one body, sensing, adapting, and responding through total presence. Across coastal and island cultures of the Pacific, Mediterranean, and Indian Oceans, people recognize octopods as masters of camouflage, strategy, and oceanic awareness. Octopus medicine centers on adaptability, perception through the whole body, and conscious relationship with change.

Strengths of the Totem

Octopus brings expansive intelligence; awareness flows through limbs, skin, and environment simultaneously.

Octopus has exceptional adaptability; shifting conditions invite creative response and strategic movement.

Octopus embodies problem-solving mastery; puzzles resolves through curiosity, experimentation, and persistence.

Octopus navigates emotional depth; water wisdom has sensitivity, empathy, and responsiveness.

Octopus holds regenerative power; renewal arises through release, resilience, and growth.

Challenges of the Totem

Octopus lives with heightened sensitivity; constant input makes for intentional grounding and rest.

Octopus moves fluidly between identities; coherence grows through self-recognition and integration.

Octopus values flexibility; sustained structure develops through conscious anchoring.

Octopus engages concealment and revelation; discernment guides timing and visibility.

Past Life Lessons Carried Forward

Octopus has learned intelligence through embodiment; the body thinks, feels, and chooses.

Octopus has learned survival through adaptation; change strengthens capabilities.

Octopus has learned strategy through movement; space, timing, and perception shape safety.

Octopus has learned regeneration; renewal follows transformation and shedding.

Recurring Patterns Across Lifetimes

Octopus souls often appear as strategists, healers, artists, innovators, counselors, or complex system navigators.

Octopus souls thrive in layered environments; synthesis and multitasking feel natural.

Octopus souls carry emotional attunement; others experience understanding and ease in their presence.

Initiations of This Lifetime

Octopus awakens during periods of rapid change, identity expansion, or emotional complexity.

Octopus activates when the soul trusts intelligence distributed throughout the body and environment.

Octopod Variations: Current Life Expression

Octopus

Common Octopus reflects adaptability within human systems; the soul engages learning, problem-solving, and social navigation across diverse environments. Mediterranean cultures associate this octopus with cleverness, sustenance, and sea mastery.

Cuttlefish

Cuttlefish reflects mastery of communication through color and pattern; the soul navigates expression, emotional signaling, and relational nuance. Many coastal traditions observe cuttlefish as a teacher of timing, camouflage, and symbolic language.

Squid

Squid reflects coordinated intelligence and momentum; the soul engages group movement, rapid response, and directional force. In many seafaring cultures, squid embody adaptability, endurance, and navigation through deep waters.

Nautilus

Nautilus reflects ancient order and sacred geometry; the soul engages continuity, memory, and the spiral of growth across time. Island cultures view this being as a living archive of oceanic lineage.

ORANGUTAN TOTEM

Core Totem Essence

Orangutan has the soul memory of solitary wisdom and deliberate presence. This totem lives through deep observation, patience, and thoughtful action created from long memory. Across the rain-forests of Borneo and Sumatra and the cultures that live in relationship with them, the orangutan appears as a forest elder, a quiet teacher, and a keeper of ancestral intelligence. Orangutan medicine centers on contemplative awareness, gentle strength, and knowledge preserved through restraint instead of display.

Strengths of the Totem

Orangutan brings profound reflective intelligence; insight forms through observation and contemplation.

Orangutan has patient endurance; long cycles unfold through steadiness and care.

Orangutan embodies gentle authority; influence arises through presence instead of force.

Orangutan has deep environmental attunement; forest rhythm guides behavior and choice.

Orangutan preserves ancestral knowledge; memory passes through lived example and quiet continuity.

Challenges of the Totem

Orangutan lives with preference for solitude; connection develops through intentional engagement.

Orangutan moves slowly through decision; timing strengthens confidence and outcome.

Orangutan has deep emotional sensitivity; expression has relational clarity.

Orangutan values continuity and habitat; disruption invites adaptation grounded in patience.

Past Life Lessons Carried Forward

Orangutan has learned wisdom through watching; silence reveals truth.

Orangutan has learned strength through gentleness; restraint refines power.

Orangutan has learned survival through memory; learned paths preserve life.

Orangutan has learned stewardship of place; care for land sustains future generations.

Recurring Patterns Across Lifetimes

Orangutan souls often appear as elders, teachers, keepers of knowledge, land stewards, or quiet leaders.

Orangutan souls influence through example; others learn by observing their choices.

Orangutan souls value depth over speed; quality guides purpose.

Initiations of This Lifetime

Orangutan awakens during periods of withdrawal, study, environmental guardianship, or return to essential values.

Orangutan activates when the soul chooses patience, contemplation, and gentle leadership.

Ostrich Totem

Core Totem Essence

Ostrich has the soul memory of grounded power, decisive movement, and survival through stamina and clear sight across open land. This totem lives where the horizon stretches wide, teaching how strength develops through endurance, speed, and unwavering awareness of surroundings. Across African savanna cultures, Egyptian symbolism, and desert and grassland traditions, the ostrich appears as a guardian of territory, a provider through feather and egg, and a keeper of balance and truth. In ancient Kemeticism, the ostrich feather represents Ma'at; order, justice, and right alignment with cosmic law. Ostrich medicine centers on a strong footing, truthfulness, and forward momentum guided by integrity.

Strengths of the Totem

Ostrich brings powerful endurance; long distances yield to steady stamina.

Ostrich has swift grounded speed; action unfolds with confidence and precision.

Ostrich embodies wide vision; awareness scans far ahead for opportunity and change.

Ostrich has protection of kin; guardianship strengthens family and community.

Ostrich has truth and balance; integrity in every step.

Challenges of the Totem

Ostrich lives through constant vigilance; rest restores clarity and ease.

Ostrich values forward motion strongly; reflection deepens wisdom and planning.

Ostrich holds strong territorial instinct; flexibility has harmony within shared space.

Ostrich has great responsibility; shared support sustains vitality.

Past Life Lessons Carried Forward

Ostrich has learned survival through stamina; persistence ensures continuity.

Ostrich has learned strength through groundedness; firm footing creates safety.

Ostrich has learned truth through alignment; integrity creates destiny.

Ostrich has learned guardianship through presence; watchfulness protects life.

Recurring Patterns Across Lifetimes

Ostrich souls often appear as protectors of family, runners or travelers, truth tellers, judges, or those who stabilize systems through honesty and endurance.

Ostrich souls maintain awareness of the big picture; decisions consider long-horizon consequences.

Ostrich souls value straightforward action; progress arises through clarity and strength.

Initiations of This Lifetime

Ostrich awakens during periods requiring stamina, relocation across vast terrain, or commitment to truth and moral clarity.

Ostrich activates when the soul stands firmly, moves decisively, and leads through integrity and strength.

Ratite Variations: Current Life Expression

Emu

Emu reflects patient endurance and paternal guardianship; the soul engages protection of young, responsibility for lineage, and steady leadership through action. Aboriginal Australian Dreaming traditions recognize the emu as a creator and celestial guide.

Cassowary

Cassowary reflects fierce boundary protection and primal authority; the soul engages strong territorial presence, direct defense, and power made with ancient forest wisdom.

Otter Totem

Core Totem Essence

Otter has the soul memory of joyful mastery. This totem lives through play as a sacred practice and skill as an embodied language. Across coastal, riverine, and wetland cultures, people recognize otter as a being of delight, clever hands, and fluid movement between realms. Otter medicine centers on pleasure aligned with competence; learning through touch, curiosity, and laughter woven into survival.

Strengths of the Totem

Otter brings embodied joy; movement, humor, and sensory engagement restore vitality and presence.

Otter has adaptive intelligence; dexterous hands and quick learning translate curiosity into effective action.

Otter has social harmony; cooperation, sharing, and playful bonding strengthen group resilience.

Otter bridges water and land; emotional intelligence and practical skill flow together with ease.

Otter honors abundance through skill; gathering, crafting, and tool use express creative competence.

Challenges of the Totem

Otter lives through pleasure and motion; energy seeks balance between play and sustained focus.

Otter follows curiosity boldly; attention expands across many interests and makes for conscious integration.

Otter thrives in connection; periods of solitude call for intentional self-companionship and grounding.

Otter holds sensitivity to environments; shifting waters shape mood and require rhythmic self-care.

Past Life Lessons Carried Forward

Otter has learned that joy sustains survival; laughter and delight strengthen endurance.

Otter has learned mastery through repetition; hands teach the mind through practice.

Otter has learned communal exchange; sharing resources and skills multiplies abundance.

Otter has learned emotional fluency; feeling and action move together as one current.

Recurring Patterns Across Lifetimes

Otter souls often appear as artists, healers, educators, craftspeople, dancers, or facilitators of group cohesion.

Otter souls bring levity into serious spaces; morale and creativity rise in their presence.

Otter souls cultivate chosen family; bonds form through shared experience and mutual support.

Initiations of This Lifetime

Otter awakens during periods of recovery, creative rebirth, or community formation.

Otter activates when the soul learns to receive pleasure as medicine and skill as devotion.

Otter Variations; Current Life Expression

River Otter

River Otter reflects adaptability within flowing change; the soul navigates transitions, learning curves, and collaborative projects with agility. Many North American Indigenous traditions honor river otters as a playful teacher and a keeper of medicine bundles tied to water.

Sea Otter

Sea Otter reflects heart-centered resilience; the soul engages nourishment, self-soothing, and community care amid powerful emotional tides. Along the Pacific Rim, sea otters appears as a symbol of stewardship, balance, and restoration within the kelp forests that sustain life.

Owl Totem

Core Totem Essence

Owl has the soul memory of quiet sight. This totem moves through darkness with precision and calm awareness. Across lands where owls live close to human settlements, cultures recognize owl as a watcher, a keeper of thresholds, and a companion of ancestral presence. Owl medicine centers on discernment, stillness, and the ability to perceive truth beyond surface movement.

Strengths of the Totem

Owl brings deep perception; attention settles into subtle sound, motion, and energetic shift.

Owl has refined intuition; inner sight guides decisions with accuracy and restraint.

Owl embodies silent authority; wisdom expresses itself through presence instead of display.

Owl navigates liminal space; transitions between life phases, worlds, and identities unfold with clarity.

Owl holds ancestral awareness; memory, lineage, and inherited knowledge remain accessible and alive.

Challenges of the Totem

Owl lives with heightened sensitivity; strong perception requires conscious grounding in the body.

Owl values solitude; social environments ask for selective engagement and energetic pacing.

Owl perceives hidden layers of reality; carrying insight invites responsibility in timing and disclosure.

Owl moves deliberately; environments driven by speed ask for adaptation without self-erosion.

Past Life Lessons Carried Forward

Owl has learned the value of silence; listening reveals truth before action.

Owl has learned the role of witness; observation preserves balance and prevents harm.

Owl has learned stewardship of knowledge; wisdom travels through careful transmission.

Owl has learned companionship with death and rebirth; cycles of ending and renewal shape soul memory.

Recurring Patterns Across Lifetimes

Owl souls often appear as seers, counselors, healers, archivists, ritual keepers, or elders in training.

Owl souls hold space during transitions; others seek their calm during crisis or change.

Owl souls cultivate inner worlds; dreams, symbols, and signs guide daily life.

Initiations of This Lifetime

Owl awakens during periods of truth seeking, grief integration, spiritual initiation, or identity refinement.

Owl activates when the soul learns to trust inner sight and honor quiet authority.

Owl Variations: Current Life Expression

Barn Owl

Barn Owl reflects guardianship of thresholds; the soul engages protection of home, family lines, and sacred space. In many European and Mediterranean traditions, barn owls stands as a watcher between worlds and a keeper of ancestral boundaries.

Snowy Owl

Snowy Owl reflects clarity within vast openness; the soul navigates isolation, vision, and purpose across wide internal landscapes. Arctic peoples recognize snowy owls as a companion of hunters and a sign of keen sight aligned with survival.

Great Horned Owl

Great Horned Owl reflects assertive wisdom; the soul integrates strength, decisiveness, and perceptive leadership. Many North American Indigenous traditions associate this owl with authority, guardianship, and powerful seeing.

Little Owl

Little Owl reflects intimate knowledge; the soul works closely with household wisdom, craft, and daily ritual. In ancient Mediterranean cultures, the little owl aligns with learning, foresight, and steady intelligence.

Ox Totem

Core Totem Essence

Ox has the soul memory of steadfast strength expressed through service, patience, and moral endurance. This totem lives through deliberate effort, reliability, and the quiet transformation of land and life through consistent labor. Across East Asian agrarian traditions, Hindu cosmology, ancient Mesopotamia, Mediterranean cultures, and Indigenous farming societies worldwide, ox appears as a sacred worker, a symbol of abundance earned through effort, and a bearer of ethical strength. Ox medicine centers on perseverance, responsibility, and power expressed through steadiness instead of force.

Strengths of the Totem

Ox brings immense endurance; sustained effort has long-term creation and stability.

Ox has grounded strength; physical and moral power remain steady under pressure.

Ox embodies reliability; others trust presence, follow pace, and build upon consistency.

Ox has abundance through labor; prosperity grows through devotion and persistence.

Ox honors sacred duty; work aligns with purpose and community well-being.

Challenges of the Totem

Ox lives through heavy responsibility; replenishment through rest and appreciation sustains vitality.

Ox values proven methods; openness has innovation alongside tradition.

Ox moves deliberately; responsiveness strengthens alignment with changing conditions.

Ox has deep commitment; delegation has balance and longevity.

Past Life Lessons Carried Forward

Ox has learned survival through perseverance; patience preserves life and legacy.

Ox has learned abundance through effort; labor transforms scarcity into stability.

Ox has learned dignity through service; responsibility has honor.

Ox has learned strength through restraint; power expressed calmly sustains harmony.

Recurring Patterns Across Lifetimes

Ox souls often appear as builders, providers, farmers, caretakers, ethical leaders, or stabilizers of systems.

Ox souls anchor families and communities; others rely on their consistency and follow their rhythm.

Ox souls carry legacy work; generations benefit from their sustained effort.

Initiations of This Lifetime

Ox awakens during periods of long-term responsibility, rebuilding, leadership through service, or commitment to foundational work.

Ox activates when the soul embraces patience, steadiness, and purpose-driven labor.

Parrot and Macaw Totem

Core Totem Essence

Parrot has the soul memory of voice as living power. This totem lives through color, sound, mimicry, and social intelligence, shaping reality through expression and relationship. Across Amazonian cultures, Caribbean islands, Central and South America, Africa, South Asia, and Oceania, parrots appear as sacred speakers, carriers of memory, and mediators between forest, sky, and people. Parrot medicine centers on communication that has spirit, repetition that preserves lineage, and expression that binds community.

Strengths of the Totem

Parrot brings vocal potency; words, sounds, and rhythm shape atmosphere and outcome.

Parrot has social intelligence; group awareness has connection, cooperation, and belonging.

Parrot embodies memory through repetition; teachings, stories, and names endure through voice.

Parrot expresses vibrant authenticity; color, personality, and presence affirm life force.

Parrot bridges human and natural worlds; communication flows across species, roles, and realms.

Challenges of the Totem

Parrot lives through heightened responsiveness to sound and attention; energetic boundaries and clarity.

Parrot mirrors environments strongly; conscious choice creates what receives amplification.

Parrot values interaction and stimulation; stillness and listening deepen wisdom.

Parrot has powerful voices; discernment guides timing and message.

Past Life Lessons Carried Forward

Parrot has learned preservation through repetition; speaking keeps knowledge alive.

Parrot has learned identity through expression; voice reveals essence.

Parrot has learned community cohesion; shared language builds belonging.

Parrot has learned spirit travels through sound; vibration has intention and memory.

Recurring Patterns Across Lifetimes

Parrot souls often appear as storytellers, teachers, performers, singers, translators, or cultural carriers.

Parrot souls animate communities; laughter, color, and speech lift collective energy.

Parrot souls protect lineage knowledge; names, songs, and rituals remain intact through their voice.

Initiations of This Lifetime

Parrot awakens during periods of voice reclamation, teaching, cultural preservation, or social leadership.

Parrot activates when the soul learns to speak truth with joy, clarity, and responsibility.

Psittacine Variations: Current Life Expression

Macaw

Macaw reflects ceremonial visibility and ancestral memory; the soul engages leadership through color, presence, and vocal authority. Amazonian cultures honor macaw feathers as sacred regalia tied to lineage, status, and spiritual power.

Amazon Parrot

Amazon Parrot reflects clarity of speech and social bonding; the soul engages teaching, conversation, and relational intelligence. Many Caribbean and South American traditions associate this parrot with village life and communal exchange.

African Grey Parrot

African Grey Parrot reflects intellectual precision and deep listening; the soul engages cognition, mimicry with understanding, and careful communication. West African cultures recognize this parrot as a being of wisdom and attentiveness.

Cockatoo

Cockatoo reflects emotional expression and cresting presence; the soul engages feeling, display, and relational honesty. Australasian cultures associate the cockatoo with community signaling and expressive leadership.

Parakeet and Budgerigar

Parakeet reflects lightness and daily communication; the soul engages joy, chatter, and social rhythm that sustains connection. South Asian traditions often associate these birds with household harmony and companionship.

Peacock Totem

Core Totem Essence

Peacock has the soul memory of radiant self-expression, sovereign beauty, and protection through presence instead of force. This totem walks the earth with royal grace while displaying the colors of the cosmos, teaching how confidence and dignity transform spaces around you. Across Indian, Persian, Greek, and Southeast Asian traditions, the peacock appears as a sacred guardian, a symbol of immortality, and a companion to deities of wisdom and compassion. In Hindu iconography, the peacock stands beside Saraswati and Kartikeya; in Persian and Byzantine art, it symbolizes eternal life; in Greek myth it bears the many eyes of divine awareness. Peacock medicine centers on authenticity, spiritual vision, and leadership expressed through luminous presence.

Strengths of the Totem

Peacock brings confident visibility; true self shines without hesitation.

Peacock has strong protective aura; beauty and presence deter harm naturally.

Peacock embodies dignity; calm authority commands respect.

Peacock has creative expression; color and artistry communicate soul truth.

Peacock has expanded perception; many eyes symbolize awareness in all directions.

Challenges of the Totem

Peacock lives within strong visibility; humility strengthens connection and balance.

Peacock values display and recognition; inner stillness deepens authenticity.

Peacock engages powerful charisma; discernment guides where energy flows.

Peacock has high sensitivity to social atmosphere; grounding preserves clarity.

Past Life Lessons Carried Forward

Peacock has learned strength through authenticity; truth radiates naturally.

Peacock has learned protection through presence; confidence establishes safety.

Peacock has learned wisdom through observation; many perspectives reveal understanding.

Peacock has learned renewal through cyclical shedding; beauty returns with each season.

Recurring Patterns Across Lifetimes

Peacock souls often appear as artists, leaders, teachers, spiritual guides, performers, or those who uplift others through inspiration and grace.

Peacock souls draw attention easily; others look to them for direction and reassurance.

Peacock souls value elegance and integrity; life organizes around meaningful expression and sacred aesthetics.

Initiations of This Lifetime

Peacock awakens during periods of stepping into visibility, reclaiming voice, sharing creative gifts, or embodying leadership with compassion and beauty.

Peacock activates when the soul claims its radiance, stands proudly in truth, and allows its presence to inspire others.

Pegasus Totem

Core Totem Essence

Pegasus has the soul memory of spiritual ascent, liberated movement, and inspiration born from the meeting of earth and sky. This totem unites the strength of the horse with the freedom of wings, teaching how grounded power rises into vision and higher consciousness. In Greek tradition, Pegasus springs from sacred waters and serves as a companion to heroes and muses, creating springs wherever his hoof touches earth. Pegasus embodies poetic inspiration, divine guidance, and the path between mortal and celestial realms. Pegasus medicine centers on freedom with purpose, imagination guided by discipline, and elevation of spirit through courage and grace.

Strengths of the Totem

Pegasus brings expansive freedom; movement unfolds without restraint or limitation.

Pegasus has visionary awareness; perspective rises above obstacles naturally.

Pegasus embodies inspiration; creativity flows like spring water from contact with earth.

Pegasus has noble strength; power expresses itself through grace and integrity.

Pegasus has spiritual ascent; consciousness lifts toward higher understanding.

Challenges of the Totem

Pegasus lives within a strong desire for open horizons; grounding in manifestation.

Pegasus values independence deeply; partnership enriches the shared journey.

Pegasus moves quickly toward vision; steady pacing sustains endurance.

Pegasus has heightened sensitivity to confinement; intentional structure has focus.

Past Life Lessons Carried Forward

Pegasus has learned freedom through trust; spirit guides safe flight.

Pegasus has learned strength through alignment; body and soul move as one.

Pegasus has learned inspiration through service; creativity uplifts many.

Pegasus has learned ascent through courage; rising above fear reveals destiny.

Recurring Patterns Across Lifetimes

Pegasus souls often appear as visionaries, artists, healers, travelers, spiritual teachers, or those who guide others toward higher possibilities.

Pegasus souls feel drawn to open landscapes, sky, wind, and movement; freedom fuels their vitality.

Pegasus souls value authenticity and expansion; life organizes around growth and exploration.

Initiations of This Lifetime

Pegasus awakens during periods of creative awakening, spiritual calling, relocation, or breaking free from limiting structures.

Pegasus activates when the soul trusts its wings, claims its strength, and rises toward vision with confidence and grace.

Pelican Totem

Core Totem Essence

Pelican has the soul memory of nourishment through generosity, guardianship expressed through selfless care, and abundance gathered from vast waters. This totem lives where ocean meets shore, teaching how provision and community sustain life together. Across the Mediterranean, Egyptian, Christian, and coastal Indigenous traditions, the pelican appears as a symbol of sacrifice, renewal, and parental devotion. Ancient lore portrays the pelican as a life-giver who feeds its young from its own body, representing profound compassion and service. Pelican medicine centers on stewardship, shared resources, and love expressed through tangible care.

Strengths of the Totem

Pelican brings generous provision; resources gather and distribute with ease.

Pelican has strong parental and communal guardianship; others feel safe and supported.

Pelican embodies cooperation; group movement strengthens hunting and survival.

Pelican has resilience; patience yields abundant return from wide waters.

Pelican has emotional openness; heart-centered care nourishes many.

Challenges of the Totem

Pelican lives through deep giving; self-nourishment sustains longevity and strength.

Pelican values community strongly; personal boundaries preserve balance.

Pelican engages large responsibilities; shared leadership lightens the load.

Pelican has steady patience; swift action enhances opportunity when needed.

Past Life Lessons Carried Forward

Pelican has learned abundance through sharing; generosity multiplies supply.

Pelican has learned strength through service; care creates lasting bonds.

Pelican has learned survival through cooperation; coordinated effort ensures success.

Pelican has learned renewal through water; tides cleanse and restore life.

Recurring Patterns Across Lifetimes

Pelican souls often appear as caregivers, teachers, providers, healers, parents, or those who support entire communities through steady generosity.

Pelican souls gather what others need and distribute wisely; prosperity flows through their hands.

Pelican souls value compassion and responsibility; life organizes around nourishment of others.

Initiations of This Lifetime

Pelican awakens during periods of family building, community support, teaching, or stepping into roles that require tangible care and provision.

Pelican activates when the soul gives freely with wisdom, protects loved ones, and trusts that generosity sustains abundance.

Penguin Totem

Core Totem Essence

Penguin has the soul memory of devotion expressed through endurance and collective care. This totem thrives within extreme environments through cooperation, ritualized movement, and unwavering commitment to kin. Across the Southern Ocean, Antarctic regions, and the cultures that live in relationship with these waters, the penguin appears as a symbol of perseverance, communal intelligence, and love sustained through hardship. Penguin medicine centers on loyalty, emotional regulation, and survival created from shared responsibility.

Strengths of the Totem

Penguin brings steadfast devotion; commitment to family and community remains constant across adversity.

Penguin has collective intelligence; group coordination has warmth, safety, and survival.

Penguin embodies emotional resilience; care and connection stabilize harsh conditions.

Penguin moves seamlessly between worlds; land and sea both serve as domains of competence.

Penguin honors ritual and rhythm; repeated actions sustain life and continuity.

Challenges of the Totem

Penguin lives within demanding environments; energy management has long-term endurance.

Penguin commits deeply to others; self-care strengthens the capacity to give.

Penguin follows collective rhythm; personal expression grows through conscious voice within the group.

Penguin faces long cycles of waiting and effort; patience in purpose.

Past Life Lessons Carried Forward

Penguin has learned survival through cooperation; unity sustains life where isolation fails.

Penguin has learned devotion as strength; love expressed through action protects lineage.

Penguin has learned endurance through ritual; consistency has life through extremes.

Penguin has learned emotional regulation; calm presence preserves warmth and clarity.

Recurring Patterns Across Lifetimes

Penguin souls often appear as caregivers, partners, community anchors, teachers, or protectors of the vulnerable.

Penguin souls form lasting bonds; partnership and shared duty shape destiny.

Penguin souls thrive within collective purpose; belonging fuels resilience.

Initiations of This Lifetime

Penguin awakens during periods of responsibility, partnership commitment, or communal survival challenge.

Penguin activates when the soul learns that devotion, cooperation, and rhythm create strength.

Penguin Variations; Current Life Expression

Emperor Penguin

Emperor Penguin reflects leadership through endurance and sacrifice; the soul engages guardianship, patience, and responsibility through extreme conditions. This expression emphasizes holding life steady through darkness and cold.

King Penguin

King Penguin reflects balanced authority and coordination; the soul engages leadership within structure, visibility, and shared effort. This expression emphasizes order, trust, and dignified presence.

Adélie Penguin

Adélie Penguin reflects courage and spirited persistence; the soul engages determination, adaptability, and active cooperation within challenging terrain.

Gentoo Penguin

Gentoo Penguin reflects agility and efficiency; the soul engages problem-solving, speed, and flexible response while remaining devoted to community.

Chinstrap Penguin

Chinstrap Penguin reflects vocal coordination and collective communication; the soul engages expression, signaling, and group cohesion through sound and presence.

Pheasant Totem

Core Totem Essence

Pheasant has the soul memory of visible beauty joined with grounded survival. This totem lives through display that arises from vitality instead of vanity, and through confidence that grows from knowing one's place within land and season. Across East Asia, Celtic lands, Indigenous European countryside lore, and agrarian cultures, the pheasant appears as a being of ceremonial presence, fertility, and attentive watchfulness. Pheasant medicine centers on standing out while remaining rooted, honoring cycles of courtship and harvest, and expressing identity with confidence and grace.

Strengths of the Totem

Pheasant brings confident visibility; presence draws attention through authenticity and vitality.

Pheasant has aesthetic intelligence; beauty communicates health, readiness, and purpose.

Pheasant embodies alert groundedness; awareness remains sharp while staying connected to earth.

Pheasant has courtship and relational signaling; connection forms through clear expression.

Pheasant honors seasonal rhythm; timing guides action, rest, and display.

Challenges of the Totem

Pheasant lives within heightened visibility; discernment guides when to display and when to remain still.

Pheasant balances show and safety; grounding has security alongside expression.

Pheasant responds quickly to disturbance; composure refines reaction into choice.

Pheasant thrives within cycles of attention; integration has stability beyond peak moments.

Past Life Lessons Carried Forward

Pheasant has learned expression as communication; visibility conveys readiness and truth.

Pheasant has learned survival through awareness; alertness preserves life amid openness.

Pheasant has learned timing through the season; display aligns with the natural cycle.

Pheasant has learned beauty as vitality; radiance reflects inner health and confidence.

Recurring Patterns Across Lifetimes

Pheasant souls often appear as performers, artists, courtiers, diplomats, or cultural representatives.

Pheasant souls carry charisma tied to embodiment; presence influences atmosphere immediately.

Pheasant souls value land and tradition; place and season shape identity.

Initiations of This Lifetime

Pheasant awakens during periods of visibility, courtship, creative display, or social emergence.

Pheasant activates when the soul claims presence confidently while remaining grounded and attentive.

Phoenix Totem

Core Totem Essence

Phoenix has the soul memory of rebirth through fire, radiant life force, and transformation that rises from ash into brilliance. This totem lives within flame and sun, teaching how endings fuel renewal and how spirit remains eternal through cycles of dissolution and creation. Across Egyptian Bennu lore, Greek and Roman phoenix myth, Persian Simurgh stories, Chinese Fenghuang tradition, Slavic Firebird tales, and many solar cultures, the firebird appears as a herald of renewal, divine authority, and immortality.

Phoenix medicine centers on regeneration, sovereign light, and the courage to release what has completed its purpose so new life may emerge.

Strengths of the Totem

Phoenix brings powerful renewal; vitality returns stronger after every cycle.

Phoenix has a radiant presence; light uplifts and energizes all nearby.

Phoenix embodies fearless transformation; change becomes a gateway to growth.

Phoenix has spiritual sovereignty; identity rises from inner truth.

Phoenix has hope and inspiration; others find courage through its example.

Challenges of the Totem

Phoenix lives through intense cycles of change; integration in stability between phases.

Phoenix values constant ascent; grounding strengthens manifestation in daily life.

Phoenix has strong independence; partnership enriches shared evolution.

Phoenix engages a powerful life force; pacing sustains endurance across many rebirths.

Past Life Lessons Carried Forward

Phoenix has learned immortality through renewal; spirit continues beyond form.

Phoenix has learned strength through surrender; release prepares the next beginning.

Phoenix has learned light through darkness; ash nourishes the next flame.

Phoenix has learned leadership through radiance; presence guides others toward hope.

Recurring Patterns Across Lifetimes

Phoenix souls often appear as healers, revolutionaries, artists, spiritual teachers, survivors of great change, or those who rebuild life repeatedly with grace.

Phoenix souls transform environments simply by entering them; stagnation dissolves, and renewal begins.

Phoenix souls value authenticity and growth; life organizes around evolution and higher purpose.

Initiations of This Lifetime

Phoenix awakens during periods of profound transformation, identity rebirth, recovery from loss, or stepping into greater spiritual authority.

Phoenix activates when the soul embraces change fully, releases old forms, and rises with renewed strength and clarity.

Firebird Variations; Current Life Expression

Bennu

Bennu reflects solar creation and divine order; the soul engages renewal through light, leadership through sacred timing, and connection to cosmic cycles. Ancient Egyptian tradition associates Bennu with the rising sun and the eternal return of life.

Greek Phoenix

Greek Phoenix reflects cyclical rebirth through flame; the soul engages dramatic transformation, purification, and radiant resurgence. This variation emphasizes personal resurrection and visible renewal.

Simurgh

Simurgh reflects ancient wisdom and maternal guardianship; the soul engages healing, protection of lineage, and guidance through deep knowledge. Persian tradition honors Simurgh as a vast, luminous bird who shelters heroes and restores life.

Slavic Firebird

Firebird reflects luminous inspiration and quest energy; the soul engages creativity, destiny seeking, and catalytic transformation that awakens others to purpose.

Pixiu Totem

Core Totem Essence

Pixiu has the soul memory of guardianship of wealth, fierce protection of lineage, and prosperity drawn through loyalty and spiritual authority. This totem stands at the threshold between heaven and earth, teaching how abundance flows toward those who guard it with integrity and purpose. In Chinese tradition, Pixiu appears as a celestial lion dragon, a protector of treasure, a ward against misfortune, and a loyal companion to emperors and warriors. It attracts fortune while defending against harmful forces. Pixiu medicine centers on the protection of resources, disciplined stewardship, and prosperity aligned with righteous conduct.

Strengths of the Totem

Pixiu brings a strong protective presence; harmful influences retreat quickly.

Pixiu has natural magnetism for prosperity; resources gather and remain secure.

Pixiu embodies loyalty and devotion; bonds strengthen through steadfast commitment.

Pixiu has courage and authority; leadership arises through confidence and integrity.

Pixiu has guardianship of sacred space and lineage; what matters most remains safe.

Challenges of the Totem

Pixiu lives with an intense guardianship instinct; generosity strengthens balanced circulation.

Pixiu values control of territory; flexibility encourages harmony with others.

Pixiu engages strong authority; compassionate listening deepens trust.

Pixiu has powerful energy; grounding has steady focus.

Past Life Lessons Carried Forward

Pixiu has learned prosperity through stewardship; wise care preserves abundance.

Pixiu has learned strength through loyalty; devotion protects family and community.

Pixiu has learned power through discipline; focus creates destiny.

Pixiu has learned guardianship of treasure; both material and spiritual wealth carry sacred value.

Recurring Patterns Across Lifetimes

Pixiu souls often appear as protectors of family wealth, business leaders, guardians of temples, strategists, or those who manage resources for many.

Pixiu souls naturally defend what they love; others rely on their strength and reliability.

Pixiu souls value integrity and prosperity; life organizes around stability and long-term security.

Initiations of This Lifetime

Pixiu awakens during periods of financial building, protecting family legacy, establishing business foundations, or strengthening energetic boundaries.

Pixiu activates when the soul claims authority, safeguards its resources, and channels abundance with discipline and wisdom.

Celestial Guardian Variations: Current Life Expression

Tianlu

Tianlu reflects wealth attraction and expansion; the soul engages prosperity growth, opportunity gathering, and confident leadership in material realms.

Bixie

Bixie reflects protective defense and warding; the soul engages clearing of harmful energy, boundary enforcement, and guardianship of sacred or ancestral spaces.

Porcupine and Hedgehog Totem

Core Totem Essence

Porcupine has the soul memory of gentle power protected through clear boundary wisdom. This totem lives through kindness paired with self-respect, teaching how softness and defense coexist in harmony. Across Indigenous North American traditions, Celtic and European folklore, African earth wisdom, and Asian countryside lore, these beings appear as teachers of peaceful confidence, self-possession, and protection without aggression. Porcupine medicine centers on quiet authority, emotional safety, and the ability to remain open-hearted while honoring personal limits.

Strengths of the Totem

Porcupine brings natural boundary mastery; protection activates through presence instead of pursuit.

Porcupine has calm confidence; strength expresses itself without dominance.

Porcupine embodies self-trust; instinct guides when to open and when to shield.

Porcupine has gentleness paired with resilience; softness remains intact alongside defense.

Porcupine has emotional safety; inner peace grows through clear personal space.

Challenges of the Totem

Porcupine lives with heightened sensitivity; grounding has ease within interaction.

Porcupine values solitude and safety; connection deepens through gradual trust.

Porcupine responds strongly to intrusion; discernment refines the response into a conscious choice.

Porcupine protects deeply; flexibility has flow without diminishing safety.

Past Life Lessons Carried Forward

Porcupine has learned protection without harm; boundaries preserve love and dignity.

Porcupine has learned power through stillness; presence deters threat.

Porcupine has learned self-respect as survival; honoring limits sustains vitality.

Porcupine has learned kindness as strength; gentleness holds enduring authority.

Recurring Patterns Across Lifetimes

Porcupine souls often appear as healers, counselors, quiet leaders, guardians of safe space, or keepers of emotional boundaries.

Porcupine souls cultivate peace around themselves; others sense safety and calm nearby.

Porcupine souls teach through example; respect arises naturally through presence.

Initiations of This Lifetime

Porcupine awaken during periods of boundary formation, emotional healing, or reclaiming personal space.

Porcupine activates when the soul learns to remain kind while standing firmly within its own territory.

Erinaceid and Hystricid Variations: Current Life Expression

Porcupine

Porcupine reflects confident defense and gentle authority; the soul engages protection through clarity, patience, and unwavering self-respect. Indigenous North American traditions honor the porcupine as a teacher of innocence preserved through boundaries and wisdom expressed without aggression.

Hedgehog

Hedgehog reflects introspection and emotional self-containment; the soul engages inner work, self-soothing, and protection through withdrawals followed by safe reemergence. Celtic and European folklore regard the hedgehog as a symbol of wisdom, hearth protection, and intuitive intelligence.

Possum Totem

Core Totem Essence

Possum has the soul memory of strategic survival through adaptability and subtle intelligence. This totem lives through timing, flexibility, and the ability to move safely within complex environments without confrontation. Across Indigenous cultures of North America, Aboriginal Australian traditions, and folk wisdom in regions where possum thrives, this being appears as a teacher of clever survival, resourcefulness, and emotional regulation under pressure. Possum medicine centers on knowing when to engage, when to withdraw, and how to remain safe while navigating unpredictable terrain.

Strengths of the Totem

Possum brings adaptive intelligence; survival unfolds through timing and situational awareness.

Possum has emotional self-regulation; a calm response preserves safety and clarity.

Possum embodies resourcefulness; nourishment and shelter appear through creative use of what exists.

Possum has flexibility; rapid adjustment has continuity within changing conditions.

Possum protects through strategy; safety arises from discernment instead of force.

Challenges of the Totem

Possum lives within heightened environmental awareness; grounding has ease and rest.

Possum values non-confrontation; assertive clarity develops through confidence and choice.

Possum navigates complex spaces; focus strengthens direction and intention.

Possum relies on withdrawal for safety; intentional engagement has growth and connection.

Past Life Lessons Carried Forward

Possum has learned survival through adaptability; flexibility preserves life.

Possum has learned safety through timing; awareness guides right action.

Possum has learned intelligence through observation; stillness reveals opportunity.

Possum has learned endurance through restraint; energy conserved has longevity.

Recurring Patterns Across Lifetimes

Possum souls often appear as survivors, strategists, mediators, quiet navigators, or protectors of vulnerable spaces.

Possum souls thrive within complexity; subtle movement avoids harm and creates continuity.

Possum souls influence outcomes indirectly; safety emerges through wise positioning.

Initiations of This Lifetime

Possum awakens during periods of instability, survival recalibration, or navigation of unfamiliar systems.

Possum activates when the soul learns to survive through awareness, restraint, and intelligent response.

Praying Mantis Totem

Core Totem Essence

Praying Mantis has the soul memory of stillness that precedes perfect action. This totem lives through contemplative awareness, precision, and spiritual alignment, teaching how patience sharpens perception and timing determines outcome. Across East Asian traditions, African symbolism, Mediterranean myth, and Indigenous African and Asian teachings, praying mantis appears as a sacred observer, a mediator between worlds, and a being whose movement reflects divine order. Praying Mantis medicine centers on presence before action, intuition refined through silence, and power expressed through exact timing.

Strengths of the Totem

Praying Mantis brings profound stillness; awareness deepens without movement.

Praying Mantis has impeccable timing; action happens at the exact moment of alignment.

Praying Mantis embodies spiritual focus; intention remains clear and undistracted.

Praying Mantis has strategic precision; effort lands cleanly and efficiently.

Praying Mantis holds meditative authority; presence alone influences environments.

Challenges of the Totem

Praying Mantis lives within deep inward focus; integration has connection and expression.

Praying Mantis waits patiently for alignment; trust has confidence within extended stillness.

Praying Mantis acts decisively; reflection has emotional integration after action.

Praying Mantis values solitude and silence; communication strengthens shared understanding.

Past Life Lessons Carried Forward

Praying Mantis has learned wisdom through observation; seeing precedes knowing.

Praying Mantis has learned power through patience; timing creates destiny.

Praying Mantis has learned alignment through stillness; silence reveals truth.

Praying Mantis has learned action as a sacred act; movement has spiritual weight.

Recurring Patterns Across Lifetimes

Praying Mantis souls often appear as monks, strategists, spiritual adepts, watchers, or guides through decision.

Praying Mantis souls influence outcome through restraint; presence alters trajectory.

Praying Mantis souls value clarity over speed; alignment defines success.

Initiations of This Lifetime

Praying Mantis awakens during periods of contemplation, spiritual refinement, or preparation for decisive action.

Praying Mantis activates when the soul trusts stillness, listens deeply, and moves only when alignment is complete.

PUFFIN TOTEM

Core Totem Essence

Puffin has the soul memory of joyful resilience, devotion to family, and mastery of two worlds: air and sea. This totem moves easily between cliff and ocean, teaching how playfulness and responsibility coexist. Across Celtic coasts, Norse shore cultures, and North Atlantic island traditions, puffin appears as a faithful partner, a diligent parent, and a symbol of endurance through harsh winds and cold seas. Puffin medicine centers on loyalty, light-hearted courage, and the ability to dive deeply for sustenance while returning safely to community and home.

Strengths of the Totem

Puffin brings cheerful resilience; joy persists even within challenging conditions.

Puffin has strong partnership bonds; devotion strengthens stability and trust.

Puffin embodies adaptability; air and water both serve as natural realms.

Puffin has resourcefulness; nourishment happens through skillful diving and timing.

Puffin has a balanced life; work and play flow together harmoniously.

Challenges of the Totem

Puffin lives within strong social bonds; personal reflection strengthens inner clarity.

Puffin values routine and nesting sites; flexibility has growth during change.

Puffin moves quickly between worlds; grounding in focus and intention.

Puffin has lighthearted energy; sustained commitment deepens long-term creation.

Past Life Lessons Carried Forward

Puffin has learned survival through cooperation; family ensures safety.

Puffin has learned nourishment through depth; diving inward reveals sustenance.

Puffin has learned joy through hardship; humor strengthens endurance.

Puffin has learned loyalty through return; home in every journey.

Recurring Patterns Across Lifetimes

Puffin souls often appear as devoted partners, caregivers, teachers, fishermen, travelers between cultures, or those who maintain strong community ties while exploring widely.

Puffin souls balance seriousness with play; morale rises through their presence.

Puffin souls value home and belonging; life organizes around chosen family and shared responsibility.

Initiations of This Lifetime

Puffin awakens during periods of building partnership, parenting, returning home after travel, or learning to balance deep work with lighthearted living.

Puffin activates when the soul commits to loyalty, dives confidently into emotional or creative depths, and returns with nourishment to share.

Puma and Cougar Totem

Core Totem Essence

Puma has the soul memory of silent authority and embodied courage. This totem lives through presence instead of display, moving with precision, patience, and unshakeable self-possession. Across the Americas, especially within Indigenous cultures of the Andes, Southwest, and Plains, puma appears as a guardian of thresholds, a teacher of leadership, and a being who walks between worlds without announcing itself. Puma medicine centers on personal power held quietly, decisive action taken at the correct moment, and sovereignty rooted in self-trust.

Strengths of the Totem

Puma brings calm confidence; authority flows through presence instead of dominance.

Puma has impeccable timing; action unfolds only when alignment and readiness converge.

Puma embodies solitary strength; self-reliance has clarity and resilience.

Puma protects territory and integrity; boundaries remain clear and respected.

Puma navigates liminal spaces; spiritual, emotional, and physical realms intersect through awareness.

Challenges of the Totem

Puma lives with deep independence; connection develops through mutual respect and chosen proximity.

Puma has intense focus; flexibility has adaptability when circumstances shift.

Puma values silence and privacy; communication strengthens influence when offered intentionally.

Puma holds powerful instinct; conscious integration refines response and direction.

Past Life Lessons Carried Forward

Puma has learned leadership without spectacle; authority rests within calm certainty.

Puma has learned the power of patience; waiting sharpens success.

Puma has learned guardianship of self and land; sovereignty preserves balance.

Puma has learned movement between worlds; unseen paths carry wisdom and safety.

Recurring Patterns Across Lifetimes

Puma souls often appear as leaders, protectors, solitary guides, spiritual guardians, or quiet path makers.

Puma souls value autonomy; they choose roles that honor independence and integrity.

Puma souls step forward during critical moments; decisive action reshapes the outcome.

Initiations of This Lifetime

Puma awakens during periods of personal power reclamation, boundary enforcement, or leadership through example.

Puma activates when the soul claims authority rooted in self-trust, patience, and quiet strength.

Felid Variations: Current Life Expression

Cougar

Cougar reflects adaptability across a wide territory; the soul navigates changing environments, roles, and identities with resilience. Many Indigenous North American cultures honor the cougar as a guardian of paths and a teacher of personal power.

Mountain Lion

Mountain Lion reflects the elevation of perspective; the soul engages leadership created from overview, strategy, and long vision. This expression emphasizes guardianship from a place of clarity and distance.

Pantherine Puma

Pantherine Puma reflects shadowed movement and stealth; the soul engages unseen influence, protection, and power expressed through subtle presence instead of visibility.

QUAIL TOTEM

Core Totem Essence

Quail has the soul memory of community safety created through attentiveness and shared vigilance. This totem lives close to the ground, teaching how survival strengthens through group awareness, rapid coordination, and devotion to family structure. Across Indigenous North American desert and grassland cultures, Mediterranean agrarian lore, and Asian countryside symbolism, quail appear as a guardian of kin, a teacher of collective movement, and a symbol of abundance sustained through cooperation. Quail medicine centers on mutual protection, emotional reassurance, and strength drawn from belonging.

Strengths of the Totem

Quail brings strong community intelligence; group awareness enhances safety and resilience.

Quail has protective devotion to family; care and vigilance extend naturally to kin and chosen circle.

Quail embodies rapid coordination; collective movement responds smoothly to changing conditions.

Quail has grounded abundance; nourishment flows through shared effort and attentiveness.

Quail maintains emotional reassurance; presence calms fear and restores stability.

Challenges of the Totem

Quail lives through heightened alertness; grounding has calm within constant awareness.

Quail values group safety deeply; personal independence develops through confidence and trust.

Quail responds quickly to perceived threat; discernment refines response into clarity.

Quail prioritizes protection of others; self-nourishment strengthens long-term care.

Past Life Lessons Carried Forward

Quail has learned survival through cooperation; togetherness preserves life.

Quail has learned protection through vigilance; awareness prevents harm.

Quail has learned abundance through sharing; provision multiplies within the community.

Quail has learned reassurance as leadership; calm presence steadies many.

Recurring Patterns Across Lifetimes

Quail souls often appear as family anchors, community caregivers, organizers, or protectors of vulnerable groups.

Quail souls strengthen group cohesion; others feel safer and more coordinated around them.

Quail souls value belonging and shared rhythm; connection creates identity and purpose.

Initiations of This Lifetime

Quail awakens during periods of family building, community reliance, or heightened responsibility for others.

Quail activates when the soul embraces collective strength, coordinated action, and reassurance offered through presence.

Rabbit Totem

Core Totem Essence

The Rabbit has the soul memory of swift life force and cyclical renewal. This totem lives close to the earth while remaining alert to subtle movement, timing, and opportunity. Across Indigenous North American nations, Celtic lands, East Asia, Africa, and Mesoamerica, the Rabbit appear as beings of fertility, moon rhythm, clever survival, and sacred timing. Rabbit medicine centers on life creation, intuitive response, and the ability to thrive through awareness and agility.

Strengths of the Totem

Rabbit brings fertile life force; creativity, growth, and multiplication flow naturally.

Rabbit has keen alertness; awareness of environments has rapid response and safety.

Rabbit embodies intuitive timing; movement aligns with cycles, seasons, and opportunity.

Rabbit has gentleness and approachability; connection forms through warmth and presence.

Rabbit expresses clever adaptability; intelligence guides survival through responsiveness instead of force.

Challenges of the Totem

Rabbit lives with heightened sensitivity; nervous energy benefits from grounding and rhythm.

Rabbit moves quickly through perception; focus has follow-through and completion.

Rabbit experiences strong reproductive and creative drive; conscious channeling has balance.

Rabbit responds immediately to stimuli; discernment refines reactions into choices.

Past Life Lessons Carried Forward

Rabbit has learned survival through awareness; alert presence preserves life.

Rabbit has learned fertility as a sacred power; creation arises through alignment with cycles.

Rabbit has learned to trust in intuition; subtle signals guide correct timing.

Rabbit has learned regeneration through repetition; life renews itself endlessly.

Recurring Patterns Across Lifetimes

Rabbit souls often appear as creators, caregivers, artists, gardeners, healers, or cycle keepers.

Rabbit souls engage themes of birth, growth, and renewal; life expands through their presence.

Rabbit souls move between vulnerability and clever strength; adaptability defines resilience.

Initiations of This Lifetime

Rabbit awakens during periods of fertility, creative expansion, family formation, or emotional sensitivity.

Rabbit activates when the soul learns to trust intuition, timing, and gentle power.

Leporid Variations: Current Life Expression

Rabbit

Rabbit reflects domestic fertility and emotional attunement; the soul engages nurturing, creativity, and close relational bonds. In East Asian traditions, the rabbit aligns with the moon, longevity, medicine preparation, and gentle wisdom. Many Indigenous cultures honor the rabbit as a clever survivor and a teacher of awareness.

Hare

Hare reflects wild vitality and lunar sovereignty; the soul engages independence, instinct, and sacred timing. In Celtic tradition, the hare serves as a creature of the Otherworld, associated with goddesses, prophecy, and transformation through moon cycles.

Jackrabbit

Jackrabbit reflects speed and heightened alertness; the soul engages rapid response, expansive perception, and survival across open terrain. Desert cultures recognize the jackrabbit as a being of awareness, agility, and endurance.

Snowshoe Hare

Snowshoe Hare reflects seasonal adaptation; the soul engages transformation aligned with environments and cycles. Northern cultures observe this hare as a teacher of camouflage, timing, and harmony with shifting conditions.

Raccoon Totem

Core Totem Essence

Raccoon has the soul memory of clever navigation through complexity using intelligence, curiosity, and adaptability. This totem lives at the edge of systems, thriving where boundaries blur between wild and human space. Across Indigenous North American teachings, forest folklore, and modern urban mythos, raccoon appears as a problem solver, a night worker, and a being who survives through ingenuity instead of force. Raccoon medicine centers on resourcefulness, flexible identity, and mastery of tools, hands, and opportunity.

Strengths of the Totem

Raccoon brings inventive intelligence; solutions arise through experimentation and curiosity.

Raccoon has exceptional adaptability; changing environments invite creative response.

Raccoon embodies tactile wisdom; hands learn through touch, manipulation, and discovery.

Raccoon has strategic opportunism; timing and positioning open access to resources.

Raccoon navigates shadow spaces; night, liminal zones, and overlooked paths offer safety and advantage.

Challenges of the Totem

Raccoon lives through constant stimulation; focus strengthens long-term creation.

Raccoon explores many possibilities; commitment deepens mastery and fulfillment.

Raccoon thrives in boundary spaces; ethical clarity has balanced interaction.

Raccoon relies on cleverness; rest and grounding sustain nervous system health.

Past Life Lessons Carried Forward

Raccoon has learned survival through ingenuity; creativity preserves life.

Raccoon has learned access through curiosity; exploration reveals hidden pathways.

Raccoon has learned intelligence through hands-on experience; doing teaches faster than theory.

Raccoon has learned identity as a flexible instrument; roles shift to meet the needs of the moment.

Recurring Patterns Across Lifetimes

Raccoon souls often appear as inventors, hackers, artists, troubleshooters, night workers, or system navigators.

Raccoon souls move easily between worlds; social, cultural, and structural boundaries soften around them.

Raccoon souls reshape environments quietly; systems adapt after their presence.

Initiations of This Lifetime

Raccoon awakens during periods of survival recalibration, system navigation, or creative problem solving.

Raccoon activates when the soul trusts curiosity, uses hands and mind together, and thrives within complexity.

RAM AND SHEEP TOTEM

Core Totem Essence

Ram has the soul memory of devotion expressed through strength and belonging. This totem lives through leadership that moves first and care that sustains many. Across the ancient Near East, the Mediterranean, Central Asia, Africa, and pastoral cultures worldwide, the Ram appear as symbols of fertility, sacrifice, guidance, and covenant between people, land, and spirit. Ram medicine centers on purposeful direction, communal responsibility, and power created from service and continuity.

Strengths of the Totem

Ram brings steadfast commitment; purpose holds firm through challenge and change.

Ram has leadership through example; movement inspires others to follow.

Ram embodies fertility and renewal; life expands through stewardship and rhythm.

Ram has communal cohesion; belonging strengthens resilience and survival.

Ram has ritual devotion; sacrifice, offering, and duty align with sacred order.

Challenges of the Totem

Ram lives with strong instinctual drive; discernment guides direction and timing.

Ram has responsibility for many; replenishment sustains long term service.

Ram values tradition and structure; flexibility has adaptation within change.

Ram responds deeply to group dynamics; personal voice grows through clarity and confidence.

Past Life Lessons Carried Forward

Ram have learned leadership through responsibility; direction has consequence.

Ram have learned sacrifice as sacred exchange; giving sustains continuity.

Ram have learned survival through cohesion; unity preserves life.

Ram have learned fertility as stewardship; abundance grows through care and timing.

Recurring Patterns Across Lifetimes

Ram souls often appear as leaders, guides, providers, ritual bearers, or cultural anchors.

Ram souls sustain communities; stability flows from their consistency.

Ram souls carry moral weight; duty and conscience shape life path.

Initiations of This Lifetime

Ram awakens during periods of leadership assumption, family responsibility, or spiritual devotion.

Ram activates when the soul accepts guidance of others while honoring shared survival.

Ovine Variations: Current Life Expression

Ram

Ram reflects initiating force and forward leadership; the soul engages courage, assertion, and decisive movement. In ancient Mesopotamian, Greek, and astrological traditions, the ram aligns with beginnings, fertility, and the power to break new ground.

Sheep

Sheep reflects communal devotion and nourishment; the soul engages care, patience, and shared belonging. Pastoral cultures worldwide honor sheep as a provider of wool, food, and stability that sustains life.

Bighorn Sheep

Bighorn Sheep reflects resilience and elevation; the soul engages endurance, balance, and mastery of difficult terrain. Indigenous cultures of the American Southwest recognize the bighorn as a teacher of strength created from perseverance.

Mountain Sheep

Mountain Sheep reflects sure footing and vigilance; the soul navigates high-stakes environments with awareness and balance. This expression emphasizes stability within exposure.

Lamb

Lamb reflects innocence, renewal, and sacred offering; the soul engages purity of intention, trust, and spiritual devotion. In many religious traditions, the lamb symbolizes covenant, rebirth, and life given for continuity.

Rat Totem

Core Totem Essence

Rat has the soul memory of survival intelligence refined through awareness, adaptability, and social attunement. This totem lives at the foundation of systems, sensing structural weakness and opportunity before others perceive change. Across Chinese, Hindu, Indigenous Asian, African, and European folk traditions, rat appears as a bringer of foresight, a companion of thresholds, and a keeper of prosperity gained through preparation and timing. Rat medicine centers on strategic thinking, collective awareness, and the ability to thrive during transition, collapse, or rapid growth.

Strengths of the Totem

Rat brings sharp anticipatory awareness; shifts register early and clearly.

Rat has exceptional adaptability; changing environments invite strategic response.

Rat embodies social intelligence; group dynamics, alliances, and resource flow reveal themselves easily.

Rat has prosperity through preparation; storage, planning, and timing secure abundance.

Rat navigates complex systems; infrastructure, supply chains, and hidden pathways remain familiar terrain.

Challenges of the Totem

Rat lives within constant stimulation; grounding has clarity and rest.

Rat engages many options at once; prioritization strengthens focus and satisfaction.

Rat values safety and continuity; trust has expansion into visibility and leadership.

Rat responds rapidly to change; reflection deepens long-term wisdom.

Past Life Lessons Carried Forward

Rat has learned survival through foresight; preparation preserves life and lineage.

Rat has learned abundance through strategy; timing multiplies effort.

Rat has learned strength through community; collective awareness ensures safety.

Rat has learned navigation of collapse and renewal; transition has opportunity.

Recurring Patterns Across Lifetimes

Rat souls often appear as planners, traders, strategists, network builders, or keepers of resources.

Rat souls thrive during change; uncertainty sharpens intelligence instead of diminishing it.

Rat souls influence systems quietly; stability follows their movement.

Initiations of This Lifetime

Rat awakens during periods of societal shift, financial recalibration, relocation, or system redesign.

Rat activates when the soul trusts foresight, honors preparation, and uses intelligence to guide collective well-being.

Raven and Crow Totem

Core Totem Essence

Raven carry the soul memory of intelligent transformation. This totem walks the threshold between worlds with alert awareness and purposeful curiosity. Across lands where corvids live beside people, communities recognize these birds as messengers, law keepers, creators, and carriers of sacred speech. Raven medicine centers on consciousness, pattern recognition, and the ability to translate unseen movement into lived meaning.

Strengths of the Totem

Raven brings keen perception; this soul reads subtle signals, social currents, and energetic shifts with precision.

Raven carry adaptive intelligence; problem solving, tool use, and strategy arise naturally.

Raven holds messenger authority; words, symbols, and timing shape reality through speech and action.

Raven steward liminal travel; this soul moves between spiritual realms, life phases, and identities with skill.

Raven expresses creative force; many cultures honor Raven as a world shaper and Crow as a keeper of sacred order.

Challenges of the Totem

Raven holds expansive awareness; constant input requires discernment and energetic management.

Raven has curiosity that seeks depth; this draws the soul toward mysteries that demand responsibility.Raven values autonomy and wit; social environments that resist insight create friction.

Raven moves quickly through ideas; grounding knowledge into embodiment makes for intentional pacing.

Past Life Lessons Carried Forward

Raven has learned the power of words; speech creates bonds, breaks illusions, and opens pathways.

Raven has learned stewardship of secrets; wisdom travels safely when timing aligns with readiness.

Raven has learned transformation through humor and trickster energy; laughter and disruption catalyze growth.

Raven has learned to guide souls; many lineages recognize these birds as psychopomp allies.

Recurring Patterns Across Lifetimes

Raven souls often appear as messengers, teachers, artists, strategists, translators, or spiritual intermediaries.

Raven souls attract liminal roles; they enter spaces of transition, death rites, initiation, and social change.

Raven souls carry visibility through voice or presence; communication creates community outcomes.

Initiations of This Lifetime

Raven activate during periods of identity change, truth telling, social restructuring, or spiritual awakening.

Raven rise when the soul must speak clearly, observe deeply, and guide others through uncertainty.

Corvid Variations: Current Life Expression

Raven

Raven reflects creation through disruption; the soul engages large-scale transformation, mythic responsibility, and world-shaping acts. In many Northern Indigenous traditions, Raven brings light, law, and the movement of culture itself.

Crow

Crow reflects social intelligence and boundary keeping; the soul navigates community dynamics, ethics, and the maintenance of sacred order. In many Plains, Celtic, and Asian traditions, Crow guard thresholds and watches over the dead.

Blackbird

Blackbird reflects liminal song and mystic voice; the soul engages threshold wisdom, enchantment, and transformation through sound. Celtic lore honors the blackbird as a bridge between worlds through music.

RHINOCEROS TOTEM

Core Totem Essence

Rhinoceros has the soul memory of immense strength guided by calm presence and unwavering direction. This totem teaches the power of grounded movement, strong boundaries, and the ability to move through life with purpose that clears obstacles naturally. Across African and South Asian symbolism, rhinoceros represents resilience, protection, and solitary authority. The rhinoceros does not seek conflict; it simply holds its ground and advances with certainty when necessary. Rhinoceros medicine centers on personal power, territorial clarity, and leadership expressed through stability instead of aggression.

Strengths of the Totem

Rhinoceros brings formidable endurance and physical strength.

Rhinoceros has natural authority; others recognize its presence immediately.

Rhinoceros embodies resilience; challenges become something to move through instead of around.

Rhinoceros has focused determination; once direction becomes clear, movement follows without hesitation.

Rhinoceros has a strong protective instinct for land, family, and community.

Challenges of the Totem

Rhinoceros lives with intense forward momentum; patience refines timing.

Rhinoceros values solitude and independence; cooperation strengthens community bonds.

Rhinoceros responds quickly to threats; measured assessment has wise action.

Rhinoceros has strong territorial instincts; flexibility has peaceful coexistence.

Past Life Lessons Carried Forward

Rhinoceros has learned strength through endurance.

Rhinoceros has learned protection through clear boundaries.

Rhinoceros has learned leadership through steady presence.

Rhinoceros has learned survival through resilience within harsh environments.

Recurring Patterns Across Lifetimes

Rhinoceros souls often appear as protectors, leaders, guardians of land, or individuals who stand firm when others retreat.

Rhinoceros souls carry a natural sense of duty toward family or community protection.

Rhinoceros souls move steadily toward long term goals instead of quick victories.

Initiations of This Lifetime

Rhinoceros awakens during times that require firm boundaries, courage, and strong personal direction.

Rhinoceros activates when the soul chooses to stand its ground, protect what matters, and move forward with calm certainty.

Rhinoceros Variations; Current Life Expression

Black Rhinoceros

Black Rhinoceros reflects fierce independence and heightened alertness. This variation often appears during periods requiring decisive action and personal sovereignty.

White Rhinoceros

White Rhinoceros reflects communal stability and calm authority. This variation emphasizes leadership through presence and cooperative survival within larger groups.

Indian Rhinoceros

Indian Rhinoceros reflects ancient endurance and protective guardianship. South Asian traditions associate this powerful animal with strength, patience, and resilience within challenging environments.

Javan and Sumatran Rhinoceros

These rare rhinoceroses reflect guardianship of ancient ecosystems and hidden strength. This variation often appears during life chapters involving preservation, protection of knowledge, or safeguarding rare resources.

Roadrunner Totem

Core Totem Essence

Roadrunner has the soul memory of swift survival, clever strategy, and grounded speed guided by sharp awareness. This totem lives in desert and scrubland, teaching how intelligence and timing outpace brute force. Across Southwestern Indigenous traditions, especially Pueblo, Hopi, and Navajo cultures, roadrunner appears as a protector against harmful forces, a guide along safe paths, and a symbol of quick thinking and good fortune. Its tracks often mark sacred direction and safe travel. Roadrunner medicine centers on agility, practical wisdom, and confident forward momentum through challenging terrain.

Strengths of the Totem

Roadrunner brings exceptional quickness; movement responds instantly to opportunity.

Roadrunner has sharp perception; threats and openings reveal themselves early.

Roadrunner embodies clever strategy; intelligence solves challenges efficiently.

Roadrunner has grounded endurance; long distances unfold through steady pace.

Roadrunner has protective guidance; safe pathways emerge clearly.

Challenges of the Totem

Roadrunner lives through constant motion; stillness strengthens integration and reflection.

Roadrunner values independence strongly; cooperation expands shared success.

Roadrunner responds rapidly to stimulus; measured pacing deepens discernment.

Roadrunner has strong self-reliance; asking for support strengthens resilience.

Past Life Lessons Carried Forward

Roadrunner has learned survival through wit; cleverness outmaneuvers difficulty.

Roadrunner has learned protection through awareness; early perception preserves safety.

Roadrunner has learned endurance through steady stride; persistence ensures arrival.

Roadrunner has learned guidance through tracks; paths reveal themselves step by step.

Recurring Patterns Across Lifetimes

Roadrunner souls often appear as scouts, guides, travelers, messengers, strategists, or those who help others navigate uncertain terrain.

Roadrunner souls move confidently through complexity; obstacles transform into routes.

Roadrunner souls value practicality and speed; life organizes around efficient action and clear direction.

Initiations of This Lifetime

Roadrunner awakens during periods requiring quick decision, relocation, desert or sparse environments, or stepping into leadership through practical wisdom.

Roadrunner activates when the soul trusts instinct, moves decisively, and follows the path that opens naturally ahead.

Robin Totem

Core Totem Essence

Robin has the soul memory of renewal expressed through voice, presence, and faithful return. This totem lives at the meeting point of earth and song, teaching how hope stabilizes life through consistency instead of spectacle. Across Celtic lands, Indigenous North American teachings, and European folk traditions, the robin appears as a dawn herald, hearth guardian, and reminder that life responds to care and participation. Robin medicine centers on emotional steadiness, renewal through daily engagement, and leadership expressed through song and visibility.

Strengths of the Totem

Robin brings renewal and reassurance; presence signals continuity and safe return.

Robin has grounded joy; happiness grows through tending land, home, and relationship.

Robin embodies vocal clarity; the song establishes rhythm, boundary, and emotional balance.

Robin has devotion to place; belonging strengthens identity and purpose.

Robin has gentle leadership; influence arises through sincerity and consistency.

Challenges of the Totem

Robin lives deeply within responsibility; replenishment through rest sustains vitality.

Robin bonds strongly to place and routine; adaptability expands opportunity.

Robin maintains a visible presence; discernment guides when to sing and when to listen.

Robin invests emotionally in cycles; perspective has resilience.

Past Life Lessons Carried Forward

Robin has learned hope through return; showing up restores trust in life.

Robin has learned leadership through voice; sound steadies communities.

Robin has learned renewal through care; tending sustains abundance.

Robin has learned courage through presence; visibility creates belonging.

Recurring Patterns Across Lifetimes

Robin souls often appear as caregivers, teachers, gardeners, morale keepers, or community anchors.

Robin souls stabilize emotional climate; others feel reassured by their constancy.

Robin souls value home, land, and rhythm; life organizes around their participation.

Initiations of This Lifetime

Robin awakens during rebuilding, seasonal transition, or restoration after hardship.

Robin activates when the soul commits to daily presence, truthful voice, and steady care.

Songbird Variations; Current Life Expression

Thrush

Thrush reflects emotional depth through layered song; the soul engages memory, storytelling, and healing through voice. Celtic and European traditions honor thrush as a keeper of ancestral feeling and melodic wisdom.

Lark

Lark reflects joy expressed through elevation and lightness; the soul engages optimism, inspiration, and spiritual uplift through song. Many cultures associate lark with dawn, hope, and connection to sky wisdom.

Nightingale

Nightingale reflects emotional truth and devotion expressed through song; the soul engages longing, love, and poetic clarity. Middle Eastern and European traditions associate nightingale with soul expression and heartfelt honesty.

Rooster and Chicken Totem

Core Totem Essence

Rooster carry the soul memory of vigilance, nourishment, and the protection of daily life. This totem lives close to the ground, teaching how safety, provision, and awareness sustain community. Across East Asian traditions, Celtic and European folk belief, African village lore, and Indigenous agrarian cultures, chicken appears as a provider and guardian of hearth, while rooster appears as a herald, protector, and keeper of time. Rooster medicine centers on watchfulness, nourishment of others, and courage expressed through consistency and voice.

Strengths of the Totem

Rooster brings constant vigilance; awareness maintains safety within shared space.

Rooster has nourishment and provision; care expressed through daily tending sustains life.

Rooster embodies courage through presence; standing one's ground protects community and home.

Rooster has rhythm and order; cycles of day, work, and rest remain clear.

Rooster holds vocal power; sound signals danger, gathers others, and restores structure.

Challenges of the Totem

Rooster live with heightened alertness; grounding has calm and rest.

Rooster respond quickly to disturbance; discernment refines reaction into leadership.

Rooster carry responsibility for others; self-care strengthens long term service.

Rooster value familiarity; confidence has expansion beyond known territory.

Past Life Lessons Carried Forward

Rooster have learned protection through vigilance; awareness preserves life.

Rooster have learned nourishment as sacred duty; feeding others sustains communities.

Rooster have learned courage through voice; sound establishes safety and order.

Rooster have learned rhythm as wisdom; time honored cycles guide survival.

Recurring Patterns Across Lifetimes

Rooster souls often appear as caregivers, household guardians, organizers, early risers, or keepers of routine and safety.

Rooster souls anchor daily life; stability grows through their consistency.

Rooster souls protect without hesitation; presence reassures others.

Initiations of This Lifetime

Rooster awaken during periods of family responsibility, home protection, or leadership rooted in routine and care.

Rooster activate when the soul accepts guardianship of daily life and uses awareness and voice to protect what matters.

Galliform Variations: Current Life Expression

Chicken

Hen reflects nourishment, protection of young, and emotional stewardship; the soul engages care-giving, resource management, and creation of safe space. Many cultures honor the hen as a symbol of fertility, provision, and maternal strength.

Rooster

Rooster reflects courage, signaling, and boundary defense; the soul engages leadership through voice, timing, and visible presence. East Asian and European traditions regard the rooster as a protector against harm and a herald of clarity and truth.

Junglefowl

Junglefowl reflects instinctual awareness and ancestral vitality; the soul engages alertness, survival intelligence, and connection to original rhythm and land.

Bantam

Bantam reflects concentrated courage and confidence; the soul engages assertiveness and protection regardless of size or status. This expression emphasizes boldness rooted in self-trust.

Salmon and River Fish Totem

Core Totem Essence

Salmon has the soul memory of return guided by endurance, purpose, and ancestral calling. This totem lives through long journeys against the current, teaching how devotion to origin and destiny creates strength. Across Pacific Northwest Indigenous nations, Celtic river lore, Nordic traditions, and northern fishing cultures, salmon appears as a sacred teacher of wisdom earned through effort, nourishment offered through sacrifice, and continuity maintained through faithful return. Salmon medicine centers on perseverance, clarity of direction, and honoring the call that draws the soul home.

Strengths of the Totem

Salmon brings unwavering determination; movement continues despite resistance.

Salmon has ancestral memory; lineage and origin guide decision and timing.

Salmon embodies purpose driven endurance; effort aligns with meaning instead of force.

Salmon has nourishment through devotion; giving sustains community and future.

Salmon navigates emotional and physical currents; depth and surface integrate smoothly.

Challenges of the Totem

Salmon lives through demanding journeys; replenishment has sustained vitality.

Salmon commits deeply to a singular path; flexibility has adaptation within purpose.

Salmon has strong ancestral pull; discernment guides balance between past and present.

Salmon invests fully in return; rest restores clarity and strength.

Past Life Lessons Carried Forward

Salmon has learned wisdom through effort; struggle refines clarity and strength.

Salmon has learned devotion through return; honoring origin sustains identity.

Salmon has learned leadership through example; perseverance teaches others.

Salmon has learned sacrifice as nourishment; giving has sacred value.

Recurring Patterns Across Lifetimes

Salmon souls often appear as teachers, elders, providers, culture bearers, or keepers of tradition.

Salmon souls answer deep callings; destiny pulls them through difficulty with purpose.

Salmon souls nourish others; their effort feeds community and continuity.

Initiations of This Lifetime

Salmon awakens during periods of return, ancestral healing, vocation calling, or commitment to long effort.

Salmon activates when the soul follows purpose despite resistance and honors where it comes from.

River and Cold Water Fish Variations; Current Life Expression

Salmon

Salmon reflects ancestral return and heroic endurance; the soul engages destiny, perseverance, and nourishment offered through devotion. Pacific Northwest Indigenous cultures honor salmon as a sacred relative whose return sustains life and law.

Trout

Trout reflects sensitivity and instinctive navigation; the soul engages awareness of subtle current, clarity within emotion, and survival guided by perception. Celtic and northern river traditions associate trout with wisdom and insight gained through attentiveness.

Char

Char reflects resilience within cold and depth; the soul engages endurance, emotional steadiness, and survival created from quiet strength. Arctic and subarctic cultures recognize char as a teacher of persistence within harsh conditions.

Steelhead

Steelhead reflects adaptive return; the soul engages flexibility within commitment, moving between worlds while honoring origin. This expression emphasizes strength refined through varied experience.

Cod

Cod reflects provision through abundance and reliability; the soul engages sustenance, stability, and responsibility to communities. North Atlantic cultures honor cod as a foundation of survival and shared prosperity.

Whitefish

Whitefish reflects nourishment and quiet continuity; the soul engages dependable contribution, clarity, and service expressed without spectacle. Many northern cultures regard whitefish as a staple of life and balance.

Grayling

Grayling reflects elegance within current; the soul engages graceful navigation, aesthetic awareness, and emotional flow guided by precision.

Scarab Beetle Totem

Core Totem Essence

Scarab Beetle has the soul memory of renewal, sacred labor, and creation guided through steady shaping of raw material into life sustaining form. This totem lives close to earth and sun, teaching how transformation unfolds through patient effort and alignment with cosmic rhythm. Across ancient Egyptian tradition, the scarab stands as Khepri; the morning sun who rolls the solar disk across the sky, symbolizing rebirth, protection, and eternal return. Scarab medicine centers on regeneration, purposeful work, and the understanding that every cycle births new light.

Strengths of the Totem

Scarab brings powerful renewal; life rises again through every cycle.

Scarab has disciplined focus; steady effort creates lasting creation.

Scarab embodies protection; sacred amulets guard body and spirit.

Scarab has transformation; waste and shadow become fertile ground for growth.

Scarab has solar vitality; energy and optimism radiate outward.

Challenges of the Totem

Scarab lives through constant labor; rest restores clarity and strength.

Scarab values self-reliance; collaboration expands possibilities.

Scarab moves methodically; flexibility enhances creative solutions.

Scarab has deep responsibility; lightness and play renew momentum.

Past Life Lessons Carried Forward

Scarab has learned rebirth through cycles; endings prepare new beginnings.

Scarab has learned strength through persistence; steady work builds legacy.

Scarab has learned protection through sacred alignment; spirit guards life.

Scarab has learned transformation through alchemy; shadow becomes nourishment.

Recurring Patterns Across Lifetimes

Scarab souls often appear as builders, healers, ritual workers, artisans, farmers, or those who restore what others discard.

Scarab souls transform environments quietly; neglected spaces become fertile through their presence.

Scarab souls value purpose and continuity; life organizes around meaningful contribution and renewal.

Initiations of This Lifetime

Scarab awakens during periods of rebuilding after loss, recovery from stagnation, or dedication to long-term goals.

Scarab activates when the soul embraces steady work, trusts cycles of renewal, and creates light from shadow.

Scorpion Totem

Core Totem Essence

Scorpion has the soul memory of contained power and sacred boundaries. This totem lives through intensity held with precision, survival created from discernment, and transformation born from self-protection. Across North Africa, the Middle East, Central Asia, Mesoamerica, and desert cultures worldwide, scorpion appears as a guardian of thresholds, a keeper of life and death knowledge, and a being whose potency commands respect. Scorpion medicine centers on mastery of personal power, emotional honesty, and transformation that arises through conscious containment instead of exposure.

Strengths of the Totem

Scorpion brings concentrated power; energy gathers inward and releases only with purpose.

Scorpion has exceptional boundary intelligence; self-protection remains clear and instinctive.

Scorpion embodies resilience; survival unfolds through adaptability and strategic response.

Scorpion holds emotional depth; feeling transforms into strength through awareness and control.

Scorpion guards sacred thresholds; initiation, intimacy, and truth remain protected spaces.

Challenges of the Totem

Scorpion lives with intense internal force; conscious integration creates stability and clarity.

Scorpion values privacy and containment; trust develops through earned proximity.

Scorpion experiences emotional extremes; regulation through embodiment has balance.

Scorpion responds decisively to threat; discernment refines timing and proportional response.

Past Life Lessons Carried Forward

Scorpion has learned survival through discernment; awareness prevents harm.

Scorpion has learned power through restraint; containment preserves potency.

Scorpion has learned transformation through intensity; pressure refines essence.

Scorpion has learned guardianship of the sacred; access requires respect and readiness.

Recurring Patterns Across Lifetimes

Scorpion souls often appear as protectors, healers, alchemists, guardians of taboo knowledge, or initiators.

Scorpion souls engage deep transformation; crisis becomes catalyst for rebirth.

Scorpion souls value truth and depth; superficial engagement holds little meaning.

Initiations of This Lifetime

Scorpion awakens during periods of boundary enforcement, emotional alchemy, or reclamation of personal power.

Scorpion activates when the soul learns to wield intensity with wisdom, timing, and self-respect.

Seahorse Totem

Core Totem Essence

Seahorse has the soul memory of gentle strength made with devotion, patience, and emotional depth. This totem lives through stillness within motion, teaching how power expresses itself through care, commitment, and subtle authority. Across ancient Greek symbolism, Chinese lore, Pacific coastal cultures, and Indigenous ocean traditions, the seahorse appears as a guardian of sacred waters, a symbol of protection, and a keeper of unusual roles within creation. Seahorse medicine centers on emotional steadiness, sacred partnership, and leadership expressed through nurturing presence.

Strengths of the Totem

Seahorse brings quiet resilience; endurance unfolds through patience and calm presence.

Seahorse has profound emotional intelligence; feeling guides decision with clarity and care.

Seahorse embodies devoted partnership; bonds strengthen through loyalty and shared responsibility.

Seahorse has protective guardianship; safety grows through attentiveness instead of force.

Seahorse navigates currents with grace; movement aligns with flow instead of resistance.

Challenges of the Totem

Seahorse lives within strong emotional bonds; self-definition has balance and clarity.

Seahorse moves slowly through change; trust in timing sustains confidence.

Seahorse values stability deeply; adaptability expands resilience within shifting currents.

Seahorse holds responsibility tenderly; replenishment through rest and support sustains vitality.

Past Life Lessons Carried Forward

Seahorse has learned strength through gentleness; care preserves life and trust.

Seahorse has learned leadership through devotion; responsibility guides authority.

Seahorse has learned emotional mastery through patience; steadiness stabilizes the outcome.

Seahorse has learned protection through presence; vigilance expressed softly remains powerful.

Recurring Patterns Across Lifetimes

Seahorse souls often appear as caregivers, partners, guardians, healers, or quiet leaders within relational systems.

Seahorse souls redefine strength; nurturing becomes command through consistency.

Seahorse souls hold sacred responsibility; others entrust them with what feels precious.

Initiations of This Lifetime

Seahorse awakens during periods of partnership commitment, emotional care-taking, or assumption of nurturing leadership.

Seahorse activates when the soul honors tenderness as strength, patience as power, and devotion as a guiding force.

Syngnathid Variations: Current Life Expression

Common Seahorse

Common Seahorse reflects emotional steadiness and partnership devotion; the soul engages loyalty, care-giving, and gentle authority within shared space.

Sea Dragon

Sea Dragon reflects mystical guardianship and ancient ocean wisdom; the soul engages enchantment, protection of sacred waters, and lineage memory through beauty and stillness.

Seal and Sea Lion Totem

Core Totem Essence

Seal carry the soul memory of emotional fluency joined with playful intelligence. This totem lives between ocean and shore, navigating feeling and form with grace and adaptability. Across Inuit, Sámi, Celtic, Polynesian, and coastal Indigenous cultures worldwide, seals appear as kin beings, shape shifters, and teachers of joy rooted in survival. Seal medicine centers on emotional literacy, balance between worlds, and resilience expressed through curiosity, connection, and delight.

Strengths of the Totem

Seal brings emotional intelligence; feeling moves freely and informs action.

Seal carries playful resilience; joy restores strength and has endurance.

Seal embodies liminal mastery; movement between inner and outer worlds flows naturally.

Seal has social bonding; community thrives through shared warmth and communication.

Seal has adaptability; shifting environments invite creative response.

Challenges of the Totem

Seal live with emotional openness; grounding has containment and clarity.

Seal value connection deeply; solitude makes for conscious cultivation.

Seal respond to atmosphere quickly; energetic hygiene has balance.

Seal balance play and responsibility; structure has long term well-being.

Past Life Lessons Carried Forward

Seal has learned joy as survival skill; delight sustains life through hardship.

Seal has learned shape shifting through context; identity adapts without loss of essence.

Seal has learned kinship across realms; land and sea remain equal homes.

Seal has learned emotional honesty; expression heals and connects.

Recurring Patterns Across Lifetimes

Seal souls often appear as healers, performers, caregivers, mediators, or emotional anchors.

Seal souls create warmth within groups; laughter and affection stabilize community.

Seal souls navigate transitions gracefully; movement between roles feels natural.

Initiations of This Lifetime

Seal awaken during periods of emotional healing, relational renewal, or return to joy.

Seal activate when the soul allows feeling, play, and connection to guide strength.

Pinniped Variations; Current Life Expression

Harbor Seal

Harbor Seal reflects gentle adaptability and emotional attunement; the soul engages quiet connection, intuition, and ease within close community. Many coastal Indigenous cultures honor harbor seal as a companion spirit and a teacher of calm presence.

Harp Seal

Harp Seal reflects migration and renewal through cycle; the soul engages transition, collective movement, and endurance created from seasonal rhythm. Arctic cultures recognize harp seal as a vital life giver and a symbol of continuity across generations.

Ringed Seal

Ringed Seal reflects survival through intimacy with environment; the soul engages precision, patience, and trust in subtle pathways. Inuit traditions honor ringed seal as a master of ice water navigation and a teacher of attunement.

Gray Seal

Gray Seal reflects emotional depth and expressive communication; the soul engages voice, individuality, and social complexity within group life.

Sea Lion

Sea Lion reflects confidence, play, and visible leadership; the soul engages expression, humor, and social coordination. Pacific coastal cultures observe sea lion as a being of bold presence, curiosity, and communal vitality.

Fur Seal

Fur Seal reflects balance between sensitivity and protection; the soul engages warmth, care, and resilience within shifting conditions.

Shark Totem

Core Totem Essence

Shark has the soul memory of primal momentum, clarity of direction, and authority expressed through continuous motion. This totem lives through instinct sharpened into mastery, teaching how survival, leadership, and purpose remain inseparable from forward movement. Across Polynesian, Hawaiian, Micronesian, African coastal, and ancient maritime cultures, shark appears as an ancestral guardian, an ocean law keeper, and a being who commands respect through presence and inevitability. Shark medicine centers on decisive clarity, emotional confidence, and the understanding that stopping weakens power while movement sustains life.

Strengths of the Totem

Shark brings unwavering forward drive; purpose sharpens through motion.

Shark has absolute clarity of direction; instinct guides decision without hesitation.

Shark embodies territorial authority; space responds to presence immediately.

Shark has emotional fearlessness; depth and intensity remain navigable.

Shark sustains life through momentum; continuous engagement preserves strength.

Challenges of the Totem

Shark lives through constant movement; conscious pacing has sustainability.

Shark values direct engagement; refinement has precision within action.

Shark holds strong territorial awareness; discernment guides interaction within shared space.

Shark has immense power; regulation strengthens longevity and impact.

Past Life Lessons Carried Forward

Shark has learned survival through motion; stopping invites vulnerability.

Shark has learned leadership through inevitability; clarity commands respect.

Shark has learned emotional mastery through immersion; depth sharpens strength.

Shark has learned guardianship through presence; authority stabilizes environment.

Recurring Patterns Across Lifetimes

Shark souls often appear as protectors, leaders, warriors, navigators, or enforcers of natural law.

Shark souls move decisively; environments reorganize around their direction.

Shark souls carry ancestral ocean memory; instinct predates language.

Initiations of This Lifetime

Shark awakens during periods requiring decisive action, boundary enforcement, or reclamation of personal power.

Shark activates when the soul commits fully to direction, maintains motion, and trusts instinct over doubt.

Shark Variations; Current Life Expression

Great White Shark

Great White Shark reflects apex authority and absolute clarity; the soul engages leadership, presence, and decisive action that reshapes entire systems.

Tiger Shark

Tiger Shark reflects adaptability and fearless exploration; the soul engages curiosity, resilience, and strength created from experience across varied terrain.

Hammerhead Shark

Hammerhead Shark reflects expanded perception and sensory intelligence; the soul engages wide awareness, strategic scanning, and emotional discernment.

Bull Shark

Bull Shark reflects territorial dominance and adaptability across environments; the soul engages boundary enforcement and authority within both emotional and practical realms.

Blue Shark

Blue Shark reflects endurance across vast distance; the soul engages long journeys, emotional stamina, and persistence created from open space.

Whale Shark

Whale Shark reflects gentle dominance and ancient wisdom; the soul engages massive presence paired with calm nourishment and non-reactive authority.

Reef Shark

Reef Shark reflects guardianship of territory; the soul engages protection, vigilance, and stewardship of shared space.

Nurse Shark

Nurse Shark reflects patience and grounded strength; the soul engages still authority, rest based power, and stability within community.

Goblin Shark

Goblin Shark reflects ancient lineage memory and deep time wisdom; the soul engages comfort within unfamiliar depth and ancestral knowledge beyond surface reality.

Saw shark

Saw shark reflects sensory precision and investigative intelligence; the soul engages exploration, detection, and strategic engagement.

Skunk Totem

Core Totem Essence

Skunk has the soul memory of sovereign self-respect expressed through calm confidence and unmistakable boundary presence. This totem lives through knowing one's worth without pursuit of dominance, teaching how clarity of identity creates safety and authority. Across Indigenous North American teachings and woodland traditions, skunk appears as a being who walks peacefully, signals clearly, and resolves conflict through certainty instead of struggle. Skunk medicine centers on dignity, personal truth, and the power of standing fully within one's own space.

Strengths of the Totem

Skunk brings absolute boundary clarity; space organizes itself around confident presence.

Skunk has fearless self-assurance; identity remains stable without comparison.

Skunk embodies calm authority; power expresses itself without escalation.

Skunk has respect through signaling; communication prevents unnecessary conflict.

Skunk has emotional independence; self-validation has decision and movement.

Challenges of the Totem

Skunk lives with strong boundary energy; discernment guides openness and connection.

Skunk signals clearly and decisively; patience has relational flow.

Skunk values autonomy deeply; collaboration expands influence when chosen consciously.

Skunk trusts self completely; listening enriches perspective without dilution.

Past Life Lessons Carried Forward

Skunk has learned protection through certainty; confidence resolves threat.

Skunk has learned peace through boundary; clarity preserves harmony.

Skunk has learned authority through identity; self-knowledge creates safety.

Skunk has learned communication as prevention; signaling replaces struggle.

Recurring Patterns Across Lifetimes

Skunk souls often appear as boundary keepers, counselors, protectors of personal space, or quiet leaders who command respect without force.

Skunk souls shift environments through presence alone; others adjust behavior instinctively.

Skunk souls value dignity above dominance; self-respect guides every interaction.

Initiations of This Lifetime

Skunk awakens during periods of boundary setting, reclamation of self-worth, or restoration of personal authority.

Skunk activates when the soul stands fully within its truth, signals clearly, and allows confidence to resolve conflict before it forms.

Sloth Totem

Core Totem Essence

Sloth has the soul memory of sacred pacing, presence rooted in the body, and wisdom revealed through unhurried living. This totem lives through deliberate movement and deep attunement to internal rhythm, teaching how life sustains itself through conservation, awareness, and patience. Across Indigenous cultures of Central and South America, rain-forest cosmology, and earth based spiritual traditions, sloth appears as a keeper of time beyond urgency, a guardian of nervous system harmony, and a being whose survival depends on moving in alignment with natural cadence.

Sloth medicine centers on honoring biological rhythm, emotional regulation through slowness, and trust in timing instead of force.

Strengths of the Totem

Sloth brings profound nervous system regulation; calm presence stabilizes body and mind.

Sloth has mastery of energy conservation; vitality sustains itself through measured movement.

Sloth embodies deep environmental attunement; body, tree, and climate communicate continuously.

Sloth has patience as wisdom; timing reveals itself through stillness.

Sloth has gentle resilience; survival unfolds through consistency instead of urgency.

Challenges of the Totem

Sloth lives within deliberate pacing; external pressure requires clear boundary holding.

Sloth values internal rhythm; communication has alignment with faster systems.

Sloth moves slowly through change; trust in self-direction sustains confidence.

Sloth has sensitivity to disruption; grounding reinforces safety and stability.

Past Life Lessons Carried Forward

Sloth has learned survival through pacing; speed yields to sustainability.

Sloth has learned wisdom through embodiment; the body has truth.

Sloth has learned safety through stillness; calm preserves life force.

Sloth has learned alignment through patience; timing emerges naturally.

Recurring Patterns Across Lifetimes

Sloth souls often appear as healers of burnout, guardians of rest, teachers of embodiment, or protectors of natural rhythm.

Sloth souls influence others through calm regulation; presence slows environments toward balance.

Sloth souls value sustainability; life organizes around what can be maintained gently.

Initiations of This Lifetime

Sloth awakens during periods of recovery, nervous system healing, rejection of urgency culture, or reclamation of bodily wisdom.

Sloth activates when the soul chooses alignment over speed and honors rest as sacred intelligence.

Snail Totem

Core Totem Essence

Snail has the soul memory of sacred pacing, portable sanctuary, and steady progress through patience and self-containment. This totem lives close to earth and moisture, teaching how life unfolds through deliberate movement and how safety arises from carrying home within. Across Celtic countryside lore, Mediterranean garden symbolism, African earth traditions, and Asian seasonal teachings, snail represents persistence, fertility, and the spiral of time. The shell mirrors cosmic geometry and the unfolding path of consciousness. Snail medicine centers on protection, introspection, and the wisdom of moving at the pace that preserves vitality.

Strengths of the Totem

Snail brings patient endurance; steady effort creates lasting achievement.

Snail has strong self-protection; boundaries remain clear and healthy.

Snail embodies portable sanctuary; inner safety travels everywhere.

Snail has deep sensitivity to environment; intuition guides safe routes.

Snail has spiral wisdom; growth unfolds through natural cycles and inner evolution.

Challenges of the Totem

Snail lives through slow deliberate rhythm; confident initiative strengthens momentum.

Snail values solitude and shelter; shared connection enriches experience.

Snail moves cautiously through change; trust has exploration and expansion.

Snail has heightened sensitivity; grounding stabilizes emotional flow.

Past Life Lessons Carried Forward

Snail has learned survival through patience; timing creates success.

Snail has learned protection through self-containment; home exists within.

Snail has learned growth through spiral cycles; life expands inward and outward together.

Snail has learned resilience through persistence; gentle motion achieves great distance.

Recurring Patterns Across Lifetimes

Snail souls often appear as healers, gardeners, monks, writers, artisans, or those who cultivate quiet spaces for reflection and growth.

Snail souls move steadily toward goals; their progress remains reliable and lasting.

Snail souls value simplicity and sanctuary; life organizes around peace and sustainability.

Initiations of This Lifetime

Snail awakens during periods of retreat, healing, home building, or reconnecting with inner life and natural rhythm.

Snail activates when the soul honors its pace, has safety within, and trusts steady consistent steps.

Snake Totem

Core Totem Essence

Snake has the soul memory of renewal through embodied wisdom. This totem moves close to the earth and within the body, guiding transformation through shedding, circulation, and life force awakening. Across Africa, Asia, the Americas, Australia, and the ancient Mediterranean, cultures recognize snake as a keeper of healing, sexuality, death rebirth cycles, and sacred knowledge. Snake medicine centers on regeneration, kundalini like vitality, and conscious relationship with instinct and power.

Strengths of the Totem

Snake brings regenerative intelligence; renewal unfolds through release and cyclical movement.

Snake has deep body wisdom; sensation, intuition, and instinct guide choice and timing.

Snake embodies healing force; many traditions associate snake with medicine, restoration, and vitality.

Snake has precision; energy flows efficiently through focus and alignment.

Snake guards sacred knowledge; mystery reveals itself through readiness and embodiment.

Challenges of the Totem

Snake lives with potent life force; conscious circulation has balance and clarity.

Snake has heightened sensual and emotional awareness; integration through movement and breath has harmony.

Snake values privacy and depth; trust creates selective sharing and visibility.

Snake awakens transformation repeatedly; grounding has stability during shedding phases.

Past Life Lessons Carried Forward

Snake has learned renewal through shedding; release restores vitality and strength.

Snake has learned healing through circulation; energy flows best when pathways remain open.

Snake has learned reverence for instinct; body knowing protects life and wisdom.

Snake has learned guardianship of sacred thresholds; initiation unfolds through readiness.

Recurring Patterns Across Lifetimes

Snake souls often appear as healers, mystics, midwives, alchemists, or keepers of sacred arts.

Snake souls move through profound transformations; identity renews through cycles.

Snake souls work closely with life force themes; sexuality, creativity, and healing intertwine.

Initiations of This Lifetime

Snake awakens during periods of healing crisis, sexual awakening, spiritual initiation, or identity transformation.

Snake activates when the soul learns to trust the body as a source of wisdom and power.

Serpent Variations; Current Life Expression

Python

Python reflects grounding and containment of power; the soul engages strength, patience, and deep embodiment. African, Southeast Asian, and Australian cultures honor python as an ancestral being tied to land, fertility, and creation.

Cobra

Cobra reflects awakened authority and protective intelligence; the soul engages leadership, vigilance, and sacred defense. In South Asian and Egyptian traditions, cobra aligns with divine protection, kundalini energy, and royal guardianship.

Rattlesnake

Rattlesnake reflects clear signaling and boundary awareness; the soul engages warning, honesty, and territorial clarity. Indigenous cultures of North America honor rattlesnake as a teacher of respect, medicine, and conscious power.

Boa

Boa reflects steady transformation and emotional depth; the soul engages slow integration, patience, and inner strength. Amazonian traditions associate boa with shamanic power and dream travel.

Viper

Viper reflects precision and potency; the soul engages focused action and decisive response. Mediterranean and Middle Eastern traditions view viper as a symbol of concentrated force and sacred danger managed through wisdom.

Rainbow Serpent

Rainbow Serpent reflects creation force and water law; the soul engages life bringing energy, land shaping, and ancestral continuity. Aboriginal Australian cultures honor Rainbow Serpent as a creator being who governs rain, rivers, and fertility.

Spider Totem

Core Totem Essence

Spider has the soul memory of creation through pattern and intention. This totem lives through weaving reality from thought, timing, and relationship. Across West African, Indigenous North American, Andean, Mediterranean, South Asian, and Pacific cultures, spider appears as a creator being, a keeper of stories, and a mediator between fate and choice. Spider medicine centers on manifestation, interconnectedness, and the intelligence that shapes life through deliberate design.

Strengths of the Totem

Spider brings masterful creation; vision translates into form through steady weaving.

Spider has pattern awareness; connections reveal themselves across people, events, and time.

Spider embodies patience and timing; action arises when alignment gathers strength.

Spider holds narrative power; story, symbol, and memory shape reality.

Spider navigates liminal space; fate and free will meet through conscious choice.

Challenges of the Totem

Spider lives within vast relational fields; clarity grows through focused intention.

Spider works with delicate balance; attunement guides tension and release within creation.

Spider has deep sensitivity to vibration; grounding through body and breath has steadiness.

Spider invests energy into long processes; renewal through rest sustains creativity.

Past Life Lessons Carried Forward

Spider has learned manifestation through consistency; small actions accumulate into destiny.

Spider has learned responsibility for creation; what the soul weaves creates experience.

Spider has learned wisdom through patience; timing refines outcome.

Spider has learned the sacredness of connection; every strand has meaning.

Recurring Patterns Across Lifetimes

Spider souls often appear as artists, weavers, strategists, ritualists, storytellers, or system builders.

Spider souls shape networks; communities and ideas organize around their designs.

Spider souls influence outcomes subtly; structure guides flow and movement.

Initiations of This Lifetime

Spider awakens during periods of creation, destiny choice, or recognition of interdependence.

Spider activates when the soul commits to weaving life with intention, ethics, and awareness.

Arachnid Variations; Current Life Expression

Orb Weaver

Orb Weaver reflects harmony and precision; the soul engages beauty, symmetry, and balanced creation. Many cultures associate this spider with cosmic order and the geometry of fate.

Tarantula

Tarantula reflects embodied patience and grounded strength; the soul engages slow power, sensory awareness, and deliberate movement. Southwestern and Mesoamerican traditions honor tarantula as a teacher of timing and earth wisdom.

Black Widow

Black Widow reflects potent boundaries and transformative intimacy; the soul engages deep relational lessons, self-sovereignty, and the power of selective connection. This expression emphasizes respect for personal force and conscious exchange.

Jumping Spider

Jumping Spider reflects curiosity and focused action; the soul engages perception, quick decision, and playful intelligence. This expression emphasizes adaptability guided by attention.

Anansi Lineage Spider

Anansi reflects story weaving and cultural memory; the soul engages wisdom through humor, narrative, and clever creation. West African traditions honor Anansi as a culture hero who shapes reality through wit and storytelling.

Dream catcher Spider

Dream catcher Spider reflects protection and spiritual filtration; the soul engages guardianship of psychic space and discernment within unseen realms. Many Indigenous North American teachings align spider with dream weaving and spiritual protection.

Squirrel Totem

Core Totem Essence

Squirrel has the soul memory of joyful preparation, agile intelligence, and abundance cultivated through steady, practical effort. This totem lives between earth and tree, teaching how foresight and play weave together to create stability and resilience. Across Indigenous North American woodland traditions, Celtic forest lore, and Eurasian countryside symbolism, squirrel appears as a gatherer, messenger, and lively keeper of seeds and stories. Squirrel medicine centers on resourcefulness, adaptability, and the understanding that small consistent actions sustain future prosperity.

Strengths of the Totem

Squirrel brings strategic preparation; resources gather steadily for coming seasons.

Squirrel has quick intelligence; problem solving flows through curiosity and experimentation.

Squirrel embodies agility; movement between levels of life remains fluid and confident.

Squirrel has joyful energy; lightness strengthens morale and creativity.

Squirrel has abundance through diligence; small efforts accumulate into security.

Challenges of the Totem

Squirrel lives within constant motion; focused pacing sustains clarity and endurance.

Squirrel values gathering strongly; circulation and sharing enrich community flow.

Squirrel responds rapidly to stimulus; calm reflection deepens discernment.

Squirrel engages many projects at once; prioritization strengthens completion and satisfaction.

Past Life Lessons Carried Forward

Squirrel has learned prosperity through preparation; foresight protects well-being.

Squirrel has learned survival through adaptability; flexibility preserves life.

Squirrel has learned joy as strength; play renews energy.

Squirrel has learned that consistency builds legacy; daily tending creates future stability.

Recurring Patterns Across Lifetimes

Squirrel souls often appear as organizers, planners, herbalists, crafters, teachers, or caretakers of home and community systems.

Squirrel souls maintain morale; enthusiasm spreads through their presence.

Squirrel souls value practicality and readiness; life organizes through thoughtful detail and steady effort.

Initiations of This Lifetime

Squirrel awakens during periods of financial planning, home building, skill development, or creating security for self and family.

Squirrel activates when the soul prepares wisely, has cheerfulness, and trusts the power of small consistent actions.

Sciurid Variations; Current Life Expression

Tree Squirrel

Tree Squirrel reflects agility and elevated perspective; the soul engages quick navigation between physical, emotional, and spiritual layers of life. This variation emphasizes adaptability and confident movement through complexity.

Flying Squirrel

Flying Squirrel reflects trust in glide and unseen support; the soul engages leaps of faith, intuitive navigation, and creative problem solving through air and space. Many Indigenous traditions view gliding animals as messengers between worlds.

Red Squirrel

Red Squirrel reflects fierce protection of resources and territory; the soul engages spirited defense, strong boundaries, and bold presence within its domain.

Gray Squirrel

Gray Squirrel reflects adaptability within human and wild environments; the soul engages coexistence, ingenuity, and thriving through changing systems.

Starfish Totem

Core Totem Essence

Starfish has the soul memory of regeneration, radial awareness, and quiet strength rooted in the ocean floor. This totem lives where tide meets stone, teaching how patience, flexibility, and renewal sustain life through constant change. Across Pacific Islander traditions, coastal Indigenous cultures, and maritime symbolism worldwide, starfish appears as a sign of guidance, healing, and connection between sea and sky through its star shape. Starfish medicine centers on self-repair, multidirectional perception, and steady presence that thrives through both movement and stillness.

Strengths of the Totem

Starfish brings powerful regeneration; body and spirit rebuild quickly after loss.

Starfish has radial awareness; perception expands in every direction at once.

Starfish embodies adaptability; form bends and flows with current and tide.

Starfish has patience; progress unfolds through steady persistence.

Starfish has emotional healing; calm presence restores balance and clarity.

Challenges of the Totem

Starfish lives within slow steady rhythm; decisive action enhances opportunity.

Starfish values stillness strongly; outward expression strengthens connection.

Starfish has quiet subtlety; confident presence increases influence.

Starfish has deep sensitivity to environment; grounding preserves stability.

Past Life Lessons Carried Forward

Starfish has learned renewal through regeneration; every loss seeds new life.

Starfish has learned wisdom through patience; time creates strength.

Starfish has learned balance through flow; cooperation with tide preserves energy.

Starfish has learned guidance through subtle presence; quiet support transforms outcomes.

Recurring Patterns Across Lifetimes

Starfish souls often appear as healers, therapists, caretakers, energy workers, or those who rebuild lives and systems gently after disruption.

Starfish souls stabilize environments through calm influence; others feel safe and supported near them.

Starfish souls value steady growth and emotional equilibrium; life organizes around restoration and harmony.

Initiations of This Lifetime

Starfish awakens during periods of healing, recovery, rebuilding identity, or learning to trust slow steady progress.

Starfish activates when the soul releases what has passed, regenerates with patience, and embraces quiet resilience.

Starling, Wren, and Small Seed Bird Totem

Core Totem Essence

Starling, Wren, and small seed birds carry the soul memory of collective intelligence, adaptive voice, and power expressed through small form and constant participation. This totem lives close to daily life, teaching how influence grows through presence, repetition, and relationship instead of size. Across Celtic lands, Indigenous European countryside traditions, East

Asian symbolism, and Indigenous North American teachings, small seed birds appear as messengers, tricksters, weather readers, and keepers of communal rhythm. Their medicine centers on cleverness, resilience, shared awareness, and the ability to shape environment through sound, movement, and cooperation.

Strengths of the Totem

This totem brings sharp social intelligence; group dynamics register quickly and accurately.

This totem has powerful voice within small bodies; sound creates mood, territory, and safety.

This totem embodies adaptability; change invites creative response and rapid learning.

This totem has collective strength; unity amplifies impact.

This totem has persistence; steady participation sustains life and belonging.

Challenges of the Totem

This totem lives within constant interaction; grounding has emotional clarity.

This totem responds rapidly to stimulation; discernment refines focus and intention.

This totem thrives in groups; solitude restores balance and self-listening.

This totem expresses continuously; silence deepens wisdom and integration.

Past Life Lessons Carried Forward

This totem has learned survival through cooperation; shared awareness preserves life.

This totem has learned influence through repetition; presence reshapes environment.

This totem has learned power through voice; sound has meaning and memory.

This totem has learned intelligence through adaptability; flexibility sustains continuity.

Recurring Patterns Across Lifetimes

Souls carrying this totem often appear as communicators, organizers, teachers, musicians, messengers, or social connectors.

These souls influence group rhythm; morale and coordination shift through their presence.

These souls value participation; life organizes through shared effort and awareness.

Initiations of This Lifetime

This totem awakens during periods of community engagement, rapid learning, communication expansion, or social navigation.

This totem activates when the soul trusts its voice, participates consistently, and honors the strength of collective motion.

Small Seed Bird Variations; Current Life Expression

Starling

Starling reflects collective intelligence and mimicry; the soul engages adaptation, pattern recognition, and influence through group movement. European traditions associate starling with transformation through unity and shared direction.

Wren

Wren reflects bold spirit within small form; the soul engages courage, cleverness, and spiritual authority expressed through voice. Celtic traditions honor wren as a sacred singer and keeper of hidden wisdom.

Sparrow

Sparrow reflects resilience and everyday courage; the soul engages survival through familiarity, cooperation, and shared space. Many cultures honor sparrow as a symbol of belonging and perseverance.

Finch

Finch reflects joy, precision, and emotional lightness; the soul engages clarity, creativity, and optimism expressed through song and color.

Chickadee

Chickadee reflects curiosity and confidence; the soul engages exploration, trust, and communication even within challenging conditions. Indigenous North American teachings associate chickadee with truth telling and alert intelligence.

Goldfinch

Goldfinch reflects abundance and vitality; the soul engages renewal, brightness, and emotional uplift through presence and movement.

Stork Totem

Core Totem Essence

Stork has the soul memory of life continuity guided by sacred timing. This totem lives through guardianship of thresholds, migration aligned with season, and devotion to lineage. Across Celtic Europe, ancient Egypt, the Mediterranean, West Africa, and Indigenous traditions of river and wetland cultures, stork appears as a bringer of blessing, a protector of home, and a guide for souls arriving into embodied life. Stork medicine centers on generational care, ethical passage, and the honoring of life transitions with reverence and steadiness.

Strengths of the Totem

Stork brings guardianship of life cycles; birth, death, and renewal unfold with protection and care.

Stork has impeccable timing; movement aligns with season, readiness, and moral clarity.

Stork embodies devotion to family and home; continuity strengthens through presence and return.

Stork has ethical stewardship; responsibility guides action and decision.

Stork navigates long journeys; migration reflects trust in ancestral pathways.

Challenges of the Totem

Stork lives with strong duty to others; nourishment of self sustains long term service.

Stork has sensitivity to disruption; grounding has steadiness amid change.

Stork values tradition deeply; flexibility has adaptation across eras.

Stork maintains watchful vigilance; rest renews clarity and strength.

Past Life Lessons Carried Forward

Stork has learned protection of the vulnerable; care preserves lineage and future.

Stork has learned transition as sacred work; passage requires guidance and patience.

Stork has learned timing as wisdom; arrival and departure shape harmony.

Stork has learned stewardship of home; place anchors identity and continuity.

Recurring Patterns Across Lifetimes

Stork souls often appear as midwives, caregivers, guardians of children, family anchors, or ritual keepers of transition.

Stork souls hold responsibility with grace; others trust their guidance during change.

Stork souls return repeatedly to themes of lineage, ancestry, and generational healing.

Initiations of This Lifetime

Stork awakens during periods of family formation, birth support, ancestral healing, or relocation tied to destiny.

Stork activates when the soul accepts guardianship of life passages and honors timing as sacred law.

Swan Totem

Core Totem Essence

Swan has the soul memory of grace made with devotion, sovereignty of the heart, and transformation expressed through beauty and discipline. This totem lives at the meeting of water and air, teaching how emotion and spirit move together through poise and intention. Across Celtic lands, Greek myth, Hindu tradition, Indigenous European waterways, and Asian symbolism, swan appears as a sacred being of fidelity, poetic voice, and spiritual passage. Swan medicine centers on lifelong devotion, emotional mastery, and leadership expressed through elegance and depth.

Strengths of the Totem

Swan brings profound grace; presence calms space and elevates tone.

Swan has unwavering devotion; bonds strengthen through loyalty and consistency.

Swan embodies emotional mastery; feeling clarity and control.

Swan has beauty as discipline; form reflects inner alignment.

Swan has spiritual passage; transitions unfold with dignity and purpose.

Challenges of the Totem

Swan lives with deep emotional investment; grounding sustains balance and clarity.

Swan holds high standards of harmony; flexibility has ease within change.

Swan expresses authority quietly; voice strengthens influence when shared deliberately.

Swan has strong attachment to partnership; self-anchoring sustains independence.

Past Life Lessons Carried Forward

Swan has learned devotion as power; commitment stabilizes destiny.

Swan has learned beauty as truth; alignment reveals itself through form.

Swan has learned leadership through grace; poise guides others safely.

Swan has learned transformation through water and song; emotion has spirit forward.

Recurring Patterns Across Lifetimes

Swan souls often appear as artists, poets, diplomats, spiritual partners, guardians of sacred unions, or guides through transition.

Swan souls elevate environments; harmony increases through their presence.

Swan souls value fidelity and refinement; relationships and purpose receive careful tending.

Initiations of This Lifetime

Swan awakens during sacred partnership, artistic calling, emotional maturation, or rites of passage.

Swan activates when the soul commits deeply, with grace, and leads through heart centered presence.

Swallow Totem

Core Totem Essence

Swallow has the soul memory of return, devotion, and hope sustained through movement. This totem lives through migration guided by trust, precision, and loyalty to place and people. Across Celtic lands, East Asia, Mediterranean cultures, and Indigenous seasonal teachings, swallow appears as a herald of renewal, a guardian of home, and a messenger that life responds to care and perseverance. Swallow medicine centers on faithful return, emotional agility, and leadership expressed through grace in motion.

Strengths of the Totem

Swallow brings assurance of renewal; presence signals continuity and safe return.

Swallow has agile intelligence; rapid movement aligns with accuracy and timing.

Swallow embodies devotion to home and kin; loyalty in long journeys.

Swallow has hope through consistency; showing up restores trust.

Swallow navigates air with mastery; emotion and action integrate smoothly.

Challenges of the Totem

Swallow lives through constant movement; grounding has rest and integration.

Swallow commits deeply to cycles of return; flexibility has expansion into new roles.

Swallow maintains visible rhythm; discernment guides pace and presence.

Swallow invests heart in place; perspective has ease during transition.

Past Life Lessons Carried Forward

Swallow has learned faith through return; devotion sustains life across distance.

Swallow has learned leadership through example; grace teaches without force.

Swallow has learned resilience through motion; momentum preserves vitality.

Swallow has learned hope as practice; consistency rebuilds belonging.

Recurring Patterns Across Lifetimes

Swallow souls often appear as travelers, messengers, caregivers, builders of home, or keepers of morale.

Swallow souls reconnect people and places; bonds strengthen through their return.

Swallow souls value timing and rhythm; life organizes around their movement.

Initiations of This Lifetime

Swallow awakens during relocation, reunion, rebuilding of home, or renewal after separation.

Swallow activates when the soul trusts the journey, honors return, and leads through grace.

Hirundine Variations: Current Life Expression

Swallow

Barn Swallow reflects devotion to home and human partnership; the soul engages rebuilding, protection of hearth, and faithful return. European and East Asian traditions honor barn swallow as a blessing upon dwelling and family continuity. Cliff Swallow reflects cooperative creation and communal safety; the soul engages group building, shared vigilance, and collective resilience. This expression emphasizes strength through coordinated effort. Tree Swallow reflects lightness and adaptability; the soul engages swift adjustment, curiosity, and joyful movement within changing environments.

Purple Martin

Purple Martin reflects leadership within community flight; the soul engages guidance, visibility, and protection of group rhythm. Indigenous North American traditions regard martin as a bringer of good season and shared prosperity.

Swift

Swift reflects endurance through sustained motion; the soul engages long arcs of effort, trust in momentum, and mastery of air over extended time. This expression emphasizes commitment through movement.

Swordfish Totem

Core Totem Essence

Swordfish has the soul memory of precision, momentum, and focused will that cuts cleanly through resistance. This totem lives in open ocean currents, teaching how clarity of purpose and streamlined action create swift progress. Across Polynesian, Mediterranean, Japanese, and coastal fishing cultures, swordfish symbolizes courage, skill, and mastery of deep waters. Its bill represents discernment and directness, a tool that parts obstacles with elegant strength. Swordfish medicine centers on decisive movement, unwavering focus, and the power of aligned intention.

Strengths of the Totem

Swordfish brings exceptional speed; action unfolds with clean forward thrust.

Swordfish has sharp precision; goals remain clear and unobstructed.

Swordfish embodies courage; vast open waters inspire confidence instead of hesitation.

Swordfish has endurance; long migrations sustain steady power.

Swordfish has strategic independence; solitary navigation strengthens self-trust.

Challenges of the Totem

Swordfish lives through constant forward drive; restorative pauses sustain longevity.

Swordfish values independence strongly; cooperation enhances shared success.

Swordfish moves directly toward objectives; flexibility refines timing and approach.

Swordfish has strong intensity; gentle presence balances energy.

Past Life Lessons Carried Forward

Swordfish has learned victory through precision; focused action yields success.

Swordfish has learned strength through endurance; distance builds resilience.

Swordfish has learned survival through clarity; decisive direction prevents confusion.

Swordfish has learned mastery of deep water; emotional depth has power.

Recurring Patterns Across Lifetimes

Swordfish souls often appear as warriors, athletes, navigators, explorers, leaders, or those who excel in high focus environments requiring speed and decisiveness.

Swordfish souls cut through complexity quickly; solutions appear clean and direct.

Swordfish souls value independence and purpose; life organizes around clear goals and forward momentum.

Initiations of This Lifetime

Swordfish awakens during periods demanding decisive action, career focus, bold travel, or committing fully to a chosen path.

Swordfish activates when the soul aligns intention sharply, without hesitation, and trusts its strength to carry it through open waters.

Billfish Variations; Current Life Expression

Marlin

Marlin reflects athletic endurance and noble pursuit; the soul engages stamina, long distance migration, and strength expressed through graceful persistence. Pacific and Caribbean fishing cultures honor marlin as a symbol of courage, respect, and partnership between human and sea.

Sailfish

Sailfish reflects coordinated speed and dynamic display; the soul engages bursts of brilliance, teamwork within motion, and swift adaptation through changing currents.

Spearfish

Spearfish reflects subtle precision and focused hunting; the soul engages quiet strategy, efficient action, and success through minimal wasted effort.

Thunderbird

Fenghuang

Roc

Thunderbird, Fenghuang, and Roc Totem

Core Totem Essence

Thunderbird, Fenghuang, and Roc carry the soul memory of cosmic force expressed through guardianship and renewal. This totem moves at the scale of myth and sky, shaping weather, fate, and moral order. Across Indigenous North American nations, East Asian cosmology, and Middle Eastern and South Asian lore, cultures recognize these great beings as regulators of balance, bearers of divine authority, and witnesses to the covenant between heaven and earth. This medicine centers on immense power guided by responsibility, justice through action, and renewal born from upheaval.

Strengths of the Totem

This totem brings command of elemental forces; storm, wind, fire, and rain respond to purpose and will.

This totem has moral authority; justice, balance, and correction move through presence and action.

This totem embodies transformative renewal; destruction clears the way for restoration and growth.

This totem holds vast vision; perspective spans generations, civilizations, and cosmic cycles.

This totem inspires awe and alignment; others respond instinctively to its call.

Challenges of the Totem

This totem lives with immense scale; translating cosmic vision into human life requires grounding and discernment.

This totem has strong corrective force; timing and precision guide effective intervention.

This totem awakens intense responsibility; leadership unfolds through humility and service.

This totem moves through upheaval; stability develops through conscious integration of power.

Past Life Lessons Carried Forward

This totem has learned stewardship of storms; power restores balance instead of chaos.

This totem has learned authority through protection; strength serves life and continuity.

This totem has learned renewal through fire and wind; endings prepare the way for rebirth.

This totem has learned covenant with the sky; alignment with higher law creates destiny.

Recurring Patterns Across Lifetimes

These souls often appear as culture shapers, reformers, protectors, spiritual leaders, or agents of change.

These souls enter moments of crisis or transition; presence catalyzes realignment and renewal.

These souls carry visible impact; actions ripple outward across systems and communities.

Initiations of This Lifetime

This totem awakens during periods of collective change, moral reckoning, or spiritual upheaval.

This totem activates when the soul accepts responsibility for influence, correction, and renewal.

Mythic Sky Variations; Current Life Expression

Thunderbird

Thunderbird reflects storm borne justice and protection; the soul engages correction of imbalance, defense of sacred law, and restoration through elemental force. Among many Indigenous nations of the Pacific Northwest and Plains, Thunderbird governs thunder, lightning, rain, and the defeat of destructive beings. This expression emphasizes guardianship of the people and enforcement of cosmic order.

Fenghuang

Fenghuang reflects harmonious renewal and virtuous rule; the soul engages balance, moral leadership, and prosperity guided by grace. In Chinese cosmology, Fenghuang arises during times of peace and righteous governance, uniting yin and yang and symbolizing renewal without domination. This expression emphasizes elegance, restraint, and benevolent authority.

Roc

Roc reflects overwhelming strength and boundary testing; the soul engages feats of scale, protection against monstrous threat, and the assertion of cosmic hierarchy. In Middle Eastern and South Asian traditions, Roc appears as a bird of immense power capable of carrying elephants and shaping destiny through sheer presence. This expression emphasizes magnitude, endurance, and the responsibility of vast force.

Tiger Totem

Core Totem Essence

Tiger has the soul memory of embodied authority fused with instinctual clarity. This totem moves through the world with alert presence, decisive timing, and deep alignment between body, emotion, and will. Across South, Southeast, and East Asia, cultures recognize tiger as a guardian of land, a protector against spiritual intrusion, and a symbol of rightful power that arises through integrity and courage. Tiger medicine centers on personal sovereignty, disciplined instinct, and the balance between ferocity and grace.

Strengths of the Totem

Tiger brings instinctual confidence; the body senses truth and responds with precision.

Tiger has fearless presence; courage arises from alignment with purpose and territory.

Tiger embodies personal authority; leadership expresses itself through self-trust and clarity.

Tiger has disciplined power; strength flows through timing, restraint, and focus.

Tiger protects life force; boundaries remain strong and responsive to threat or imbalance.

Challenges of the Totem

Tiger lives with intense instinctual energy; conscious direction channels power into constructive expression.

Tiger values autonomy; environments that press conformity invite discernment and boundary reinforcement.

Tiger has emotional heat; integration through movement and breath has balance.

Tiger walks a solitary path; relationship grows through mutual respect and earned trust.

Past Life Lessons Carried Forward

Tiger has learned mastery of fear; presence transforms threat into grounded action.

Tiger has learned the ethics of strength; power serves protection and balance.

Tiger has learned territory as sacred; land, body, and spirit align as one domain.

Tiger has learned restraint; patience sharpens effectiveness and authority.

Recurring Patterns Across Lifetimes

Tiger souls often appear as protectors, leaders, warriors, advocates, or path clearers.

Tiger souls confront injustice directly; action restores balance within systems.

Tiger souls value integrity; alignment between word, action, and instinct guides life choices.

Initiations of This Lifetime

Tiger awakens during periods of power reclamation, boundary definition, or leadership emergence.

Tiger activates when the soul claims authority rooted in embodied truth and disciplined instinct.

Tiger Variations; Current Life Expression

Bengal Tiger

Bengal Tiger reflects active guardianship and visible leadership; the soul engages protection of family, community, and ancestral land. In South Asian traditions, this tiger aligns with goddess power, courage, and righteous action.

Siberian Tiger

Siberian Tiger reflects endurance and sovereignty across vast terrain; the soul navigates isolation, long vision, and strength created from patience. Indigenous peoples of the Russian Far East honor this tiger as a forest guardian and a being of spiritual authority.

Sumatran Tiger

Sumatran Tiger reflects adaptability within dense environments; the soul works with stealth, precision, and protection of delicate ecosystems. In Indonesian cosmology, this tiger serves as an ancestral guardian and mediator between worlds.

Malayan Tiger

Malayan Tiger reflects agility and territorial intelligence; the soul engages boundary maintenance, quick decision making, and protection within complex social landscapes.

White Tiger

White Tiger reflects rare clarity and spiritual authority; the soul engages heightened awareness, sacred responsibility, and initiation into visible guardianship. In Chinese cosmology, White Tiger aligns with the West, autumn, metal, and the protection of spiritual thresholds.

Turkey Totem

Core Totem Essence

Turkey has the soul memory of abundance shared through generosity, grounded leadership, and reverence for the land. This totem lives through nourishment offered to the collective, teaching how prosperity multiplies when care, humility, and stewardship guide action. Across Indigenous North American nations, turkey appears as a sacred provider, a teacher of gratitude, and a being whose presence reminds community to honor cycles of giving and receiving. Turkey medicine centers on communal well-being, embodied humility, and leadership expressed through service.

Strengths of the Totem

Turkey brings generous provision; abundance flows through sharing and gratitude.

Turkey has grounded confidence; presence commands respect through steadiness.

Turkey embodies communal leadership; well-being strengthens through coordination and care.

Turkey has gratitude as practice; thankfulness stabilizes prosperity and harmony.

Turkey has land stewardship; nourishment aligns with respect for earth and cycle.

Challenges of the Totem

Turkey lives with strong responsibility to others; replenishment through rest sustains vitality.

Turkey values collective rhythm; discernment has personal pacing within group need.

Turkey has visible presence; humility refines influence and balance.

Turkey commits to provision; delegation strengthens continuity and ease.

Past Life Lessons Carried Forward

Turkey has learned abundance through generosity; giving sustains life.

Turkey has learned leadership through service; care creates authority.

Turkey has learned gratitude as law; reverence maintains balance.

Turkey has learned strength through humility; steadiness preserves harmony.

Recurring Patterns Across Lifetimes

Turkey souls often appear as providers, organizers, hosts, land stewards, or cultural keepers of ceremony and feast.

Turkey souls anchor community gatherings; nourishment and morale rise around them.

Turkey souls value reciprocity; exchange creates identity and purpose.

Initiations of This Lifetime

Turkey awakens during periods of community building, care-giving leadership, or renewed relationship with land and food-ways.

Turkey activates when the soul practices gratitude, shares resources wisely, and leads through service.

Turtle and Tortoise Totem

Core Totem Essence

Turtle has the soul memory of endurance created from patience, protection through wisdom, and creation made with time. This totem lives through ancient rhythm, teaching how life unfolds steadily when grounded in purpose and inner stability. Across Indigenous North American nations, Polynesian ocean cultures, Hindu and Chinese cosmology, African creation stories, and

Mediterranean myth, turtle appears as Earth bearer, world foundation, and keeper of ancestral law. Turtle medicine centers on longevity, emotional steadiness, sacred boundaries, and the understanding that progress deepens through consistency instead of speed.

Strengths of the Totem

Turtle brings profound endurance; time becomes ally instead of obstacle.

Turtle has natural protection; boundaries remain clear, calm, and effective.

Turtle embodies patience as wisdom; steady movement sustains creation.

Turtle has grounded presence; body, land, and spirit align naturally.

Turtle has ancestral memory; lineage and law guide direction and identity.

Challenges of the Totem

Turtle lives within slow rhythm; responsiveness has engagement within faster systems.

Turtle values safety and structure; flexibility expands range and expression.

Turtle has deep responsibility; delegation has balance and longevity.

Turtle commits to long vision; celebration along the path nourishes spirit.

Past Life Lessons Carried Forward

Turtle has learned survival through patience; steady effort preserves life.

Turtle has learned authority through stability; grounded presence commands respect.

Turtle has learned creation through time; what lasts grows slowly.

Turtle has learned protection through boundary; self-containment sustains harmony.

Recurring Patterns Across Lifetimes

Turtle souls often appear as elders, culture keepers, land stewards, healers, or long vision leaders.

Turtle souls stabilize systems; others rely on their calm and continuity.

Turtle souls build legacies; future generations benefit from their pace.

Initiations of This Lifetime

Turtle awakens during periods of long commitment, ancestral healing, land connection, or rebuilding after upheaval.

Turtle activates when the soul honors timing, maintains boundaries, and trusts steady progress.

Chelonian Variations; Current Life Expression

Sea Turtle

Sea Turtle reflects emotional endurance and ancestral navigation; the soul engages long journeys, memory through water, and return guided by instinct. Polynesian and Indigenous coastal cultures honor sea turtle as a sacred navigator and guardian of ocean law.

Green Sea Turtle

Green Sea Turtle reflects nourishment and life cycle continuity; the soul engages healing, balance, and restoration through gentle persistence.

Leatherback Turtle

Leatherback Turtle reflects extreme endurance and ancient lineage; the soul engages depth, resilience, and survival created from vast emotional terrain.

Hawksbill Turtle

Hawksbill Turtle reflects precision and sacred craftsmanship; the soul engages discernment, detail awareness, and protection of delicate systems.

Freshwater Turtle

Freshwater Turtle reflects adaptability within emotional and relational systems; the soul engages balance between inner world and external demand. Many Indigenous river cultures honor freshwater turtle as a teacher of harmony and patience.

Snapping Turtle

Snapping Turtle reflects boundary enforcement and protective authority; the soul engages defense of space, clarity of limit, and strength expressed when required. Indigenous teachings regard snapping turtle as a keeper of law and consequence.

Box Turtle

Box Turtle reflects self-containment and inner sanctuary; the soul engages solitude, reflection, and protection through withdrawal and grounding.

Painted Turtle

Painted Turtle reflects beauty through resilience; the soul engages self-expression created from endurance and quiet confidence.

Softshell Turtle

Softshell Turtle reflects sensitivity paired with adaptability; the soul engages responsiveness, emotional awareness, and flexibility within protection.

Tortoise

Tortoise reflects mastery of land based endurance and longevity; the soul engages patience, stability, and creation made with body and earth. African, Mediterranean, and Asian traditions honor tortoise as a symbol of wisdom, time, and grounded authority.

Giant Tortoise

Giant Tortoise reflects extreme longevity and legacy consciousness; the soul engages slow mastery, generational impact, and responsibility across time.

Desert Tortoise

Desert Tortoise reflects survival through conservation; the soul engages resilience, boundary intelligence, and endurance created from minimal resource environments.

Galapagos Tortoise

Galapagos Tortoise reflects ancient sovereignty and evolutionary patience; the soul engages leadership through presence, memory through form, and continuity through stillness.

Unicorn Totem

Core Totem Essence

Unicorn has the soul memory of purity, sovereignty, and untouchable magic. This totem teaches alignment with truth so clear that distortion cannot attach. Unicorn exists within myth, yet its presence moves through spiritual systems across cultures as a symbol of sacred power that answers only to integrity. This is not softness; this is precision. Unicorn energy does not bend. It refines. It selects. It allows access only where resonance exists. Unicorn medicine centers on energetic discernment, spiritual authority, and the embodiment of a field so coherent that lower frequencies dissolve on contact.

Strengths of the Totem

Unicorn has absolute energetic clarity; illusion reveals itself immediately.

Unicorn embodies sovereignty; influence from outside forces holds no authority.

Unicorn has purity of intention; action aligns with truth instead of approval.

Unicorn channels high frequency magic; manifestation occurs through alignment instead of force.

Unicorn protects through refinement; only what matches its field gains access.

Challenges of the Totem

Unicorn maintains high standards; connection deepens through allowing imperfection within human experience.

Unicorn stands apart; community strengthens through selective openness.

Unicorn rejects distortion quickly; patience has growth in others.

Unicorn holds intense frequency; grounding in power into physical reality.

Past Life Lessons Carried Forward

Unicorn has learned purity through devotion to truth.

Unicorn has learned protection through energetic refinement.

Unicorn has learned power through alignment instead of domination.

Unicorn has learned discernment through exposure to illusion.

Recurring Patterns Across Lifetimes

Unicorn souls often appear as mystics, seers, healers, or individuals who hold a strong internal compass that guides every decision.

Unicorn souls resist corruption; environments that demand compromise create friction.

Unicorn souls attract projection; others place fantasy or expectation onto them due to their presence.

Initiations of This Lifetime

Unicorn awakens during periods that require absolute authenticity, energetic boundaries, and refusal to dilute truth.

Unicorn activates when the soul steps fully into sovereignty and allows alignment to guide relationships, work, and spiritual practice.

Urchin Totem

Core Totem Essence

Sea Urchin has the soul memory of sacred boundaries, quiet defense, and hidden beauty protected within a strong outer field. This totem lives among reefs, stone, and tidal pools, teaching how sensitivity and protection work together. Across Pacific Islander, Mediterranean, and coastal Indigenous traditions, urchin symbolizes self-preservation, resilience, and the wisdom of guarding one's center. Its spherical form mirrors the sun and the circle of wholeness, while its spines create a natural energetic shield. Sea Urchin medicine centers on healthy boundaries, inner sanctuary, and strength expressed through stillness instead of force.

Strengths of the Totem

Sea Urchin brings powerful boundary awareness; personal space remains clear and respected.

Sea Urchin has quiet resilience; survival thrives through steadiness and patience.

Sea Urchin embodies self-protection; natural defenses maintain safety without aggression.

Sea Urchin has inner richness; beauty and nourishment grow within protected space.

Sea Urchin has grounding; close contact with stone and sea stabilizes energy.

Challenges of the Totem

Sea Urchin lives within strong protective field; openness deepens connection and trust.

Sea Urchin values stillness strongly; gentle movement expands opportunity.

Sea Urchin moves cautiously through environment; confident exploration broadens experience.

Sea Urchin has heightened sensitivity; balanced exposure strengthens adaptability.

Past Life Lessons Carried Forward

Sea Urchin has learned safety through boundaries; protection preserves vitality.

Sea Urchin has learned strength through stillness; calm presence deters disruption.

Sea Urchin has learned abundance through conservation; energy stores wisely.

Sea Urchin has learned wholeness through circular awareness; center remains constant.

Recurring Patterns Across Lifetimes

Sea Urchin souls often appear as guardians, empaths, therapists, archivists, or those who protect sacred spaces and maintain energetic boundaries for others.

Sea Urchin souls create sanctuaries; environments feel safe and contained around them.

Sea Urchin souls value privacy and integrity; life organizes around inner richness instead of outward display.

Initiations of This Lifetime

Sea Urchin awakens during periods of boundary building, emotional protection, home creation, or learning to guard personal energy.

Sea Urchin activates when the soul claims its space confidently, protects its center, and trusts the strength of quiet presence.

Vulture Totem

Core Totem Essence

Vulture has the soul memory of sacred purification and reverent completion. This totem lives through the honoring of endings as necessary acts of love that sustain life. Across ancient Egypt, Tibet, the Andes, Mesoamerica, Africa, and Indigenous cultures worldwide, vulture appears as a holy cleaner, a guardian of transition, and a being entrusted with what others turn away from. Vulture medicine centers on reverence for death as transformation, responsibility to the collective cycle, and wisdom gained through service at the edge of life.

Strengths of the Totem

Vulture brings profound purification; decay transforms into nourishment for the living world.

Vulture has fearless presence with endings; completion unfolds with dignity and care.

Vulture embodies ecological and spiritual stewardship; balance restores through responsible removal.

Vulture has vast perspective; distance reveals truth beyond emotion or attachment.

Vulture holds sacred responsibility; service sustains life cycles and ancestral order.

Challenges of the Totem

Vulture lives close to death and transition; grounding has emotional integration.

Vulture has collective burden; ritual and rest sustain longevity of service.

Vulture values distance and clarity; intimacy grows through chosen descent and connection.

Vulture moves deliberately through purpose; patience in authority within human pace.

Past Life Lessons Carried Forward

Vulture has learned reverence for endings; completion preserves life and balance.

Vulture has learned service through humility; essential work requires presence without recognition.

Vulture has learned purification as sacred act; removal creates space for renewal.

Vulture has learned guardianship of thresholds; passage demands respect and responsibility.

Recurring Patterns Across Lifetimes

Vulture souls often appear as death workers, healers of grief, spiritual cleaners, elders, or guardians of transition.

Vulture souls stabilize systems through unseen labor; balance returns quietly through their work.

Vulture souls carry ancestral duty; lineage healing and completion repeat across incarnations.

Initiations of This Lifetime

Vulture awakens during periods of grief work, ancestral release, ecological service, or spiritual leadership tied to endings.

Vulture activates when the soul accepts responsibility for clearing, purification, and reverent closure.

Walrus Totem

Core Totem Essence

Walrus has the soul memory of ancestral endurance, communal protection, and wisdom through survival at the edge of ice and sea. This totem lives where ocean, land, and frozen world meet, teaching how strength, cooperation, and memory sustain life in demanding environments. Across Inuit, Yupik, Chukchi, and Arctic coastal cultures, walrus serves as provider, teacher, and respected elder of the sea. Its presence has entire communities through nourishment, shelter, and tools. Walrus medicine centers on stewardship, grounded authority, and loyalty to kin and lineage.

Strengths of the Totem

Walrus brings immense physical and emotional strength; stability in every situation.

Walrus has communal loyalty; group bonds create safety and continuity.

Walrus embodies ancestral memory; wisdom flows through generations.

Walrus has resource stewardship; care for what is given sustains the whole community.

Walrus has calm authority; presence alone establishes order and protection.

Challenges of the Totem

Walrus lives within strong responsibility to others; personal replenishment sustains vitality.

Walrus values close group structure; independence has balanced identity.

Walrus moves deliberately; adaptability enhances responsiveness during change.

Walrus has powerful protective instinct; gentleness strengthens harmony within community.

Past Life Lessons Carried Forward

Walrus has learned survival through cooperation; collective strength preserves life.

Walrus has learned wisdom through endurance; time creates understanding.

Walrus has learned prosperity through stewardship; respectful use sustains abundance.

Walrus has learned guardianship of lineage; elders guide the future.

Recurring Patterns Across Lifetimes

Walrus souls often appear as elders, providers, protectors of family, craftspeople, teachers of tradition, or those who hold communities together through practical care.

Walrus souls naturally stabilize groups; others rely on their reliability and strength.

Walrus souls value heritage and continuity; life organizes around family, memory, and service.

Initiations of This Lifetime

Walrus awakens during periods of stepping into elder roles, supporting extended family, preserving tradition, or creating stability during harsh conditions.

Walrus activates when the soul embraces responsibility with dignity, protects its people, and offers strength through calm presence.

Whale Totem

Core Totem Essence

Whale has the soul memory of planetary consciousness. This totem lives at the scale of oceans, migration, and ancestral time, holding memory that predates human record. Across Polynesian, Inuit, Northwest Coast, Norse, and many coastal cultures worldwide, whale appears as an ancestor, a navigator, and a keeper of sacred sound. Whale medicine centers on deep emotional intelligence, lineage memory, and the ability to carry vast knowing with grace and calm authority.

Strengths of the Totem

Whale brings profound emotional depth; feeling moves through the soul with maturity and compassion.

Whale has ancestral memory; lineage wisdom flows through body, voice, and instinct.

Whale embodies sacred sound; voice, song, and vibration heal, guide, and connect across distance.

Whale has steady power; immense strength expresses itself through gentleness and precision.

Whale navigates vast journeys; long vision and endurance shape destiny and purpose.

Challenges of the Totem

Whale lives with expansive emotional capacity; integration through expression and movement has balance.

Whale has deep memory; processing grief and inherited experience requires ritual and time.

Whale moves at deliberate pace; environments driven by urgency invite grounding and self-advocacy.

Whale holds collective awareness; boundaries and clarity between personal and ancestral emotion.

Past Life Lessons Carried Forward

Whale has learned stewardship of memory; the past informs healing instead of burden.

Whale has learned guidance through sound; voice has truth, comfort, and direction.

Whale has learned navigation through trust; inner compass aligns with oceanic rhythm.

Whale has learned guardianship of life; presence stabilizes community and lineage.

Recurring Patterns Across Lifetimes

Whale souls often appear as elders, healers, singers, storytellers, navigators, or lineage keepers.

Whale souls carry gravitas; others sense depth and safety in their presence.

Whale souls work with collective healing; family, culture, and community themes shape life path.

Initiations of This Lifetime

Whale awakens during periods of ancestral healing, grief integration, or calling into deep service.

Whale activates when the soul uses voice, memory, and presence to guide others through vast emotional waters.

Whale Variations: Current Life Expression

Blue Whale

Blue Whale reflects planetary scale awareness; the soul engages responsibility, humility, and presence within immense systems. Many oceanic cultures view this whale as a living embodiment of Earth's heartbeat and deep order.

Humpback Whale

Humpback Whale reflects healing through song and creativity; the soul engages expression, teaching, and emotional release through voice and art. Polynesian and Northwest Coast traditions honor the humpback as a singer, storyteller, and ceremonial guide.

Gray Whale

Gray Whale reflects endurance and ancestral migration; the soul navigates long journeys created from memory, return, and persistence. Coastal Indigenous peoples recognize the gray whale as a symbol of survival, navigation, and cyclical wisdom.

Sperm Whale

Sperm Whale reflects deep diving consciousness; the soul engages exploration of profound inner realms, mystery, and concentrated intelligence. Many maritime cultures associate the sperm whale with depth mastery and powerful inner vision.

Orca

Orca reflects family intelligence and coordinated power; the soul engages leadership within kin groups, strategy, and communal protection. Northwest Coast cultures honor orca as a clan ancestor, guardian, and embodiment of family strength.

Beluga Whale

Beluga Whale reflects joy and communication; the soul engages adaptability, social bonding, and emotional expression through sound. Arctic cultures recognize the beluga as a friendly messenger and a bridge between ice, water, and people.

Narwhal

Narwhal reflects sacred singularity and mystery; the soul engages uniqueness, spiritual focus, and the honoring of rare gifts. Inuit traditions regard the narwhal as a being of deep-sea magic and ancestral significance.

Wolf Totem

Core Totem Essence

Wolf has the soul memory of relational intelligence. This totem lives through the balance of individuality and belonging, instinct and ethics, survival and devotion. Across the Northern Hemisphere, including Indigenous North American nations, Siberian cultures, Central Asian steppe peoples, and Northern European traditions, the wolf appears as a teacher of kinship, law, and sacred order. Wolf medicine centers on loyalty guided by discernment, communication rooted in honesty, and leadership that serves the whole.

Strengths of the Totem

Wolf brings social intelligence; awareness of group dynamics has cohesion and mutual protection.

Wolf has instinctual wisdom; sensing danger, opportunity, and alignment arises naturally.

Wolf embodies loyalty; bonds strengthen through trust, consistency, and shared purpose.

Wolf communicates clearly; voice, signal, and presence guide collective movement.

Wolf balances autonomy with belonging; strength grows through both independence and cooperation.

Challenges of the Totem

Wolf lives with strong relational bonds; loss, separation, or betrayal shape deep emotional responses.

Wolf holds a heightened awareness of hierarchy; leadership and followership require ethical clarity.

Wolf senses threat acutely; regulation has calm assessment and grounded action.

Wolf commits to the pack; personal needs ask for conscious expression within group life.

Past Life Lessons Carried Forward

Wolf has learned survival through cooperation; shared effort multiplies strength.

Wolf has learned leadership through service; guidance protects instead of dominates.

Wolf has learned the power of voice; sound has identity, warning, and belonging.

Wolf has learned respect for natural law; territory, order, and rhythm sustain life.

Recurring Patterns Across Lifetimes

Wolf souls often appear as leaders, protectors, mediators, teachers, or guardians of the community.

Wolf souls form chosen family; loyalty defines the relationship more than blood alone.

Wolf souls navigate boundary spaces; wildness and civilization meet through their presence.

Initiations of This Lifetime

Wolf awakens during periods of community formation, leadership responsibility, or identity within group life.

Wolf activates when the soul aligns personal truth with collective well-being.

Canid Variations: Current Life Expression

Gray Wolf

Gray Wolf reflects balanced leadership and pack harmony; the soul engages cooperation, ethical authority, and shared survival. Many Indigenous North American and Eurasian cultures honor the gray wolf as a teacher of law, kinship, and endurance.

Dire Wolf

Dire Wolf reflects ancestral memory and primal strength; the soul engages deep lineage power, collective survival instinct, and ancient identity brought forward. This expression emphasizes roots, continuity, and resilience.

Arctic Wolf

Arctic Wolf reflects endurance and cohesion in extreme conditions; the soul navigates scarcity, clarity, and loyalty under pressure. Northern cultures associate this wolf with perseverance and communal reliance.

Zebra Totem

Core Totem Essence

Zebra has the soul memory of individuality within community, protective patterning, and strength expressed through coordinated movement. This totem lives across open plains and savanna, teaching how identity and belonging thrive together. Across African savanna cultures, the zebra symbolizes balance, cooperation, and the wisdom of blending into collective rhythm while maintaining distinct self-expression. Its stripes create natural camouflage and energetic harmony, reflecting unity through diversity. Zebra medicine centers on social intelligence, group protection, and confident authenticity.

Strengths of the Totem

Zebra brings strong communal awareness; safety emerges through coordinated group movement.

Zebra has balanced individuality; self-expression thrives within shared belonging.

Zebra embodies alertness; perception remains sharp across wide horizons.

Zebra has endurance; long migrations unfold through a steady rhythm.

Zebra has energetic camouflage; harmony with the environment provides natural protection.

Challenges of the Totem

Zebra lives within a strong herd connection; solitude deepens self-reflection.

Zebra values constant vigilance; relaxation restores vitality and trust.

Zebra responds quickly to disturbance; measured pacing refines direction.

Zebra has complex social bonds; clear communication strengthens stability.

Past Life Lessons Carried Forward

Zebra has learned survival through unity; herd strength ensures continuity.

Zebra has learned authenticity through pattern; uniqueness enhances collective beauty.

Zebra has learned awareness through observation; wide vision prevents danger.

Zebra has learned rhythm through migration; steady movement fulfills destiny.

Recurring Patterns Across Lifetimes

Zebra souls often appear as community builders, mediators, artists, teachers, or those who celebrate diversity while fostering cohesion.

Zebra souls thrive within networks; collaboration energizes their purpose.

Zebra souls value fairness and equality; life organizes around shared strength and mutual respect.

Initiations of This Lifetime

Zebra awakens during periods of building community, balancing individuality with belonging, or learning to move confidently within group dynamics.

Zebra activates when the soul honors its unique pattern, aligns with collective rhythm, and advances with awareness and cooperation.

Bibliography and Cited Sources

Allen, Tony, Fergus Fleming, Charles Philips. *Voices of the Ancestors: African Myth.* London: Duncan Baird Publishers, 1999.

Apostal, Virgil Mayor. *Way of the Ancient Healer, Sacred Teachings from the Philippine Ancestral Traditions.* Berkley, CA: North Atlantic Books, 2010.

American Psychiatric Association. *Diagnostic and Statistical Manual of Mental Disorders Fifth Edition DSM-5.* Washington, DC: American Psychiatric Publishing, 2013.

Andrews, Ted. *Animal Speak: The Spiritual & Magical Powers of the Creatures Great & Small.* St. Paul, MN: Llewellyn Worldwide, 2003.

Barrabbas, Frater. *Spirit Conjuring for Witches: Magical Evocation Simplified.* Woodbury, MN: Llewellyn Worldwide, 2017

Berney, Charlotte. *Fundamentals of Hawaiian Mysticism.* Berkeley, CA: Crossing Press, 2000.

Cowan, Tom. *Shamanism as a Spiritual Practice for Daily Life.* New York, NY: Crown Publishing, 1996.

Crawshaw, Ralph. *Compassion's Way: A Doctor's Quest into the Soul of Medicine.* Bloomington, IL: Medi-Ed Press, 2002.

Cunningham, Scott. *Cunningham's Guide to Hawaiian Magic & Spirituality.* Woodbury, MN: Llewellyn Publications, 1994.

Eliade, Mircea. *Shamanism Archaic Techniques of Ecstasy.* Princeton, NJ: Princeton University Press, 1964.

Ellwood, Taylor. *Walking with Spirits, How to Work with Spirits and Get Consistent Results.* Portland, Oregon: Magical Experiments Publication, 2020.

Fortune, Dion. *Psychic Self Defence, A Study in Occult Pathology and Criminality.* Naples, Italy: Albatross Publishers, 2018

Greer, Carl. *Change the Story of Your Health: Using Shamanic Techniques for Healing.* Scotland, UK: Findhorn Press, 2017.

Hall, Manly P. *The Secret Teachings of All Ages, An Encyclopedic Outline of Masonic, Hermetic, Qabbalistic, and Rosicrucian Symbolical Philosophy.* Mineola, NY: Dover Publications, Inc., 2010.

Harner, Michael. *The Way of the Shaman.* New York, NY: Harper One, 1980.

Horne, Roger. *Folk Witchcraft, a Guide to Lore, Land, and Familiar Spirit for the Solitary Practitioner.* Moon Over Mountain Press, 2019.

Ingerman, Sandra. *Shamanic Journeying: A Beginner's Guide.* Boulder, CO: Sounds True, Inc., 2004.

Ingerman, Sandra. *Soul Retrieval, Mending the Fragmented Self.* New York, NY: Harper Collins, 1991.

Inkwright, Fez. *Folk Magic and Healing, An Unusual History of Everyday Plants.* Turkey: Liminal11, 2019.

Kelden. *The Crooked Path, An Introduction to Traditional Witchcraft.* Woodbury, MN: Llewellyn Publications, 2020.

King, Serge Kahili. *Urban Shamanism.* New York, NY: Fireside, 1990.

Konstantinos. *Summoning Spirits, the Art of Magical Evocation.* Woodbury, MN: Llewellyn Worldwide, 2002.

Lecouteux, Claude. *Witches Werewolves and Fairies, Shapeshifters and Astral Doubles in the Middle Ages.* Rochester, Vermont: Inner Traditions, 1992.

Leland, Charles Godgfrey. *Etruscan Roman Remains in Popular Tradition.* London, England: T Fisher Unwin Paternoster Square, 1892.

Long, Max Freedom. *Huna, An Introduction.* Midwest Journal Press, 2015.

Long, Max Freedom. *The Hula Code In Religions.* Marina Del Rey, CA: Delors's & Co., Publishers, 1982.

Long, Tracie. *In Focus: Shamanism & Your Personal Guide.* New York, NY: Zambezi Publishing, 2020.

Mackesy, Charlie. *THE BOY, THE MOLE, THE FOX AND THE HORSE.* New York, NY: HarperOne, 2019

Madden, Kristin. *The Book of Shamanic Healing.* Woodbury, MA: Llewellyn Publications, 2002.

Mantles, Doc. *Shamanism for Beginners! How to Understand and Implement a Shaman Way of Living.* CreateSpace, 2018.

Martinie, Dr. Louie. *Talking to the God with Food, Questioning Animal Sacrifice.* Cincinnati, Ohio: Black Moon Publishing, 2019.

Masters, Robert Augustus. *Spiritual Bypassing: When Spirituality Disconnects Us From What Really Matters.* Berkley, CA: North Atlantic Books, 2010.

Oesterley, W.O.E.. *Sacred Dance in the Ancient World.* Mineola, NY: Dover Publications, Inc., 2002.

Pearson, Nigel G.. *Treading the Mill, Workings in Traditional Witchcraft.* Woodbury, MN: Llewellyn Publications, 2020

Penczak, Christopher. *The Temple of Shamanic Witchcraft, Shadows, Spirits, and the Healing Journey.* Woodbury, Minnesota: Llewellyn Publications, 2016.

Phelan, Rev. Arlene.. *Hawaiian Shamanism, Secrets of the Modern Shaman.* DM Bookpro, 2018.

Powell, Wayne Kealohi and Patricia Lynn Miller. *Hawaiian Shamanistic Healing, Medicine Ways to Cultivate the Aloha Spirit.* Woodbury MN: Llewellyn Publications, 2018.

Power, Tomas. *Morbid Magic, Death Spirituality & Culture From Around the World.* Woodbury, MN: Llewellyn Publications, 2019.

Rezentes, William C., III. *Ka Lama Fukui, Hawaiian Psychology: An Introductions.* Honolulu, HI: 'A'ali'i Books, 1996.

Rodman, Julius Scammon. *The Kahuna Sorcerers of Hawaii, Past and Present.* Smithtown, NY: Exposition Press, 1979.

Rosean, Lexa. *The Encyclopedia of Magical Ingredients, A Wiccan Guide to Spellcasting.* New York, NY: Pocket Books, 2005

Rysdyk, Evelyn C.. *Spirit Walking, A Course in Shamanic Power.* Newburyport, MA: WeiserBooks, 2013.

Sarangerel. *Chosen by the Spirits: Following Your Shamanic Calling.* Rochester, VT: Destiny Books, 2001.

Scully, Nicki. *Alchemical Healing.* Rochester, MT: Bear & Company, 2003.

Warner, Michael. *The Way of the Shaman.* New York, NY: Harper Collins Publishers, 1980.

Wesselman, Hank. *The Journey to the Sacred Garden: A Guide to Traveling in the Spiritual Realms.* Hay House, Inc., 2003.

Wesselman, Hank. *Spiritwalker: Message From The Future.* New York: NY: Bantam Books, 1995.

Wesselman, Hank and Jill Kuykendall. *Spirit Medicine, Healing in the Sacred Realms.* Carlsbad, California: Hay House, Inc, 2004.

White, Gordon. *Star.Ships, A Prehistory of the Spirits.* UK: Scarlet Imprint, 2016

ALY CARDINALLI

Author Bio

Aly Cardinalli is an accomplished witchdoctor, performing arts specialist, psychic, and master educator with over twenty five years of experience in his fields. He has dedicated his life to promoting traditional practices and spreading knowledge about culture.

Born a dark medium and oversensitive psychic, Aly grew up surrounded by spirits and natural remedies that were used to cure both physical and spiritual ailments. He learned from various family members the art of healing, witchcraft, and spirituality, gradually developing a deep passion for indigenous and creolized practices.

As a young man, Aly decided to pursue a career in the performing arts. He studied music, dance, and theatrical directing, and quickly made a name for himself as a talented performer, exceptional choreographer (an expert in over eighteen styles of dance), and an award winning director. His unique knowledge of the arts and culture, along with his exceptional stage presence, made him an instant hit with audiences across the globe, artistically influencing over 135 productions and performing in over 200.

Despite his success in the performing arts, Aly continued to practice traditional shamanic techniques. Aly has also developed an innovative training and classification system for psychics, mediums, and sensitives. Because of his genius and prodigy youth, his knowledge and aptitude in the inclusive disciplines of culture, healing, spirituality, mysticism, and storytelling is unmatched.

Over the years, Aly has gained immense popularity as a master educator in his fields. Aly has been the dean of education for a performing arts school, a teacher trainer, the headmaster at a witchcraft and psychic development school, and the education director for a healing arts institute.

Thanks to his dedication and hard work, Aly Cardinalli is now widely recognized as a commodity to cultural education. His talent, passion, and expertise have inspired countless people to embrace rich and vibrant culture and to embrace the power of spiritual arts and ancient cultural expression.

Substack/YouTube: @alycardinall

www.ingramcontent.com/pod-product-compliance
Lightning Source LLC
LaVergne TN
LVHW090543110826
845146LV00001B/3

* 9 7 9 8 9 5 0 9 0 5 0 0 1 *